Patriation and Its Consequences

Patriation and Its Consequences

Constitution Making in Canada

EDITED BY LOIS HARDER
AND STEVE PATTEN

UBCPress · Vancouver · Toronto

23 22 21 20 19 18 17 16 15   5 4 3 2 1

Printed in Canada on FSC-certified ancient-forest-free paper (100% post-consumer recycled) that is processed chlorine- and acid-free.

Library and Archives Canada Cataloguing in Publication

Patriation and its consequences : constitution making in Canada / edited by Lois Harder and Steve Patten.

Includes bibliographical references and index.
Issued in print and electronic formats.
ISBN 978-0-7748-2861-1 (bound).—ISBN 978-0-7748-2862-8 (pbk).—
ISBN 978-0-7748-2863-5 (pdf).—ISBN 978-0-7748-2864-2 (epub)

1. Canada. Constitution Act, 1982. 2. Constitutional history – Canada. 3. Constitutional amendments – Canada. 4. Canada – Politics and government – 1980-1984. 5. Federal-provincial relations – Canada. I. Patten, Steve, author, editor II. Harder, Lois, author, editor

KE4199.P38 2015   342.7102'9   C2015-900732-1
KF4482.P38 2015   C2015-900733-X

Canadä

UBC Press gratefully acknowledges the financial support for our publishing program of the Government of Canada (through the Canada Book Fund), the Canada Council for the Arts, and the British Columbia Arts Council.

This book has been published with the help of a grant from the Canadian Federation for the Humanities and Social Sciences, through the Awards to Scholarly Publications Program, using funds provided by the Social Sciences and Humanities Research Council of Canada.

Printed and bound in Canada by Friesens
Set in Sabon by Apex CoVantage, LLC
Copy editor: Frank Chow
Proofreader: Marnie Lamb
Indexer: Judy Dunlop

UBC Press
The University of British Columbia
2029 West Mall
Vancouver, BC V6T 1Z2
www.ubcpress.ca

TO PATRICIA PARADIS,

FOR HER VISION AND INSPIRATION

Contents

Acknowledgments

The completion, let alone the success, of an edited volume relies on the enthusiasm and goodwill of many people. As the editors of this collection, we have been fortunate to work with an amazing group of scholars, practitioners, and specialists. Our first debt of gratitude is owed to the volume's contributors, whose insights and careful scholarship shed new light on the law and politics of patriation. We are also grateful to Peter Meekison, Howard Leeson, and Oryssia Lennie for providing the initial inspiration that ultimately led to this book. The Centre for Constitutional Studies at the University of Alberta, including its board of directors and especially its executive director, Patricia Paradis, provided the intellectual home for this initiative. Emily Andrew and Megan Brand of UBC Press have been outstandingly supportive and patient in assisting us to navigate the publishing and editorial process. We are also extremely grateful to the Social Sciences and Humanities Research Council for a generous Public Outreach Grant (608-2010-0021), and to the Awards to Scholarly Publications Program of the Canadian Federation of the Humanities and Social Sciences for its contribution to the costs of publication. Finally, we would like to thank our families for their support and good humour through the many hours we spent putting this book together.

Patriation and Its Consequences

PART I
Introduction: The Significance of Constitution Making

Looking Back on Patriation and Its Consequences

1

Lois Harder and Steve Patten

On 3–5 November 2011, the Centre for Constitutional Studies at the University of Alberta hosted the Patriation Negotiations Conference to mark the thirtieth anniversary of the fateful deliberations that culminated in the *Constitution Act, 1982.* The speakers' roster included many of the key players involved in those 1981 negotiations, including Premiers Peter Lougheed (Alberta), John Buchanan (Nova Scotia), and Brian Peckford (Newfoundland), then Saskatchewan Attorney General Roy Romanow, and many political advisers and public servants who were intimately engaged in the strategizing, dealmaking, and agreement drafting. The conference provided a fascinating opportunity to reflect on Canadian "constitutional lore" associated with the patriation negotiations – the accepted stories about the role of the Kitchen Accord, the marginalizing of Quebec during the "Night of the Long Knives," the exclusivity of executive federalism, and the single-mindedness of Prime Minister Pierre Trudeau. Interestingly, many of the key players remembered those events differently, and for some the desire to "set the record straight" was intense.

Repeated with sufficient frequency, particular narratives of historical events become authoritative, while alternative readings are regarded as self-serving revisionism. Yet what lore, revisionism, and record straightening demonstrate is the very elusiveness of one shared truth through which to understand momentous historical events. In the case of the patriation negotiations, we do, of course, have a document whose signatories and terms attest to the dynamics of the bargaining. Yet the dry formality of the agreement's provisions obscures much of the passion that infused the negotiations themselves, the long history that had precipitated them, and the struggles of Indigenous peoples, women's groups, and Canadians generally to see themselves reflected in their constitution.

The Patriation Negotiations: A Synopsis

Patriation refers to the effort to "retrieve" Canada's constitution from the British Parliament. Because Canadian governments had never managed to agree on a domestic process for amending the constitution, it remained a British statute for half a century after the 1931 *Statute of Westminster* granted independent self-governance to the dominions of the British Empire. This situation was increasingly untenable for a modern nation-state, particularly for the francophone province of Quebec, where the spectre of British colonial domination was especially galling.

Prime Minister Trudeau imagined that patriation, an amending formula, and a constitutionally entrenched charter of rights would engage Quebec more fully in the Canadian federation and articulate a national vision of Canada through the shared values of liberal rights. Throughout the 1970s and in 1980, Trudeau and the provincial premiers tackled this agenda, but mutually agreeable terms proved elusive. In October 1980, therefore, Trudeau threatened to act without the provinces – to patriate the constitution unilaterally. This gambit was ultimately blocked when, in September 1981, the Supreme Court of Canada handed down its ruling on the *Patriation Reference,* holding that while a unilateral action would not be illegal, it would offend a constitutional convention requiring substantial provincial consent in order to secure a constitutional amendment. That ruling forced Trudeau back to the bargaining table in one last, and not especially hopeful, effort to realize his constitutional ambitions.

The constitutional negotiations of 2–5 November 1981 were, on the surface, a classic example of executive federalism, with First Ministers debating in front of television cameras while their officials negotiated in the corridors of Ottawa's National Conference Centre. Of course, the negotiations were inflected by the long-standing animosity between Trudeau and Premier René Lévesque and doubt about whether terms could be found that Quebec's separatist premier would ever accept. However, seven other provincial premiers also resisted Trudeau's agenda, and, along with Quebec, had formed the "Gang of Eight" provinces to oppose many aspects of the federal government's unilateral patriation initiative. Agreement seemed unlikely, and never more so than when the prime minister proposed a referendum on the amending formula and on a charter of rights as a way of breaking the deadlock. The premiers were well aware that the Canadian public supported a charter, and they worried that Trudeau's appeal to the people would undermine their own desire to protect provincial autonomy and parliamentary supremacy. As the conference progressed, the search for common ground included the so-called Kitchen Accord discussions among federal minister of justice Jean Chrétien and the attorneys general of Saskatchewan and Ontario (Roy Romanow and Roy McMurtry), as well as a proposal from Premier Peckford of Newfoundland. During the night of 4 November, premiers and officials from Alberta, Saskatchewan, Newfoundland, and British Columbia gathered to work on these terms and develop a new proposal. Representatives of all of the remaining provinces except Quebec were informed of the developments over the course of those late hours, while Quebec learned of the new proposal only at a premiers' breakfast meeting on 5 November. Lévesque was livid (Leeson 2011, 59–66). A bargain had been worked out, but Quebec felt it had been abandoned during a "Night of Long Knives" and refused to support the plan. Canada would patriate its constitution with a "made in Canada" amending formula and an entrenched charter of rights and freedoms, but this impressive political feat was also deeply scarred by Quebec's missing signature. As scholars Keith Banting and Richard Simeon (1983) poignantly observed, "no one cheered."

Negotiating Constitutional Lore

In this brief précis of the patriation negotiations, we have encountered constitutional lore regarding the importance of the Kitchen Accord and the extent to which the other premiers abandoned Quebec by excluding Lévesque from negotiations during the Night of the Long Knives, the extent to which the content of the deal emerged from the actors and processes of executive federalism, and the importance of Trudeau's obsession with patriation and entrenching a charter of rights. We now reflect on these elements of Canadian constitutional lore.

The Role of the Kitchen Accord

The November 1981 Federal-Provincial Conference of First Ministers on the Constitution was convened out of necessity, not hope. Given the Supreme Court's *Patriation Reference* decision, Trudeau was obliged to consult with his provincial colleagues, and the premiers had little choice but to engage in another round of negotiations. The conference had no formal agenda and began with no new proposals on the table. No meaningful progress was made during the first full day of negotiations on 3 November. In fact, when three premiers approached Trudeau with a British Columbia–sponsored proposal, the prime minister angrily rejected it. A second provincial proposal, this one offered by Saskatchewan premier Allan Blakeney, died a similar death early the following day. The mood turned even gloomier when Lévesque appeared to break with his Gang of Eight colleagues by agreeing to Trudeau's surprise suggestion of a referendum to address the constitutional impasse. The Gang of Eight had agreed that any change in their strategy would require consultation, and Lévesque's sudden concession to Trudeau appeared to crack their united front (Clarkson and McCall 1990, 378–80). Arguably, Trudeau successfully used his referendum proposal to split the Gang of Eight and frustrate any chance of making progress towards a negotiated amending formula and charter.

Less than twenty-four hours later, however, an agreement to patriate the constitution with an amending formula and charter of rights was signed by the prime minister and nine provincial premiers. How did a settlement emerge from a conference that appeared doomed to failure? According to a CBC news special, the seeds of this momentous compromise were sown during a brief meeting in a kitchen on the fifth floor of the National Conference Centre (CBC 1981). As Canadians watched, Jean Chrétien, Roy Romanow, and Roy McMurtry re-enacted their historic kitchen meeting for the news cameras, and in that moment the mythology of the Kitchen Accord was born. Canadian constitutional folklore now tells us that these three ministers saw an opportunity to bridge the divide between the federal government and the Gang of Eight. On two pages ripped from a notepad, they recorded what they believed would be a workable trade-off that combined elements of the Gang of Eight's preferred amending formula, Trudeau's rights charter with a notwithstanding clause, a commitment to the principle of equalization payments, provincial control of nonrenewable resources, allowances for affirmative action policies that conflict with mobility rights when a province's employment rate is below the national average, and a compromise approach to implementing minority language rights. This accord, the story goes, was the focus of a long night of backroom negotiations and resulted in an agreement that, by the morning of 5 November, all First Ministers other than Lévesque were prepared to sign.

But not everyone is comfortable with the narrative that credits the Kitchen Accord trio with seizing an otherwise unrecognized opportunity for a breakthrough in the constitutional negotiations. Former Newfoundland premier Brian Peckford claims that the seeds of the compromise were actually sown early in the afternoon of 4 November, when he turned his mind to compiling the points of potential agreement. In his contribution to the University of Alberta's 2011 Patriation Negotiations Conference, Peckford was adamant that the Kitchen Accord story was a "myth." It was his proposal, fleshed out by Newfoundland officials, that he claimed was taken forward, fine-tuned in negotiations with other members of the Gang of Eight, and then prepared and presented to the conference on 5 November.

Perhaps the truth is less dramatic than the Kitchen Accord story, or even Peckford's narrative of a lone premier drafting a proposal that his colleagues eventually rallied around. It seems clear that a lot of ideas and proposals were being shared between delegations. In a paper delivered at the 2011 conference, Romanow continued to argue that the ideas he documented in the fifth-floor kitchen were the "key catalyst" that made agreement possible, but he was also quick to credit ideas put forward by others, including Peckford. He prefers to refer to the ideas that he, Chrétien, and McMurtry advanced as the "kitchen proposals," one among many noteworthy pieces in the constitutional jigsaw (Romanow 2012). By November 1981, there were very few First Ministers or constitutional advisers who had not participated in, or been briefed on, the substance of dozens of constitutional meetings and likely hundreds of draft proposals. Some had been involved as far back as the nearly successful Victoria conference of 1971. It must have been clear to everyone that Trudeau and the federal delegation were most fixated on entrenching a charter of rights, while Gang of Eight premiers worried at least as much about the amending formula. So long as the principle of equalization, western demands regarding provincial control of nonrenewable resources, and Newfoundland's request for some flexibility on mobility rights were also addressed, the key to an agreement would be giving Trudeau his charter (with a sufficiently comprehensive notwithstanding clause to calm provincial skeptics) and giving the Gang of Eight their amending formula (minus the fiscal compensation for opting out to which Trudeau objected).

Howard Leeson's retelling of the backroom negotiating during the evening of 4 November 1981 reveals how agreement emerged from multiple sources. Saskatchewan officials had drafted proposals based on Romanow's meeting with Chrétien and McMurtry. Newfoundland had a draft proposal based on Peckford's scheme. Alberta officials laid out a position that was "substantially the same as that of Newfoundland and Saskatchewan" (Leeson 2011, 60). There were, of course, points of disagreement – for example, Newfoundland had originally included language on Aboriginal rights to which BC officials objected – but everyone was working with the same constellation of approaches to the set of constitutional issues that needed to be addressed. Premier Peckford and the ministers who drafted the kitchen proposals certainly deserve recognition for putting to paper the elements of a compromise that would save another First Ministers' conference on the constitution from failure, but neither the story of the Kitchen Accord nor Peckford's narrative deserves to be privileged by Canadian constitutional mythology. Why, then, has the story of the Kitchen Accord been retold in a manner that seems to suggest that the patriation agreement was drafted by three ministers meeting in a kitchen at the National Conference Centre? The answer may lie in the desire of officials from other provinces not to allow a single premier (Peckford) to take credit for the agreement. The *Globe and Mail*'s Rosemary Speirs reported that officials from Saskatchewan and Ontario circulated among reporters on 5 November, saying that they had orchestrated the compromise and suggesting that Peckford was merely the front man for the consensus (Speirs 1981). However, as was evident in the CBC news special the day the conference concluded, the degree of popular attention given to the Kitchen Accord might be explained by the fact that there is something attractive and convenient – and redolent of Canada – about the story of three innovative individuals (French, Anglo, Ukrainian; federal and provincial; central Canadian and regional), hammering out an accord that would define Canada's new constitution.

The Night of the Long Knives

To many observers, the patriation agreement represented an abandonment of Quebec by the other members of the Gang of Eight. As Alain-G. Gagnon and Alex Schwartz argue in Chapter 12, the settlement evidenced a general failure – perhaps a refusal – to acknowledge the constitutional significance of Quebec's distinctive national reality. Without consulting Lévesque, Canada's English-speaking First Ministers and their advisers drafted a constitutional proposal that included elements – such as an amending formula that failed to include a commitment to provide financial compensation to provinces that opt out – that Quebec was unlikely to accept. Lévesque said that when he was presented with the proposal on the morning of 5 November, he felt abandoned, as though he had been stabbed in the back during the night – the Night of the Long Knives.

Several observers and participants in the 1981 conference dispute this interpretation. Alberta premier Peter Lougheed wrote that there was "no attempt to develop something behind the back of any province in the Group of Eight" (cited in Meekison 1999, 26). Because Lougheed, like several other premiers, had not been physically present in the hotel suites where negotiations and drafting had occurred during the evening of 4 November, he could claim, in correspondence with Lévesque, that the document outlining the proposed agreement was "first presented" to the Gang of Eight premiers at an 8:00 a.m. breakfast meeting on

5 November – implying that Lévesque had the same opportunity as others to discuss, amend, and accept or reject the proposal. All of this is technically true, but it is also clear from accounts of the events of the evening of 4 November that the premiers and officials involved in the negotiations were aware of Quebec's absence from the discussions (Graham 2011; Leeson 2011). Thus, it is disingenuous to assert that Quebec was not excluded from a key moment in the constitutional negotiations. But why was Quebec excluded? To what extent was Quebec's exclusion a calculated risk that Donald Smiley would later label a "dangerous deed" (Smiley 1983)? Was Quebec's exclusion an inevitable consequence of what many participants assumed to be Lévesque's aversion to ever agreeing to any constitutional package? To what extent were Lévesque and his advisers actually responsible for Quebec's exclusion from the negotiations and agreement?

Howard Leeson's *The Patriation Minutes* (2011) includes a revealing outline of his recollection, as a deputy minister and constitutional adviser to Saskatchewan premier Allan Blakeney, of the negotiations on the evening of 4 November. Leeson details how and when different delegations were brought into the discussions and the distinct roles they played. He reports that shortly after midnight, when the deal was being completed and the final strategic decisions were being made, there was a discussion of what to do about Quebec:

> The general conclusion was that Québec could never agree with anything, and specifically would not agree to this package, because of the lack of compensation in the Amending Formula. Nevertheless, it was agreed that the proposal must be put to Québec at the already scheduled 8am meeting of the "Gang of Eight." (64)

Pierre Trudeau (1993, 246) echoed this view when he later wrote that it was always unrealistic to believe a separatist premier could be persuaded to participate in the renewal of the Canadian constitution. If designing a successful compromise was not, in fact, on Lévesque's agenda, Leeson is likely correct that Quebec's exclusion from the negotiations until a nearly finalized proposal was presented to the premiers was essential to success. Not everyone accepts this assessment, however. In Chapter 11 of this volume, Peter Russell argues that given space and time to negotiate, the Quebec premier may have been willing to come on side. Lévesque had already accepted the April 1981 Gang of Eight amending formula, a procedure that did not include a Quebec veto. Perhaps if a real effort to negotiate with Lévesque had been undertaken, Quebec could have been convinced to come on side. Lévesque did, after all, support the Meech Lake Accord six years later.

In Chapter 8, however, Guy Laforest and Rosalie Readman offer a different perspective on Quebec's exclusion. They contend that "René Lévesque and his government must also be held responsible for the constitutional isolation of Quebec." Lévesque arrived at the conference with a "weak team" that allowed him to make a number of strategically inept and fateful decisions. Greatest of all was his decision to signal that he was breaking from the Gang of Eight by accepting Trudeau's proposal to submit an entrenched charter and amending formula to the people in a referendum. This departure from the Gang of Eight's April 1981 accord allowed other provinces to assume that Quebec was no longer committed to working with the "gang." Then, Laforest and Readman point out, on the evening of 4 November – when, as Peter Lougheed says, "every premier would have expected a great deal of lobbying and exchanges of views" (cited in Meekison 1999, 25) to be occurring – Lévesque and his delegation spent the night at their Hull hotel without making any effort to communicate with either their allies or adversaries. Of course, it is difficult to predict what would have happened if the Quebec delegation had been actively engaged in negotiations that evening. In the event, they were not, and most other premiers believed that Lévesque was unwilling to sign any sort of deal. Moreover, after he expressed his willingness to accept patriation followed by a referendum, many of the premiers wanted to seize the moment and take control of the conference agenda. They were willing to exclude Quebec if that made agreement more likely. Clearly, in terms of Quebec's exclusion, there was plenty of blame to go around.

Patriation as a Product of Executive Federalism

The patriation story is typically told with a focus on the role played by Canada's First Ministers and the formal, often secretive processes of executive-level intergovernmental relations known as "executive federalism" (Sheppard and Valpy 1982; Graham 2011). Clearly, the prime minister, premiers, and their advisers were centre stage as the patriation agreement was negotiated, but understanding this key moment in Canadian constitutional history requires that attention be paid to the interface between the politics of executive federalism and the constitutional engagement of organized interests and ordinary citizens. Indeed, actors who played no formal role at the First Ministers' conference first raised some of the core issues, perspectives, and language under consideration. Advocacy organizations had become increasingly attentive to constitutional politics during the 1970s, and citizen engagement was particularly apparent after Trudeau launched his unilateral patriation initiative in October 1980. Although few demonstrations matched the November 1980 Constitution Express that brought Aboriginal peoples from across Canada to Ottawa to participate in public demonstrations and constitutional workshops, or the February 1981 women's conference that led to the creation of the feminist Ad Hoc Committee on the Constitution, Canadians from all walks of life sought to have their voices heard.

When the Special Joint Committee on the Constitution (the Hays-Joyal Committee) was established to seek public input into the federal government's draft constitutional provisions, over 200 groups made oral presentations to televised committee hearings, and over 900 groups and individuals submitted written briefs. These interventions had an impact on the content and language of the constitutional proposals that would be debated by the First Ministers in November 1981. By addressing issues ranging from the wording of a "reasonable limits" clause to the specification of equality rights and approaches to recognizing and protecting Aboriginal and treaty rights, groups as diverse as organizations of persons with disabilities, the National Action Committee on the Status of Women, the National Indian Brotherhood, the Canadian Civil Liberties Association, and the Canadian Association of Lesbians and Gay Men were an important part of the patriation story.

By November 1981, constitutional politics was no longer the exclusive domain of the political elite. As Penny Bryden argues in Chapter 5, Canada had entered an era of "spectator constitutionalism" in which ordinary citizens followed the twists and turns of constitutional politics and realized they had a stake in the outcome of negotiations. Canadians wanted to see their constitution patriated, and they strongly supported entrenching a charter of rights. Trudeau used this popular support for the constitutionalization of rights and freedoms to his strategic advantage by proposing immediate patriation followed by a referendum to legitimize an amending formula and charter. In addition to splitting the Gang of Eight, this proposal also increased the pressure on the other premiers by introducing the possibility of breaking from the traditions of executive federalism and allowing the people to decide. If a deal had not been struck, the premiers would have risked losing their capacity, derived from the processes of executive federalism, to be the constitution makers.

Following the First Ministers' constitutional agreement of 5 November 1981, attention turned to preparation of the legal language of the *Constitution Act, 1982*. The drafting process created an opportunity for organized interests to shape the final document. Two of the most significant changes made during the weeks after 5 November would not have occurred if not for pressure from such interests. First, the language regarding Aboriginal and treaty rights that was added to federal proposals in April 1981 was dropped from the 5 November agreement but restored later in November (Hogg 2010). First Nations organizations had developed working relationships with a number of provincial delegations and most certainly played a role in the decision to include section 35 of the *Constitution Act, 1982*. An even clearer case of citizens influencing the drafting of the constitution was the successful feminist lobby that ensured that the sex equality guarantee in section 28 would be protected from the section 33 notwithstanding clause. Marilou McPhedran, Judith Erola, and Loren Braul's contribution in Chapter 8 is particularly instructive on the important interaction between the politics of executive federalism and the constitutional activism of citizens. Their insights underscore the extent to which the lens of executive federalism is insufficient to the task of understanding the patriation negotiations.

Trudeau's Magnificent Obsession

Another prevailing narrative defines patriation and the entrenchment of the *Canadian Charter of Rights and Freedoms* as one of Pierre Trudeau's great accomplishments. In this narrative, it was Trudeau's single-minded pursuit of a particular constitutional vision for Canada that shaped the patriation agreement. In their expression of this narrative, Stephen Clarkson and Christina McCall (1990) examine Trudeau's dogged pursuit of his constitutional obsession, beginning with his appointment as justice minister under Prime Minister Lester Pearson. They describe the November 1981 conference as the

> week that saw the climax of the great drama of [Trudeau's] public life ... However large the cast of characters that gathered in Ottawa for the event ... however flamboyantly the bit players strutted on the stage (and at least a dozen of them claimed afterwards that *his* role had been crucial in reaching the final outcome), there was no question who was the star. It was Trudeau who physically and figuratively wielded the gavel that caused the proceedings to unfold. (357)

There is no doubt that Trudeau was the driving force behind constitutional renewal in Canada, a fact explicitly acknowledged by Saskatchewan premier Allan Blakeney and BC premier Bill Bennett, among others (Cohen, Smith, and Warwick 1987, 84). However, none of the parties expressed much optimism that a deal was likely when Trudeau initiated the November 1981 conference (Romanow, Whyte, and Leeson 2007, 192), and few close observers of the negotiations attribute the conference's eventual success to Trudeau.

Indeed, one of the persistent themes to emerge from the 2011 Patriation Negotiations Conference was that 4 November 1981 marked a pivotal moment in the patriation process. Before that date, constitutional politics was defined in response to Trudeau's agenda and concerns about national unity. Sometime during 4 November, however, the initiative shifted from Trudeau and his nemesis, René Lévesque, to the other nine premiers. Trudeau's body language at the conclusion of the conference spoke volumes; he did not appear to be a man triumphant. Many will recall Trudeau's lament that Canada got "a Charter," but not "the Charter." The prime minister was clear that the final compromise was "not of my making" (CBC 1981).

In an era of political celebrity, it is hardly surprising that someone with the charisma of Pierre Trudeau would come to embody the patriation moment, but students of constitutional history are ill served by a diet of great-man invocations. The complicated and contradictory details of the constitutional negotiations reveal a much richer and more complex story.

Patriation and Its Consequences

The chapters that comprise this volume elaborate the patriation moment. Rather than "setting the record straight," these analyses offer a range of perspectives, attesting to the contested character of the patriation negotiations and the *Constitution Act, 1982.* Several chapters indulge elements of the patriation lore even as they seek to subvert it, but perhaps such indulgences are unavoidable. After all, they carry their own preferred versions of events, and they make a great story.

The Significance of Constitution Making

This book begins with Janine Brodie's overview and assessment of the patriation negotiations and the politics they have wrought. Drawing on Raymond Williams's theory of dominant, residual, and emergent forces (1977), Brodie asks: "How do we go about recalling this moment, which was so rife with conflicting motivations, visions, and memories, so contradictory and equivocal in its outcomes, and yet so integral to our collective present and future?" She begins with the dominant forces – with Trudeau's desire to secure Quebec's place in Confederation through constitutional renewal and Lévesque's challenges in balancing sovereigntist objectives with a pro-federalist provincial referendum outcome. In Brodie's estimation, by 1981 Quebec's claims to a special place in Confederation were a residual though still influential force in Canadian politics. From there, she considers "the people" as emergent forces. However, in contrast to scholars who argue that the *Constitution Act, 1982* produced "Charter Canadians" who made their claims through a Charter-invigorated Supreme Court (Cairns 1992; Morton 1995), Brodie insists that claims makers were part of the political process well before the early 1980s, and that the Charter has been both a blessing and a curse to progressive movements for social change. While the constitution might have freed Canada from Britain, Brodie argues it still requires substantive recognition of the relationship between the Canadian state and Indigenous peoples. If Canada is to be freed of its colonial heritage – one of the espoused goals of patriation – respect for treaties and new relationships with Indigenous peoples are a necessity. In that broader project, the accomplishment marked by patriation may well be a footnote.

Tracing the Long Road to Patriation

The next three chapters provide some of the history and motivating concepts for the patriation negotiations themselves. In Chapter 3, on constitutional nationalism, Eric Adams traces the patriation objective back through a long and fractious set of political and legal/scholarly conversations, first initiated at Confederation. Without an amending formula in the *British North America Act* (*BNA Act*), with an adjudicative structure in which Britain's Judicial Committee of the Privy Council (JCPC) served as Canada's highest court, and lacking foreign policy autonomy, Canada remained tethered to Britain in ways that would become increasingly contentious for the aspiring nation-state. As Adams points out, defenders of the status quo asserted that Britain served as a neutral arbiter for a linguistically and ethnically divided dominion. Moreover, the role of the British Parliament in adjudicating and amending Canada's constitution expressed Canada's respect for the British Empire and its parliamentary traditions. By contrast, Canada's constitutional nationalists regarded the continued British role as an intolerable expression of the dominion's infantilized status and as a barrier to Canada's abilities to develop policies, institutions, and constitutional practices that reflected the desires of Canadians themselves. As Adams observes, however, insight into who "Canadians themselves" might be was as shallow among constitutional nationalists as it was among the anglophiles. Certainly from the provinces' perspective, the tendency of the JCPC to affirm their powers and representative capacities was every bit as supportive of Canadian identity as the federalist/centrist ambitions that prevailed among constitutional nationalists. While it is undoubtedly important that Canada attained foreign policy autonomy (1931), the "supremacy" of the Supreme Court (1949), and subsequently its own amending formula(s), ultimately, Adams concludes, the patriation of 1982 resolved fewer problems than constitutional nationalists might have hoped, and generated several others in the bargain.

No volume (or conference) on the patriation negotiations would be complete without some consideration of the *Canadian Charter of Rights and Freedoms*. We are extremely fortunate to have in Chapter 4 the insights of Barry Strayer, who served as associate counsel on the constitution for Prime Minister Trudeau and was directly engaged in drafting the Charter. Strayer traces the long road of Canada's rights regime from the Westminster system of parliamentary sovereignty (or supremacy) – namely, that the people's representatives should be the ultimate authority for the laws of the land – to the adoption of a constitutionally entrenched charter that positioned the Supreme Court as the arbiter of parliamentary decision making. As Strayer points out, this shift was a matter of ongoing debate and struggle, and, as section 1 (rights are subject to reasonable limits in a free and democratic society) and section 33 (the notwithstanding clause, enabling fundamental freedoms, legal rights, and equality rights to be subject to legislative override) demonstrate, the tension or balance between the authority of Parliament and that of the courts remains very much alive in the Charter. Strayer provides an illuminating discussion of the debate and drafting decisions concerning sections 1, 7, 15, and 33. The politics of rights are apparent in his recollections, but it is also clear that democratic engagement provided Canada with a better Charter than executive federalism alone would have done.

Executive federalism was, of course, the primary mode for engaging Canada's constitution in the run-up to and throughout the patriation negotiations. The prime minister and premiers felt themselves empowered to bargain on behalf of their respective geographical (if not electoral) constituencies, an assumption of representative legitimacy that was facing growing scrutiny, as Penny Bryden observes in Chapter 5. While situating the process of constitutional negotiations firmly in the context of executive federalism, Bryden shines her analytical light on the role of citizens who, as interested spectators, became increasingly engaged with and important to the possibility of constitutional change. Televised segments of First Ministers' meetings, charismatic political personalities, and high-stakes bargaining helped fuel Canadians' interest in the debates. Federal and provincial leaders felt the weight of popular expectations, and understood the appeal to popular support as a key element of the constitutional negotiating strategy. Of course, most of the negotiating took place behind closed doors, but Bryden demonstrates how, as the pressure to reach an agreement intensified, citizen-spectators became potential players when Trudeau proposed the ultimate appeal to popular support – the prospect of a referendum.

Shaping Patriation: Law, Political Vision, Political Actors, and Political Struggle

In Chapter 6, Philip Girard's discussion of the *Patriation Reference* of 1981 considers the political legitimacy of constitutional renewal in the context of the relationship between law and politics. Girard joins with others in concluding that law (i.e., the ruling on the *Patriation Reference*) affected politics by forcing Trudeau to abandon unilateral patriation and obliging him instead to secure political and constitutional legitimacy for his package. However, Girard points out, holding another First Ministers' conference was not the only option open to the governing Liberals. Indeed, Girard contends that if adequate ground rules had been in place – if, for example, the 1979 legislation on constitutional referenda had been enacted before Parliament was dissolved and an election called – Trudeau might have opted to appeal over the heads of the courts and the premiers and seek consent from the Canadian people. A federally initiated referendum would have resulted in a constitutional package quite different from the one that resulted from the First Ministers' conference of November 1981. With regard to the impact of politics on law, Girard contends that the Supreme Court of Canada's finding of a convention requiring provincial consent in the constitutional amendment process was affected by the political context, but he disputes Trudeau's characterization of this ruling as "blatant manipulation" (Trudeau 1996, 256). Girard argues that because the *Patriation Reference* was a *reference* – a question to the court about the legality and constitutionality of a unilateral approach to patriation – the court is empowered to advise governments rather than simply adjudicate the question and thus is able to articulate political views that would be inappropriate in non-reference situations.

Broadening the discussion of the role of the courts, Chapter 7 by David Schneiderman considers the intellectual foundations of Trudeau's proposal to entrench a charter of rights within the constitution and thus override parliamentary sovereignty. Schneiderman argues that Trudeau, in fact, did not give much intellectual attention to judicial review in the run-up to patriation, primarily because he was not concerned about it. Certainly, his education and his mentors at Harvard and the London School of Economics would have acquainted him with arguments outlining the tendency of courts to block progressive social change. Yet, Schneiderman argues, various influences, including the constitutional thinking of F.R. Scott, Trudeau's admiration for the US Constitution, and inattention to the adjudicative function in the work of Trudeau's intellectual touchstone, Jacques Maritain, as well as in the instruments of the postwar international human rights regime, may have encouraged Trudeau's heedlessness regarding the development of a full-blown theory of the judicial role in rights enforcement. Chapter 7 concludes with the suggestion that Trudeau's vision of the judicial role is best understood as Madisonian – that is, as emphasizing the cultural role of rights in articulating shared values and curbing factionalism, rather than the power of the courts as ultimate arbiters.

In Chapter 8, Guy Laforest and Rosalie Readman outline some of the core causes and consequences of the 1981 patriation agreement, but the chapter's most significant contribution is the new light it sheds on Pierre Trudeau and René Lévesque. Drawing on the work of philosopher and former Trudeau confidante and speech writer André Burelle, Laforest and Readman explore the ways in which Trudeau's political philosophy was for several decades shaped by a blend of anti-nationalist individualism and a less individualistic "communitarian personalism." They contend, however, that understanding Trudeau's role during the patriation negotiations requires an examination of the reasons for his eventual abandonment of his more communitarian ideas during the 1980–81 period. As for Lévesque, Laforest and Readman judge his performance on the constitutional file during 1980 and 1981 to be disastrous. They criticize Lévesque for, among other things, seeming to give up on Quebec's historic constitutional veto in his deal with the Gang of Eight, failing to make use of potential federalist constitutional allies such as Claude Ryan, and arriving at the November 1981 conference with a weak and indecisive team that failed to prevent him from undermining any alliances he had formed by accepting Trudeau's offer of a referendum to break the constitutional impasse.

Taking up the fascinating story of Indigenous peoples' engagement in the patriation process in Chapter 9, Louise Mandell and Leslie Hall Pinder describe the Constitution Express and the efforts of Aboriginal leaders and activists to persuade British parliamentarians to honour the historic relationship between the Crown and First Nations. Through a first-hand account of mobilization efforts in Canada and months of negotiating in London, this chapter illuminates the political and legal strategies employed by Aboriginal leaders to focus international attention on the First Ministers' failure to include Indigenous peoples in the constitutional negotiations. The hope was that if Canadian politicians were unwilling to respect the constitutional status of treaties or acknowledge the existence of Aboriginal rights, the British Crown would do so. Legal challenges were brought to contest the transfer of authority from the British Crown to the Canadian government. Although these arguments were ultimately unsuccessful, they served an important educative function for British jurists and parliamentarians and the public, and reinforced solidarity among Indigenous activists.

In Chapter 10, Marilou McPhedran, Judith Erola, and Loren Braul also offer first-hand accounts of the patriation moment, this time from the perspective of feminist efforts to free section 28 – which guarantees Charter rights to men and women equally – from the constitutional override of section 33. The women's movement had been deeply involved in the constitutional negotiations of the early 1980s, and its influence was evident in the sex equality clauses of the various proposals for a charter. In the last minute dealmaking in November 1981, the section 33 notwithstanding clause was developed as a means of striking a balance between parliamentary sovereignty and an entrenched charter of rights. As Trudeau's minimum ante, language and mobility rights were not subject to the section 33 override, but equality rights (section 15) were. This situation might have been tolerable to the women's movement, given that the new deal also included a paramountcy clause (section 28) that ensured that all rights in the Charter would be guaranteed to men and women equally. As it turned out, however, even the paramountcy clause was subject to the override in the November 1981 agreement. Minister Responsible for the Status of Women Judith Erola immediately set about mobilizing her contacts in the women's movement, with the aim of persuading each of the premiers to free section 28 from the notwithstanding clause. The hard-fought battle resulted in an important symbolic victory even if, as McPhedran, Erola, and Braul note, there is uncertainty about the substantive contribution of an unfettered section 28 to equality of the sexes in Canada.

The Political and Constitutional Consequences of Patriation

The agreement reached in November 1981 left a lot of unfinished business. In addition to the immediate post-patriation mobilization of the women's movement, Indigenous peoples, insulted by their exclusion from the constitutional negotiations, continued their efforts to lobby the British Parliament to reject patriation until treaties and Indigenous rights were properly incorporated into the amended constitution. And in the ensuing decade of "mega-constitutional politics" (Russell 1993), efforts to include Quebec within the Canadian constitution were attempted and failed. Has the *Constitution Act, 1982* made a difference to Canada? Absolutely. The Charter has had an enormous impact on Canadian politics and society, ranging from stronger rights protections for people accused of crimes to marriage rights for same-sex partners. Paradoxically, Quebec's exclusion has compelled long and important discussions about the character of the federation. Also paradoxically, the strictures of the amending formula, as well as a contemporary political class that insists on Canada's constitutional fatigue, have meant that changes of a constitutional character often happen in small, incremental, and circuitous ways (e.g., the parliamentary recognition of Quebec as a distinct society; the Conservative government's plans for Senate reform). Clearly, many of the consequences were neither intended nor anticipated, but they have, nonetheless, reshaped Canada and the vision through which it imagines its future.

In Chapter 11, the first of the chapters exploring politics in the wake of patriation, Peter Russell examines two of the most significant unintended consequences of the patriation settlement. First, by agreeing to a constitutional package that was rejected by Premier Lévesque and the Quebec National Assembly, the patriation process alienated Quebec nationalists and put Canadian unity at risk. As a consequence, Canadians found themselves launched into a decade-long season of mega-constitutional politics that included the Meech Lake Accord, the so-called Quebec round of constitutional negotiations, and a nationwide referendum on the Charlottetown Accord, known as the Canada Round. The second unintended consequence was a set of important gains made by Aboriginal peoples. Russell argues that although the patriation process was initiated to deal with Quebec's aspirations, the final package included important advances in the recognition of Aboriginal and treaty rights of First Nations peoples.

In Chapter 12, Alain-G. Gagnon and Alex Schwartz contend that many of the deficiencies of Canadian federalism stem from, follow, or were reinforced by the 1981 patriation agreement. They argue that the agreement represented a denial of the constitutional significance of Quebec's distinctiveness. The lack of "recognition" is only a part of the problem, however; Gagnon and Schwartz champion a "federalism of empowerment" that looks beyond recognition and focuses on maintaining an open space where multiple orders of government are effectively empowered to move in response to the changing needs of governance. Such a pluralistic federalism of empowerment must be flexible, robust, and versatile in pursuit of the various utilitarian, liberal, and democratic communitarian values of federalism. Gagnon and Schwartz's analysis of the past thirty years suggests that Canadian federalism has failed. Rigidity has trumped flexibility, centralization has trumped robustness, and monism has trumped versatility – and all in the name of a single-minded focus on utilitarian goals of functional efficiency.

In Chapter 13, Kiera Ladner accepts Russell's contention that the inclusion of sections 25 and 35 in the *Constitution Act, 1982* was a significant achievement with very real transformative potential. In practice, however, this monumental achievement accomplished very little for Aboriginal peoples. With no precision or agreement on the meaning and content of the Aboriginal and treaty rights recognized and affirmed by section 35, non-Indigenous officials, politicians, lawyers, and judges have been able to vitiate and even undermine the supposed constitutional achievement of First Nations. In the absence of the political will and inclination to make section 35 transformative of western, Eurocentric constitutionalism, optimism has been dashed and what appeared to be an achievement to some has, in the end, been the monumental defeat that most Aboriginal leaders thought it was when they refused to endorse the 1981 constitutional settlement.

Finally, in Chapter 14, Alexandra Dobrowolsky considers the post-patriation transformation in Canadian politics with regard to the political efficacy and legitimacy of the women's movement. From the heady days of the section 28 mobilization, through a federal leaders' debate on women's issues in the 1984 election, to the steady decline in government support for women's organizations and for matters of gender equality generally, Dobrowolsky paints a grim picture of a shrinking opportunity structure in which the claim that "we are all equal now" obscures ongoing practices and structures of oppression. For all of the attention paid to rights and equality spawned by the patriation moment and the operation of the Charter, the longer term has been marked by efforts to delegitimize women's claims making. Whether mobilization efforts on the part of Indigenous peoples and "the 99 percent" will inspire a more engaged relationship between citizens and the Canadian state remains an open question.

Conclusion

The negotiations of 2–5 November 1981 marked a key moment in Canadian constitutional history. The resulting constitutional agreement led to the passage of the *Constitution Act, 1982,* including its amending formula, entrenched charter of rights, and commitment to Aboriginal and treaty rights (section 35). This volume revisits the patriation moment with the goal of understanding the long road to patriation, the legal and political forces that shaped patriation, and the political and constitutional consequences of patriation. The essays contributed by political scientists, legal scholars, historians, and individuals who were involved in partisan, feminist, and First Nations politics associated with the patriation negotiations make a unique contribution to our understanding of patriation and its consequences.

References

Banting, Keith, and Richard Simeon. 1983. *And No One Cheered: Federalism, Democracy and the Constitution Act.* Toronto: Methuen.

Cairns, Alan. 1992. *Charter versus Federalism: The Dilemmas of Constitutional Reform.* Montreal/Kingston: McGill-Queen's University Press.

CBC. 1981. "Canada's Constitution: The Kitchen Accord." *CBC Digital Archives.* http://www.cbc.ca/archives/categories/politics/the-constitution/charting-the-future-canadas-new-constitution/the-kitchen-accord.html.

Clarkson, Stephen, and Christina McCall. 1990. *The Magnificent Obsession.* Vol. 1, *Trudeau and Our Times.* Toronto: McClelland and Stewart.

Cohen, Lenard, Patrick Smith, and Paul Warwick. 1987. *The Vision and the Game: Making the Canadian Constitution.* Calgary: Detselig Enterprises.

Graham, Ron. 2011. *The Last Act: Pierre Trudeau, the Gang of Eight, and the Fight for Canada.* Toronto: Allen Lane Canada.

Hogg, Peter. 2010. "The Constitutional Basis of Aboriginal Rights." *Lex Electronica* 15 (1) Centre de recherché en droit public (CRDP). https://papyrus.bib.umontreal.ca/xmlui/handle/1866/9303.

Leeson, Howard. 2011. *The Patriation Minutes.* Edmonton: Centre for Constitutional Studies, Faculty of Law, University of Alberta.

Meekison, J. Peter. 1999. *Constitutional Patriation: The Lougheed-Lévesque Correspondence.* Kingston: Institute of Intergovernmental Relations, Queen's University.

Morton, F.L. 1995. "The Effect of the Charter of Rights on Canadian Federalism." *Publius* 25 (3): 173–88.

Romanow, Roy J. 2012. "Reflections on the Kitchen Accord." *Constitutional Forum* 21 (1): 1–6.

Romanow, Roy, John Whyte, and Howard Leeson. 2007. *Canada ... Notwithstanding: The Making of the Constitution 1976–1982.* 25th anniversary ed. Toronto: Thomson Carswell.

Russell, Peter. 1993. "The End of Mega Constitutional Politics in Canada?" *PS: Political Science and Politics* 26 (1): 33–37.

Sheppard, Robert, and Michael Valpy. 1982. *The National Deal: The Fight for a Canadian Constitution.* Toronto: Fleet Books.

Smiley, Donald. 1983. "A Dangerous Deed: The Constitution Act, 1982." In *And No One Cheered: Federalism, Democracy and The Constitution Act,* edited by Keith Banting and Richard Simeon, 74–95. Toronto: Methuen.

Speirs, Rosemary. 1981. "The Constitutional Surprise – 'Bad Boy' Peckford Helped Pull Rabbit from the Hat." *Globe and Mail,* 6 November, A1.

Trudeau, Pierre Elliott. 1993. *Memoirs: Pierre Elliott Trudeau.* Toronto: McClelland and Stewart.

—. 1996. *Against the Current. Selected Writings 1939–1996.* Toronto: McClelland and Stewart.

Williams, Raymond. 1977. *Marxism and Literature.* Oxford: Oxford University Press.

Constituting Constitutions: The Patriation Moment

2

Janine Brodie

The 1981 Federal-Provincial Conference of First Ministers on the Constitution was a defining moment in Canadian political development. In the early days of November, Canada's First Ministers and their closest advisers gathered in the Centennial Room on the fifth floor of Ottawa's National Conference Centre to reimagine Canada's constitutional future. Although the months preceding the conference had offered little prospect that intergovernmental consensus could be reached on a new constitutional order, it was hoped that Canada's First Ministers – eleven white men in suits, as they came to be known in some circles – could at least agree to dust off the *British North America Act (BNA Act)*, which had sat on the storage shelves of the British Parliament for 115 years, and build a consensus on a homegrown constitutional amending formula. Since 1927, successive federal governments had tried no fewer than ten times to bring Canada's founding constitutional document home, but each of these constitutional adventures had foundered on the contentious question of an amending formula. After over a century of statehood and fifty years after the United Kingdom had formally acknowledged the legislative autonomy of its dominions with the *Statute of Westminster* (1931), Canada held the dubious distinction of being the only country in the world with a constitution "living abroad."

Although the impasse over the amending formula had been differently configured in earlier federal-provincial negotiations, the core of the debate invariably revolved around contests over the respective powers and legislative autonomy of Canada's federal and provincial governments. As the eminent constitutional scholar Frank Scott explained to a gathering of the Royal Society in 1961, these were effectively struggles about sovereignty. The "repatriation of the constitution involves replacing the theory of the legal sovereignty of the United Kingdom, on which the BNA Act now rests, with a new theory." "The amending clause," he added, "will imply that theory" (Scott 1977, 402). Where would ultimate authority rest in a new constitutional order – with the federal government or the provinces, with the courts and rights-bearing citizens or legislatures, or with nations, and, if so, which ones? This chapter traces the competing claims to power that collided behind the closed doors of the National Conference Centre, as well as the compromises and discursive formulations that constructed a new but still incomplete constitutional order in Canada. It outlines the compelling developments leading to the November meeting and then explores the dynamic interplay of dominant, residual, and emergent forces that configured this watershed event. The chapter concludes with some thoughts about the anticipated and unanticipated legacies of the patriation moment.

Prelude: The Making of a Constitutional Moment

Canada's First Ministers gathered in Ottawa in November 1981 with a "mixed mood of grudging necessity, persistent mistrust, and moderate hope" (Romanow, Whyte, and Leeson 1984, 193). The pressure to come to a new constitutional consensus was greater than in previous eras, and the stakes were higher. After Quebec's referendum on sovereignty association was defeated in 1980, Prime Minister Pierre Trudeau set in motion a constitutional process to make good on his promise to Quebec voters, pledged in the heat of the referendum campaign, that a no vote was a vote for change. Trudeau then informed the House of Commons that the constitution would be renewed and that he would not stop "until it was done" (quoted in Graham 2011, 29). His plan was to unveil a new constitution, complete with an amending formula and a charter of rights and freedoms, on Canada Day 1981, the fiftieth anniversary of the *Statute of Westminster* (Graham 2011, 68).

Trudeau's broader vision of constitutional renewal prioritized pan-Canadian minority language rights, a stronger economic union, and an entrenched charter of rights and freedoms. His agenda, however, faced immediate resistance from a tapestry of dissenters, among them Québécois nationalists, western province builders, Indigenous leaders, and parliamentary traditionalists. Some saw the patriation moment as an opportunity to bargain for a better constitutional deal; others were wary of the implications of constitutional change for the powers and protections they already had under the status quo. For the federal government, however, constitutional failure was not an option this time around. Within the inner circles of the federal government, the central issue on the table in November 1981 was no longer simply an amending formula but "the very nature of Canada" (Chrétien 1990, 284).

Although this round of constitutional reform involved an expanding cast of constitutional claims makers, the federal and provincial governments, the privileged subjects of the *BNA Act*, were the dominant players. They had engaged in a constitutional poker game over veto powers and amending formulas, devolution, and new fiscal formulations of the federal bargain for over a year, but these discussions and shuttle diplomacy only seemed to further entrench opposing positions and increase polarization. Trudeau's promise of constitutional renewal appeared to be slipping from his hands as one obstacle blended into another. A First Ministers' meeting in Ottawa in September 1980 ended in abject failure. In October, Trudeau raised the stakes by circumventing the premiers and addressing the Canadian public directly. He announced on national TV that he was prepared to act unilaterally on what he termed the "People's Package" – patriation with an all-Canadian amending formula and an entrenched bill of rights. The so-called Powers Package, involving various provincial demands associated with jurisdictional realignments, would be tabled for future federal-provincial negotiations. In November 1980, a Joint Committee of the House of Commons and the Senate launched televised hearings on the proposed Charter; the committee ultimately heard from 914 individuals, 294 groups, and 104 witnesses, the vast majority of whom supported the constitutional entrenchment of a charter of rights and freedoms (Graham 2011, 87). In fact, most lobbied for a broader menu of rights than those included in the draft Charter document. On the basis of these consultations, the Joint Committee submitted an amended and, most would say, vastly improved version of the Charter to the House of Commons in April 1981.

The prime minister's threat of unilateral action and partitioning of the constitutional agenda met with immediate resistance from a coalition of provinces. These provinces condemned Trudeau's People's Package as a thinly disguised federal power grab. They saw the Charter as a violation of the federal principle of divided sovereignty and a potential threat to provincial legislative autonomy, especially with respect to the provision of minority language rights. Three provincial court challenges quickly ensued. As Philip Girard explains in Chapter 6, the lower courts split 2–1 on the legality of federal unilateralism and so the question was put to the Supreme Court of Canada (SCC), which rendered its decision in late September 1981. It ruled that federal unilateralism was technically legal but unconstitutional in a broader sense, violating both the spirit of federalism and Canadian constitutional convention, which, the SCC ruled, anticipated a substantial degree of provincial consent (Graham 2011, 72–73). This decision effectively sent the First Ministers back to the bargaining table for a last try at forging an intergovernmental consensus on the patriation of the *BNA Act.*

In preparation for the November meeting, the federal government shaved its constitutional agenda to a short list of three deeply contentious items: patriation, an amending formula, and a charter of rights and freedoms (Graham 2011, 73). When the doors closed at the National Conference Centre on 2 November, however, few were optimistic that a deal could be struck. Provincial demands for a significant redistribution of jurisdictional power had been effectively put on hold, but Quebec was represented by the recently re-elected Premier René Lévesque, who was committed to the dissolution of the federation rather than its constitutional renewal. Trudeau reflected in his *Memoirs* that the election of the Parti Québécois (PQ) in 1976 made negotiations both unavoidable and unlikely to succeed. Although Peter Russell takes issue with the rush to certainty on this matter (see Chapter 11), Trudeau (1993, 246) concluded: "It is clear that there never was a realistic chance of persuading a separatist party to renew the constitution of Canada." The consensus seemed to be that the Quebec delegation was prepared to walk out if no meaningful concessions were put on the table, effectively shutting down the process, as previous experience had demonstrated. After all, both the 1964 Fulton-Favreau formula and the 1971 Victoria Charter had been shelved after Quebec withdrew its support.

The separatist drama was not the only reason for skepticism during those chilly days of early November. Quebec had joined forces with seven other increasingly muscular provinces to form the so-called Gang of Eight. These provinces were determined to wrest more jurisdictional power from the federal government, or, at the very least, block any perceived encroachment on their existing powers. Still stinging from the National Energy Program and distrustful of Trudeau's vision of a reinvigorated economic union and his resolve to constitutionally entrench a national minority language rights regime, these provincial leaders welcomed René Lévesque as an ally in their united front against the federal government. As noted earlier, they were wary of the implications of the constitutional entrenchment of a charter of rights, none more vehemently than Manitoba's Sterling Lyon, who never deviated from his position that the Charter violated the fundamental premises of Canadian democracy – parliamentary sovereignty and representative democracy. And, after over a decade in power, Trudeau had more than his fair share of enemies. As is so often the case in Canadian politics, nationalism, political economy, and private animosities were interwoven in complex and unpredictable ways.

Despite all of this, a deal was struck on patriation, an amending formula, and a charter of rights and freedoms, albeit one partially tempered by a notwithstanding clause. New language on the principle of equalization and provincial jurisdiction over natural resources was added, while affirmation of existing Aboriginal and treaty rights would be included later, together with the assurance that the First Ministers would meet with Aboriginal leaders to give substance to these constitutional guarantees. In the weeks following the November conference, an unprecedented mobilization of the women's movement would secure constitutional protection of sexual equality from the notwithstanding clause. After over a year of discussions and four days of intense in-camera negotiations, Trudeau had been remarkably successful in achieving his constitutional agenda. At the conclusion of the conference, he announced to the press that he only had "one regret" to put "on the record ... we have not kept in the amending formula a reference to the ultimate sovereignty of the people as could be tested in a referendum" (Trudeau 2010, 258). Yet the prime minister's obvious bravado could not and would not conceal the agreement's glaring shortcoming. A patriation process that had begun with a pledge to Quebec to affect meaningful constitutional renewal concluded without the consent of the Quebec government. A visibly stunned René Lévesque responded with an air of resignation: "All of this is sad ... for Quebec; perhaps even sadder for Canada ... Quebec finds itself alone. It will be up to the Quebec people to draw their conclusions" (Lévesque 2010, 259). Success and failure stared at each other across the negotiating table, and, to borrow a line from Banting and Simeon (1983), "no one cheered."

No one could predict whether or when the seismic shift in Canadian constitutional politics endorsed at the First Ministers' conference would generate political tsunamis on different political shores. In the past three decades, the 1981 constitutional reforms, especially the *Canadian Charter of Rights and Freedoms*, have generated divisive political debates about, among other things, the supremacy of the SCC over elected legislatures, the ascendency of an unelected "Court Party," the judicialization of politics, a reframing of the relationship between the courts and legislatures, and the emergence of new identities and new forms of claims making in Canadian politics (Arthurs 2003, 10). The echoes of this constitutional moment also have reverberated through many of the most significant and often antagonistic developments in Canadian politics in the past thirty years: the failed Meech Lake and Charlottetown Accords, a nearly successful secession referendum in Quebec in 1995, the fracturing of the federal party system, and ongoing tensions with Aboriginal peoples. On so many terrains, November 1981 was a critical juncture in Canadian political development, establishing new pathways for political contestation, political decision making, and conflict resolution. But how do we go about recalling this moment, which was so rife with conflicting motivations, visions, and memories, so contradictory and equivocal in its outcomes, and yet so integral to our collective present and future?

Dominant, Residual, and Emergent Forces

The late British cultural theorist Raymond Williams (1977, 121–27) argued that such significant cultural and political moments defy singular authoritative narratives because each is uniquely configured and constituted by a dynamic interplay among dominant, residual, and emergent political imaginaries and social forces. The *dominant*, according to Williams, embodies and advances the perspectives of the ruling political class and social majorities, but it is always partial, contested, and unstable. The dominant, by definition, is unable to incorporate all of the conflicting claims to power that configure the politics of an era, and thus must continuously defend its authority from contending meanings, some with deep roots in the past, and others only beginning to take form (Williams 1977, 123). The dominant, however, is fortified by particular discursive and institutional configurations and power relations that enable it to neglect, exclude, or refuse to recognize either *residual* claims, which have been formed in the past but remain active and effective elements of the present, or *emergent* perspectives, which offer competing diagnoses of what is at stake and unsettling, if not disruptive, political solutions (Williams 1977, 121). At any given moment, these three forces can be found in dynamic interplay, shaping the future in often unanticipated ways.

The Dominant

The 1981 patriation conference stirred a potent and volatile mixture of the dominant, residual, and emergent, each advancing a particular conception of sovereignty and the ultimate power to decide. In fact, there were at least four different claims to foundational constitutional authority vying for affirmation in this round of constitutional negotiations, only three of which were represented at the negotiating table. Did Canadian sovereignty ultimately emanate from citizens, provincial governments, or two founding settler societies? Or, as the Aboriginal leadership, who were excluded from the negotiations, contended, was Canada founded on the idea of treaty relationships between settler and Indigenous peoples, each with legitimate claims to their own legal traditions and governmental institutions? The dominant narrative, which divided the ruling class into federal and provincial camps, framed this constitutional moment as a stark and uncompromising choice between two very different visions of the essence of Canada's constitutional order. "Did Canadian sovereignty," Trudeau asked, "emanate from a people with a collective will to live as a nation, seeking a common good throughout the country, and governing themselves under a federative form of Constitution?" Or was it "the creature of ten provinces (some would say two nations), dependent on them for its existence and governed by the consensus of its eleven governments – ten provincial and one federal?" (Trudeau 1990, 375; Graham 2011, 17). These two visions, Trudeau added, had "hardened, crystallized, and clashed" throughout the constitutional renewal process that effectively began "with the interprovincial meeting of 1967 and ended with the federal-provincial conference of November 1981" (Trudeau 1990, 376).

Trudeau's unequivocal juxtaposition of the will of the Canadian people against the prerogatives and interests of governments reflected his fundamental commitment to individual rights, but it also misrepresented the theoretical and historical complexities of the sovereignty question that was intractably burrowed in constitutional reform in 1981. Trudeau had been a champion of individual rights as a shield against the abuses of power and the pathologies of ethnic nationalism since his earliest encounters with the Duplessis regime in the late 1940s. He later wrote that he "saw the *Charter* as an expression of my long-held view that the subject of law must be the individual" (Trudeau 1993, 322). He also was convinced that a constitutionally entrenched bill of rights could offset growing centrifugal pressures in Canada, whether emanating from Quebec nationalists or resource-rich province builders. He believed that a bill of rights was the best way to begin a dialogue of constitutional reform with the provinces, explaining to the Canadian Bar Association in 1967 that "essentially we will be testing – and, hopefully, establishing – the unity of Canada" (quoted in Russell 2010b, 317). As a governing instrument, a charter promised to transcend claims to historical compacts between peoples or levels of governments by guaranteeing all national citizens, regardless of ethnicity or region, the same constitutional protections. Through judicial review, the courts could regulate common standards across provincial jurisdictions with respect to, for example, minority language and mobility rights and, in time, mould new political allegiances to a pan-Canadian political culture grounded in the idea of "rights bearing citizens of equal status" (Choudhry 2009, 239).

The dissenting provinces were quick to point out that this formulation of the ultimate sovereignty of the rights-bearing citizen, protected by an entrenched charter and unelected, federally appointed judges, violated the principles of parliamentary supremacy and federalism (divided sovereignty), which were embedded in the *BNA Act* and in Canadian constitutional convention. Canada's founding documents and subsequent political developments provided ample justification for the argument that Confederation was built on the idea of a compact, either between two founding peoples or between the federal and provincial governments. The former had a pre-Confederation lineage, hailing back to the *Quebec Act, 1774* and the 1840 *Act of Union*, and claims to special status for Quebec within Confederation had been an enduring thread in Canadian political discourse for over a century. After Quebec's Quiet Revolution in the 1960s, however, its premiers had demanded ever-greater jurisdictional and fiscal powers from Confederation in order to build a new Quebec that embodied the aspirations of an increasingly ambitious and vibrant Québécois nationalism (Choudhry 2009, 236). The tug of war for allegiances, legitimacy, and power between the national government and the provinces also had a long lineage in Canadian federalism and constitutional politics, stretching back to the Confederation debates. The arguments of earlier champions of provincial power, such as Ontario's Oliver Mowat, reappeared with particular clarity and commitment among the resource-rich provinces of the 1980s. These decentralizing pressures in the federation increased exponentially in the 1970s when postwar economic strategies, which had privileged central Canada, began to unravel. After a decade of international oil shocks, economic power was clearly shifting to the resource-rich provinces.

The promise of greater jurisdictional autonomy – what Trudeau derisively called the "patriation for power" game – was the glue that bonded the dissenting provinces in the months leading up to the patriation conference. The constitutional agenda presented to the premiers in November 1981 critically disrupted their claims to greater jurisdictional power. The dominant framing of a singular choice between a pan-Canadian rights regime and a dysfunctional and colonial constitutional status quo was uniquely Trudeau's. In the People's Package, the Charter of Rights and Freedoms was a proxy for federal power while the case for provincial power and autonomy was represented as short-sighted and parochial. As Clarkson and McCall (1990, 357) argue, Trudeau viewed the premiers as "small-minded, self-interested, and regional barons." He came out swinging at the dissenting provinces, charging that the "greed of the provinces was a bottomless pit" (quoted in Graham 2011, 68). In his opening statement to the conference, he rejected the provinces' patriation plan as "incremental separatism" (Leeson 2011, 17). Leeson notes that during the closed-door negotiations, Alberta premier Peter Lougheed confronted Trudeau directly, asking, "You don't believe in the equality of provinces?" Trudeau responded, "I believe in the equality of people" (quoted in Leeson 2011, 39). As noted above, Trudeau's response was deeply rooted in his political world view, but he was also a brilliant strategist and keenly aware of the power of popular appeals to individual rights. The provinces were unlikely to prevail in negotiations framed as a zero-sum battle between the Canadian people and greedy provinces, especially as the People's Package increasingly captured the public imagination. With the notable exceptions of Bill Davis of Ontario and Richard Hatfield of New Brunswick, both of whom supported the federal agenda, the premiers had been herded into a discursive corner to shadow-box with federal power.

The Residual

The People's Package, backed up with the threat of unilateralism and a referendum, was a shrewd manoeuvre that temporarily diverted, but could not suppress, robust constitutional residuals, the most powerful of which was the special status of Quebec in Confederation. Although Trudeau resisted the legitimacy of all compact theories, whether grounded in territorial or nationalist claims, Canadian politics, especially in the aftermath of Quebec's Quiet Revolution, told a very different story. As Prime Minister Lester Pearson explained to the House of Commons in late 1962, "Confederation may not have been technically a treaty or a compact between states" but "it was an understanding or a settlement between the two founding races of Canada made on the basis of an acceptable and equal partnership" (Graham 2011, 22). The Royal Commission on Bilingualism and Biculturalism, which issued its preliminary report in 1965, was mandated to recommend "what steps should be taken to develop the Canadian Confederation on the basis of an equal partnership between the two founding races" (quoted in McRoberts

1997, 117). More tangibly, the idea that Quebec was a province *pas comme les autres* had been progressively written into the federal bargain through opting-out and compensation provisions, jurisdiction sharing, and fiscal transfers. The 1971 Victoria Charter had included a veto for Quebec (and Ontario) in its proposed amending formula. Moreover, the constitutional renewal process ground to a halt when Quebec withdrew its consent, just as it had when Quebec withdrew from the 1964 Fulton-Favreau formula. Quebec governments "from Lesage to Johnston to Bertrand to Bourassa" had insisted that they would agree to patriation only on the conditions of a guaranteed veto and enhanced powers, and this had been the position of the Parti Québécois government until early 1981 (McRoberts 1997, 165).

In this round of constitutional negotiations, however, René Lévesque effectively ceded claims to Quebec's special status when he joined forces with the other dissenting provinces, the Gang of Eight, in April 1981. Lévesque endorsed an amending formula that, on most matters, would require the consent of two-thirds of the provinces, representing over 50 percent of the population, along with an opt-out with compensation provision that could be exercised by all provinces (McRoberts 1997, 165). Trudeau (1993, 313) later recalled that in so doing Lévesque had "accepted the principle of provincial equality," so that now Quebec was a "province like the others." It is generally agreed that joining the other dissenting provinces was a risky gamble, perhaps even evidence, as Trudeau (1993, 241; see Chapter 8) said later, that Lévesque was a "good tactician" but "not much of a strategist." Through this alliance, Lévesque had effectively taken the residual constructions of special status, the double contract, and sovereignty association off the negotiating table, implicitly endorsing the idea of Confederation as a compact between governments rather than between peoples.

In retrospect, however, Lévesque had little choice but to throw Quebec's hat in the ring with the other dissenting provinces. The progressive erosion of Quebec's special status in constitutional politics had begun much earlier, when Robert Bourassa walked away from the Victoria Charter in 1971. At that time, the other premiers had been willing to concede a constitutional veto to Quebec and Ontario, but this particular centre-periphery configuration of Confederation was rapidly dissolving in the political economy of the 1970s. Soon after, British Columbia argued that it should be considered a fifth region in any future amending formula, prompting oil-rich Alberta to demand that all provinces have a veto. Ontario was losing its command over the Canadian economy and Lévesque had lost too much political currency with the recent defeat of the sovereignty association referendum to reassert the veto provisions agreed upon only ten years earlier.

There was always the possibility that a strong coalition of dissenting provinces might succeed in wresting more jurisdictional power from the federal government as a condition of their support for patriation. In the end, however, the federal government did not offer significant concessions to the Gang of Eight or to Quebec. In the immediate aftermath of the conference, the PQ government tried to recover its claims to special status with a reference to the Quebec Court of Appeal, arguing specifically that "the consent of the Province of Quebec is required, by constitutional convention, for constitutional amendments affecting the legislative competence of the Quebec legislature, or the status or role of Quebec's government or legislature" *(Quebec Veto Reference)*. In 1982, however, both the Quebec Court of Appeal and the SCC held that Quebec did not have a veto by constitutional convention. The ship of state had already set sail on new constitutional waters.

In his accomplished three-part documentary *The Champions*, which chronicles the political careers of Pierre Trudeau and René Lévesque, Donald Brittain (1978, 1988) made an astute observation. For most of their lives, these two men had been champions of different visions of the future of Quebec, but they also were "prisoners of each other." Howard Leeson makes a similar point. Both men, he argues, were "rather sad figures, so engrossed in their own fight that they [forgot] that they [were] dealing with other political leaders who [did] not agree with either of them" (Leeson 2011, 2). The November 1981 First Ministers' conference marked the beginning of Lévesque's disturbing descent into political obscurity (Poliquin 2009). Trudeau, in contrast, assumed the posture of the victor. Dismissing denunciations of the backroom deals, he quipped that Lévesque had "tried to destroy our vision with his referendum and he failed" and he failed with the gang of 8 (Trudeau 1993, 326–27). But history would prove that Trudeau's vision of "transcending the linguistic divide" and "Québécois nationalism" with a charter of rights also failed (Choudhry 2009, 235). The 1981 agreement prompted a series of half measures, constitutional and legislative, to draw Quebec into a new constitutional order, among them the failed Meech Lake and Charlottetown Accords and two resolutions in the House of Commons, the first in 1995, following a nearly successful referendum on sovereignty, which recognized Quebec as a "distinct society," and the second in 2006, which recognized the Québécois as "a nation within a united Canada." Recognition of the identities and aspirations of a people, residual compacts in a sense, remain an effective element of the present, living alongside and in conversation with the rights-bearing individual of the Charter.

The Emergent

There was a broad spectrum of emergent actors in dynamic interplay with dominant and residual forces during this constitutional moment, but their representatives were not included at the negotiation table. Nevertheless, groups speaking for women, the disabled, the poor, minority religious and ethnic groups, and Aboriginal peoples were an integral part of the constitutional renewal process, lobbying MPs, mobilizing supporters, and engaging in education campaigns. The joint parliamentary committee on the constitution was the primary focus of this variegated campaign for recognition and rights, however. As Jean Chrétien (1990, 298), minister of justice in 1981, later explained, the Joint Committee provided a forum for the "normally unpowerful and unorganized" to have some input into the Charter. In subsequent years, some political analysts have argued that the Charter created political spaces for a new class of claims makers in Canadian politics – so-called Charter Canadians (Cairns 1999) – and that the equality-seeking groups recognized in the Charter have colluded with the judiciary to form a "Court Party." It is alleged that this unelected alliance has achieved political outcomes that would never have passed through legislatures representing political majorities and "ordinary" Canadians (Morton and Knopff 2000). Contrary to such accounts, however, these emergent forces were neither products of the Charter nor dependent on the judiciary for claims to recognition and equality. Instead, equality-seeking groups helped to fertilize the political ground for the Charter, and their subsequent victories and defeats in the courts, as other chapters in this book describe, demonstrate both the possibilities and limits of constitutionally entrenched liberal rights regimes for inclusion and equality.

Raymond Williams (1977, 123) argued that truly oppositional emergent forces, which promote visions of a political future that exceed the imagination and horizons of the dominant order, are typically excluded, diverted, forgotten, and repressed. They are relegated to the margins, where, in time, they may gather sufficient momentum to transform the dominant forces or, alternatively, fade into the annals of history. Aboriginal groups represented just such an emergent oppositional force and attest to the resilience (and reconfiguration) of the idea of "peoples" in contemporary Canadian politics. Aboriginal groups approached the constitutional renewal process with different agendas, but each saw the process as a way of redefining settler-Indigenous relationships. As Ladner and McCrossan (2009, 267) recall, Inuit representatives sought constitutional recognition of their land rights, representatives of Métis and non-status Indians wanted to be recognized as Aboriginal peoples, and the flagship organizations of status Indians "viewed the Constitution as an opportunity to negotiate the 'terms and conditions' of their relationship with Canada." To realize these ends, as Chapter 9 details, Aboriginal groups engaged in a multistage lobbying campaign: organizing a "Constitution Express" via rail across Canada, presenting briefs to the joint parliamentary committee, and petitioning the British Parliament and Queen Elizabeth II.

After substantial resistance from several premiers, the 1981–82 constitutional moment did launch a new era of Aboriginal politics in Canada. Section 25 of the Charter ensured that Charter guarantees "of certain rights and freedoms shall not be construed so as to abrogate or derogate" from any Aboriginal and treaty rights. A First Ministers' consensus on the language of section 35 of the *Constitution Act, 1982* was reached in the weeks following the conference. This section "recognized and affirmed" the "existing aboriginal and treaty rights of the aboriginal peoples of Canada." It was agreed that Canada's First Ministers and Aboriginal leaders would meet to give substance to section 35, thereby, Aboriginal leaders hoped, laying the foundations for a new post-colonial constitutional order in Canada. However, these meetings and another, convened by Brian Mulroney in 1987, ended in obstruction and failure.

Maurice Bulbulian's two-part series *Dancing around the Table* (1983, 1987) documents these meetings, demonstrating, in stark relief, the ways in which Aboriginal claims to self-determination exceeded the constitutional imagination and ambitions of the early 1980s. The footage also reveals a "motivated ignorance" on the part of the First Ministers that ensured that Aboriginal leaders' vision of a Canada with multiple and/or divided sovereignties was never seriously entertained (Calhoun 1989). Prime Minister Trudeau, for example, began the 1983 conference with a series of parameter statements: Aboriginal rights "must not violate the rights of other Canadians"; "we are going to bargain what your rights are" and "in what way you will be integrated into Canadian society" (Bulbulian 1983). Each of these pronouncements obscured the fact that Aboriginal peoples were seeking to recover their own constitutional order, which had been suppressed through colonization and the *Indian Act.* For many of their leaders, the question was not how Aboriginal peoples could be integrated into the new liberal rights regime entrenched in the Charter but rather how sovereignty might be multiplied and redistributed between settler and Indigenous constitutional orders.

One after another, Aboriginal leaders responded that their goal was self-government and that there was "more than one way to understand equality." But Trudeau, a disciple of liberal individualism, could not see them. At the end of the 1984 conference, and at the end of his political career, he told Mary Simon, then an Inuit representative, that "in a sense you are equal when you think you are equal and the law won't change much" (Bulbulian 1987). The contrast between this dismissive statement and his celebration of the ultimate sovereignty of individual rights only two years earlier could not have been more telling. The resistance of the premiers to Aboriginal demands, in contrast, was more firmly grounded in political economy and self-interest. This was especially clear at the 1987 conference convened by Conservative Prime Minister Brian Mulroney, a meeting that Premier Bourassa of Quebec did not even bother to attend. "Whose land?" the premiers demanded; "who would pay?" "Self-determination is an empty concept," they asserted, but also added, "don't provinces also have a right to self-determination?" In 1987, the premiers simply refused to negotiate a new beginning, hiding behind the catchphrase "define before we sign" (Bulbulian 1987).

Having failed to put flesh on section 35 through good faith political negotiations with Canada's First Ministers, Aboriginal groups have had to rely on a series of SCC decisions to rectify this. Many believe that this has been a costly strategy that has pushed the goal of self-determination further out of reach. Although the SCC has determined that section 35 constrains the exercise of sovereign power (*R. v. Sparrow*), the court has taken the position that section 35 primarily offers cultural protection, specifically to those practices, customs, and traditions that were integral to Aboriginal peoples and societies prior to contact with Europeans (*R. v. Van der Peet;* Dick 2009). Thus, the courts have not only taken on the role of deciding what is integral to Aboriginal cultures but also constructed the authentic Aboriginal as an artifact of the past, not a vibrant partner in our collective present (Dick 2009, 973–74; Borrows 2010, 11, 15). Just as important, Caroline Dick argues, the SCC singular emphasis on the cultural protections offered by section 35 has "allowed the Court to avoid the issue of Aboriginal sovereignty and the legitimacy of the Canadian state's authority over Aboriginal peoples" (Dick 2009, 972–73; Ladner and McCrossan 2009, 272). At the same time, John Borrows (2010, 197) contends that strong arguments can also be made that Indigenous law and self-governance "were integral to the organization of the distinctive cultures of aboriginal peoples throughout Canada prior to the arrival of Europeans." In other words, even a circumscribed reading of section 35 could support Aboriginal aspirations to self-government.

Trudeau once confessed that he "honestly [did not] know what the Indians want" (quoted in Ladner and McCrossan 2009, 269). Self-determination for "peoples" and multiple/divided sovereignty based on treaty relationships between nations, although implied in sections 25 and 35, fell outside the constitutional imagination of the 1980s and was resisted. Emergent struggles for a more robust understanding of settler-Aboriginal relations have repeatedly run up against what Dale Turner aptly describes as the "walls of resistance" of settler societies, especially the doctrines of *terra nullius* and extinguishment, and the "salt water thesis" (Turner 2006). Paradoxically, the *Constitution Act, 1982*, which affirms the inherent rights of Aboriginal peoples, now serves as another brick in that wall. In 2007, Canada, together with three other settler societies – Australia, New Zealand, and the United States – refused to sign the United Nations *Declaration on the Rights of Indigenous Peoples* (UNDRIP). Chuck Strahl, then minister of Indian Affairs and Northern Development, explained that the declaration was "fundamentally incompatible with Canada's constitutional framework." "By signing on," he said, "you default to this document by saying that the only rights in play here are the rights of First Nations. And, of course, in Canada, that's inconsistent with our constitution" (Canwest 2007). Subsequently, the federal government signed on to UNDRIP, but only conditionally.

This, of course, is a convenient but specious argument. The UNDRIP is not a legally binding document under international law but national constitutions can be changed to respect and hopefully advance international norms, such as those contained in the *Universal Declaration of Human Rights*. The *Canadian Charter of Rights and Freedoms* is a testament to this. Perhaps more to the point, Canada has a history of conventional practice with compacts between peoples, divided sovereignty, and multilevel governance. Canada also has internationally lauded political theorists and constitutional scholars who have written comprehensively about blending rights and recognition as well as the traditions and assumptions of western and Indigenous governance (Borrows 2010; Tully 1995). Most important, the recommendations of the 1996 Royal Commission on Aboriginal Peoples clearly envision a template for a new compact and new Aboriginal order of government within Canada's constitutional framework. These remain emergent forces, but they do outline pathways around some walls of resistance. In a sense, the page on Aboriginal rights that was opened in the 1981 patriation moment remains unwritten.

Conclusion

Constitutions are both nouns and verbs. They are celebrated public documents that set out the supreme rules and fundamental values by which we govern ourselves. Constitutions also embody the results of previous struggles over sovereignty, recognition, and citizenship. However, constitutions also always actively constitute and reconstitute. Through political, not solely judicial, processes and decision making, constitutions open and close spaces for political mobilization and claims making for residual and emergent forces; they form and reform the public body and public bodies, and they articulate and rearticulate public imaginaries about nationhood, inclusion, and equity.

The patriation moment can be assessed through both lenses. The agreement struck by the First Ministers in November 1981 formed the template for the *Constitution Act, 1982,* which has rewritten and continues to rewrite the rules by which we govern ourselves. At the same time, the experience of the past three decades also indicates that few of these changes were as dramatic as those feared by the early critics of constitutional reform. The constitutional entrenchment of the *Canadian Charter of Rights and Freedoms* has resulted in a renegotiation of the rules of engagement between the state and citizens. Broader legal protections have been granted to a diverse range of claims makers, among them the accused and convicted; women; minority language, ethnic, and religious groups; and gays and lesbians. The courts' rulings are rarely definitive, however, and, as discussed above with respect to Aboriginal claims to self-determination, the decisions have been decidedly ambiguous, tenuous, and framed in the language of culture rather than sovereignty. Moreover, there is little evidence to suggest that the courts have usurped the power and prerogatives of elected legislatures or hijacked the policy process and the public purse. Instead, they have established a dialogue with legislatures and bureaucracies and have been reluctant to render decisions, especially with respect to social rights claims, that imply fiscal commitments from governments (Hogg and Bushnell 1997; Kelly 2005).

In the intervening years, prominent constitutional scholars have wondered aloud whether the era of mega-constitutional politics of the 1980s and early 1990s was worth the political wounds that it inflicted (Russell 1992). The patriation process, followed by the unsuccessful Meech Lake and Charlottetown Accords, failed to draw Quebec under a renewed constitutional umbrella. Harry Arthurs argues that these struggles largely succeeded in generating a "cult of constitutionalism," which transformed "legal practice and scholarship" rather than society itself. While our attentions were diverted by constitutional reform, the power to shape the norms that govern the possibilities and constraints of the daily lives of Canadians shifted elsewhere, specifically to processes of globalization, international trade agreements, and neoliberalization, all of which fall outside the purview of the new constitutional order (Arthurs 2003, 5–6;

Schneiderman 2003). Roderick Macdonald and Robert Wolfe (2008, 69) similarly argue that economic development paradigms or "national policies" are "more constitutive of the Canadian state and its policy instruments than any of its renamed Constitution Acts." Others suggest that the centre of power has shifted in recent decades, not from elected legislatures to the judiciary but instead from all branches of government to the executive, specifically to the Prime Minister's Office and the political operatives and senior mandarins housed therein (Savoie 2008; Martin 2010).

Few would dispute Peter Russell's astute observation (2010a, 289) that the failure of the Charlottetown Accord in 1992 brought to an end the era of mega-constitutional politics in Canada "with a whimper rather than a bang." Russell (2010a, 289) continues to argue that the idea of big constitutional change has fallen into a "deep freeze" but that Canada's constitution continues to evolve "through the quieter, incremental, and sunnier ways of organic constitutionalism – the very ways in which our constitutional system evolved through the first century." Recent decades provide many examples of what is sometimes termed "legislative constitutionalism" – that is, constitution-like proclamations and rules emanating from legislatures and intergovernmental agreements rather than from constitutional negotiation and change. The recognition of Quebec as a "distinct society" and the Québécois as a "nation within a united Canada," the *Clarity Act*, the residential schools apology, and recent proposals to establish an elected Senate through federal legislation are examples of this trend. It is not clear, however, whether bypassing the difficult politics of constitutional change is indeed, as Russell puts it, a "sunnier way." The growing devolution of immigrant selection to the provinces and the unfolding instruments of open federalism, for example, may soothe provincial demands for greater autonomy, perhaps most especially in Quebec, but such incremental changes generate legal tapestries, unanticipated consequences, and policy incoherence. Incremental change also effectively places the power to determine the content and pace of change back in the hands of governments that can choose to act on some unfulfilled constitutional futures while ignoring, perhaps even attempting to reverse, others. The ongoing struggle of Aboriginal peoples for recognition and self-determination is a glaring example. The legacies of the patriation moment are many. There have been victories, setbacks, improvisations, and difficult lessons learned in the past thirty years. One of these lessons, undoubtedly, is that the patriation of the *BNA Act* from the dusty vaults of Imperial Britain did not sever Canada from its colonial past. This break can come only when, through meaningful negotiations with Aboriginal peoples, Canada begins to build the foundations for a new post-colonial constitutional future.

Acknowledgments

This research was supported by the Canada Research Chair Program, in which I hold a Tier 1 Chair in Political Economy and Social Governance, and the Pierre Elliott Trudeau Foundation, which awarded me a fellowship in 2010. I also thank Brent Epperson for his capable research assistance.

References

Arthurs, Harry. 2003. "Constitutional Courage." *McGill Law Journal/Revue de droit de McGill* 49 (1): 1–22.

Banting, Keith, and Richard Simeon. 1983. *And No One Cheered: Federalism, Democracy and the Constitution Act*. Toronto: Methuen.

Borrows, John. 2010. *Canada's Indigenous Constitution*. Toronto: University of Toronto Press.

Brittain, Donald. 1978. *The Champions*. Part 1, *Unlikely Warriors;* Part 2, *The Trappings of Power.* https://www.nfb.ca/film/champions_part_1/.

—. 1988. *The Champions.* Part 3, *The Final Battle.* https://www.nfb.ca/film/champions_part_3

Bulbulian, Maurice. 1983. *Dancing around the Table.* Part 1. http://www.nfb.ca/film/dancing_around_the_table_1.

—. 1987. *Dancing around the Table.* Part 2. https://www.nfb.ca/film/dancing_around_the_table_part_two

Cairns, Alan. 1999. *Charter versus Federalism.* Montreal/Kingston: McGill-Queen's University Press.

Calhoun, Cheshire. 1989. "Responsibility and Reproach." *Ethics* 99 (2): 389–406. doi:10.1086/293071.

Canwest. 2007. "Native Rights Declaration Inconsistent with Legal Tradition: Strahl." *National Post,* 13 September. http://www.canada.com/nationalpost/news/story.html?id=23df9769-3423-4f43-b828-a755725c2719&k=23677.

Choudhry, Sujit. 2009. "Bills of Rights as Instruments of Nation-Building in Multinational States: The Canadian Charter and Quebec Nationalism." In *Contested*

Constitutionalism: Reflections on the Canadian Charter of Rights and Freedoms, edited by James Kelly and Christopher Manfredi, 233–50. Vancouver: UBC Press.

Chrétien, Jean. 1990. "Bringing the Constitution Home." In *Toward a Just Society: The Trudeau Years*, edited by Thomas Axworthy and Pierre Elliot Trudeau, 282–310. Toronto: Viking Press.

Clarkson, Stephen, and Christina McCall. 1990. *The Magnificent Obsession.* Vol. 1, *Trudeau and Our Times.* Toronto: McClelland and Stewart.

Dick, Caroline. 2009. "Culture and the Courts Revisited: Group Rights Scholarship and the Evolution of S. 35(1)." *Canadian Journal of Political Science* 42 (4): 957–78. doi:10.1017/S0008423909990655.

Graham, Ron. 2011. *The Last Act: Pierre Trudeau, the Gang of Eight, and the Fight for Canada.* Toronto: Allan Lane Canada.

Hogg, Peter, and Allison Bushnell. 1997. "The Charter Dialogue between Courts and Legislatures." *Osgoode Hall Law Journal* 35 (1): 75–124.

Kelly, James. 2005. *Governing with the Charter: Legislative and Judicial Activism and Framers' Intent.* Vancouver: UBC Press.

Ladner, Kiera, and Michael McCrossan. 2009. "The Road Not Taken: Aboriginal Rights after the Re-Imagining of the Constitutional Order." In *Contested Constitutionalism: Reflections on the Canadian Charter of Rights and Freedoms*, edited by James Kelly and Christopher Manfredi, 263–83. Vancouver: UBC Press.

Leeson, Howard. 2011. *The Patriation Minutes.* Edmonton: Centre for Constitutional Studies.

Lévesque, René. 2010. "'Quebec Finds Itself Alone.' Excerpt from Public Statement, November 6, 1981." In *Essential Readings in Canadian Government and Politics*, edited by Peter Russell, François Rocher, Debra Thompson, and Linda White, 259–60. Toronto: Emond Montgomery Publications.

Macdonald, Roderick, and Robert Wolfe. 2008. "The Real Constitutional Question: Canada's 21st Century National Policy." *Policy Options* 30(1): 68–76.

Martin, Lawrence. 2010. *Harperland: The Politics of Control.* Toronto: Penguin Group Canada.

McRoberts, Kenneth. 1997. *Misconceiving Canada: The Struggle for National Unity.* Toronto: Oxford University Press.

Morton, F.L., and Rainer Knopff. 2000. *The Charter Revolution and the Court Party.* Peterborough: Broadview Press.

Poliquin, Daniel. 2009. *René Lévesque*. Toronto: Penguin Canada.

R. v. Sparrow, [1990] 1 S.C.R. 1075 [*Sparrow*].

R. v. Van der Peet, [1996] 2 S.C.R. 507 [*Van der Peet*].

Re: Objection by Quebec to a Resolution to Amend the Constitution, [1982] 2 S.C.R. 793 [*Quebec Veto Reference*].

Reference re Amendment of the Constitution of Canada, [1982] Que. C.A. 33, 134 D.L.R. (3d) 719.

Romanow, Roy, John Whyte, and Howard Leeson. 1984. *Canada Nothwithstanding: The Making of the Constitution, 1976–1982*. Toronto: Carswell/Methuen.

Russell, Peter. 1992. *Constitutional Odyssey: Can Canadians Become a Sovereign People?* Toronto: University of Toronto Press.

—. (2006) 2010a. "Constitutional Politics: In a New Era Canada Returns to Old Methods." In *Essential Readings in Canadian Government and Politics*, edited by Peter Russell, François Rocher, Debra Thompson, and Linda White, 289–92. Toronto: Emond Montgomery Publications.

—. (1983) 2010b. "The Political Purposes of the Canadian Charter." In *Essential Readings in Canadian Government and Politics*, edited by Peter Russell, François Rocher, Debra Thompson, and Linda White, 315–27. Toronto: Emond Montgomery Publications.

Savoie, Donald. 2008. *Court Government and the Collapse of Accountability in Canada and the United Kingdom*. Toronto: University of Toronto Press.

Schneiderman, David. 2003. "The Old and New Constitutionalism." In *Reinventing Canada*, edited by Janine Brodie and Linda Trimble, 243–58. Toronto: Prentice Hall.

Scott, Frank R. 1977. "Our Changing Constitution." In *Essays on the Constitution: Aspects of Canadian Law and Politics*, 390–404. Toronto: University of Toronto Press.

Tully, James. 1995. *Strange Multiplicity: Constitutionalism in an Age of Diversity*. Cambridge, UK: Cambridge University Press.

Turner, Dale. 2006. *This Is Not a Peace Pipe: Toward a Critical Indigenous Philosophy*. Toronto: University of Toronto Press.

Trudeau, Pierre Elliott. 1990. "The Values of a Just Society." In *Toward a Just Society: The Trudeau Years*, edited by Thomas Axworthy and Pierre Elliot Trudeau, 357–88. Toronto: Viking Press.

—. 1993. *Memoirs*. Toronto: McClelland and Stewart.

—. 2010. "'I Am Happy to Report That a Consensus Has Been Reached.' Excerpt from Public Statement, Friday, November 6, 1981." In *Essential Readings in Canadian Government and Politics*, edited by Peter Russell, François Rocher, Debra Thompson, and Linda White, 258–59. Toronto: Emond Montgomery Publications.

Williams, Raymond. 1977. *Marxism and Literature*. Oxford: Oxford University Press.

PART 2
Tracing the Long Road to Patriation

Constitutional Nationalism: Politics, Law, and Culture on the Road to Patriation

3

Eric M. Adams

Pierre Trudeau did not like the word "patriation." Acutely aware of the power of words – whether describing his constitutional reforms as the "People's Package" or deriding his opponents' view of federalism as a "confederation of shopping centres" – in his memoirs Trudeau dismissed "patriation" as an "ugly formal term" (Trudeau 1993, 250, 302). And so it was that in the scattered rain of 17 April 1982, just before the Queen signed the constitution into law, Trudeau spoke instead of the "bringing home of our constitution ... and the beginning of a new spring" (CBC 1982). Such metaphors were intended to attract and hold the Canadian public to a particular constitutional ideal, one intimately rooted to place, sealed by identity, and enlivened by future possibilities. Ignoring his earlier disdain for nationalism (which he likened to superstition and magic), Trudeau as prime minister frequently invoked a spirit of *constitutional nationalism* in his quest for constitutional change (Trudeau 1965, 34). In doing so, he drew on a long tradition in Canadian constitutional politics, law, and culture. In this chapter, I argue that constitutional nationalism and its attendant rhetoric of home, nation, and identity played a critical role in setting the intellectual foundations and creating some of the fissures in the patriation negotiations of 1981.

Constitutional nationalism locates its demand for national self-determination, ideology, and sovereignty in formal constitutional instruments. It takes seriously not only the *legal* authority of the constitution to effect change but also the *symbolic* role of the constitution as an instrument to construct and cement national identity, unity, and purpose. Canadian constitutional nationalism bears some affinity with Jürgen Habermas's modern concept of "constitutional patriotism" as the attachment to constitutionally inscribed liberal norms (Habermas 1998, 500; Müller and Scheppele 2008). For Habermas, by transcending ethnic nationalism as the basis for constitutional democracy, constitutional patriotism and its attachment to constitutional rights offers hope for political cohesiveness among multinational states or federations of states. For much of the twentieth century, however, Canadian constitutional nationalists downplayed pluralism and rights-based constitutionalism in favour of the singularity, symbolism, legality, and sovereignty of nationhood. As the other chapters in this volume amply reveal, constitutional nationalism, although dominant among many political, legal, and cultural elites, was but a single thread in a larger tapestry of Canadian political thought in the decades leading to patriation. Powerful challenges to constitutional nationalism emanated from Quebec, feminists, and Aboriginal peoples, among others. Undoubtedly, the blunt, monolithic nationalism inherent in the discourse adopted among constitutional nationalists explains in part why many felt increasingly alienated by Canada's twentieth-century constitutional project. As we shall see, from its earliest days, Canadian constitutional nationalism revealed signs of the constitutional clashes to come.

This chapter explores the role of constitutional nationalism especially among anglophone politicians, lawyers, and the public in setting Canada on the road to the momentous constitutional changes of 1982. Constitutional nationalism first gained force in parliamentary debates following the end of the First World War. Buoyed by arguments that emphasized the need for Canada's constitutional status to match its growing spirit of independence and self-confidence as a nation, the demand for the formal power of constitutional amendment and self-determination quickly won converts across the political spectrum. In making their arguments, constitutional nationalists drew upon emerging ideas in Canadian constitutional scholarship similarly premised on the desire to recognize the distinctiveness of Canadian constitutional purpose, and the impossibility of achieving it under the legal, judicial, and constitutional oversight of Great Britain. When Canada moved increasingly towards such independence with the Balfour Declaration, the *Statute of Westminster, 1931*, and the ending of appeals to the Judicial Committee of the Privy Council (JCPC), Canadian constitutional culture came to reflect the emerging consensus that Canada's national identity was intimately tied to its constitutional documents and, crucially, the ability to alter them.

"[A] nation does not remain a nation only because it has roots in the past," George Grant noted. "Memory is never enough to guarantee that a nation can articulate itself in the present. There must be a thrust of intention into the future" (Grant 1965, 12). A fully Canadian constitution provided constitutional nationalists with the opportunity to remake the past, define the present, and re-envision the future. And yet for all of constitutional nationalism's legal, rhetorical, symbolic, and cultural force, Quebec's dissent in the patriation negotiations of 1981, and the failures of the Meech Lake and Charlottetown Accords in their aftermath, revealed the stark reality that Canada's fundamental constitutional principles – their past, present, and future – remained contested, elusive, and uncertain.

Constitutional Nationalism in Politics

Canada's original constitutional framers planted the seeds of future controversy. The *British North America Act* (*BNA Act;* now known as the *Constitution Act, 1867*) that they drafted contained no amending formula. The omission could not have been an oversight since other constitutions available at the time of drafting – notably those of New Zealand and the United States – included amending formulas. Furthermore, the Canadian framers included a provision dealing with the amendment of provincial constitutions (what was then section 92[1]), and specified where Parliament retained the power to amend individual sections (section 40, for example, defined electoral districts "until the Parliament of Canada otherwise provides"). Although the historical record is opaque, the scholarly consensus is that the framers likely regarded a general amending formula as unnecessary since the British Parliament would continue its role as the ultimate source of legal sovereignty for the new

Dominion of Canada (Oliver 2005, 111). Earlier constitutional acts in British North America – the *Quebec Act, 1774*, the *Constitutional Act, 1791*, the *Act of Union* of 1840 – had not contained amendment provisions either. As Thomas D'Arcy McGee expressed it: "We go to the Imperial Government, the common arbiter of us all, in our true Federal metropolis – we go there to ask for our fundamental Charter. We hope, by having that Charter that can only be amended by the authority that made it, that we will lay the basis of permanency for our future government" (cited in Gérin-Lajoie 1950, 34).

As D'Arcy McGee implied, given the fragile bonds of constitutional consensus achieved at Confederation, the responsibility of arbitrating future disputes concerning constitutional change might be better left to a disinterested party. In addition, the attachment to the historical cultural, political, and constitutional link between the "mother country" and the new dominion that some of the framers retained cemented the desire to maintain the colonial constitutional tie. During the Confederation deliberations, for example, John A. Macdonald asserted that "the desire to remain connected with Great Britain and to retain our allegiance to Her Majesty was unanimous" (Ajzenstat et al. 2003, 204). Finally, Norman McLean Rogers posits that Macdonald may have desired to leave the contentious issue of amendment unresolved so that the federal government might, over time, simply claim the amending power as exclusively its own (Rogers 1934, 482).

Whatever the reason, the amending formula's absence from the *BNA Act* has haunted Canadian constitutional law and politics ever since. From the outset, the "complex and difficult problem" of Canadian constitutional amendment "has been surrounded with a certain mysterious imprecision," William Livingston (1951, 437), the American political scientist, observed. How, in short, were constitutional amendments to be made? What was Parliament's role in securing constitutional change? Did the provinces need to agree on proposed amendments? These fundamental questions could not be avoided since, almost immediately, constitutional changes were required to address Canada's geographic and demographic expansion. The Government of Canada accomplished its first amendments by direct appeals to Britain without Parliament's approval, but by the end of the nineteenth century, joint approval from the

House of Commons and Senate became the practice (Gérin-Lajoie 1950, 50–93; Favreau 1965, 10–16; Hurley 1996, 19). Sometimes, Canada consulted provinces on proposed amendments; other times, it did not. The result was continuing confusion over Canada's amending procedure, a controversy that ultimately landed on the doorstep of the Supreme Court of Canada in the *Patriation Reference* and *Quebec Veto Reference* (see Chapter 6).

As early as 1883, however, observations began to be made that Canada should be amending its own constitution, with a Toronto periodical, *The Bystander,* arguing that the constitutional power of amendment ought to be vested in Canadian hands (Gérin-Lajoie 1950, 221). Such arguments were forcefully taken up by the lawyer, journalist, and nationalist John Skirving Ewart early in the twentieth century: "Canada has commenced to believe in herself, and to recognize ... the feelings and aspirations and the strong strivings of strenuous nationhood," he claimed, "and, on the other hand, of the utter impossibility of full expression and assertion in mere colonial status" (Ewart 1908, 1). The ideals of nationhood, he argued, could be achieved by ending legal appeals to the British JCPC, Canada's highest appellate judicial body, and by taking full control of the power of constitutional amendment. Ewart's views, though challenged by his contemporaries, steadily became orthodoxy in debates between nationalists and imperialists (Berger 1970). Changes at the level of governmental practice mirrored the intellectual shift as Canada began to negotiate its own international commercial treaties and exhibit greater autonomy in foreign affairs. When Canada signed the Treaty of Versailles in 1919 to end the First World War, many remarked on the beginning of a new era of independence in Canada.

It is no coincidence that the following year, opposition leader Mackenzie King brought the issue of Canada's emerging national status to the House of Commons. "If you take the letter of the constitution alone," he argued, "will anyone for one moment contend that this country is a sovereign nation ... when we have to go to the British Parliament to ask for an amendment to our Constitution?" (Canada 1920, 468). King recommended that work commence immediately on a domestic constitutional amending formula. Over the next decade, a host of voices took up King's demand, most notably the "prophet" of Canadian politics and founding leader of the Co-operative Commonwealth Federation (CCF), J.S. Woodsworth (McNaught 2001).

Beginning in 1924, Woodsworth repeatedly introduced motions in the House of Commons seeking agreement that Canada needed a domestic amending formula. His motives, he freely admitted, were driven by practical politics rather than constitutional theory. A pacifist, Woodsworth was keen to disassociate Canada from imperial politics (and the attendant wars) of the British Empire. More specifically, however, he and other progressives from English Canada wanted the federal government to possess clear jurisdiction over economic matters. Despite existing federal jurisdiction over "trade and commerce" and "peace, order, and good government," the Privy Council, under the intellectual leadership of Lords Watson and Haldane, had narrowed the scope of those provisions so that provincial jurisdiction covered the majority of economic matters (Saywell 2002). For politicians like Woodsworth, the JCPC had effectively blocked construction of the welfare state. "The oldtime constitutional provisions are quite inadequate to meet the needs of the present," he claimed time and again. "If we want to fix an automobile why should we be forced to go back to an ox-cart in order to get our models and our tools?" (Canada 1924, 511). For progressives outside of French-speaking Quebec, an amended constitution would provide the means of addressing the interpretive deficiencies of the JCPC and of implementing the centralization of economic matters.

In advocating for constitutional change, Woodsworth consistently expounded on the constitution as a symbol of nationhood extending beyond the world of formal law. "I am well aware that it is a matter that, perhaps, ought to be dealt with by a constitutional lawyer," he coyly conceded. But legal niceties, he made clear, should not obscure the fact that "Canada regards herself as grown up." That spirit of independence, he claimed, granted "the full right of deciding upon the destinies of the people of Canada just as the British Parliament has the full right of deciding the destinies of those who live in the Motherland" (Canada 1924, 508). Equality of rights became a recurring refrain in the debate. Why should Canadians not exercise control over their constitutional document as British citizens did theirs? And, for that matter, why should Canada not have the equal rights of Australia, South Africa, and Ireland, which possessed the constitutional power to amend? The logic of this line of argument, the rhetorical power of the language of rights, and the appeal to national pride, enabled Woodsworth to move the debate beyond his more specific agenda for federal economic intervention.

Such arguments could – and did – appeal across partisan lines. Although many Quebec MPs remained wary of the centralizing motives infusing the rhetoric, Henri Bourassa supported the spirit of constitutional independence, so long as minority and provincial rights were protected in any proposed amending formula. "We must look forward to the day," Bourassa agreed, "when in Canada our constitution will be dealt with by power arising from the will of the people of Canada, without the interference of the British Parliament" (Canada 1927b, 1048). Andrew McMaster, a Liberal, pleaded for a non-partisan approach to finding an amending formula and called for unity on the "desire to see Canada grow to the full stature of nationhood" (Canada 1924, 518). Those sharing Woodsworth's politics extended his arguments into other facets of British constitutional control. Joseph Shaw opined that "another difficulty in connection with this constitution ... is that it is interpreted three thousand miles away ... I think that our constitution should be interpreted in Canada, and I think that our jurists are just as competent to interpret it." More emphatically still, he concluded that "constitutions are made for people; not people for constitutions. Constitutions must be just and must be interpreted not to bind and shackle the people, but to meet the changing conditions of the times" (Canada 1924, 530–31). Thus, constitutional nationalism bound two distinct constitutional concerns: the absence of an amending formula and the Privy Council as Canada's highest appellate authority.

Parliamentary opponents initially attacked Woodsworth and his allies for fanning non-existent flames. The constitutional amendment process involved "mere academic questions ... to which no one in the country is at all excited and no substantial body of people want any alteration," Conservative MP John Baxter argued (Canada 1924, 517). Others, extolling the genius and security of the British Empire, stressed the need to retain all ties, constitutional and otherwise, to Great Britain. "No, Canada is not a sovereign state," Thomas Langton Church declared, "and it is a good thing that it is not ... We are a nation in name only" (Canada 1925,

294). Still others pointed out that the system of seeking amendments from Britain actually worked pretty well. "Are we not free enough?" Sir Henry Drayton queried. "Any request that comes from Canada to the British House will be respected," he pointed out (Canada 1925, 305). Now wedded to the status quo alongside the Conservatives, Prime Minister Mackenzie King and his justice minister, Ernest Lapointe, responded that Woodsworth had based his arguments on a mistaken premise. "The British North America Act and the limitations which are imposed upon our powers, if there are such limitations, are made of our own free will," Lapointe argued. "There is no inferiority in that" (Canada 1924, 520). Others wondered whether the power of constitutional amendment might be dangerous. Would Parliament be in a position to alter the division of powers to the detriment of the provinces? Confederation was a hard-earned compromise, some argued; better not reopen the bargain lest consensus and cool heads fail Canada this time around.

William Irvine likely spoke for others in characterizing this volley of debate as confounding. "On the one hand we are told that we are not independent and must not be independent. On the other hand we are told that we are absolutely free and ought to be free ... will any member tell us what status we do have? I think the Canadian status ... is just about as clear as mud" (Canada 1924, 538–39). By 1927, an exasperated Robert Manion complained of the "constitution mongers": "People who are so worried about the constitution of our country, or so worried about the autonomy of Canada and so much afraid that we are subservient to some other part of the empire that they wish to put all the power of our people in the hands of this Parliament" (Canada 1927a, 517). And yet the issue simply would not die. Disenchantment with the Privy Council continued to grow, especially after its decisions declaring *ultra vires* federal labour legislation (*Toronto Electric Commissioners v. Snider*) and ruling "void and inoperative" Parliament's attempt to block criminal appeals to the Privy Council (*Nadan v. The King*). In addition, Governor General Julian Byng's refusal to follow Mackenzie King's advice to dissolve Parliament in 1926 emboldened those advocating for Canada's greater constitutional independence, King now chief among them.

At the 1926 Imperial Conference, Canada's growing spirit of constitutional nationalism contributed to the Balfour Declaration, which proclaimed that Canada and the other Commonwealth dominions were "autonomous Communities within the British Empire, equal in status, in no way subordinate to one another in any respect of their domestic or external affairs, though united by a common allegiance to the Crown" (Ollivier 1954, 146). The spirit of the declaration was enshrined in law by the *Statute of Westminster, 1931*, which ended the reign of the British Parliament over Canadian legislation, with the notable exception of the *BNA Act.* At this critical juncture, fundamental disagreement on the nature of Canadian federalism prevented Canadian politicians from agreeing on an amending formula to replace British oversight. Was Confederation a contract, or treaty, or compact that entitled the original colonies to veto proposed alterations? Which provinces qualified as the original colonies, given that the Province of Canada, having been divided into Ontario and Quebec, no longer existed? What role should the post-Confederation provinces play in the amending process? Should Parliament be able to amend some features of the constitution alone, and others with provincial consent? If so, which ones? And how much provincial consent was necessary? The historical record offered no clear precedents and politicians remained divided on the overarching principles that might lead them to an agreed solution.

Despite disagreement on the particulars, the fact that Canada needed an amending formula was now beyond debate. "The record of Canadians in two world wars," Prime Minister Louis St. Laurent told Canadians just before the 1949 federal election, "demonstrated beyond any question our ability and our capacity to bear the responsibilities of full nationhood. But our adult nationhood is not yet fully recognized in our constitution and our laws ... A method should be worked out to amend our constitution in Canada" (Canada 1949c, 833). At Canada's request, the British Parliament did enact a constitutional amendment enabling the Canadian Parliament to unilaterally amend matters of exclusive federal jurisdiction, *The British North America (no. 2) Act, 1949.* Referencing Canada's "perhaps not altogether proud or enviable distinction ... of being the only sovereign state without the power to amend its own constitution," St. Laurent described the new power "as one of the most important steps in the constitutional development of Canada ... since Confederation." Simply put, he explained, "Canada must act as an adult nation and assume her own responsibilities" (Canada 1949c, 832). "Thus was completed," Frank Scott surmised, "the first stage in the transfer of the amending power"; the second stage, agreement on the general amending formula, would begin as early as the Dominion-Provincial Conference of 1950 (Scott 1977, 203). But that meeting too, like previous attempts and like the efforts that would follow over the next two decades, ended in failure.

Even the formula that emerged at the November 1981 patriation negotiations – now enshrined as Part V of the *Constitution Act, 1982* – has failed to settle the matter, as the Supreme Court tacitly acknowledged in the *Quebec Secession Reference.* In setting the constitutional framework to enable a province to secede from Canada, the court turned not to the amending formula but rather to the constitution's more amorphous "unwritten principles." In the event that "a clear majority on a clear question in favour of secession" arises, the court held, the constitution's unwritten principles call for a duty to negotiate among all the relevant political actors. Such negotiations would take place in a complex "political process" that could "only be resolved by means of political judgments and evaluations." In other words, the negotiations surrounding a fundamental alteration of the constitution would directly engage competing visions of constitutional nationalism. Even in periods of relative quiet, the politics of constitutional nationalism remain fundamentally unsettled.

Constitutional Nationalism in the Law

Coinciding with the rise of constitutional nationalism in Canadian politics, "Canada's newer constitutional law" began to reshape the foundational assumptions and orientations of Canadian constitutional thought (Adams 2006). Scholars such as W.P.M. Kennedy and later Bora Laskin at the University of Toronto, Frank Scott at McGill, and Vincent Macdonald at Dalhousie issued the same battle cry in the classroom, in law journals, and in addresses to the public: Canadian constitutional law had its own unique and distinct purpose, identity, and destiny; appeals to the JCPC must be abolished to allow that destiny to be fulfilled; the constitution must be changed to meet new theories of government and to address new economic realities; and a domestic constitutional amending formula was needed as a symbol of Canada's status as a nation. Variations of these issues dominated Canada's constitutional scholarship from the 1920s into the 1950s (Risk 2006, 233).

In making such constitutional claims, scholars ran against the content and tone of established Canadian constitutional thought. For example, in *The Law of Legislative Power in Canada* (1897), A.H. Lefroy argued that Canada's constitutional framers had "faithfully followed by preference ... the principles of the British Constitution" in adopting Westminster-style legislatures, responsible government, and the principle of parliamentary supremacy (Lefroy 1897, xxlv; Risk 2006, 66). Accordingly, Lefroy, like his contemporaries, approached Canadian constitutional law as an emanation of British constitutionalism and the Diceyan rule of law. The constitutional sovereignty of the British Parliament over the Dominion of Canada, with the Privy Council atop the hierarchy of the Canadian judiciary, was simply beyond question. Not surprisingly, the judges of the Privy Council agreed. As Lord Haldane explained in his admiring reflection on Lord Watson's tenure as "an Imperial judge of the very first order," the "function" of a judge on the Privy Council

> is to be a statesman as well as a jurist, to fill in the gaps which Parliament has deliberately left in the skeleton constitutions and laws that it has provided for the British Colonies ... Lord Watson made the business of laying down the new law that was necessary his own. He completely altered the tendency of the decisions of the Supreme Court ... In a series of masterly judgments he expounded and established the real constitution of Canada. (Haldane 1899, 278)

Aiming to follow in Watson's footsteps, Haldane clearly relished his own reputation as an expert in Canadian constitutional affairs. "Last night the Canadian lawyers entertained me at dinner and treated me with reverence like a father," he noted with pleasure (Vaughan 2010, 175). Haldane's decentralist views may have been feted among provincial politicians and their lawyers, but his reputation as "the wicked step-father of the Canadian Constitution" (Eugene Forsey's famous appellation) was nearly universally held among Anglo-Canadian constitutional scholars, particularly his decisions favouring provincial jurisdiction in *Reference re The Board of Commerce Act* (1922), *Fort Frances Pulp and Paper Company* (1923), and *Toronto Electric Commissioners* (1925). Fuelled by a growing sense of Canadian nationalism and increasing frustration at what they regarded as the regressive decentralism inherent in the Privy Council's jurisprudence, scholars like Kennedy, Scott, Macdonald, and Laskin turned Lefroy's scholarship on its head: replacing faith in the British constitutional connection with skepticism, and admiration for the Privy Council with resentment.

Initially, the Privy Council appeared impervious to such rumblings of discontent. In striking down section 1025 of the *Criminal Code*, which blocked Canadian criminal cases from being appealed to the Privy Council, Viscount Cave noted that "in His Majesty's Dominions beyond the seas the method of appeal to the King in Council has prevailed and is open to all the King's subjects." "Under what authority, then," the Lordships inquired, "can a right so established and confirmed be abrogated by the Parliament of Canada?" (*Nadan v. The King*, [1926]). The simple answer was that British laws constituting the Privy Council and its right to hear appeals trumped any Canadian laws to the contrary. *Nadan v. The King* may have been right at law in 1926, but it revealed a tin ear to the stirrings of constitutional nationalism, and signalled a colonial attitude that many Canadian lawyers increasingly resented.

When a similar effort to ban criminal appeals returned to the Privy Council nine years later in *R v. British Coal*, but now with the *Statute of Westminster, 1931* in effect, the Privy Council altered course. "Such appeals," it held, "seem to be essentially matters of Canadian concern, and the regulation and control of such appeals would thus seem to be a prime element in Canadian sovereignty as appertaining to matters of justice." Such logic suggested that civil appeals should follow. That issue presented greater legal difficulty since the typical matters of civil law – claims in contract, property, tort, or the *Civil Code* in Quebec – engaged subject matters of clear provincial jurisdiction, arguably including provincial control over the "administration of justice in the province." Further, provincial governments justifiably regarded the Privy Council as historically supportive of provincial rights. The widely negative reaction to the Privy Council's decisions striking down Canada's New Deal legislation, however, emboldened the federal Parliament to push ahead with its plan to abolish all appeals.

In response to the ongoing economic devastation wrought by the Depression, R.B. Bennett's Conservative government sought to criminalize anti-competitive practices, provide credit protection to farmers, establish minimum wages and maximum hours of work, and create a system of unemployment and social assistance. When the Liberals defeated the Conservatives in the 1935 federal election, Prime Minister Mackenzie King referred the bundle of legislation to the Supreme Court for a decision on its constitutionality. A divided court struck down most of the legislation. The Privy Council, on appeal, did likewise in 1937, providing the opportunity for Lord Watson's famous admonition to Parliament that "although the ship of state now sails on larger ventures and into foreign waters she still retains the watertight compartments which are an essential part of her original structure" (*Labour Conventions Case*).

The reaction of Anglo-Canadian constitutional scholars was swift and vitriolic. In a special issue of the *Canadian Bar Review* dedicated to the decisions, W.P.M. Kennedy (1937, 398) took direct aim at the "bastard loyalty which gave [the *BNA Act*] the doubtful devotion of primitive ancestor worship." Frank Scott (1937, 494) repeated his decade-old argument that "the Privy Council is and always will be a thoroughly unsatisfactory court of appeal for Canada." In working notes penned in 1932, Scott pointed out that "the interpretation of the Constitution is a matter that cannot be left to judges who are unfamiliar with Canadian traditions and with the Canadian situation. In addition, the existence of the appeal is now seen to be inconsistent with the achievement of full national status" (Scott Papers, Library and Archives Canada). By contrast, and in keeping with a history of support for the Privy Council's jurisprudence, many French-speaking lawyers in Quebec enthusiastically greeted the New Deal decisions. Léo Pelland defended the judgments as respecting the true nature of Canadian federalism, just as he had earlier criticized the New Deal legislation for violating "*la lettre et l'esprit de la Constitution*" (Pelland 1936–37, 214; Pelland 1937–38). Constitutional nationalists either ignored such views or dismissed them as outdated and regressive. Charles Cahan, a Conservative MP from Montreal and former secretary of state, sought the advice of both Kennedy and Scott in drafting his bill to abolish appeals to the Privy Council (Canada 1938, 2157). The fate of the Privy Council, already weakened by a decade of attack, was sealed by the New Deal cases.

In the ensuing reference case concerning the constitutionality of legislation banning all Privy Council appeals, Parliament asked the Supreme Court of Canada to rule on its own superiority. Chief Justice Lyman Duff, for the majority, upheld Parliament's amendments to the *Supreme Court Act* as *intra vires.* Notably, in doing so Duff employed some of the constitutional nationalists' arguments to repel the provinces' efforts to retain their right of appeal to the Privy Council. His judgment began by noting the nation-building jurisdiction of the federal Parliament to govern territories outside of the original provinces and to create new provinces; "responsibilities," Duff held, "of the very highest political nature." From the domestic capacity to grow and govern a nation, the chief justice turned to the distant location of the Privy Council. "The members of His Majesty's Privy Council, as everybody knows, are nominated by the King on the advice of the Prime Minister of the United Kingdom," Duff observed. "The constitution and organization of the Court in every respect is exclusively subject to the Parliament of the United Kingdom ... No legislature in Canada has, of course, anything to say about the constitution of the Judicial Committee or about its organization." Accordingly, Duff reasoned, the Privy Council, by definition, could not fall within the ambit of provincial jurisdiction. Moreover, since the *Statute of Westminster, 1931* had removed "the obstacles ... which prevented the Parliament of Canada giving full effect to legislation for objects within its powers," Parliament must possess the authority to abolish all appeals to the Privy Council (*Reference re: Supreme Court Act Amendment Act*).

On an appeal delayed by the war until 1947, the Privy Council agreed. In *Ontario (Attorney General) v. Canada (Attorney General),* Lord Jowitt began by noting the "transcendent constitutional importance" of the *Statute of Westminster, 1931* and the significance of the "short, but pregnant" legislative provision before them. Jowitt pointed out that the attorney general in England "took no part in the controversy, which has throughout been between the Dominion of Canada and certain of the provinces." In other words, even Britain seemed to recognize that times had changed – that its colonial relationship with Canada was ending. For its part, the Privy Council approached the matter as a relatively straightforward and constitutional assertion of national independence. Emphasizing the role of the *Statute of Westminster, 1931* and the plenary federal jurisdiction under section 101 of the *BNA Act*, which granted the federal government jurisdiction over "a General Court of Appeal," Lord Jowitt simply surmised that "it must be within the power of the Dominion Parliament to enact that the jurisdiction of its Supreme Court shall be ultimate. No other solution is consonant with the status of a self-governing Dominion." "The regulation of appeals is," the Privy Council concluded "a 'prime element in Canadian sovereignty', which would be impaired if at the will of its citizens recourse could be had to a tribunal, in the constitution of which it had no voice." That such an outcome was unthinkable at the time of the *BNA Act*'s drafting was of no consequence, Lord Jowitt held. The constitution of Canada, he implied, must keep pace with the international status of the nation and the constitutional nationalism of its people.

The ending of appeals to the Privy Council gave constitutional nationalists a certain satisfaction, but considerable work remained. Bora Laskin (1951, 1057, 1076), for example, counselled the newly supreme Supreme Court of Canada to embrace "the spirit of its new status" by freeing themselves from the "shadow" cast by the Privy Council's federalism jurisprudence. In Parliament, the minister of justice and the prime minister similarly heralded the "historic" occasion as a further step towards Canada's independence, while the opposition Progressive Conservatives struck a more cautious tone, siding with the Canadian Bar Association, which urged that the court continue to be bound by the Privy Council's precedents (Canada 1949a, 75; 1949b, 189–99). Initially, the Supreme Court justices themselves appeared reluctant to abandon the stable foundations of constitutional jurisprudence laid by the Privy Council, but, in the years that followed, they slowly and steadily crafted a jurisprudence often more sympathetic to federal jurisdictional claims. "The powers of this Court in the exercise of its jurisdiction," Justice Ivan Rand declared in *Re The Farm Products Marketing Act* in 1957, "are no less in scope than those formerly exercised in relation to Canada by the Judicial Committee." Change in judicial interpretation, he argued, is "a function inseparable from constitutional decision" and inevitable given the "evolving features and aspects of matters which the intensive and extensive expansion of the life of the country inevitably presents." For constitutional nationalists, the singular authority of the Supreme Court and its drift to a more centralized view of federalism was a triumph, but they continued to regret that "one badge of colonialism remains – the formal amendment of the British North America Act by the Parliament of Great Britain" (Laskin 1951, 1038). In their eyes, the Canadian constitutional project remained incomplete.

Constitutional Nationalism in Constitutional Culture

It has often been argued that Canada's constitutional history before 1982 was overwhelmingly driven by political elites. Ordinary Canadians simply were not interested in the *BNA Act,* Reginald Whitaker argues, and Canada's constitution was not much interested in ordinary Canadians (Whitaker 1983, 240–41; Russell 2004). This assertion of constitutional elitism understates the powerful force of constitutional nationalism in influencing political, legal, and popular debates about the constitution. Canada's constitution, what it meant for nationhood, what body should be responsible for its interpretation, and how it might better reflect a changing world were matters of deep and abiding concern in Canadian politics, law, and constitutional culture more generally.

Most Canadians did not subscribe to law journals, parse constitutional judgments, or pore over Hansard, but they certainly read newspapers. The King-Byng Affair, the Balfour Declaration, the *Statute of Westminster, 1931,* Dominion-Provincial constitutional conferences, and the ending of Privy Council appeals were front-page news across the country. Reporters and editorialists generally framed such moments in constitutional terms, characterizing much of Canada's politics as intimately bound up in the *BNA Act* and Canada's evolution towards national independence. Leading the charge, the influential *Manitoba Free Press* (1927, 13) championed constitutional nationalism by castigating the "anomalous and humiliating position of being the only country on earth claiming to be a nation which has to have its constitution patched up ... by an external parliament." Nearly twenty-five years later, despite the constitutional changes in the interim, the *Winnipeg Free Press* (1950, 1) could still lament the "humiliation to every Canadian" of their powerlessness to amend their own constitution. The *Free Press* did not speak for all, of course, and the reliably conservative *Globe and Mail* tended to regard constitutional independence with greater skepticism. The *Globe*'s editors (1936, 4) attributed early efforts to abolish appeals to the Privy Council as "common blather," but after the Second World War they acknowledged that opinion, including theirs, had shifted. "Appeals to the Privy Council, in the opinion of many Canadians not Socialists, are inconsistent with our position as a free, self-governing nation," the editors wrote, notably keen to distance constitutional nationalism and its policies from their origins in progressive politics (*Globe and Mail* 1948, 6). At *Le Devoir*, André Laurendeau wrote about these issues too, although refracted through a different set of constitutional concerns. From his editorial desk in Montreal, the early champion of Quebec nationalism cautioned that the development of Canadian constitutional independence should not come at the cost of federalism. The Privy Council, he feared, had slyly been replaced by a "federally founded tribunal" that was likely to centralize constitutional interpretation against the interests of the provinces. Where others saw constitutional development and progress towards nationhood, Laurendeau saw the erosion of federalist principles and the Confederation compromise (Laurendeau 1976, 186).

Confederation had become, as perhaps it always was, a constitutional moment open to sharply conflicting interpretations. For historian and unabashed constitutional nationalist Arthur Lower, "the purpose of Confederation was to establish a national unit and ... to obliterate the provincial boundaries and fuse the colonial units then existing." Thus understood, the Privy Council had erroneously interpreted the *BNA Act*, inattentive to the "present conditions in Canada, physical, economic, social and psychological." "The abolition of Privy Council appeals," Lower and his colleagues concluded in their submission to the Royal Commission on Dominion-Provincial Relations (Rowell-Sirois Commission), "is one of the essentials for the establishment of national unity ... and for having a constitution that will be and remain comfortable to our needs" (Lower, Coyne, and MacFarlane. 1937, 21–25). Media reports of Lower's arguments generated a flood of requests for copies of his presentation. Copies of his submission were duly sent to the United Farmers of

Manitoba, the City of Moose Jaw, the Canadian Chamber of Agriculture, the Canadian Institute of International Affairs, the Winnipeg Electric Company, Professor Frank Underhill (who promptly assigned it to his students at the University of Toronto), and Jack Pickersgill, so that its arguments might be passed along to Mackenzie King (Lower Papers, Queen's University Archives). Whatever might be said about the sagacity of Lower's constitutional arguments, they clearly struck a chord.

From the late 1920s to the 1950s, the arguments of Canadian constitutional nationalism could be found in a variety of public discourses. Along with Lower, professors like Frank Scott and W.P.M. Kennedy circulated their arguments as widely as they could. They corresponded with politicians. They gave public addresses. And, of course, they taught generations of students. Bora Laskin emerged from the influence of Kennedy's law school at the University of Toronto to don the mantle of Canada's leading constitutional thinker (Girard 2005). Frank Scott's passion for Canadian constitutional law captivated the young law student Pierre Trudeau, and left an indelible imprint on Trudeau's constitutional thought (Djwa 1987, 326). As Gerald Le Dain recalled, "[Scott's] teaching had an energizing as well as an illuminating effect ... What he was talking about, broadly speaking, was the nature of Canada and what it meant to be Canadian, and the role of constitutional law in relation to the supreme values, as he saw them, of Canadian life" (Le Dain 1981, 1). From the classroom and arguments in law journals and newspaper editorials, constitutional nationalism became a more widely shared understanding of Canadian constitutional culture, particularly in anglophone Canada. In the postwar decades, a new generation emerged from Canadian universities ready to complete the unfinished constitutional project that was Canada; they wanted to bring the constitution home.

Conclusions

During the Second World War, the magazine *Canadian Affairs* provided soldiers serving overseas with a connection to events in the country they had left behind. I. Norman Smith's article "Canada's Constitution" appeared in the spring of 1944. "You might argue that Canadians are fighting this war to protect their constitution," the *Ottawa Journal*'s editor wrote. "The thing Canadians are really fighting for is the right to do what they want with their constitution. In Naziland Hitler decides what the Constitution is to be. In Canada the people decide" (Smith 1944, 1). Constitutional nationalists applauded the spirit of the article but pointed out that Smith's last point would not be true until Canada possessed its own constitutional amending formula. If the right of the people to control their constitution was worth fighting and dying for, surely it was worth bridging political and jurisdictional divides to agree on the means of constitutional change. Yet even the powerful trope of nationhood could not resolve the differences between provinces and the federal government about the relationship between constitutional change and federalism. In their exuberance to remake Canadian constitutional law under a singular identity and purpose, constitutional nationalists from Woodsworth to Trudeau too often ignored federalism and the deep diversity that lay beyond their gaze.

Nonetheless, buried in the history of Canadian constitutional thought may lie intriguing lessons from paths not taken. In the spring of 1948, Jean Lesage, prior to serving as premier of Quebec and securing his historic place in Quebec's Quiet Revolution, rose in the House of Commons to support the abolition of appeals to the Privy Council. "If we are proud of our Canadian status, if we are proud of our nationhood, if we are proud of our country," Lesage declared, "the least we can do, the first step we can take is to have our own courts render conclusive decisions." But, Lesage continued, ending appeal was itself insufficient. "We shall," he predicted, "face endless constitutional problems as long as we are devoid of a Canadian constitution enacted by the Canadian people." "I realize that it involves no small task since a constitution could be drafted only through an assembly or a national constituent convention. Although the task is long, arduous, and difficult, I am confident that Canadian patriotism is now sufficiently developed" (Canada 1948, 3381–83). Lesage was certainly right about the difficulties of the journey. Nevertheless, his remarkable speech also illuminates a critical feature of constitutional democracy too often ignored by the constitutional nationalists – the need for constitutional participation and legitimacy among the people and provinces of Canada.

Whatever its deficiencies, the ideals of constitutional nationalism established in Canadian constitutional politics, law, and culture in the mid-twentieth century provided the unseen foundations for the patriation politics in the decades that followed. Although it is the *Canadian Charter of Rights and Freedoms* that has drawn much of the academic attention since 1982, it was the yearning for patriation that created the imperative for constitutional change. When Trudeau spoke of bringing the constitution home, he relied on the evocative language, metaphor, and aspirations of sixty years of Canadian constitutional thought. Nevertheless, as happy as the outcome of the patriation negotiations would have made many of the early constitutional nationalists, there would have been disappointment, too, that the dangers signalled by their critics had, indeed, come to pass.

Acknowledgments

A Killam Grant from the University of Alberta generously supported the research for this project. I am also indebted to the excellent research assistance of Kaylyn Johnson, Brett Grierson, and Kelsey Robertson.

References

Adams, Eric M. 2006. "Canada's 'Newer' Constitutional Law and the Idea of Constitutional Rights." *McGill Law Journal/Revue de droit de McGill* 51 (3): 435–74.

Ajzenstat, Janet, Paul Romney, Ian Gentles, and William D. Gairdner. 2003. *Canada's Founding Debates.* Toronto: University of Toronto Press.

Berger, Carl. 1970. *The Sense of Power: Studies in the Ideas of Canadian Imperialism.* Toronto: University of Toronto Press.

Canada. House of Commons. 1920. *Debates.* 13th Parliament, 4th Session. 16 March.

—. House of Commons. 1924. *Debates.* 14th Parliament, 3rd Session. 20 March.

—. House of Commons. 1925. *Debates.* 14th Parliament, 4th Session. 18 February.

—. House of Commons. 1927a. *Debates.* 16th Parliament, 1st Session. 21 February.

—. House of Commons. 1927b. *Debates.* 16th Parliament, 1st Session. 9 March.

—. House of Commons. 1938. *Debates.* 18th Parliament, 3rd Session. 8 April.

—. House of Commons. 1948. *Debates.* 20th Parliament, 4th Session. 27 April.

—. House of Commons. 1949a. *Debates.* 21st Parliament, 1st Session. 20 September.

—. House of Commons. 1949b. *Debates.* 21st Parliament, 1st Session. 23 September.

—. House of Commons. 1949c. *Debates.* 21st Parliament, 1st Session. 17 October.

CBC 1982. "Trudeau Brings Home the Constitution." *CBC Digital Archives*. http://www.cbc.ca/archives/categories/politics/prime-ministers/pierre-elliott-trudeau-philosopher-and-prime-minister/bringing-home-the-constitution.html.

Constitution Act, 1867 (U.K.), 30 & 31 Vict., c. 3, reprinted in R.S.C. 1985, App. II, No. 5.

Constitution Act, 1982, being Schedule B to the *Canada Act, 1982* (U.K.), 1982, c. 11.

Djwa, Sandra. 1987. *The Politics of the Imagination: A Life of F.R. Scott.* Toronto: Douglas and McIntyre.

Ewart, John S. 1908. *The Kingdom of Canada, Imperial Federation, the Colonial Conferences, the Alaska Boundary and Other Essays.* Toronto: Morag and Co.

Favreau, Guy. 1965. *Amendment of the Constitution of Canada.* Ottawa: Queen's Printer.

Fort Frances Pulp and Paper Company v. Manitoba Free Press Company, [1923] A.C. 695.

Gérin-Lajoie, Paul. 1950. *Constitutional Amendment in Canada.* Toronto: University of Toronto Press.

Girard, Philip. 2005. *Bora Laskin: Bringing Law to Life.* Toronto: University of Toronto Press.

Globe and Mail. 1936. "The Inferiority Bogy." 1 July, 4.

—. 1948. "Blueprint for a Revolution." 24 August, 6.

Grant, George. 1965. *Lament for a Nation: The Defeat of Canadian Nationalism.* Toronto: McClelland and Stewart.

Habermas, Jürgen. 1998. *Between Facts and Norms: Contributions to a Discourse Theory of Law and Democracy.* Translated by. William Rehg. Cambridge, MA: MIT Press.

Haldane, R.B. 1899. "Lord Watson." *Juridical Review* 11 (3): 279–81.

Hurley, James. 1996. *Amending Canada's Constitution: History, Processes, Problems and Prospects.* Ottawa: Government of Canada.

Kennedy, W.P.M. 1937. "The *British North America Act:* Past and Future." *Canadian Bar Review* 15 (6): 393–400.

Labour Conventions Case, [1937] A.C. 326.

Laskin, Bora. 1951. "The Supreme Court of Canada: A Final Court of and for Canadians." *Canadian Bar Review* 29 (10): 1038–79.

Laurendeau, André. 1976. *The Essential Laurendeau.* Edited by Ramsay Cook and Michael Behiels. Toronto: Copp Clark.

Le Dain, Gerald. 1981. "F.R. Scott and Legal Education." *McGill Law Journal/Revue de droit de McGill* 27 (1): 1–13.

Lefroy, A.H.F. 1897. *The Law of Legislative Power in Canada.* Toronto: Toronto Law Book.

Livingston, William S. 1951. "The Amending Power of the Canadian Parliament." *American Political Science Review* 45 (2): 437–49. doi:10.2307/1951470.

Lower, Arthur., J.B. Coyne, and R.O. MacFarlane on behalf of the Native Sons of Canada. 1937. Brief submitted to the Royal Commission on Dominion-Provincial Relations. Winnipeg.

Manitoba Free Press. 1927. "How to Amend the Constitution." 7 November, 13.

McNaught, Kenneth. 2001. *A Prophet in Politics: A Biography of J.S. Woodsworth.* Toronto: University of Toronto Press.

Müller, Jan-Werner, and Kim Lane Scheppele. 2008. "Constitutional Patriotism: An Introduction." *International Journal of Constitutional Law* 6 (1): 67–71. doi:10.1093/icon/mom039.

Nadan v. The King, [1926] A.C. 482.

Oliver, Peter. 2005. *The Constitution of Independence: The Development of Constitutional Theory in Australia, Canada, and New Zealand.* Oxford: Oxford University Press.

Ollivier, Maurice. 1954. *The Colonial and Imperial Conferences from 1887 to 1937*, vol. 3. Ottawa: Queen's Printer.

Ontario (Attorney General) v. Canada (Attorney General), [1947] A.C. 127.

Pelland, Léo. 1936–37. "Problèmes de droit constitutionnel." *Revue de droit* 15: 5–27, 65–86, 194–214.

—. 1937–38. "Problèmes de droit constitutionnel." *Revue de droit* 16: 86–103.

R v British Coal Corp., [1935] A.C. 500.

Re The Farm Products Marketing Act, [1957] S.C.R. 198.

Reference re Secession of Quebec, [1998] 2 S.C.R. 217.

Reference re: Supreme Court Act Amendment Act (Canada), [1940] S.C.R. 49.

Reference re The Board of Commerce Act, 1919 & The Combines and Fair Prices Act, 1919, [1922] 1 A.C. 191.

Risk, R.C.B. 2006. *A History of Canadian Legal Thought: Collected Essays.* Toronto: University of Toronto Press.

Rogers, Norman McLean. 1934. "Constitutional Impasse." *Queen's Quarterly* 41.4: 475–86.

Russell, Peter H. 2004. *Constitutional Odyssey: Can Canadians Become a Sovereign People?* 3rd ed. Toronto: University of Toronto Press.

Saywell, John. 2002. *The Lawmakers: Judicial Power and the Shaping of Canadian Federalism.* Toronto: University of Toronto Press.

Scott, Frank. 1937. "The Consequences of the Privy Council Decisions." *Canadian Bar Review* 15.6: 485–92.

—. 1977. *Essays on the Constitution: Aspects of Canadian Law and Politics.* Toronto: University of Toronto Press.

Smith, I. Norman 1944. "Canada's Constitution." *Canadian Affairs* 8: 1–4.

Statute of Westminster, 1931, 22 & 23 Geo. 5 c. 4 (U.K.).

Toronto Electric Commissioners v. Snider, [1925] A.C. 396.

Trudeau, Pierre Elliott. 1965. "Federalism, Nationalism, and Reason." In *The Future of Canadian Federalism/L'Avenir du federalism canadien*, edited by Paul-André Crépeau, 16–35. Toronto: University of Toronto Press.

—. 1993. *Memoirs.* Toronto: McClelland and Stewart.

Vaughan, Frederick. 2010. *Viscount Haldane: "The Wicked Step-Father of the Canadian Constitution?"* Toronto: University of Toronto Press.
Whitaker, Reginald. 1983. "Democracy and the Canadian Constitution." In *And No One Cheered: Federalism, Democracy and the Constitution Act*, edited by Keith Banting and Richard Simeon, 240–60. Toronto: Methuen.
Winnipeg Free Press. 1950. "The Quebec Conference." 25 September, 1.

4 The Evolution of the Charter

Barry L. Strayer

The original nineteenth-century constitution of the Canadian Confederation was, jurisprudentially, a product of its time. It was a legal positivist document based on the assumption that Britain enjoyed sovereignty over its remaining colonies, and that Parliament at Westminster could exercise that sovereignty through binding legislation, including constitutional legislation. Although in the mid-nineteenth century Britain would perhaps not have been able, or even disposed, to enforce those laws by force of arms, it was understood on both sides of the Atlantic that most Canadians accepted the laws of Westminster as legitimately binding on them. As a result, Westminster could authorize law-making by the Canadian Parliament and legislatures, and as long as those bodies stayed within the fields of jurisdiction assigned to them, they in turn would pass laws binding on their Canadian subjects. They would, like Westminster, enjoy legislative sovereignty in their respective spheres. This thinking owed much to the writings of Jeremy Bentham and John Austin, and, after Confederation, was reinforced in both countries by the writings of A.V. Dicey, who expounded a theory of parliamentary sovereignty in which there was no room for a quasi–natural law appeal to universal values to hamper law-making. The majority of statesmen in both Britain and British North America had little interest in theories of natural law or the inherent rights of man as extolled in the American and French Revolutions of the eighteenth century; indeed, to many those revolutions exemplified the dangers inherent in such notions.

The journey from Canadian politicians' early attachment to parliamentary sovereignty to the entrenchment of a charter of rights and freedoms in Canada's constitution in the 1980s tracks significant shifts in thinking about the relationship between the state and citizens. These shifts were driven by historical events, scholarly and political debates, and the increased participation of citizen groups in the political process. This chapter recounts this journey, demonstrating the transition in Canada's legal culture from a dedication to parliamentary sovereignty to a system of constitutional guarantees of individual rights protected against legislative or administrative interference. I will also relate some of the reasons that the *Canadian Charter of Rights and Freedoms* came to have its present content – reasons that relate to the intense struggle between parliamentary sovereignty and guaranteed rights. I write this account from my perspective as an active participant in the drafting of the Charter and an observer of the compromises and struggles inherent in the constitutionalization of rights.

The Rights Regime of the *British North America Act*

It is not surprising that few limitations were imposed on Canadian legislatures by the *British North America Act, 1867* (*BNA Act*) as long as they stayed within the limits of the federal-provincial distribution of powers. At Confederation, the exceptions to this were only two: the guarantees in section 93 of Roman Catholic separate schools in Ontario and Protestant separate schools in Quebec; and the guarantees in section 133 of the right to use both English and French in Parliament and in the legislature of Quebec, with bilingual records to be kept by those bodies, as well as the right to use either language in federal or Quebec courts.

It is true that in the mid-twentieth century, the Supreme Court of Canada did make some important decisions that had the effect of protecting fundamental freedoms (e.g., *Reference re Alberta Statutes* in 1938 and *Switzman v. Elbling and A.G. Quebec* in 1957), but the results were really based on division of powers grounds. A few judges and at least one writer (Brewin 1957) found an implied bill of rights, guaranteeing freedom of speech, conscience, association, and so on, in the preamble to the *BNA Act*, which cited the desire of the confederating provinces to have "a constitution similar in principle to that of the United Kingdom." This theory did not find widespread approval as a basis for guaranteeing freedom from legislative interference with fundamental and political rights. In fact, it was devoid of historical substance. This phrase in the preamble was, it is generally agreed, an elliptical adoption by the Fathers of Confederation of the unwritten principle of responsible government so recently achieved in the North American colonies in belated imitation of Britain.

Growth in Human Rights Protection

There was little political interest in the protection of fundamental freedoms and legal rights until after the First World War. Labour agitation caused Parliament to impose restraints through such measures as section 98 of the *Criminal Code*, which suppressed "unlawful associations" that advocated governmental change by force or violence. In response, the Co-operative Commonwealth Federation (CCF), the forerunner of today's New Democratic Party (NDP), adopted the Regina Manifesto at its founding convention in 1933. The manifesto called for guarantees of fundamental freedoms and non-discrimination "irrespective of race, nationality or religious or political beliefs." No specifics were provided as to how this would be achieved – whether by constitution or legislation. As will be seen, however, the CCF and the NDP were later in the vanguard of the movement for a constitutional bill of rights, with the exception of the NDP government in Saskatchewan during the constitutional negotiations of 1978–82. Frank R. Scott, a leading constitutional lawyer who was an intellectual leader of the CCF and later its national president, advocated a constitutional bill of rights in a 1935 essay (League for Social Reconstruction 1935).

In 1945, a CCF Member of Parliament introduced a resolution calling for a constitutional bill of rights to protect fundamental liberties and legal and equality rights (Canada 1945, 900). The drafting of the *Universal Declaration of Human Rights* by the United Nations was the subject of ongoing study by a parliamentary committee. That declaration had many sweeping economic rights, but MPs were unwilling to accept any binding international obligation that might prevent domestic legislatures from acting or, indeed, that might require them to implement provisions such as "the right to social security" or "the right to work." The traditional culture of parliamentary sovereignty was very much alive. Parliament finally endorsed the declaration in 1948, but on the understanding that it was simply a statement of goals. In the meantime, many provinces had adopted legislative measures (not, of course, constitutionally entrenched) to prohibit various forms of discrimination (Tarnopolsky 1975, 3–14; MacLennan 2003, 66–99).

The *Canadian Bill of Rights* and the Prospects of Entrenchment

Saskatchewan premier T.C. Douglas proposed a constitutional bill of rights at a federal-provincial conference in 1950 (Canada 1950, 32–40) but received no support from other heads of government. The next major initiative in the human rights field did not occur until after the election of the federal Progressive Conservative government in 1957. Its leader, John Diefenbaker, had long been an advocate of a federal statutory bill of rights, and he achieved his goal with the adoption of the *Canadian Bill of Rights, 1960.* The public debate on this bill stirred up aspirations for the better protection of rights, but many of these aspirations were unrealized because the *Bill of Rights* lacked important rights guarantees, did not apply to provincial governments, and was not constitutionally entrenched so as to override federal legislation inconsistent with its terms. As a statute, it could be amended or repealed by Parliament. Further, the bill had built-in qualifiers: section 2 allowed Parliament to avoid its authority by declaring particular legislation to be operative notwithstanding the bill, and section 6 allowed the federal cabinet to proclaim the *War Measures Act,* which allowed the government to circumvent the legal protections afforded by the *Canadian Bill of Rights.*

The parliamentary debate on the bill marked the first time the Liberal Party declared its support for entrenching rights protections in the constitution. Until then, the Liberals had hewed to the conventional doctrine of parliamentary sovereignty, not least in their approach to obligations such as the recognition of economic rights in the *Universal Declaration of Human Rights,* which they refused to accept as binding on Parliament or provincial legislatures (MacLennan 2003, 123). Presumably, the Liberals' support for entrenchment was a political strategy, since Diefenbaker – who had doubtless concluded that federal-provincial agreement on a constitutional amendment was highly unlikely – was not prepared to advocate entrenchment of the *Bill of Rights* in the constitution.

A federal-provincial conference was held in 1960 as the *Canadian Bill of Rights* was being enacted. At this conference, the newly elected premier of Quebec, Jean Lesage, suggested that there should be a constitutionally entrenched bill of rights. Premier Douglas agreed, but no one else supported the idea. There were, however, other discussions about the constitution and the desirability of "repatriation," as it was then known. Subsequently, Diefenbaker issued an invitation to a Conference of Attorneys-General on Repatriation, to be chaired by his minister of justice, Davie Fulton.

Trudeau and the Politics of Rights

In 1967, Canada's centennial year, there was a renewed sense of pride in the country, a self-confidence that Canada would enter its second century in improved form. It was widely assumed that the time had come to rethink nineteenth-century imperial law and update the constitution. The recently appointed minister of justice, Pierre Trudeau, now had responsibility for the constitutional file, and he instructed his counsel and me, as associate counsel on the constitution, to prepare proposals for a constitutional bill of rights or charter.

Pierre Trudeau had a natural intellectual affinity for the legal protection of the fundamental rights of the individual. He had read extensively in the works of the Enlightenment and in more contemporary works of religious philosophy underpinning individual rights. He had come to believe that the individual was the fundamental unit in our polity, not governments. He admired the instruments of the American and French Revolutions, the *US Bill of Rights*, and the French *Declaration of the Rights of Man*. For some years in the 1940s and 1950s in Montreal, he had come to be influenced by the constitutional views of Frank Scott. It seems probable that Trudeau finally became convinced of the need for a constitutional bill of rights during a boat trip the two took together down the Mackenzie River in 1956 (Djwa 1987). Trudeau subsequently published several articles advocating such an instrument. During the same period, he was disputing the need for a major change in the distribution of powers, much to the annoyance of his nationalist contemporaries in Quebec.

The conjunction of Canada's centennial year and his position as minister of justice provided Trudeau with the opportunity to persuade his cabinet colleagues to embrace a constitutional bill of rights. From my vantage point as associate counsel on the constitution, Trudeau had two main reasons for pressing the issue at this time. The first was strategic. He knew that constitutional discussions would begin soon. Premier John Robarts of Ontario had already issued invitations to his fellow First Ministers to a Confederation of Tomorrow Conference in Toronto in November 1967. The federal government intended to decline this invitation on the grounds that the prime minister of Canada should be the one to call constitutional conferences. Ultimately, Ottawa sent only observers to Toronto. The federal government needed to regain the initiative by calling a federal-provincial conference of its own. Trudeau had argued for years, as an academic and a political writer, that a constitutional charter should have a higher priority than changes in the distribution of powers, yet he knew that the provinces' vision of constitutional renewal really meant a series of transfers of federal powers to the provinces. As a matter of strategy, he wanted Ottawa to seize the initiative by proposing a constitutional charter as a first item of business, and he believed the public would be attracted to this as a priority.

His second reason involved his concept of national unity. Trudeau wanted constitutional protection for both official languages on a national basis, and guarantees of individual minority language rights for French and English across the country. This was his pan-Canadian approach to the protection of those languages. In particular, it would mean that a Quebec francophone should be able to use French anywhere in Canada. In this, of course, Trudeau challenged those who saw Quebec as the only safeguard for the French language, and the only place where francophones could expect these rights to be protected. As for the inclusion of other rights in a charter, he saw this as a definition through dialogue of Canadians' fundamental values. In sum, he saw a charter as an important instrument of national unity, expounding shared values rather than emphasizing forces of division. It was obvious that such a charter would require the Supreme Court of Canada to apply the same rules to the interpretation of legislation of all provinces and of the Parliament of Canada, thus promoting a consistent, rights-based legal regime across the country and increasing the prominence of the Supreme Court in the national culture.

In laying the groundwork for the federally convened constitutional conference, Trudeau charged his constitutional advisers with preparing a discussion paper on a charter. *A Canadian Charter of Human Rights* was published in early 1968, just before the federal-provincial conference from 5 to 7 February (Canada 1968). This hastily drafted paper was intended to identify the main issues that would have to be considered for entrenchment. It explained the significance of a constitutional bill of rights as compared with statutory instruments existing at the federal and provincial levels (Canada 1968, 13–14). It obliquely referred to the "frozen rights" problem that had arisen through the interpretation of the *Canadian Bill of Rights, 1960:* the idea that the bill protected only rights as they stood at the time of its adoption, even if by that time those rights had been heavily qualified by accepted limitations (Canada 1968, 14; see *Robertson and Rosetanni v. the Queen*). It also pointed out that such an instrument would apply equally to all legislatures and governments, federal or provincial. As for suggestions of possible rights for inclusion, the paper borrowed Bora Laskin's categorization of rights and freedoms: political, legal, egalitarian, and economic (Canada 1968, 15–27; Laskin 1959). To this were added language rights at the specific direction of the minister. Working with Carl Goldenberg and a group of outside expert advisers, we also looked at a number of other documents for inspiration, including the *US Bill of Rights*, the *Universal Declaration of Human Rights*, the *European Convention on Human Rights*, the *International Covenant on Civil and Political Rights*, and the *International Covenant on Economic, Social and Cultural Rights*. The paper raised issues such as possible permitted limitations to some or all rights, the idea of a notwithstanding clause in some form (Canada 1968, 30), and the problems of using any language that might allow the courts to require substantive due process (Canada 1968, 20). In the discussion paper, we warned of the problems of economic rights and advised against including them, because they could have the effect of constitutionally compelling legislatures and governments to spend money or provide services (Canada 1968, 27). We knew that their inclusion would meet with strong resistance from some provinces, given the still pervasive culture of legal positivism and parliamentary supremacy. While we believed that our political culture could accept constitutional strictures to make governments refrain from certain evils (negative rights), we did not think it right or appropriate that parliamentary sovereignty should be further suppressed by enabling the constitution and the courts to oblige governments to do good (through positive rights).

The Constitutional Conference of February 1968 chaired by Prime Minster Pearson determined that there should be a comprehensive review of the constitution, and ongoing machinery was established to that end. At a further meeting in February 1969, Prime Minister Trudeau tabled *The Constitution and the People of Canada*, which amplified the government's views on various subjects, including "fundamental rights," and outlined, in draft form, the specific rights and freedoms that should be protected (Trudeau 1969, 50–63). In this conference and in subsequent meetings of officials, it became clear that there was no consensus among the provinces on the concept of entrenchment or on the rights that should be included. The culture of parliamentary sovereignty strongly informed these discussions.

Political Priorities and Constitutional Renewal

By September 1970, many First Ministers were becoming impatient with the constitutional review process and urged that priority be given to an amending formula and patriation. This was agreed to, along with an understanding that progress would be made through bilateral federal-provincial discussions. The results of these discussions were articulated in the Victoria Charter and approved at a First Ministers' conference in Victoria on 14–16 June 1971. The Victoria Charter was a fairly limited document, but it did contain an agreed method of patriation, an amending formula (giving a veto to Quebec and Ontario), and a few basic, fundamental rights (the right to vote and freedoms of thought, conscience, and religion, of opinion and expression, and of peaceful assembly and association) (Bayefsky 1989, 1: 214). These rights were "subject only to such limitations as are prescribed by law and as are reasonably justifiable in a democratic society in the interests of national security, public safety, health or morals or the fundamental rights and freedoms of others" – language borrowed from article 9 of the *European Convention on Human Rights.* The Victoria Charter also contained some language rights. While all First Ministers gave tentative approval to this charter, they had twelve days to confirm whether or not they would recommend it to their legislatures. Within a few days, Premier Bourassa of Quebec said he would not. The systematic federal-provincial discussion of constitutional reform ground to a halt for the next seven years.

The negotiations resumed in 1978 after the introduction of Bill C-60 in the federal Parliament (Bayefsky 1989, 1: 340). In order to revive constitutional discussions, this bill was drafted as a comprehensive revision of the constitution, including efforts to crystallize certain constitutional conventions (or practices) so that a reader would have a more complete view of how the constitution actually worked. The theory was that Parliament would proceed to enact those portions within its sole jurisdiction, and the remainder would require the consent of the provinces to varying degrees, in accordance with the existing rules of constitutional amendment. The provincial reaction to Bill C-60 ranged from surprise to suspicion to outright hostility. For present purposes, we need only mention the draft on rights and freedoms. For the first time in a federal draft, the government included a general remedies clause that allowed for the exclusion of evidence that had been obtained in violation of charter rights – the predecessor of subsection 24(2) of the present Charter. Section 25 also included a limitation of rights clause similar to the permitted limitations on political and democratic rights provided in the Victoria Charter, but in Bill C-60 such limitations could be applied to all rights and freedoms.

Immediately after the release of Bill C-60 in June 1978, a spate of federal-provincial discussions at the ministerial and official level ensued, but such discussions on a bill of rights were desultory at best, at least until early 1980. Some provinces would accept entrenchment for certain rights, while others totally rejected the concept. Those provinces that could accept some entrenchment usually made their acceptance subject to radical revision of the language proposed by Ottawa. During this period, only Ontario among the provinces proposed a partial charter text, at a meeting of ministers on 22–24 January 1979. Ontario's draft was limited to fundamental freedoms, democratic rights, and language rights. In the meantime, the federal government revised its draft in an effort to respond to provincial concerns. Even though Bill C-60 was ultimately a non-starter, its dissection by various federal-provincial subject matter committees certainly focused attention on the subject of rights.

Between the Quebec Referendum and Adoption of the Joint Resolution for Patriation

After the Trudeau government returned to power with a majority in March 1980 and the "No" vote claimed victory in the Quebec referendum on secession in May, the prime minister made it clear that the Charter was one of his top priorities. This focused the minds of negotiators, but it took a number of drafts before the federal government was ready to table a charter in Parliament in October 1980, and even that iteration did not represent all of its drafters' aspirations. On the one hand, a number of sections had been weakened in the hope of meeting the concerns of some of the provinces and gaining their support, thus enhancing the prospects of patriation and the adoption of the Charter. On the other hand, some sections were strengthened in response to growing popular support for the Charter, fuelled by the nationally televised hearings of the Special Joint Committee on the Constitution (Hays-Joyal Committee). Indeed, those of us close to the project on the federal side welcomed the contributions of the public and parliamentarians who advocated for a robust set of rights guarantees.

Evolution of Key Sections

The remainder of this chapter considers some of the most significant debates and reworkings of Charter provisions that occurred in the period immediately preceding patriation. In considering the contestation surrounding sections 1, 7, 15, and 33, it is clear that tensions between the provinces' desire to maintain parliamentary sovereignty and popular advocacy for meaningful rights guarantees pervaded these discussions, and that the resulting interpretations of these clauses have sometimes varied from our initial intentions.

Section 1

> The *Canadian Charter of Rights and Freedoms* guarantees the rights and freedoms set out in it subject only to such reasonable limits prescribed by law as can be demonstrably justified in a free and democratic society.

The opening words of Section 1 were intended to overcome the "frozen rights" concept that had been applied to the interpretation of the *Canadian Bill of Rights.* Section 1 of that instrument "recognized and declared that in Canada there have existed and shall continue to exist ... the following human rights and fundamental freedoms." This was interpreted to mean that the rights that were "continued" were rights in the form and with the qualifications that had been accepted in Canada at the time of that bill's passage. During the long debate over the Charter, we had concluded that the courts should be free to define the content of rights by their fundamental meaning. Hence, in our draft of 22 August 1980, we opened the section with these words: "The *Canadian Charter of Rights and Freedoms recognizes* the following rights and freedoms" (emphasis added) without reference to how they might have existed in Canada – an invitation to the courts to determine their universal meaning. As modified in the final version, the same concept remains: a general *guarantee* of these rights and freedoms without tying them to past practice in Canada.

Perhaps more importantly, section 1 makes the general provision for permitted limitations on rights. The need for these limitations had initially been outlined in *A Canadian Charter of Human Rights* (Trudeau 1968, 17–19) and was present in the *European Convention on Human Rights* and the *International Covenant on Civil and Political Rights.* Such limitations are, in effect, a recognition that individual rights are not absolute but on rare occasions must be trumped by communal needs in the form of laws for the protection of the wider society. The *European Convention* permitted the most limitations, including the capacity to restrict rights in the interest of morality, public order, national security, public safety, protection of the rights or freedoms of others, territorial integrity, prevention of disorder or crime, and protection of the reputation or rights of others. Each kind of limitation had to be prescribed by law and determined to be "necessary in a democratic society." Such provisions inspired us in our drafting of the Charter, but we also wanted to respond to the provinces' apprehensions regarding rights guarantees. We hoped that including many permissible grounds of limitation would preserve some reassurance of legislative sovereignty. Our initial approach to a limitation clause appeared in Bill C-60, which was given first reading in June 1978 (Bayefsky 1989, 1: 340). Section 25 of that bill included a single clause applying to all rights, permitting such limitations "as are justifiable in a free and democratic society in the interest of public safety or health," etc., "whether such limitations are imposed by law or by virtue of the construction or application of any law." As the debate surrounding the Charter proceeded, many provinces wanted specific limitations permitted on certain rights. In response, the federal draft of 4 July 1980 included several limitation clauses, phrased somewhat differently and attached to fundamental freedoms, legal rights, mobility rights, and property rights (Bayefsky 1989, 2: 599).

This approach faced two criticisms. Those supportive of an effective charter ridiculed the number of possible limitations, suggesting that the permitted exceptions would devour the rights that were supposedly guaranteed. But the provinces opposed to a charter thought our limitations did not go far enough, and on 28 August 1980, they proposed only one limitation clause in section 1, as follows:

> The *Canadian Charter of Rights and Freedoms* recognizes the following rights and freedoms subject only to such reasonable limits *as are generally accepted in a free society living under a parliamentary democracy* (emphasis added). (Bayefsky 1989, 2: 678)

This being the last word from the provinces before discussions broke off, the federal government adopted most of this language as part of the proposed Resolution for a Joint Address to Her Majesty the Queen tabled in Parliament on 6 October 1980 (Bayefsky 1989, 2: 743). We substituted the word "guarantees" for "recognizes," but we included the final words "in a free and democratic society with a parliamentary system of government." This latter phraseology soon attracted critics in the parliamentary committee itself and from civil liberties groups appearing before the committee (Canada 1981: Canadian Civil Liberties Association 7: 9; Advisory Council on the Status of Women 9: 129). The criticism was simple and telling: the phrase preserved parliamentary supremacy. Any limit imposed on rights by a competent legislature would naturally prevail in a state "with a parliamentary system of government." There was also criticism that the federal draft was insufficiently specific on the nature of permissible limitations and the burden of proof required to establish that the limitations were justified (Canada 1981: Canadian Civil Liberties Association 7: 10). After several weeks of hearings, the minister of justice announced that he would accept section 1 as the text we know today:

> The *Canadian Charter of Rights and Freedoms* guarantees the rights and freedoms set out in it subject only to such reasonable limits *prescribed by law as can be demonstrably justified* in a free and democratic society (emphasis added). (Bayefsky 1989, 2: 766)

Section 7

> Everyone has the right to life, liberty and security of the person and the right not to be deprived thereof except in accordance with the principles of fundamental justice.

Section 7 had its intellectual origins in the Fifth and Fourteenth Amendments to the US Constitution and in section 1 of the *Canadian Bill of Rights*. The US amendments guarantee the individual the right to life, liberty, and enjoyment of property, to which the *Canadian Bill of Rights* added "security of the person." In all these instruments, the individual is not to be denied such rights except by "due process of law." In 1967, as we considered which matters were to be protected by a charter, we certainly could not ignore this collection of rights, a centrepiece of the *Canadian Bill of Rights*. In the discussion paper *A Canadian Charter of Human Rights*, we explained that "due process" had at times been interpreted by the US courts as having a substantive content: that is, it could be interpreted to require that legislation, to be valid in the courts' eyes, must be intrinsically fair and just and not merely provide a fair procedure (Canada 1968, 19–20). In our view, "due process" in this sense had been more problematic in connection with the guarantee of "enjoyment of property" and less so with the rights to life and liberty. Hence, we recommended that if all such rights were to be put in a charter, the criteria for their deprivation should be different: "due process" for deprivation of life, liberty, and security of the person; and "in accordance with law" for denial of property. Bill C-60 (1978) adopted this structure (Bayefsky 1989, 1: 348). The next federal draft, published on 4 July 1980, retained the separate treatment for "life, liberty and security of the person" and "enjoyment of property," but property was protected from denial by the "due process of law" requirement, and "due process" was defined in essentially procedural terms (Bayefsky 1989, 2: 599). In essence, that process would encompass the legal rights now found in sections 8 to 14 of the Charter. A separate subsection provided everyone a right to a fair hearing "in accordance with the principles of fundamental justice." This formulation was designed to gain the provinces' acceptance by defining the "due process" concept by reference to familiar legal rights. During that summer's discussion, however, there were still provincial objections to any guarantee of property rights, for fear that these could interfere with legitimate provincial legislation in areas such as zoning, expropriation for public purposes, and environmental management. Nor did the attempt to define "due process" reassure the premiers. In the next federal draft (22 August 1980), there was no general right to the enjoyment of property, and the right to "life, liberty and security of the person" was simply protected by "due process" (Bayefsky 1989, 2: 669). This phrase remained a problem for many provinces (see Romanow, Whyte, and Leeson 1984, 245–46). As a result, in the 3 September draft, the last before the meeting of the First Ministers scheduled for 8–12 September, "except by due process of law" was replaced with "except in accordance with the principles of fundamental justice" (Bayefsky 1989, 2: 704). The term "principles of fundamental justice" was borrowed from paragraph 2(e) of the *Canadian Bill of Rights*, which required that federal statutes be interpreted so as not to "deprive a person of a fair hearing in accordance with the principles of fundamental justice for the determination of his rights and obligations." In 1972, in *Duke v. The Queen*, the Supreme Court of Canada had interpreted this language to refer to procedural fairness, not substantive due process (*Duke v. the Queen*, 923). In hindsight, perhaps we should have been more hesitant to use this phrase from a paragraph that specifically referred to a fair hearing, but in our haste we assumed that the Supreme Court would see it as an apt expression to describe matters of procedure. Certainly, the provinces saw it as an improvement, and it was in the text approved in November 1981 by nine of the premiers. Meanwhile, as the text was examined by the joint parliamentary committee, both Roger Tassé, the deputy minister of justice, and I testified to the committee that the intention of this wording was to avoid substantive due process and simply to provide for procedural fairness, and it was presumably on the basis of that information that the committee and Parliament ultimately approved the text (Canada 1981, 46: 32–34). As early as 1985, however, in the *BC Motor Vehicle Act Reference,* the Supreme Court ignored the drafting history and interpreted section 7 to embrace substantive due process, thus empowering itself to decide whether a law was valid or not depending on whether or not the judges approved of the policy embodied in the statute. To this day, the Supreme Court and all courts obliged to follow it, exercise this policy-reviewing power.

Section 15

> 15(1) Every individual is equal before and under the law and has the right to the equal protection and equal benefit of the law without discrimination and, in particular, without discrimination based on race, national or ethnic origin, colour, religion, sex, age or mental or physical disability.
>
> (2) Subsection (1) does not preclude any law, program or activity that has as its object the amelioration of conditions of disadvantaged individuals or groups including those that are disadvantaged because of race, national or ethnic origin, colour, religion, sex, age or mental or physical disability.

The *Canadian Bill of Rights* stated that the particular rights named in that document (legal rights and fundamental freedoms) should be enjoyed without discrimination based on specified grounds. It did not include ethnic origin, age, or mental or physical disability as prohibited grounds of discrimination. We first added ethnic origin and age in Bill C-60, 1978. As a result of federal-provincial discussions over a year and a half, we came to the conclusion that this format was too restrictive and that there should be a general prohibition against discrimination by governments. This resulted in a new draft of 4 July 1980, which eliminated named grounds of discrimination: it provided that "everyone has the right to equality before the law and to equal protection of the law without distinction or restriction other than any distinction or restriction provided by law that is fair and reasonable having regard to the object of the law" (Bayefsky 1989, 2: 599). This was an early attempt at a general limitations concept that later became part of section 1. Subsection (2) of the 4 July draft had a brief affirmative action exception. By 22 August 1980, we put forward our first draft with a general limitations provision in section 1, having dropped the "fair and reasonable" limitation in section 15 on the basis that the new section 1 would permit limitations on non-discrimination rights where necessary (Bayefsky 1989, 2: 669). This version, as submitted on 22 August 1980, appeared with minor modifications in a subsequent federal draft and in the proposed Resolution for a Joint Address to the Queen tabled by the prime minister on 6 October 1980. It was the subject of much discussion in the joint committee and Parliament: representations to the committee by concerned groups and individuals resulted in major improvements in what was to become section 15. Intriguingly, in the only draft charter ever submitted by the provinces as a whole, there were no equality rights (Bayefsky 1989, 2: 678).

Women's groups were extremely effective in advocating for changes in section 15, as is clear from Chapters 10 and 14 in this volume. Besides their contributions, another profound change in section 15 that evolved during the committee stage was to make the prohibited grounds of discrimination open-ended. As tabled initially, section 15 specified the prohibited grounds of discrimination as race, national or ethnic origin, colour, religion, age, and sex. Mental or physical disability were added as specific prohibited grounds when the resolution was before Parliament between February and April 1981. From time to time, there would be questions in committee about why other grounds had not been included, notably sexual orientation. Though there was some support for this suggestion, the majority of the committee felt that there was no national consensus for its express inclusion. The problem was met by changing the section to read "without discrimination *and, in particular*, without discrimination based on race." Thus, the named identities were only examples of the prohibited grounds, not an exhaustive list. This has allowed the courts to extend equality protections by finding analogous grounds.[1]

Because of its great concern over the breadth of the new section 1, ending with "a parliamentary system of government," the Canadian Advisory Council on the Status of Women (CACSW) wanted to specify that certain forms of discrimination could never be reasonable: those based on sex, race, colour, national or ethnic origin, or religion (Canada 1981, 9: 127–28). In this, they sought to replicate the US principle of strict scrutiny, the requirement that the state produce a compelling rationale for discrimination when applying the equal protection clause of the Fourteenth Amendment of the US Constitution. This concept was not included, but the committee supported a strengthening of section 1 by removing the phrase "with a parliamentary system of government" and placing the burden of proof on governments invoking section 1 to justify a limitation of any right. Feminists remained concerned, however. The government had accepted the addition of what is now section 25 – that the Charter should not be construed so as to abrogate any Aboriginal rights. This section was designed to meet the concerns of Aboriginal groups that the equality provisions in section 15 might undermine specific Aboriginal rights and title. Some ethnic groups feared that section 15 might deny them the right to practise their own cultural traditions. This concern prompted the addition of what is now section 27 – the obligation to interpret the Charter "in a manner consistent with the preservation and enhancement of the multicultural heritage of Canadians." Feminist groups saw these changes as possible guarantees of male dominance in, for example, Aboriginal governance and status or in ethnic cultural practices (Canada 1981: CACSW 9: 141–43; NAWL 22: 59–61; IRIW 17: 71–72, 92). As a result, section 28 was urged upon the committee, as follows: "Notwithstanding anything in this Charter, the rights and freedoms referred to in it are guaranteed equally to male and female persons." In achieving this, many women felt that they had obtained the equal rights amendment to the Canadian constitution that had eluded their American counterparts.

Other concerns were raised by the prospect of constitutionally guaranteed equality. The Roman Catholic hierarchy feared that equal rights to education might abolish publicly funded Catholic separate schools already guaranteed in various constitutional documents. We sought to persuade them that the Charter would not override these existing rights, but they were not convinced.[2] The federal government accepted an amendment stating that the Charter did not affect rights in respect of denominational, separate, or dissentient schools (section 29). Yet another group expressed concern about the possible dangers of equality: the monarchists. They feared that section 15 would render the *Act of Settlement, 1701* discriminatory on the basis of sex and religious grounds. The *Act of Settlement* sets out the rules of descent for the Canadian Crown – through the male line and with the provision that the monarch must be a Protestant. Again, we sought to reassure the monarchists that the Charter would not override other parts of the Constitution, an argument that they ultimately accepted.[3]

Section 33: The "Notwithstanding Clause"

> (1) Parliament or the legislature of a province may expressly declare in an Act of Parliament or the legislature, as the case may be, that the Act or a provision thereof shall operate notwithstanding a provision included in section 2 or sections 7 to 15 of this Charter.
>
> (2) An Act or a provision of an Act in respect of which a declaration made under this section is in effect shall have such operation as it would have but for the provision of this Charter referred to in the declaration.
>
> (3) A declaration made under subsection (1) shall cease to have effect five years after it comes into force or on such earlier date as may be specified in the declaration.
>
> (4) Parliament or the legislature of a province may re-enact a declaration made under subsection (1).
>
> (5) Subsection (3) applies in respect of a re-enactment made under subsection (4).

This section was adopted by the First Ministers on 5 November 1981 and was a vital part of the compromise that enabled patriation. To many, the notwithstanding clause was a surprise, a kind of deus ex machina, but the idea was not new. As noted above, the *Canadian Bill of Rights* had a similar provision in section 2, and it also provided that the lawful invocation of the *War Measures Act* effectively negated the rights protections of the *Bill of Rights. A Canadian Charter of Human Rights* (Trudeau 1968, 30) also raised the question of whether some notwithstanding clause might be needed, at least to enable governments to deal with emergencies.

As we have seen, many of the provinces were extremely reluctant to entrench a charter of rights in the constitution. At a meeting of First Ministers on 5–6 February 1979, Premier Peter Lougheed of Alberta attempted to break the logjam by suggesting a notwithstanding clause that would allow a legislature to decide, openly, to evade the strictures of the Charter. In the summer of 1980, a notwithstanding clause was again considered, first at the officials' level, and then by the ministers in the Continuing Committee of Ministers on the Constitution (CCMC). That committee referred several questions concerning the Charter for determination by the First Ministers. Should it be entrenched? What categories of rights should it contain? Should there be an override clause allowing legislatures to pass laws expressly overriding Charter rights and, if so, which rights (Bayefsky 1989, 2: 709)? While no consensus was reached at the September 1980 First Ministers' meeting, this preliminary work was in the record and available to those who were seeking a compromise in November 1981. Pierre Trudeau remained reluctant to accept such a clause but finally did so on 5 November, insisting on a five-year limit for declarations, and requiring that a legislature re-enact the declaration in order to continue to override the Charter (Leeson 2011, 70).

Conclusion: The Cost and the Value of Evolution

The *Canadian Charter of Rights and Freedoms* was the product of many diverse pressures and many compromises. The result contains some latent ambiguities. Despite the successful effort to free section 28 from section 33, evocatively described by Marilou McPhedran, Judith Erola, and Loren Braul in Chapter 10, ambiguity continues to surround the section's meaning. For while section 28 ensures equality of rights between men and women "notwithstanding anything in this Charter," section 1 allows legislatures to impose "reasonable limits" on *any* of the rights in the Charter. Subsection 15(2) permits affirmative action; does section 28 nevertheless prohibit any affirmative action for groups defined by gender?

These are the inevitable results of political compromises in the course of drafting. On balance, however, it was worth it. The Charter is an imperfect document produced by an imperfect political system, but nonetheless a giant step forward for our society.

Notes

1 See, for example, *Andrews v. Law Society of British Columbia* at para. 152.

2 I believe we were later vindicated by the Supreme Court of Canada in *Adler v. Ontario.*

3 Happily, the Commonwealth countries of which the Queen is head of state have agreed to desegregate the succession to the throne.

References

Act of Settlement, 1701, 12 & 13 William III, c. 2.

Adler v. Ontario, [1996] 3 S.C.R. 609.

Andrews v. Law Society of British Columbia, [1989] 1 S.C.R. 143.

Bayefsky, Anne. 1989. *Canada's Constitution Act 1982 and Amendments: A Documentary History.* 2 vols. Toronto: McGraw-Hill Ryerson.

Brewin, Andrew. 1957. "Case Comment." *Canadian Bar Review* 35 (5): 554–58.

British North America Act, 1867, 30 & 31 Vict., c.3 (U.K.).

Canada. Constitutional Conference (1950). 1950. *Proceedings of the Constitutional Conference of Federal and Provincial Governments.* Ottawa: E. Cloutier, King's Printer.

Canada. Department of Justice. 1968. *A Canadian Charter of Human Rights.* Ottawa: Department of Justice.

Canada. House of Commons. 1945. *Debates.* 20th Parliament, 1st Session. 10 October.

Canada. Parliament. Special Joint Committee on the Constitution of Canada (Hays-Joyal Committee). 1981. *Minutes of Proceedings and Evidence.* Ottawa: Queen's Printer.

Canadian Bill of Rights, 1960, 8–9 Eliz. II, c. 44.

Canadian Charter of Rights and Freedoms, Part 1 of the *Constitution Act, 1982,* being Schedule B to the *Canada Act, 1982* (U.K.), 1982, c. 11.

Duke v. the Queen, [1972] S.C.R. 917.

Djwa, Sandra. 1987. *The Politics of the Imagination: A Life of F.R. Scott.* Toronto: McClelland and Stewart.

European Convention on Human Rights (Convention for the Protection of Human Rights and Fundamental Freedoms), 4 November 1950, E.T.S. No. 5; 213 U.N.T.S. 221.

International Covenant on Civil and Political Rights, New York, 16 December 1966, 999 U.N.T.S. 171 (entered into force 23 March 1976).

International Covenant on Economic, Social and Cultural Rights, New York, 16 December 1966, 993 U.N.T.S. 3 (entered into force 3 January 1976).

Laskin, Bora. 1959. "An Inquiry into the Diefenbaker Bill of Rights." *Canadian Bar Review* 37 (1): 77–134.

League for Social Reconstruction. Research Committee. 1935. *Social Planning for Canada.* Toronto: Thomas Nelson and Sons.

Leeson, Howard. 2011. *The Patriation Minutes.* Edmonton: Centre for Constitutional Studies.

MacLennan, Christopher. 2003. *Toward the Charter: Canadians and the Demand for a National Bill of Rights.* Montreal/Kingston: McGill-Queen's University Press.

Romanow, Roy, John Whyte, and Howard Leeson. 1984. *Canada ... Notwithstanding: The Making of the Constitution 1976–1982.* Toronto: Carswell/Methuen.

Re B.C. Motor Vehicle Act, [1985] 2 S.C.R. 486.

Reference re Alberta Statutes, [1938] 2 S.C.R. 100.

Robertson and Rosetanni v. the Queen, [1963] S.C.R. 651.

Switzman v. Elbling and A.G. Quebec, [1957] S.C.R. 285.

Tarnopolsky, Walter. 1975. *The Canadian Bill of Rights.* 2nd ed. Toronto: McClelland and Stewart.

Trudeau, Pierre Elliott. 1968. *Federalism and the French Canadians.* Toronto: Macmillan.

—. 1969. *The Constitution and the People of Canada: An Approach to the Objectives of Confederation, the Rights of People and the Institutions of Government.* Ottawa: Queen's Printer.

Universal Declaration of Human Rights. GA Res. 217(III). UNGAOR. UN Doc. A/810 (1948).

The Rise of Spectator Constitutionalism, 1967–81

5

P.E. Bryden

Canadians have a peculiar fascination with constitution making. We have paid close attention to the negotiations, deals, slights, and animosities that have characterized the process of writing – and rewriting – our constitution in all its various forms, and we have happily revisited those events on anniversaries both new and old. The constitution is our never-ending story, with enough heroes and villains and plot changes to keep everyone interested, even when feigning boredom. That Canadians could be so entranced by the details of prorogation in the winter of 2008, as evidenced by both the traditional and social media coverage, demonstrates that even when there is little enthusiasm for mega-constitutional change, there is still a broadly based interest in more modest constitutional gymnastics. In a list of things that make Canadians distinct, surely this constitutional obsession must rank at least as high as three-down football and "zed" at the end of the alphabet.

The period between 1967 and 1982 marked the rise of a particular form of constitutional fascination, one that would have interesting repercussions for years after the passage of the *Constitution Act, 1982*. During these years, Canadians were spectators – but active and enthusiastic spectators – to the unfolding constitutional drama. The real players were professionals and included the prime ministers and premiers, their advisers, and the judicial referees, but the amateurs had an increasingly important role to play. The politicians, in particular, used the spectators to secure their particular constitutional positions and to undermine their adversaries' positions, and, in the final gambit that secured patriation, they brought the spectators in to become implicit players in the outcome. While this has been accurately portrayed as a period of mega-constitutional politics (Russell 1993, 75), when the whole document was on the table, rather than the bits and pieces that had been debated separately since Confederation, it was also a period during which the Canadian public played an increasingly determinative role in the outcome of negotiations. This curious sort of spectator constitutionalism paved the road to patriation, but it also ensured that the efforts to correct the shortcomings of the *Constitution Act, 1982* with the Meech Lake and Charlottetown Accords would themselves fall short.

The Confederation of Tomorrow Conference: An Audience Is Born

The story of mega-constitutional change in Canada began somewhat inadvertently. A disillusioned Premier John Robarts of Ontario, witnessing both the Quiet Revolution in Quebec and a federal government that seemed ill equipped to respond, called for a full-blown intergovernmental meeting to discuss the very nature of Confederation (Saywell 1967, 76). It was a suggestion made in anger, but he followed it through after the passion had cooled, making clear in his government's 1967 Speech from the Throne that Ontario would convene a First Ministers' conference to discuss the future of Confederation (Robarts 1966; Ontario 1967a). Robarts imagined that this Confederation of Tomorrow Conference would end the isolation of Quebec (Pearson 1967). He believed Ontario was the obvious province to initiate a public discussion of the future of Confederation because it "has a special role to play as an outstanding and an understanding interpreter of the view of Quebec to some of the other parts of Canada" (Ontario 1967b, 3570). No one anticipated that the conference would set the nation on a fifteen-year path towards constitutional renewal.

The weeks leading up to the opening of the conference were filled with optimistic anticipation (H.I. Macdonald, interview with author, 1996). Officials from Ontario's intergovernmental affairs office scurried across the country, meeting their counterparts and key politicians in an effort to pave the way for agreement at the conference. There might have been some uncertainty about the goals of the conference in other parts of Canada – New Brunswick officials, for example, seemed to agree with Ottawa that a province had no business calling a conference of this sort, and Premiers Ernest Manning of Alberta and Ross Thatcher of Saskatchewan doubted the relevance of the "deux-nations" theory so popular in Quebec (Bryden 2011, 119–21) – but the naysayers were, for the most part, won over. The spirit that had motivated the meeting was positive, so there was no reason to think that the results should be otherwise.

The conference would do more than answer the question of what Quebec wanted. It would also, Robarts hoped, showcase Ontario at its best. The host himself was well positioned: he had "the power to communicate goodwill and confidence" (*Globe and Mail* 1967, 6) and a strong provincial treasury. The conference was held on the fifty-fourth floor of the new Toronto-Dominion Centre, and the Ontario government footed the bill for the grand banquets, intimate lunches, and television coverage of both the spectacular location and the progress of discussions (Wills 1967, 8). Canadians were invited into the conference – at least from the safe distance of their living rooms – to watch some of the steps towards reshaping the constitution. While not part of the careful groundwork that had taken place largely unnoticed, or the closed sessions where much of the real discussion took place, Canadians nevertheless began to scrutinize what was happening to their constitution.

The conference got off to a shaky start. At the televised opening session, Quebec premier Daniel Johnson indicated that profound constitutional change was necessary in order to accommodate Quebec, and on the second day the two main players, Robarts and Johnson, disagreed over whether simple amendment to the constitution was sufficient or whether a complete rewriting would be necessary. Robarts's statement that Ontario "was not necessarily anxious for a complete revision" aligned him with Alberta's Ernest Manning and Newfoundland's Joey Smallwood. Johnson eventually relaxed his hard line. By asserting that a solution could be achieved through a series of amendments that "could later be consolidated," Johnson was essentially conceding that rewriting the constitution was unnecessary. When he explained his position with a metaphor, the tension broke with laughter: "Some people in Quebec want to divorce Canada and then remarry the same woman with a new marriage contract," he declared. "I want to see if we can't amend the marriage contract, rather than take the chance of a divorce and having the woman meet someone else" (Stevens and Saywell 1968, 90; Pape 1967).

Perhaps intergovernmental conferences always contain an element of showmanship, but by allowing television cameras onto the fifty-fourth floor of the TD Centre, Robarts was creating an audience for constitutional acrobatics as much as he was showcasing the modern wonder of Toronto's newest office tower. The Confederation of Tomorrow Conference, therefore, had several important implications for the future of constitutional discussions. First, it resulted in a significant provincial agreement to band together in the face of Ottawa's reluctance to initiate a constitutional review process. Second, it created "key players" in the constitutional drama: Robarts's "expert handling" of the "risky venture" elevated his stature, and a conference essentially called to discuss Quebec's concerns quite naturally provided a platform for Daniel Johnson, that province's chief spokesperson (Goldenberg 1967). Finally, it brought constitutional discussions, which had normally been the quintessence of backroom debates, into the light, showcasing the participants and their arguments and turning the rest of Canada into an audience. The mega-constitutional discussion that was opened up with the Confederation of Tomorrow Conference would follow a profoundly different course from any of the more modest constitutional dialogues of the past.

Towards the Victoria Charter: Players, Plotlines, and Spectators

Lester Pearson's Liberal government had not been in favour of the Confederation of Tomorrow Conference, believing that constitutional matters should properly remain areas of federal initiation. Having lost that position to an eager Premier Robarts, the federal contingent was not about to stay on the sidelines for long. Indeed, Robarts anticipated as much, declaring in the provincial legislature that the "decision to call the Confederation of Tomorrow Conference made it possible for the federal government, if it chose to, to resume its primary role in these matters, and I think that events have proved us to be correct" (Ontario 1968, 263). At Ottawa's instigation, the informal discussions that the premiers had undertaken in Toronto were followed, in February 1968, with a full federal-provincial conference on the constitution. This more formal intergovernmental conference, coming barely two months after the opening act in the constitutional saga, produced new stars and a clearer plotline for the Canadian audience to follow.

The situation in Quebec remained a crucial factor in the timing and content of the conference. As Pearson told cabinet, "the balance between unity and secession may depend on what the Conference does or fails to do" (Cabinet Document 1968). Citing de Gaulle's "Vive le Québec libre" speech, the split between federalists and separatists within the Quebec Liberal Party, and the pressure that René Lévesque's brand of separatism had placed on Premier Daniel Johnson, Pearson impressed upon his colleagues the need to tread carefully. But such soft diplomacy was Pearson's style and not that of his justice minister, Pierre Trudeau. While the latter's "gunslinger" image had not yet been developed, it surely had its origins at the constitutional conference in February 1968, where Trudeau and Daniel Johnson exchanged pointed barbs over the future of Canada. Trudeau had long made known his commitment to a charter of rights, writing to his provincial counterparts in the fall to include it on the constitutional agenda (Posen 1968b). For Johnson, however, the charter was nothing more than a tool for achieving Trudeau's leadership ambitions. According to Trudeau's later biographers, at the conference itself "in response to Johnson's needling, he repeated his arguments, giving back barb for barb until there was general agreement that he had carried the exchange and the conference" (Clarkson and McCall 1990, 110). His "magnetic television presence" (Newman 1968) gained the attention of the English Canadian constitutional spectators. Trudeau rode that enthusiasm on to a victory – and the prime ministership – at the Liberal leadership convention two months later.

Constitutional agreement was not as easy to secure, and the provincial positions diverged in the antagonistic environment of the Ottawa-Quebec battle. The most positive result of the February meeting was that, at the very least, all the participants agreed to continue the dialogue at a later date. But the conference marked a shift from the Confederation of Tomorrow experience by bringing new players to the forefront and, according to the now marginalized Robarts, ending "Ontario's role as a helpful middle man. From here on in, it is going to be a battle between two varieties of French-speaking Quebeckers" (Stevenson 1988). Like the earlier informal discussions, however, this too had been televised, and the existence of spectators transformed the nature of the proceedings. Like any drama, the constitutional negotiations needed protagonists, and Trudeau's performance put him clearly on centre stage.

The spectacle was difficult to maintain, however. Ultimately, real work needed to be done on hammering out an agreement on an amending formula, a charter of rights, and the vexatious division of powers. For the more prosaic work of constitution making, a Continuing Committee of Officials on the Constitution (CCOC) was struck at the conclusion of the February conference; the committee would meet dozens of times over the next three years. Working from provincial proposals for amendments, it quickly discovered the dilemmas of reform: where Ontario submitted twelve propositions dealing with the objectives of Confederation, official languages, and fundamental rights (Greathed 1968), Quebec submitted fifty proposals that envisioned "a wholly new constitution for Canada based on a set of principles that would explicitly recognize a country of two nations as well as ten provinces," and many others submitted nothing at all (Posen 1968a). The uneven responses of the provinces made the work of the CCOC all the more difficult.

Inevitably, as the constitutional road show continued through conferences in December 1968, February 1969, and September 1970, and culminated in Victoria in June 1971, public – and political – enthusiasm waned. Other priorities impinged on the constitutional agenda, and the conferences became more vitriolic and less fruitful. Once Trudeau became prime minister, for example, he moved very quickly on medicare, the timing of which had been the subject of much internal debate under Pearson. Imposing a hasty 2 percent social development tax, Trudeau and Finance Minister Edgar Benson determined that federal health funding would begin forthwith, forcing participating provinces to also begin funding immediately. Opposition from the provinces was immediate and intense. Robarts spoke for many of the premiers when he demanded that the Trudeau government stop forcing the provinces into medicare: "Don't drive us into a corner; above all don't take advantage of [Quebec] Premier Bertrand's weakness." Later, he added, "and don't try it with the other provinces either" (Posen 1968a). With jurisdiction at the root of so many issues of Canadian public policy, discussions of the constitution in its entirety were bound to become confused with the day-to-day issues of the federation, like health care provision and, increasingly, tax reform, pollution, First Nations, and housing (Robarts 1969).

But this wasn't what the pubic wanted. According to NDP leader Tommy Douglas, by adopting "a very dull and pedestrian approach" the federal Liberals had succeeded in "throw[ing] a smokescreen of boredom around the subject [of constitutional review] and have really turned the people off" (Canada 1970, 148). In the decades of constitutional conversations prior to the inclusion of spectators, little concern had been expressed about either what the public wanted or whether or not they were bored. But once the spectators, with their predilection for heroes and villains, quantifiable successes and obvious failures, had been brought into the process, constitutional negotiations needed to advance accordingly. Naturally, there continued to be frenetic discussion behind the scenes in CCOC and various other intergovernmental meetings, but when the First Ministers met, the expectation was that there would be measurable progress.

In pursuit of the finale that the spectators demanded, the federal government adopted an innovative approach to constitutional discussions. Rather than allowing an open discussion with all the premiers present, by 1970 Ottawa was merely giving the appearance of endorsing an open discussion of the amending formula; in reality, it was pushing for "high level bilateral discussions with two or three of the key provinces to find out how much room for compromise there was" (Stevenson 1970). Minister of Justice John Turner was the key federal point man in these meetings with the provinces, joined in his early 1971 tour of the capitals by a powerful collection of bureaucrats, including Gordon Robertson, Bob Bryce, Gérard La Forest, and Barry Strayer. Gordon Robertson in the Prime Minister's Office concluded that "there was general unanimity that real progress must be achieved, at this juncture, in the Constitutional discussions" and that "all provinces indicated a better and more sympathetic realization of the situation in Quebec and, in particular, of [Quebec

Premier] Bourassa's position" (Hunter 1971; Macdonald 1971a). But if there was sympathy towards Quebec across the country, there could be no real understanding of the federal position, as Ottawa refused to show its hand in any of the bilateral conversations that took place through the spring of 1971 (Stevenson 1971).

This new approach may have permitted the constitutional conversation to continue away from the spotlight, and may have been pursued in an honest effort to secure the agreement that the public so dearly wanted, but without a clear statement of federal intentions, and no way of knowing the position that other provinces were taking in these bilateral conversations, rumours and suspicions were bound to grow (Macdonald 1971b). As the Victoria conference in June 1971 approached, a few things were clear, perhaps none more so than that social policy was going to be a key topic of debate. The federal government's use of the spending power throughout the previous decade, and Quebec's exercise of its right to opt out of national social programs, had put the two levels of government on a collision course. Quebec regarded social policy as an integral component of the constitutional review process, whereas the federal government consistently sought to separate the two issues. The two levels of government appeared to be spiralling into a constitutional abyss.

The Canadian spectators clearly had hoped that something would come out of Victoria. The sense of anticipation was greatest in Quebec, where Premier Bourassa was faced with extraordinarily high expectations from all sides. The nationalists "regard the constitutional meeting as crucial for Confederation in the sense that its outcome represents the crucial test of the federal system's ability to satisfy cultural and regional aspirations" (Clift 1971); similarly, the federalists, who normally counted Bourassa among their numbers, looked to Victoria for evidence that Confederation could be redesigned to satisfy the needs of Quebec, most particularly through the crucible of social policy. When the conference opened on 14 June, all eyes – both in Victoria and across the nation, where viewers tuned in to the televised opening statements – were on Trudeau and Bourassa.

Following the standard opening remarks of each of the First Ministers, the group retired to "begin a long, and amazingly secret, debate" (Saywell 1972, 52). That the discussion could be described in such terms only highlights the degree to which the public expected to bear witness to the constitutional dialogue. Thirteen hours of closed-door discussions later, the premiers and prime minister finally appeared with the Victoria Charter in hand. In addition to the amending formula, political and language rights, and statements on regional disparities and continuing federal-provincial consultation, it also included a revised section 94A dealing with the crucial matter of social policy. Precisely how the agreement was reached, how much strong-arming was necessary, and which provinces – if any – were reluctant to sign on were unclear.

This was the moment that everyone had been waiting for: the unveiling of a constitutional agreement in front of the crowd of expectant spectators. But the mood was curiously subdued at the close of the conference as the Victoria Charter was introduced to the public. Each government had until 28 June to secure legislative agreement on its terms, and Premier Bourassa was already showing signs of discomfort with the agreement. His unease was well founded. Commentators in Quebec were quick to pounce on Bourassa's agreement to "La Charte à Trudeau," and by 23 June the already weakened premier was forced to withdraw his support, torpedoing the Victoria Charter and leaving the eleven ministers with nothing to show for their years of work (Saywell 1972, 60). By removing his signature from the document, Bourassa appealed to his own Quebec audience: he was "thunderously applauded by all four parties when he entered the National Assembly" (*Globe and Mail* 1971a). But other audiences were watching with equal anticipation, and they were far less receptive to the results. In English Canada, the rejection of the Victoria Charter was met with irritation and an increasingly intransigent attitude towards constitutional renewal. The *Globe and Mail*'s lead editorial, for example, announced that

> "we have been foolish in Canada, and weak. With the best of intentions, and feeling that Quebec has been short-changed in the past, we have submitted to round after round of gouging, hoping to salvage the country. But nothing grows strong by yielding indefinitely. If the country is worth salvaging it is only as a federation in which the various parts negotiate and compromise, give as well as take" (*Globe and Mail* 1971b).

The English audience for the constitutional follies was, it seemed, tired of giving.

The Waning of Spectator Constitutionalism in the 1970s

The expenditure of energy on the constitutional file had been enormous in the four years since mega-constitutional discussions began in Toronto in 1967, and the deflation that followed the collapse of Victoria was palpable. Justice Minister Turner made clear in discussions with provincial officials that "constitutional talks were dead for the time being" (Stevenson 1972). Intergovernmental attention, just like that of the Canadian public, turned to the escalating oil and gas crisis, inflation, and the Trudeau government's proposed wage and price controls. The constitution shifted to the background, but it was never far from anyone's mind. In October 1974, for example, Trudeau announced in Parliament his intention to secure the patriation of the constitution within four years (Canada 1974). Gordon Robertson followed up on this announcement with a spring 1975 tour of most of the provincial capitals in his new position as secretary to the cabinet for federal-provincial relations, discussing the various views on constitutional reform, presumably preparatory to another round of intergovernmental negotiations (Robertson 2000, 286). A great deal of work would need to be done if any agreement was to be reached: Quebec wanted guarantees in areas of immigration and communications, the premiers of Manitoba and Alberta expressed some concern over the proposed amending formula, and Alberta and Saskatchewan both wanted "a clearer definition of provincial control over natural resources" (Robertson 2000, 286).

Increasingly fed up with the lack of progress towards his stated goal of patriation – and aware of the public's expectation of a constitutional deal – Trudeau announced in February 1976 the possibility that the federal government might pursue patriation unilaterally. As he stated in a detailed letter to all the provincial premiers, "if unanimity" on a variety of alternatives – ranging from simple patriation to a combination of patriation, a revised amending formula, and changes to those parts of the *BNA Act* on which agreement had already been secured – "does not appear possible," the federal government would have to consider a joint address from the Senate and House of Commons "to the Queen, requesting appropriate legislation by the British Parliament to end its capacity to legislate in any way with respect to Canada" (Trudeau 1976). Was it a bluff designed to increase pressure on the provinces? Perhaps, but it served both to bring the First Ministers back to the bargaining table and to buttress Trudeau's reputation for toughness, which had been waning in the face of mounting economic problems.

The constitutional gambit "posed a political dilemma for each province ... To oppose the federal threat to act unilaterally ran the risk of seeming to oppose patriation per se," which put the provinces "in the position of appearing to be against motherhood" (Posen 1976). The solution was for the provinces to agree on a patriation package among themselves and then present the federal government with the way forward. Starting with proposals from Ontario and Alberta, the premiers met at their annual conference in Edmonton in the summer of 1976 and came away with some significant constitutional accomplishments. Language rights, the protection of French culture, equalization, permanent mechanisms for intergovernmental agreements and constitutional review, and the creation of new provinces were all agreed to by the assembled leaders. Some big issues remained outstanding, however, including the amending formula, the Supreme Court, and the taxation of corporations and natural resources (Davis 1976). Far from being dejected about their failures, the premiers focused instead on their irritation with the federal government's insistence on "pursuing policies which were seriously straining the negotiating climate," and committed themselves to continuing their discussions later in the fall (Annual Premiers' Conference 1976).

Many other issues moved to the forefront: the November 1976 election of a separatist government in Quebec; the report of the Pépin-Robarts Task Force on Canadian Unity, which proposed a more decentralized federation; and, in May 1979, the election of the Joe Clark Progressive Conservative minority government. Not only was the election in many ways a rejection of Trudeau's constitutional vision, but it also suggested that Canadians were ready for Clark's new province-friendly approach to intergovernmental relations. The Conservative leader had campaigned in part on establishing a new "community of communities" approach to Canadian federalism. He seemed to speak the language of cooperation and conciliation: "The Government of Canada neither can, nor should, attempt on its own to resolve the problems and develop the opportunities before us," Clark wrote to provincial premiers. "We must involve, much more deeply than in the past, both the provinces and the private sector in developing approaches" (Clark 1979). After establishing that his government was prepared to shift the balance of power towards the provinces, however, provincial premiers were quick to start demanding even more – more control over energy, health, and ultimately the constitution (Peckford 1979; Vaughan 2004, 250–52). But the hand-lettered sign that Trudeau's staff had left for Clark in the Prime Minister's Office – "We'll be back" – proved prophetic, and after only nine months in power, the Clark Conservatives were defeated on a vote of confidence, and the Liberals resumed their place in Ottawa (Clarkson 2005, 87).

The Final Act: Patriation and Spectator Constitutionalism

It seemed that spectator constitutionalism was on the wane through the heart of the 1970s. The public was just as disillusioned as the politicians by the collapse of the Victoria Charter, and all backed off the constitutional file. The conversations continued in the premiers' offices and the offices of attorneys general across the country, but they were quiet and low-key and rarely produced results that made it into the public consciousness. All that changed in 1980. Two narratives, each compelling enough to engage Canadians' attention, collided in a particularly public manner.

René Lévesque's election in 1976, and the establishment of a Parti Québécois government, brought with it the promise of a referendum on separation, but the timing was never quite right. Trudeau's resignation as leader of the Liberal Party following his electoral defeat – which ultimately proved to be quite temporary – provided the right circumstances for scheduling the referendum. Called for May 1980, it asked Quebecers whether they would give the PQ government the authority to negotiate a new relationship – called sovereignty association – with the federal government and the rest of Canada. The sovereigntist side took an early lead in the polls, despite some missteps along the way, but in April, two months after returning to power, Trudeau stepped into the fray. He gave three major speeches in Quebec in support of Claude Ryan and the federalist "non" side; in the first and second, he linked a "non" vote to the renewal of the federal system. In the final speech, delivered six days before the referendum, he was even more explicit:

> I know that I can make the most solemn commitment that following a No vote, we will start immediately the process of renewing the Constitution, and we will not stop until it is done ... We are putting ourselves on the line, we Quebec MPs, because we are telling Quebeckers to vote NO, and we are saying to you in other provinces that we will not accept that you interpret a No vote as an indication that everything is fine, and everything can stay as it was before. We want change, we are putting our seats [in Parliament] on the line to have change. (McRoberts 1997, 158)

It was a direct appeal to the Quebec people, an acknowledgment that they had been watching constitutional developments in the past. When the sovereignty association option garnered little more than 40 percent of the vote just days later, it was a humiliation for Lévesque but opened the door for Trudeau's renewed federalism.

For many observers, this meant that the constitutional train was back on track: renewed federalism surely meant constitutional renewal, and a return to the negotiating table that had largely been left vacant since Victoria. In preparation for a meeting of First Ministers, the CCOC spent the summer trying to facilitate some agreement among the various government positions, but it was ultimately unsuccessful (Ontario 1980). The First Ministers' conference in the fall of 1980 revealed even more disagreement. It was, according to observers, "one of the most acrimonious [constitutional conferences] on record" (Russell 1993, 110). The complete lack of progress boded ill for patriation, and did nothing to satisfy a public increasingly hungry for a constitutional deal. At the beginning of October, Trudeau made it clear that he was through negotiating with the provinces, which had perhaps been his plan all along. A memorandum leaked just days prior to the opening of the 1980 conference indicated that the federal government should be prepared, as it had been in 1976, to act unilaterally if no agreement could be reached with the provinces. This time, Trudeau made good on the threat.

There was very little private space left for constitutional manoeuvring: Trudeau's strategy was to have the proposed legislation, including the Charter and the amending formula, first publically debated and passed by the House of Commons, where his "People's Package" could gain some legitimacy. On the other hand, three provinces – Manitoba, Quebec, and Newfoundland – began court proceedings on the constitutional viability of unilateral patriation. By the spring of 1981, the mixed results were in, and the stage was set for an appeal of the three provincial court decisions to the Supreme Court of Canada. Like the debate in Parliament, where the Conservatives were filibustering the bill, the court decisions were eagerly awaited, and Canadians watched the results across the country. As the spectacle took shape, positions were identified and solidified in the public eye. The two sides were easy to spot: on one side were Trudeau and his two provincial allies, Ontario and New Brunswick; on the other side were the remaining premiers, the notorious "Gang of Eight."

Nothing was more eagerly awaited than the Supreme Court decision, which was issued on 28 September 1981 in a historic manner. The justices announced their complex decision before a television audience. On the question of whether the federal government could legally initiate patriation of the constitution unilaterally, the Supreme Court declared, in a 7–2 decision, that the answer was yes. But the court also chose to answer the question of whether constitutional convention allowed the federal government to seek patriation without the agreement of the provinces; on this question, a majority of 6–3 found that the answer was no. The simple explanation of the court's forty-five-minute decision was that while it would be legal for Trudeau's government to act unilaterally, it wouldn't be nice (Russell 1983, 210–38). Ontario's minister of intergovernmental affairs, Tom Wells, and attorney general, Roy McMurtry, were quick to offer the province's opinion on the decision at a press conference that afternoon, noting, on the question of convention, that "it was always known that this was a departure from general precedent in order to break a logjam" (Stevenson 1981). With a unilateral initiative constitutionally discredited, however, the First Ministers would have to return to the negotiating table.

The excitement around spectator constitutionalism was reaching its peak, and the First Ministers knew that they would need to keep their audiences interested and supportive if a deal was ever going to be struck. This was as true for Trudeau and his two allies as it was for the so-called Gang of Eight, whose alliance was rooted in opposition to Trudeau's strong-arm tactics and the threat of unilateral patriation. Both sides needed to appeal to the bleachers, either by making progress towards a constitution or by demonstrating that the terms of such progress were unacceptable. In its public appeal, however, the federalist side had the advantage and used it.

With so much riding on the evolution of negotiations, and so many people watching, the First Ministers moved carefully, carving out a few days of private consultation following the judicial decision. During this period of court-encouraged transition from the unilateral gambit of the federal government to the negotiated agreement that would be attempted in November, Ontario politicians and bureaucrats played a key role, fielding calls from other provinces, making sense of rumours that individual premiers were prepared to move on one or another part of the patriation package, and assessing how their intelligence on the position of the various members of the Gang of Eight might fit in with what they knew first-hand about the federal position. Although many commentators have focused attention on the events of 2–5 November, calling it "the week that was" (Romanow, Whyte, and Leeson 1984, 188–215), it was really the period between 19 and 26 October over the telephone, and between 28 and 31 October in various hotels in downtown Toronto, that the constitutional deal first began to take shape. Key conversations were held between Ontario, Saskatchewan, British Columbia, and New Brunswick officials; Alberta's team offered some key interventions. A Quebec presence was notably non-existent in the back and forth over what might be possible in the context of a First Ministers meeting; instead, Quebec was "lobbying with other members of the seven [provinces] to hold tough" (Stevenson 1981).

By the week before the opening of the conference, BC point man Jim Matkin could report that British Columbia, Saskatchewan, Nova Scotia, and Prince Edward Island were all willing to make substantive compromises. That left Manitoba, Alberta, and, least surprisingly, Quebec all "sticking to the confrontation." While the preparatory meetings were being held in Toronto, Quebec's minister of intergovernmental affairs,

Claude Morin, expressed his concern about the conversations to his Alberta counterpart, making it "clear that if even one more province broke with the Accord [of the Gang of Eight] then Quebec would no longer be bound by it and would move independently" (Morin, quoted in Lougheed 1999, 22). From Quebec's perspective, then, any willingness to compromise was regarded as a betrayal of the original alliance of the Gang of Eight. For its part, the federal government sounded less and less interested in "any exercises in cooperative federalism" (Stevenson 1981). Nevertheless, although the work done behind the scenes was crucial to arriving at a deal in November 1981, the role that the public played, even implicitly, was determinative.

The first three days of meetings went predictably, with arguments circulating about the amending formula and the Charter of Rights – the two components of a constitutional agreement that posed the greatest difficulty for one side or the other – and little progress being made on either. The possibility of compromise was in the air, however, as Ontario officials agreed that they could accept the so-called Alberta amending formula that eliminated their province's traditional veto over constitutional change, and Trudeau was persuaded by Ontario premier Bill Davis to accept a limitation on his Charter of Rights (McMurtry 1982–83, 63–64). Through it all, Canadians sat glued to their nightly news and devoured newspapers, keenly following the latest twists in the constitutional plot. The public fascination with a story that was taking place largely behind closed doors even gave rise to a new strategy in Canadian journalism – the "scrum," in which journalists surround politicians in hopes of a "quote that may turn out to be historic or spectacularly banal" (*Globe and Mail* 1981).

Beyond its interest in constitutional progress, though, the public became part of the strategy that finally secured a deal – and part of the process that left Quebec isolated and kept its signature off the final document. During the negotiations on 5 November, Trudeau suggested a referendum to decide the fate of both the amending formula and the proposed Charter of Rights. In effect, he suggested giving a say to all those people who had been watching the increasingly public antics of the constitution makers – they were interested enough to watch; let's let them play. It was a strategy that would ultimately let the public make the final constitutional decision, and Lévesque took the bait. Looking "enthusiastic" about the possibility, the Quebec premier appeared to break with his English-speaking colleagues in considering a mechanism that had long been opposed by the Gang of Eight because it eliminated the important role of premiers and provincial legislatures in amending the constitution. The threat of a referendum set the stage for the final middle-of-the-night agreement between seven of the dissenting provinces and the three governments on the federalist side (Clarkson and McCall 1990, 357–86).

The deal itself, then, was clearly a function of spectator constitutionalism. The role the public played had been growing since the advent of mega-constitutional negotiations at the Confederation of Tomorrow Conference in 1967. John Robarts invited the public to watch at least part of the answer to the question he asked of his provincial counterparts: "What does Quebec want?" From that moment, a constitutional audience existed where there had been none. For the first time in the long history of constitutional debates, the story was a compelling one. People were interested in its outcome just as much as they were interested in the ups and downs of the process, and those few people who were actual participants were forced to take the public interest into account. Television cameras were allowed into parts of the constitutional conferences, the questions themselves were framed in terms of one side versus another, and Trudeau and Lévesque proved to be well-matched combatants in a constitutional narrative that appeared more pugilistic than judicial.

With the public let in and the spectators given a role to play, the Canadian constitutional process was inexorably changed. Mega-constitutional negotiations remained the mainstay of the process for at least another decade following patriation, but now the spectators wanted in, too. Not only had we become, as Alan Cairns has argued so persuasively, "Charter Canadians," included in the constitutional process because of the entrenched *Charter of Rights and Freedoms*, we had been brought into the drama over the course of fifteen years as engrossed spectators. After 1982, the spectators had as much of a stake in the constitutional drama as the professionals.

References

Annual Premiers' Conference. 1976. *Communique.* Federal-Provincial Financial Negotiations, August. *Canadian Annual Review* papers, Private Collection.

Bryden, P.E. 2011. "Intergovernmental Guardians: Treasury's Role in Setting the National Agenda, 1959–1967." In *The Guardian: Perspectives on the Ministry of Finance of Ontario,* edited by Patrice Dutil, 109–30. Toronto: University of Toronto Press.

Canada. Cabinet Document. 1968. 9 January. Document 10–68. File: 5517–04(68–1)-1. Vol. 4720. Library and Archives Canada.

Canada. House of Commons. 1970. *Debates.* 28th Parliament, 3rd Session. 15 October.

—. 1974. *Debates.* 28th Parliament, 2nd Session. 2 October.

Clark, Joe. 1979. Letter to William Davis. 26 July. File: Ontario. TL 85–830, FD-1, box 1. RG 58-9-1. Archives of Ontario.

Clarkson, Stephen. 2005. *The Big Red Machine: How the Liberal Party Dominates Canadian Politics.* Vancouver: UBC Press.

Clarkson, Stephen, and Christina McCall. 1990. *The Magnificent Obsession.* Vol. 1, *Trudeau and Our Times.* Toronto: McClelland and Stewart.

Clift, Dominique. 1971. "Confederation '71: Quebec." *Montreal Star,* 12 June, 17.

Davis, William. 1976. Report to Cabinet on Discussions at the 17th Annual Premiers' Conference, 25 August. File: Constitutional Conferences, General. Container 27. RG 50-5-1. Archives of Ontario.

Globe and Mail. 1967. "In Confidence and Goodwill." 28 November, 6.

—. 1971a. "Bourassa Is Applauded by National Assembly for Rejecting Charter." 24 June, 1.

—. 1971b. "No Victoria Charter and No More Yielding." 24 June, 6.

—. 1981. "News Scrum: Chaotic and Usually Useless." 5 November, 1.

Goldenberg, Carl. 1967. Letter to John Robarts. 4 December. File: Goldenberg, Carl, 1967–69. Box 2, Series F-15-4-3. MU 7998. John Robarts Papers, Archives of Ontario.

Greathed, Ed. 1968. Letter to Keith Reynolds. 18 July. File: Propositions – Constitutional Committee of Officials. Box 110. RG 6-14. Archives of Ontario.

Hunter, Michael. 1971. Letter to Keith Reynolds. 22 January. File: Federal Government, Constitution Correspondence, January-February 1970. Vol. 485. RG 3-26. Archives of Ontario.

Lougheed, Peter. 1999. *Constitutional Patriation: The Lougheed-Lévesque Correspondence.* Kingston: Institute of Intergovernmental Relations, Queen's University.

Macdonald, H. Ian. 1971a. Letter to John P. Robarts. 5 February. File: Federal-Provincial Conference, Constitution, Victoria. Box 1. RG 3-59. Archives of Ontario.

—. 1971b. Letter to Darcy McKeough. 1 April. File: FP 7-1 Fed/Prov Affairs Secretariat, 1971 – Organization. Box 9. RG 3-49. Archives of Ontario.

McMurtry, R. Roy. 1982–83. "The Search for a Constitutional Accord – A Personal Memoir." *Queen's Law Journal* 8: 28–73.

McRoberts, Kenneth. 1997. *Misconceiving Canada: The Struggle for National Unity.* Toronto: Oxford University Press.

Newman, Peter. 1968. "The Impact of Television." *Montreal Star,* 7 February, 13.

Ontario. 1967a. *Legislative Debates.* Speech from the Throne. 25 January.

—. 1967b. *Legislative Debates.* 18 May.

—. 1968. *Legislative Debates.* 27 February.

—. Ministry of Intergovernmental Affairs. 1980. "Report to Cabinet on the Discussions to Date of the Continuing Committee of Ministers on the Constitution." 30 July. File: Constitutional Matters, General. Box 17, FP 4. RG 3-49. Archives of Ontario.

Pape, Gordon. 1967. "Johnson Relaxes Hard Line Policy." *Montreal Gazette,* 30 November, 1.

Pearson, L.B. 1967. Letter to John Robarts. 26 January. File: Correspondence, 1965–1971. MU 5311. Gathercole Papers. Archives of Ontario.

Peckford, Brian. 1979. Letter to Joe Clark. 23 August. File: Intergovernmental Affairs. Vol. 8. RG 55. Nova Scotia Archives and Records Management.

Posen, Gary. 1968a. "Report of the Meeting of the Continuing Committee ... July 25–26 1968." File: Constitutional Conference, Continuing Committee, 1968. Box 116. RG 6-14. Archives of Ontario.

—. 1968b. Letter to Ed Greathed. 13 December. File: Constitutional: Federal-Provincial Conference, February 1968. Box 113. RG 6-14. Archives of Ontario.

—. 1976. Draft Memo for Darcy McKeough to William Davis. 14 May. File: 705-2: Constitutional Conferences, General. Box 27. RG. 50-5-1. Archives of Ontario.

Robarts, John P. 1966. "Remarks to the Advertising and Sales Executives' Club in Montreal, Wednesday, November 23rd, 1966." Private collection, Canadian Annual Review papers, unorganized material.

—. 1969. "Draft letter to the Hon P.E. Trudeau from the Hon. J.P. Robarts." 3 November. UB 130–31. RG 6-14. Archives of Ontario.

Robertson, Gordon. 2000. *Memoirs of a Very Civil Servant: Mackenzie King to Pierre Trudeau.* Toronto: University of Toronto Press.

Romanow, Roy, John Whyte, and Howard Leeson. 1984. *Canada ... Notwithstanding: The Making of the Constitution, 1976–1982.* Toronto: Carswell/Methuen.

Russell, Peter H. 1983. "Bold Statescraft, Questionable Jurisprudence." In *And No One Cheered: Federalism, Democracy and the Constitution Act,* edited by Keith Banting and Richard Simeon, 210–38. Toronto: Methuen.

—. 1993. *Constitutional Odyssey: Can Canadians Become a Sovereign People?* 2nd ed. Toronto: University of Toronto Press.

Saywell, John, ed. 1967. *Canadian Annual Review for 1966.* Toronto: University of Toronto Press.

—. 1972. *Canadian Annual Review for 1971.* Toronto: University of Toronto Press.

Stevens, Paul, and John Saywell. 1968. "Parliament and Politics." In *Canadian Annual Review, 1967,* edited by John Saywell, 3-99. Toronto: University of Toronto Press.

Stevenson, Donald W. 1970. Letter to H. Ian Macdonald. 20 November. File: CCO, Constitutional Conference, November-December 1970. Box 3. RG 3-105. Archives of Ontario.

— 1971. Letter to H. Ian Macdonald. 6 January. File: Federal-Provincial – Meetings. Vol. 28. RG 50-33. Archives of Ontario.

—. 1972. Memo to file. 14 March 1972. File: Federal-Provincial Series, Minister's Meeting with Mr. Turner, March 11–12/72. Box 26. RG 50-33. Archives of Ontario.

—. 1981. "Chronology of Steps Leading to Constitutional Agreement on November 5th, 1981." Private Collection.

—. 1988. "Notes for Use by Don Stevenson at the Federal-Provincial Conference Simulation, University of Waterloo, December 12, 1988." Private Collection.

Trudeau, Pierre. 1976. Letter to William Davis. 31 March. File: FP 4-1, Constitution – Amendment to the Constitution of Canada '76. Box 29, trans. 80–1156. RG 3-49. Archives of Ontario.

Vaughan, Frederick. 2004. *Aggressive in Pursuit: The Life of Justice Emmett Hall.* Toronto: University of Toronto Press, for the Osgoode Society for Legal History.

Wills, Terrence. 1967. "A Gourmet's Canadiana with a Choice of Views." *Globe and Mail,* 28 November, 8.

PART 3

Shaping Patriation: Law, Political Vision, Political Actors, and Political Struggle

Law, Politics, and the *Patriation Reference* of 1981

6

Philip Girard

Adam Dodek (2011, 117) has called the *Patriation Reference* decision of 1981 one of the "most important and least read" of all the constitutional law decisions of the Supreme Court of Canada. Pierre Trudeau (1996, 248) called it the most important decision that the Supreme Court ever rendered or ever would render. It seems that, like Trudeau himself, the *Patriation Reference* "haunts us still."[1] Legal commentators were generally not positive about the decision when it came out (e.g., Hogg 1982), and most have remained skeptical and wary of it, though a new attitude of grudging respect may be emerging (Hogg 2006). Political scientists, by contrast, were more positive about the decision and, if Peter Russell (2011b) can be taken as an example, have maintained that position over time.

In this chapter, I come at the *Patriation Reference* from two angles. First, I ask whether law affected politics: that is, I analyze the effect of the decision on the political actors. Then I look at whether politics affected law: that is, whether the shape of the decision was affected by the highly volatile political climate in which it was argued, considered, and rendered. Along the way, I also ask two questions that are seldom posed: Why did this matter end up going to the Supreme Court at all when Trudeau was so determined not to have the courts involved? And why did he not call a referendum, as he threatened to do at several junctures in the constitutional saga?

It was the dissenting premiers (initially, the "Gang of Six," later Eight) who developed the initial court strategy in response to Trudeau's 2 October 1980 announcement that he would proceed unilaterally with his People's Package of patriation, a charter of rights, and an amending formula. Trudeau's proposal was that patriation and the charter would become law immediately upon passage of the implementing law by the British Parliament, but the amending formula proposal contained some flexibility. The rule of unanimity would prevail for two years, during which there would be further negotiations. If no agreement could be reached, two proposals would be presented to the people of Canada in a binding referendum: the federally supported Victoria formula,[2] and a proposal agreed to by at least eight provinces representing 80 percent of the population.

While the idea of giving the people of Canada the final say on a constitutional amending process was new, a process for consulting citizens on constitutional matters through non-binding referenda had been a priority of the Trudeau government in 1978–79. A *Canada Referendum Bill*, Bill C-9, was extensively debated in the House of Commons and in the Standing Committee on Justice and Legal Affairs in early 1979, but failed to become law before an election was called on 26 March. It would have allowed the cabinet to initiate a consultative referendum on any topic relating to the constitution of Canada, including – interestingly, in view of later events – any "custom, convention, or enactment" that comprised the constitution of Canada. The significance of the bill's failure to pass will become apparent later.

In developing their court strategy in response to Trudeau's unilateral patriation initiative, the premiers ensured that the questions referred to the courts of appeal of Manitoba, Quebec, and Newfoundland raised issues of both law and convention. They hoped that even if they lost on the law, they might secure a win in the court of public opinion if the decision on the convention issue went in their favour. As the provincially initiated references were heard, the federal government sent counsel to oppose the provincial arguments but did not take steps to initiate a competing reference to the Supreme Court, as it might have done, or announce that it would appeal any decision with which it did not agree. In December 1980, a senior British minister was sent to Ottawa to urge the government to refer the matter to the Supreme Court, but without success (Marshall 1984, 191). Meanwhile, on the parliamentary front, the New Democratic Party supported the resolution introduced in the House of Commons in the fall of 1980, but the Progressive Conservatives opposed it and began a filibuster that stretched debate into the spring.

In February 1981, the Manitoba Court of Appeal decided 3–2 in favour of the federal government. It took until the end of March before the second provincial court ruled. On 31 March, the Newfoundland Supreme Court held unanimously that the federal government had no right to proceed as a matter of either law or convention. Up to this point, the federal government was resolved to go to London without waiting for any decision of the Supreme Court of Canada, in spite of the extreme reluctance of the British government to proceed without knowing the views of the court (Strayer 2013, 173; McMurtry 2013, 297–99). However, when news of the Newfoundland decision was conveyed to a federal cabinet meeting then in progress, it took only twenty minutes to decide to appeal (Sheppard and Valpy 1982, 233). Still, there was no official announcement about the matter until the 8 April pact that saw the opposition Progressive Conservatives agree to end their parliamentary filibuster and all three parties agree to await the Supreme Court ruling, which the government formally agreed to seek before voting on the Trudeau government's draft resolution on patriation. The dissenting provinces had already given notice that they would appeal the Manitoba Court of Appeal ruling, so it was not difficult to append to it the federal appeal of the Newfoundland decision. The Quebec Court of Appeal's mid-April ruling in favour of the federal government's position came too late to affect the decision to put the questions before the Supreme Court of Canada. The Supreme Court hearings extended over five days, beginning in late April. The *Patriation Reference* decision followed almost exactly five months later, on 28 September.

As is well known, the court issued two majority decisions. The first found that Trudeau's plan to unilaterally request passage of his package by the British Parliament was legal, with seven justices concurring and two dissenting. The second, with six justices concurring and three dissenting, was that, with regard to the relevance of provincial consent, there was a convention, albeit unenforceable in the courts, requiring the consent of a substantial number of provinces. Following tradition, I refer to the decision on the law as Majority I, and the decision on convention as Majority II, as that is the order in which they appear in the case reports.

Did Law Affect Politics? The Political Aftermath of the *Patriation Reference*

There is really no doubt about the ultimate answer to this question. As Peter Russell (2011a, 22) said recently in a review of Ron Graham's book *The Last Act*, the First Ministers' meeting of November 1981 "took place only because of a decision of the Supreme Court of Canada in September 1981." Nonetheless, the way in which that decision's impact manifested itself in politics and public opinion is of interest to anyone seeking to understand not just the patriation process but Canada itself. A question that is seldom asked about the patriation saga is how such a major change to the constitution of a developed democracy could take place without the direct participation of the Canadian public. The Supreme Court's decision led to a new round of negotiations among Canada's political leaders, but it is not quite right to say that it forced the players to return to the negotiating table. The legitimacy requirement that the judgment highlighted might have been satisfied in other ways, such as an election or a referendum, either before, after, or without further negotiations. Both federal and provincial politicians considered these possibilities in the wake of the decision, but in the end the traditional tools of executive federalism were employed to bring about constitutional change. Thus, while it is clear that the *Patriation Reference* had a huge impact on events, the nature and form of that impact was not inevitable. This section will consider both the path taken and those not taken as the political actors reacted to the new environment created by the Supreme Court's intervention. The analysis will demonstrate that the lack of direct recourse to the people was partly due to contingent factors such as the absence of a referendum law, and was partly a result of Canadians' historical lack of direct engagement in constitutional change and their acquiescence in the leading role of politicians in accomplishing it.

Trudeau was informed of the Supreme Court's decision in Seoul, South Korea, on a stopover to a Commonwealth Conference in Melbourne,

Australia. Although the timing of the conference was extremely inconvenient, he did not want to cancel his trip lest it seem to accord too much importance to the Supreme Court decision, whose delivery date had been announced before his departure (Burelle 2005, 345). Holding the Supreme Court at arm's length was consistent with Trudeau's long-standing position that patriation was a political matter and the courts should stay out of it. For a while, Justice Minister Jean Chrétien and Trudeau played a good cop/bad cop routine, with Chrétien taking the hard line that Ottawa's "win" on the legal question was all that counted, while Trudeau dangled hints that he might be willing to consider more negotiations with the premiers. In fact, Trudeau had decided by the end of the day that he would meet the premiers one more time, but he continued to consider other options and waited for two weeks to gauge public reaction to the ruling before announcing his decision on 13 October (English 2009, 503).

The extent to which the Supreme Court decision functioned as a "game-changer," as Carissima Mathen (2011, 163) has termed it, quickly became apparent. Within two days, the reaction seemed to throw the unilateral train right off the tracks, and indeed to threaten the future of the entire patriation enterprise. On 30 September, the NDP caucus met and announced that the party would withdraw its support of Trudeau's package unless the prime minister made one more attempt to negotiate with the premiers (Walkom 1981). This was highly significant, as the Liberals held only two seats in Manitoba and no seats further west. The NDP's backing of Trudeau's package had provided at least the illusion of western support, but even that was now jeopardized. René Lévesque wrapped himself in the mantle of Majority II, and called the Assemblée nationale into special session to debate a resolution condemning the federal government's unilateral plan as unconstitutional, a resolution supported by Claude Ryan and all but nine of his Liberal Members of the National Assembly (MNAs) when the vote was taken on 2 October. Joe Clark, leader of the federal Progressive Conservatives and the Official Opposition, denounced reliance on Majority I as "legal trickery" on the part of the government. Clark noisily threatened to withdraw from the agreement he had previously made with Trudeau (McArthur 1981). Virtually unanimous editorial opinion across the country called on

Trudeau to take the hint in the Majority II judgment and engage in one more round of negotiations. The irrepressibly Liberal *Toronto Star* was the only exception (*Toronto Star*, 1981a). Even the *Times* of London weighed in, calling on Trudeau to secure more provincial support before coming to the United Kingdom (United Press International 1981).

According to André Burelle, Trudeau's French speechwriter of the period, Lévesque's response caused a "quasi-panique" among the federal Liberal caucus in Quebec, who began a week-long meeting in Orford, Quebec, on 28 September (Burelle 2005, 345). The whip of the Quebec Liberals arrived soon after the decision was released, and reported that the Parti Québécois (PQ) was considering a referendum on Trudeau's unilateral patriation package should Trudeau attempt to invoke the legal power that the Supreme Court decision seemed to accord him; moreover, Quebec Liberal leader Claude Ryan would join Lévesque in condemning Ottawa's action. Burelle, who kept the prime minister briefed on events as they unfolded, was astonished and dismayed at how quickly the caucus seemed prepared to abandon the Charter in light of Lévesque's threat (347). He worried that if Lévesque even announced his referendum, the British Parliament would wait to learn its results before considering whether to pass Trudeau's package. He noted that a federal election might be needed to enhance the legitimacy of Trudeau's own package, but asserted that "*nous ne pouvons même pas songer à un référendum pan-canadien étant donné l'absence d'une loi-cadre fédérale sur le référendum*" (346).[3] The failure to pass the *Canada Referendum Bill* in February–March 1979 thus played a critical role at this juncture (Boyer 1992, 42–46). Given the speed at which events were unfolding, there was no time to reintroduce the bill and get it passed. Had it been at the ready, Trudeau might well have decided to leap over the heads of both the dissenting premiers and the Supreme Court to see whether he could garner sufficient support from the Canadian people to proceed to London.

A week later, Burelle himself seemed to have succumbed to the panic he had earlier decried. In his view, the Supreme Court decision had given the PQ a very powerful weapon: "*celle de la moralité vs la légalité*" (Burelle 2005, 351). He feared that the current federal public relations campaign was too mild and that stronger measures would be needed to counter Lévesque's strong pushback. Even before the Supreme Court decision,

Quebec had started its "Minute Ottawa" campaign, whose principal visual image was a fist crumpling a Quebec flag. Against this, the federal government ads, to be run at first only in Quebec, featured "wholesome people like a saleslady in a store and a man stacking cord wood. Each emphasized a constitutional theme such as equality, mobility, equalization payments, and language rights," topped with the anodyne slogan "With our new constitution, everybody wins" (Bauch 1981, 2). Polling seemed to suggest that two-thirds of Quebecers would support Lévesque in any referendum opposing the federal charter *"aux droits collectifs des Québécois"* (Burelle 2005, 351).

As for federal countermeasures, Burelle also counselled that an election was probably out of the question, because Trudeau's management of the economy had not been popular, and it would not be possible to confine the ballot question solely to the constitutional issue (Burelle 2005, 352–54). With no referendum machinery at the ready, and an election inadvisable for a variety of reasons, the Canadian people would not, in the end, be directly consulted about the People's Package.

When the Assemblée nationale passed its 2 October resolution condemning any unilateral federal action that would diminish the powers of the Assemblée without its consent, the Supreme Court decision was front and centre: "The Supreme Court, having decided that the federal proposals respecting the constitution of Canada decrease the powers of the National Assembly of Quebec and that unilateral action by the federal government, although legal, is unconstitutional, being contrary to the conventions, this assembly demands." (Canadian Press 1981, 10; O'Neill 1981). Lévesque's embrace of Majority II provides additional evidence confirming the thesis of Guy Laforest and Rosalie Readman in Chapter 8 that the Quebec premier's strategy at this time was somewhat haphazard and improvised. Majority I had given the federal government the formal power to effect constitutional change without Quebec's consent, while the requirement of "substantial consent" declared to be conventionally required said nothing about the specificity of Quebec. Lévesque and his advisers appeared not to be alert to the danger that the substantial consent requirement might be met by a group of provinces without Quebec.

On the same day as the vote in the Assemblée nationale, the Liberal caucus at Orford decided, with only one dissenting vote, to urge Trudeau to proceed with unilateral patriation only if one more round of negotiations with the premiers failed (Fox 1981). Thus, within a few days of the Supreme Court decision, Trudeau's unilateralist policy appeared to be in tatters. On the plus side, however, Quebec seemed to step back from the brink. Following some impressive sabre rattling in the first week after the *Patriation Reference* was released, Lévesque toned down the rhetoric and showed more willingness to play by the existing rules – including considering the possibility of having PQ candidates run federally to take the fight to Ottawa (Picard 1981b). Certainly, francophone media opinion in Quebec was alarmed by the degree of anti-Ottawa hostility displayed by Lévesque in the days after the court decision, and strongly counselled engaging in further negotiations. *La Presse*, *Le Soleil*, and *Le Devoir* all found Lévesque's recall of the Assemblée nationale unnecessarily provocative, and warned – presciently – that if the government continued in this vein, it risked finding itself isolated should the other premiers decide to negotiate a deal. Lévesque's advisers doubted whether a referendum would have much impact in London, and within a week the idea had been quietly dropped (Picard 1981a; Chambers 1981).

Ultimately, Trudeau did obtain the consent of nine premiers to a revised package that was passed into law. At the empirical level, then, it is clear that the *Patriation Reference* had an enormous impact on the political outcome of the constitutional reform package. Unlike the *Quebec Secession Reference* seventeen years later, which could be analogized to a dose of preventive medicine, the *Patriation Reference* was more like a shot of adrenaline administered in the midst of an allergic reaction. It forced Trudeau to alter his plans, consider the alternatives, and ultimately reengage with the premiers. In that sense, it is often regarded as a defeat for Trudeau.

However, the decision did, in fact, confirm that Trudeau possessed a powerful weapon – the legal right to proceed unilaterally to Westminster. He later recalled that had the last round of negotiations in November 1981 failed after good-faith participation by the federal government, he would have relied on Majority I to go to Westminster and take his chances with the British Parliament, which, at that point, might well have acquiesced. If not, Trudeau asserted, "we would have [had] the option of a massive demonstration of national will, leading to a unilateral declaration of constitutional independence from Britain." He went on to say that he instructed his principal secretary, Tom Axworthy, to "start making contingency plans for a referendum or an election in 1982" (Trudeau 1993, 316).

Had this route been successfully taken, Canada would have had a truly autochthonous constitution. Judging from the opinion polls of the day, the package might well have won a majority in all provinces, including Quebec, and Canadians might have been spared the subsequent years of wrangling that included Meech Lake, Charlottetown, and the 1995 Quebec referendum. A poll held in November 1981 showed that a majority of voters in Quebec would not oppose patriation and a charter of rights if a referendum were held (English 2009, 516). It is impossible to tell how much public opinion might have been swayed during any such campaign, especially in Quebec, where the PQ would have vigorously resisted the federal initiative. It is worth noting, however, that when Trudeau was preparing his "plan B" referendum in case negotiations with the premiers failed, he asked Burelle whether he thought the constitutional package would achieve a majority in Quebec. Burelle's response in early November 1981, unlike his prediction a month earlier (though that prediction related to a Quebec-run referendum), was that it would indeed achieve a majority in Quebec (Burelle 2005, 355).

Later in life, after seeing how the exclusion of Quebec from the November 1981 deal had played out politically, Trudeau expressed regret that he had not followed the referendum path. In an interview with Ron Graham in 1992, he said that he felt he had had "no choice but to accept the provinces' deal after Davis's call on the evening of November 4th. But now I think it was a mistake. I should have gone for an election or a referendum. Quebec wouldn't have been able to say it was 'left out,' because everybody [i.e., all the premiers] would have been 'left out,' and Canada would have got a better amending formula and a better charter" (Graham 2011, 260).

That may well be, but Trudeau would have had an uphill battle convincing his own government and possibly even the people of Canada that a referendum was the best way out of such a political impasse. Although a poll held a week after the Supreme Court decision suggested that 60 percent of Canadians thought there should be a referendum on the package before Trudeau went to London, there were few letters to the editor on the subject, very few editorials favouring such a move – the *Toronto Star*, again, being the exception – and no discernible popular movement promoting it (*Toronto Star*, 3 October 1981b). Moreover, key players in Trudeau's own cabinet and virtually all the premiers were opposed to a referendum. Curiously, Joe Clark, after relentlessly opposing the Liberals' referendum bill in 1978–79, subsequently came around to the idea that, if the final round of negotiations failed, there should be a referendum or an election on the constitutional package, though he probably favoured the latter (Malarek 1981).

Michael Valpy's views were representative of media opinion on the subject of referenda: in a country where relations between majorities and minorities and between regions were strained and required constant adjustment and compromise, the referendum was too blunt and, therefore, too dangerous an instrument to use. Previous referenda in 1898 (on temperance) and 1942 (on conscription) had been hugely divisive and counterproductive (Valpy, October 1981). The *Gazette* even managed to find psychologists who opined that a preference for compromise was deeply rooted in the "Canadian character," making the winner-take-all tool of the referendum unsuitable for Canadian politics (Wills 1981).

Among legal scholars, only Laval professor Gil Rémillard foreshadowed Trudeau's later regrets by pointing out, in the wake of the *Patriation Reference*, that a referendum with concurrent majorities in the Atlantic provinces, the West, Ontario, and Quebec would have been the only way to settle conclusively the issue of legitimacy that was raised by the Supreme Court. The court itself stated that "the constitutional value which is the pivot of the conventions stated above and relating to responsible government is the democratic principle: the powers of the state must be exercised in accordance with the wishes of the electorate" (*Patriation Reference*, 880). According to Rémillard, this was "the first time that the democratic principle ha[d] been so clearly stated in a Canadian legal decision ... [and] situated not exclusively in relation to the sovereign authority of Parliament or the state, but directly in relation to the people" (Rémillard 1983, 191–92). Subsequent events proved him correct: the nagging doubt about the legitimacy, as opposed to the legality, of imposing a major constitutional change on Quebec without its consent haunted

Canadian politics for the next fourteen years, and cannot be said to have disappeared even today (Rémillard 1983; see also McWhinney et al. 1981).

Accustomed to seeing the constitution as belonging not to the people but to the political class, Canadians acquiesced in allowing the latter, with some coaching from the Supreme Court, to carry out the process of constitutional reform. Mostly, they wanted a conclusion to the controversy so the politicians could focus on the grave economic problems of the early 1980s. They liked the idea of a charter of rights but did not see the mechanics of its adoption as their affair. Canadians wanted to air their views on the content of the Charter and the package as a whole to their political representatives, and did so, but they did not see themselves – yet – as the decision makers.

Did Politics Affect Law? The Legal Aftermath of the *Patriation Reference*

Legal scholars have not been kind to the *Patriation Reference.* Many were and still are convinced that it was wrong for the Supreme Court to pronounce on the convention issue. Doing so, the argument goes, allowed politics and law to affect one another in inappropriate ways. Peter Hogg said at the time that the only reason for the court to have done so was to influence the political outcome. Much less politely, Pierre Trudeau a decade later asserted, with retired Supreme Court Justice Brian Dickson in attendance, that the judges of Majority II "blatantly manipulated the evidence before them so as to arrive at the desired result. They then wrote a judgment which tried to lend a fig-leaf of legality to their preconceived conclusion" (Trudeau 1996, 256). Recently, Adam Dodek (2011) has stated that the justiciability of constitutional conventions recognized in the *Patriation Reference* represents "the continuing constitutional danger of the decision." Others have been critical from the opposite end of the legal spectrum, arguing that the court was wrong to draw such a bright line between convention and law, and should have recognized that conventions can become legally binding – "crystallize" – over time (Gélinas 1997; Lederman 1978, 1983).

My own view lies between these two. As a legal pluralist, I find the bright-line division between law and not law unsatisfying, and agree with Heard that there are varieties of conventions that may differ in their obligatory character (Heard 1991). I would urge that at least some constitutional conventions be seen as a kind of law, and therefore the subject of court recognition and commentary in appropriate instances, even without benefit of the doctrine of crystallization. Below, I develop the argument that although the Supreme Court's handling of the convention issue was indeed affected by the political context in which it arose, it was not an illegitimate exercise.

After the initial version of this chapter was written, allegations were published that politics had affected law in an entirely illicit fashion during the writing of the *Patriation Reference*. In his book *La Bataille de Londres: Dessous, secrets et coulisses du rapatriement constitutionnel*, Frédéric Bastien (2013) alleged that Chief Justice Bora Laskin and Justice Willard Estey had had back-channel communications with the federal and British authorities before the hearing and during the writing of the decision.[4] In his view, these alleged improprieties rendered the decision null and void. In a recent publication, I argued that Dr. Bastien's allegations were unsustainable, being based on a combination of incomplete research and faulty interpretation (Girard 2014). In addition, over 2,000 pages of government documents recently released to the government of Quebec pursuant to a freedom of information request demonstrate that the federal government was entirely unaware of the content of the Supreme Court's decision before its release (Bellavance 2013). I refer the interested reader to these sources for further detail.

If the nature of conventions is one aspect of the interface between politics and law, the procedural context of the *Patriation Reference* is another. I will argue that in reference cases, where courts are advising governments rather than adjudicating on well-understood rights derived from common law or statute, they can legitimately take into account more of the political context than they normally would. Carissima Mathen (2011) has recently drawn attention to the reference context of the *Patriation Reference*. She notes that the reference power was included in the original *Supreme Court Act* of 1875, that it was unsuccessfully challenged by the provinces before the Privy Council in 1912, and that, over time, the idea that such opinions were no more than advisory became replaced by the notion that they were binding. This is not surprising given that the notion of binding precedent was itself largely a late nineteenth-century invention that reached its heyday in the 1950s (Dawson 1968). In 1957, the Supreme Court of Canada mitigated this doctrine somewhat by signalling that reference decisions should not render future litigation on the same topic *res judicata;* some commentators have gone further and advocated a return to the idea that such opinions are advisory only (Strayer 1988, 331–32).

Strayer (1988, 317) has observed that both provincial and federal politicians came to view the reference procedure as "an integral part of the functioning of the constitution." Peter Hogg (2006, 59) has stated that references are "uncommon." While this is true in terms of absolute numbers, the observation is misleading with regard to the overall significance of reference cases in our constitutional jurisprudence: over a quarter of all constitutional decisions rendered by the Supreme Court between 1875 and 1986 were reference decisions, a substantial proportion by any standard (Strayer 1988, 311). It is true that the relative frequency of reference decisions has declined in recent decades, from 35 percent of all constitutional decisions appealed to the highest court before 1967 to 15 percent thereafter, but some of the most important constitutional cases of recent years have originated as references, such as the *BC Motor Vehicle Act Reference,* the *Quebec Secession Reference,* and the *Same-Sex Marriage Reference.*

The very ubiquity of the reference jurisdiction probably explains why none of the judges in the *Patriation Reference* drew much attention to it as the means by which the matter had come before them. The authors of Majority I laconically characterized the provincial legislation authorizing the instant references as "wide enough to saddle the respective courts with the determination of questions which may not be justiciable," although they went on to note that the Supreme Court retained a discretion to refuse to answer such questions (*Patriation Reference,* 768).

Not so the judges in the *Quebec Secession Reference,* who were more forthcoming about the nature of references. They noted that as "the Canadian Constitution does not insist on a strict separation of powers[,] Parliament and the provincial legislatures may properly confer other legal functions on the courts, and may confer certain judicial functions on bodies that are not courts." Thus, there was "no constitutional bar to this Court's receipt of jurisdiction to undertake such an advisory role" (*Quebec Secession Reference,* 233).

I read the Supreme Court here as returning to that initial idea of the reference jurisdiction as advisory, and signalling that it might be willing to be more adventurous in a reference case than it would in ordinary litigation. Although the judges in Majority II did not say this expressly, I believe this is what they were doing.

Given that critics such as Hogg and Trudeau speak to the motivations of the justices, it is useful to ask whether biographical writings devoted to the judges who decided the *Patriation Reference* might provide any insight into the drafting of the decision; in particular, do they reveal anything about the impact of the political context on the decision? Canadian judges have typically been reticent in sharing their views on important cases after retirement, and the *Patriation Reference* is no exception in that regard. Of the nine judges who decided the case, three have book-length biographies: Chief Justice Bora Laskin (Girard 2005) and Justices Brian Dickson (Sharpe and Roach 2003) and William McIntyre (McConnell 2000). There are, in addition, transcripts of interviews with Justices Ronald Martland, Willard Estey, Antonio Lamer, and Dickson, conducted by representatives of the Osgoode Society for Canadian Legal History. The first two are accessible to researchers; the latter two are still embargoed. Although the book-length biographies provide no startling revelations about their subjects' views, Dickson's biographers reported to this author that he was uncharacteristically defensive about his role in the *Patriation Reference*, and would neither discuss it nor provide his file on the case, even though he had meticulously preserved virtually all his other case files and allowed Sharpe and Roach free access to them. This suggests a certain uneasiness with his own role in the case. Robert Sharpe conducted his interviews with Dickson between 1991 and 1993, just after the retired chief justice had endured a public thrashing by Trudeau in March 1991. It would not be surprising if Dickson was highly sensitive about his role in the case at this time, and fearful of revealing anything that might be perceived as giving credence to Trudeau's critique.

The Osgoode Society's interview with former justice Estey, conducted in 1993, reveals that it was Supreme Court Justice Jean Beetz who was attracted by the Saskatchewan proposal relating to a convention of "substantial consent," and who persuaded most of his colleagues to adopt it.

In a powerful statement concerning the effect of politics on law, Estey reported that Beetz "was the intellectual leader of the idea that we should soften the approach, make it possible, let everybody back down a wee bit, force another rung on the ladder for the aggressive feds who just wanted to snap it [off]" (Estey 1993, 162–63). And twelve years after the fact, though of course with the benefit of hindsight, Estey found himself thinking that that had probably been the better course.

Many critics of the *Patriation Reference* decision contend that ruling on the convention issue was both inappropriate and overly political. However, of the twenty-two judges who heard the arguments in this case, thirteen in provincial courts of appeal and nine in the Supreme Court of Canada, only one refused to address the convention issue. Only one behaved the way that Peter Hogg said he should behave. The fact that twenty-one out of twenty-two judges believed that they could and should answer the reference question on conventions (although three admittedly did so reluctantly in the Supreme Court) must tell us something. What it tells us, in my view, is that it is not just Canadian politicians who believe that the reference procedure is "an integral part of the functioning of the constitution." Judges, too, have internalized this idea and accept that this advisory role is one that may lead them into penumbral areas of the law, whether those be constitutional conventions or unwritten constitutional principles. The issue of convention was put squarely on the table in all three provincial references in the context of a great national debate about the legality and legitimacy of Trudeau's proposed method of patriating the constitution. To refuse to answer the question would have failed the people of Canada in their hour of need, and all the judges except Manitoba's Justice Gordon Hall seemed to realize this.

This need not mean that the courts will answer any old question about any old convention any old time someone raises one. The courts have the discretion to refuse to answer reference questions and may do so based on an understanding of the political context. In this sense, a refusal to answer can be just as "political" as a decision to answer. In assessing how well the courts deal with politically charged references, it is useful to look at two others with some similarity to the *Patriation Reference:* the *Manitoba Language Rights* and *Quebec Secession* references. In referring to these along with the *Patriation Reference,* Peter Hogg (2006, 96) has written that "in each case, the Court came up with a solution that arguably exceeded the normal limits of judicial power, but the solution was a clever one that defused the crisis." Now, "clever" is not exactly a resounding compliment. It suggests a response that is glib and superficially attractive, but ultimately not well founded because it exceeds "the normal limits of judicial power." But reference cases *do* authorize the Supreme Court to go beyond "the normal limits of judicial power," or what I would prefer to call the normal parameters of the judicial function: in reference cases, we are in the realm of judicial exhortation rather than power. So it cannot be a valid critique of the court merely to observe that it has answered the questions posed in a reference, even if some of those questions deal with a convention. It is valid to critique the judges' handling of those questions, as many have with regard to the court's invocation of "substantial consent" and its handling of the Quebec veto issue. But if the judges are giving advice on non-justiciable issues rather than deciding rights, then surely they are entitled to discuss soft law as well as positive law.

With regard to the content of the convention, this is not the place to discuss whether the Supreme Court "got it right." Rather, I will address only the issue of whether Majority II's declaration of a convention of "substantial consent" was affected by the political context in an illegitimate way. Estey's recollections suggest a high level of awareness of the political context and discomfort with the confrontational politics of patriation. It is also true that most observers thought that if a convention existed, it was one of unanimity (McMurtry 2013, 300, 303). But it is not as if Majority II made up the idea of substantial consent on its own. Two highly regarded constitutional scholars, John Whyte and Ken Lysyk, put the argument before the court, and the 1965 white paper prepared for Minister of Justice Guy Favreau had indeed found instances where the federal government had requested constitutional amendments affecting provincial powers without the provinces' consent (Girard 2005, 512–13). Thus, there was definitely evidence that any convention in this regard could not be one of unanimity. Whether it had crystallized into a pattern of the federal government's seeking a set number less than unanimity was really the nub of the issue.

But here the historical evidence was ultimately ambiguous: the minority saw no crystallized pattern at all, the majority one of substantial consent. While one cannot exclude the possibility that the Majority II judges were unduly influenced by the political context in finding the pattern they did, this is not an inference that has to be drawn. Judges interpret ambiguous evidence in different ways all the time without being charged with illicit motivations. That is part of judging. There is no reason to give credence to Trudeau's charge of "blatant manipulation" of the evidence.

In the court of public opinion, the Supreme Court's decision was sometimes criticized for being unclear or confusing, but the judges were never reproached for answering the convention question.[5] If anything, they were sometimes reproached for not providing enough guidance. Their role in advising the political actors about both the positive law and the conventions of political behaviour was seldom questioned and, as indicated above, the message of Majority II was immediately and enthusiastically taken up by editorial writers across the country in both the English and French media. Clearly, the court enjoyed a great deal of legitimacy, even, perhaps especially, in the opinion of René Lévesque, who had previously castigated it for "always leaning, like the Tower of Pisa, in one direction." And while some thought that the court should have defined "substantial provincial consent" more precisely, most thought it was wise to hand this issue back to the politicians. In this, the court foreshadowed the [undefined] "clear majority on a clear question" doctrine that it enunciated seventeen years later in the *Quebec Secession Reference.*

Conclusion

Did law – the *Patriation Reference* – affect politics in 1981? Unquestionably, though not in as straightforward a way as has often been asserted. There were other alternatives that Trudeau might have pursued, which he later regretted not pursuing. Majority II's observation that the "pivot" of the relevant constitutional conventions was "the democratic principle" opened up the possibility that a referendum or an election might clothe the constitutional reform with the necessary legitimacy. As it was, the option of the First Ministers' conference provided the means for the premiers of English

Canada to seize the initiative, as Laforest and Readman argue in Chapter 8, leading to a short-term victory with long-term political consequences.

Did politics affect law? This is a much more controversial question, to which the answer is expected to be "no" in a constitutional order where the separation of powers is supposed to be a fundamental characteristic. But the reference procedure provides for a limited exception to the separation of powers, one where the courts may be asked to advise governments on both justiciable and non-justiciable issues rather than adjudicate on rights. This chapter has argued that in such cases, the courts not only can but also should assess the political context in which the reference arises, and in answering the questions posed should take into account manifestations of law beyond the traditional sources. This inevitably gives rise to a danger that courts will be seen as acting outside their proper sphere of competence or for inadmissible motives, but that is part and parcel of the reference jurisdiction.

As to whether the Supreme Court allowed itself to be influenced by the political context of the *Patriation Reference*, there is no doubt that the context influenced the judges' decision to discuss the convention issue at all. The more difficult question is whether – and if so, how – Majority II might have been influenced by the political context in declaring that the relevant convention was one of substantial consent rather than unanimity. While it is not possible to settle this question definitively, I would conclude that the evidence on the convention issue was sufficiently ambiguous that Trudeau's charges of "blatant manipulation" on the part of Majority II cannot be supported. When interviews with Justice Lamer – the only judge to sit on both the *Patriation Reference* and the *Quebec Secession Reference* – become available, perhaps we will have more evidence on this issue.

What one can say with more certitude about the *Patriation Reference* is that, in retrospect, it marked a turning point with regard to the role of the Supreme Court in Canadian constitutionalism, one that, as Edward McWhinney said at the time, was "suited to the particular political temper of our times in Canada, and transcend[ed] the more obvious imperfections of literary style and legal rationalization [contained] in it" (McWhinney 1981, A6).

Acknowledgments

I would like to thank the Social Sciences and Humanities Research Council of Canada for research funding pursuant to standard research grant 410-2008-1398, and Anders Knudsen, Nikki Petersen, and Megan Simpson for research assistance in the preparation of this chapter. I also thank Peter Carver for delivering an earlier version on my behalf at the Patriation Negotiations Conference organized by the Centre for Constitutional Studies in November 2011.

Notes

1 After writing these words, I found that Jean-François Gaudreault-DesBiens had invoked the same phrase in describing the legacy of the *Patriation* and *Quebec Veto* references (Gaudreault-DesBiens 2011, 113).

2 The Victoria formula of 1971 required, for most constitutional amendments, the consent of any province with more than 25 percent of the population of Canada, two provinces in Atlantic Canada, and two of the western provinces having more than 50 percent of the population of those provinces.

3 "We cannot even think of mounting a cross-Canada referendum given the absence of a federal referendum law" (author's translation).

4 Bastien's book was published as an English translation in 2014. See references.

5 This statement is based on a scan of all issues of seven newspapers between 28 September and 10 November 1981, for any content relating to the *Patriation Reference*, whether in the form of reporting, editorials, or letters to the editor: *Vancouver Sun*, *Winnipeg Free Press*, *Globe and Mail*, *Toronto Star*, *Montreal Gazette*, *La Presse*, and *Le Devoir*.

References

Bastien, Frédéric. 2014. *The Battle of London: Trudeau, Thatcher, and the Fight for Canada's Constitution*. Translated by Jacob Hemel. Toronto: Dundurn.

Bastien, Frédéric. 2013. *La Bataille de Londres: Dessous, secrets et coulisses du rapatriement constitutionnel*. Montreal: Boréal.

Bauch, Hubert. 1981. "Quebec Caucus Backs PM." *Montreal Gazette*, 2 October, 1–2.

Bellavance, Joël-Denis. 2013. "Repatriation de la Constitution: Trudeau n'aurait pas reçu d'infos privilégiées." *La Presse*, 7 December, A24.

Boyer, Patrick. 1992. *Direct Democracy in Canada: The History and Future of Referendums*. Toronto: Dundurn.

Burelle, André. 2005. *Pierre Elliott Trudeau: L'intellectuel et le politique*. Montreal: Fides.

Canadian Press, The. 1981. "The Resolution Before the National Assembly." *Montreal Gazette*, 1 October, 10.

Chambers, Gretta. 1981. "Premier on the Spot too." *Montreal Gazette*, 10 October, 19.

Dawson, John. 1968. *The Oracles of the Law*. Westport, CT: Greenwood Press.

Dodek, Adam. 2011. "Courting Constitutional Danger: Constitutional Conventions and the Legacy of the *Patriation Reference*." *Supreme Court Law Review* 54: 117–42.

English, John. 2009. *Just Watch Me: The Life of Pierre Elliott Trudeau 1968–2000*. Toronto: Alfred A. Knopf Canada.

Estey, Willard Z. 1993. *Interview*. Osgoode Society for Canadian Legal History, http://www.osgoodesociety.ca/Home.html.

Fox, Bill. 1981. "Give Provinces Last Chance to Negotiate, PM Urged." *Toronto Star*, 3 October, A1.

Gaudreault-DesBiens, Jean-François. 2011. "The 'Principle of Federalism' and the Legacy of the *Patriation* and *Quebec Veto* References." *Supreme Court Law Review* 54: 77–116.

Gélinas, Fabien. 1997. "Les conventions, le droit et la Constitution du Canada dans le renvoi sur la « sécession » du Québec: le fantôme du rapatriement." *Revue du Barreau du Québec* 57: 291–342.

Girard, Philip. 2005. *Bora Laskin: Bringing Law to Life*. Toronto: University of Toronto Press, for the Osgoode Society for Canadian Legal History.

—. 2014. "A Tempest in a Transatlantic Teapot: A Legal Historian's Critical Analysis of Frédéric Bastien's *La Bataille de Londres*." *Osgoode Hall Law Journal* 51: 673–99.

Graham, Ron. 2011. *The Last Act: Pierre Trudeau, the Gang of Eight, and the Fight for Canada*. Toronto: Allen Lane.

Heard, Andrew. 1991. *Canadian Constitutional Conventions: The Marriage of Law and Politics*. Toronto: Oxford University Press.

Hogg, Peter W. 1982. "Comments on Legislation and Judicial Decisions: Constitutional Law – Amendment of the British North America Act – Role of the Provinces." *Canadian Bar Review* 60: 307–34.

—. 2006. "Canada: From Privy Council to Supreme Court." In *Interpreting Constitutions: A Comparative Study*, edited by Jeffrey Goldsworthy, 55–105. Oxford: Oxford University Press.

Lederman, William. 1978. "Constitutional Amendment and Canadian Unity." In *The Constitution and the Future of Canada. Special Lectures of the Law Society of Upper Canada 1978*, 17–36. Toronto: DeBoo.

—. 1983. "The Supreme Court of Canada and Basic Constitutional Amendment." In *And No One Cheered: Federalism, Democracy and the Constitution Act*, edited by Keith Banting and Richard Simeon, 176–88. Toronto: Methuen.

Malarek, Victor. 1981. "Clark Favors Quebec Call for a Vote." *Globe and Mail*, 3 November, 2.

Marshall, Geoffrey. 1984. *Constitutional Conventions: The Rules and Forms of Political Accountability*. Oxford: Clarendon Press.

Mathen, Carissima. 2011. "'The Question Calls for an Answer, and I Propose to Answer It': The *Patriation Reference* as Constitutional Method." *Supreme Court Law Review* 54: 143–68.

McArthur, Jack. 1981. "How Legal Rights Can Melt Away." *Toronto Star*, 30 September, C12.

McConnell, Howard. 2000. *William McIntyre: Paladin of the Common Law.* Montreal/Kingston: McGill-Queen's University Press.

McMurtry, Roy. 2013. *Memoirs and Reflections.* Toronto: University of Toronto Press, for the Osgoode Society for Canadian Legal History.

McWhinney, Edward. 1981. "'A Homily on Constitutional Good Manners." *Vancouver Sun*, 29 September, A6.

McWhinney, Edward, et al. 1981. "The How, When and Why of Constitution-Making: The Machinery for Developing a New Constitution." In *Mécanismes pour une nouvelle constitution,* edited by Edmond Orbon et al., 65–88. Ottawa: Éditions de l'Université d'Ottawa.

O'Neill, Pierre. 1981. "Une motion sur les pouvoirs du Québec." *Le Devoir*, September 30, 1.

Picard, Jean-Claude. 1981a. "L'Assemblée débattra une motion de résistance au Projet Trudeau" *Le Devoir*, 30 September, 1.

—. 1981b. "Le Parti québécois envisage de s'engager dans l'arène fédérale." *Le Devoir*, 5 October, 1.

Re B.C. Motor Vehicle Act, [1985] 2 S.C.R. 486 [*BC Motor Vehicle Act Reference*].

Re Manitoba Language Rights, [1985] 1 S.C.R. 721 [*Manitoba Language Rights Reference*].

Re: Objection by Quebec to a Resolution to Amend the Constitution, [1982] 2 S.C.R. 793 [*Quebec Veto Reference*].

Re: Resolution to Amend the Constitution, [1981] 1 S.C.R. 753 [*Patriation Reference*].

Reference re Same-Sex Marriage, [2004] 3 S.C.R. 698 [*Same-Sex Marriage Reference*].

Reference re Secession of Quebec, [1998] 2 S.C.R. 217 [*Quebec Secession Reference*].

Rémillard, Gil. 1983. "Legality, Legitimacy and the Supreme Court." In *And No One Cheered: Federalism, Democracy and the Constitution Act,* edited by Keith Banting and Richard Simeon, 189–209. Toronto: Methuen.

Russell, Peter. 2011a. "Showdown in Ottawa." Review of *The Last Act: Pierre Trudeau, the Gang of Eight and the Fight for Canada,* by Ron Graham. *Literary Review of Canada,* September 2011, 22–23.

—. 2011b. "The *Patriation* and *Quebec Veto References:* The Supreme Court Wrestles with the Political Part of the Constitution." *Supreme Court Law Review* 54: 69–76.

Sharpe, Robert, and Kent Roach. 2003. *Brian Dickson: A Judge's Journey.* Toronto: University of Toronto Press, for the Osgoode Society for Canadian Legal History.

Sheppard, Robert, and Michael Valpy. 1982. *The National Deal: The Fight for a Canadian Constitution.* Toronto: Macmillan.
Strayer, Barry. 1988. *The Canadian Constitution and the Courts.* 3rd ed. Toronto: Butterworths.
—. 2013. *Canada's Constitutional Revolution.* Edmonton: University of Alberta Press.
Toronto Star. 1981a. "A Legal Go-Ahead." *Toronto Star*, 29 September, A8.
—. 1981b. "Let's Have a Referendum on the Constitution." *Toronto Star*, 3 October, A1.
Trudeau, Pierre Elliott. 1993. *Memoirs.* Toronto: McClelland and Stewart.
—. 1996. *Against the Current: Selected Writings 1939–1996.* Toronto: McClelland and Stewart.
United Press International. 1981. "Get Provincial Support, 'Times' Tells Trudeau." *Montreal Gazette*, 1 October, 10.
Valpy, Michael. 1981. "A Human Dilemma." *Globe and Mail*, 21 October, 6.
Walkom, Thomas. 1981. "Strings Attached to NDP's Backing." *Globe and Mail*, 1 October, 1.
Wills, Terrance. 1981. "It's Just Not the Canadian Way, Pierre." *Montreal Gazette*, 3 October, 23.

The Judiciary in Trudeau's Constitutional Vision: Intellectual Trajectory and the Origins of the Charter

7

David Schneiderman

With their open-ended commitments to freedom, liberty, and equality, bills of rights are instruments of imprecise meaning. They inevitably require interpretation by independent third parties, typically national high courts such as the Supreme Court of Canada. In the Anglo-American tradition, judges use text, history, and precedent to aid in their interpretive tasks. Yet these devices are not usually determinative in vexing constitutional cases (Posner 2008, 82). Instead, constitutional questions are resolved with reference to non-legal considerations as often as to legal ones. For this reason, Peter Russell (1983, 51–52) could insist early on in the life of the *Canadian Charter of Rights and Freedoms* that its principal impact would be to "judicialize politics and [to] politicize the judiciary."

Surely, this prospect was foreseeable to those involved in the patriation process of 1980–82, particularly the self-described "lawyer ... a teacher of constitutional law, and former minister of justice" Pierre Elliott Trudeau (1993, 316). In his 1967 talk to the Canadian Bar Association (CBA) titled "A Constitutional Declaration of Rights," then Minister of Justice Trudeau declared that one must speak with precision for "in this area, more than any other, one must know where a policy leads" (Trudeau 1968a, 53).[1]

This speech signalled that constitutional reform would therefore be approached carefully: "We have not supported vague and contradictory formulas designed to change everything all at once without really knowing what would follow" (Trudeau 1968a, 59). With few exceptions, however, the judicial function under a bill of rights did not concern the constitutional negotiators of the early 1980s. Russell (1983, 52) observed that the "political leaders who led the campaign for the Charter gave little attention to this consequence." Premiers Allan Blakeney of Saskatchewan and Sterling Lyon of Manitoba unquestionably placed the "judicialization of politics" squarely on the table (Blakeney 2010), yet these concerns played little role in the public debates leading up to patriation. Howard Leeson, then Saskatchewan's deputy minister for intergovernmental affairs, observed that what "was missing was the broader political discussion in Canada of the desirability of having a court administered society, a court judge-made law" (Cohen, Smith, and Warwick 1987, 88).

This chapter inquires into the place of judicial review under a bill of rights in the thinking of Pierre Trudeau, the Charter's principal architect. Trudeau studied and taught constitutional law and worked on the constitutional dossier throughout much of his intellectual, political, and bureaucratic career. What place did the judiciary have in his constitutional thinking and, in particular, in the events leading to the November 1981 accord? I argue that the judiciary inhabited a marginal place in his constitutional thinking, attracting some sustained reflection only after 1981. During debates over the Meech Lake and Charlottetown Accords, Trudeau offered detailed consideration of the judicial role under written constitutions, yet his sudden interest seemed opportunistic, serving the strategic end of undermining public support for these constitutional initiatives. Trudeau later offered a scathing critique of the Supreme Court's decision in the *Patriation Reference* of 1981, where a majority of the justices held that constitutional convention required the prime minister to obtain a "substantial degree of provincial consent" before proceeding with patriation (*Patriation Reference*, 905). This acknowledgment of the judicial function, however, was not in regard to rights but concerned a bet – unilateral patriation of the constitution – on which Trudeau and his government had staked their political future. My claim is that while Trudeau was interested in the judicial function in a constitutional democracy, he did not take an intellectual interest in judicial review under a bill of rights in the context of the constitutional reform efforts leading up to patriation. I aim to fill a gap in the literature by undertaking a sort of mini-intellectual biography focusing on Trudeau's thinking – or not thinking – about judicial review under an entrenched rights document.

Few scholars have considered the judicial role in Trudeau's constitutional thinking. Typically, scholars point to the main elements of his project – official minority language rights and modest mobility rights, both of which are excluded from section 33's override – to which everything else is superfluous. Tom Flanagan (2002, 134), for this reason, maintains that judicial review under the Charter was an "idiosyncratic outcome of Trudeau's desire" to entrench bilingualism. Gordon Robertson, Don Lenihan, and Roger Tassé (1994, 35) assume that there was some implied but never fully elaborated constitutional theory at work. Only Lorraine Weinrib (1998, 263) has sought to understand the judicial role, in an essay devoted to Trudeau's constitutional project of a bill of rights. Drawing from Trudeau's three-page review of Edward McWhinney's *Comparative Federalism* (1962), published in a 1963 issue of *Revue du notariat,* Weinrib isolates an argument about the institutional benefits of a bill of rights. The "existing constitutional system," she writes, "burdened the Supreme Court with political responsibilities because it was judging legislation without being restricted by the norms of public law that a constitutional bill of rights would provide" (Weinrib 1998, 263). For this reason, she maintains, an entrenched bill of rights for Trudeau "would have benign institutional effects" (263). Although a fair summary of Trudeau's book review, Weinrib's account tells us little about the influences Trudeau embraced and resisted in coming to this view about the judiciary's "benign effects" in the realm of rights.

The paucity of references to the role of judicial interpretation in Trudeau's writings and public statements provides one explanation of why the subject has not received more sustained analysis. I argue that he did not give much thought to this question, because he did not worry about it. The success of his project turned on securing a permanent shift in Canada's constitutional culture rather than any particular judicial approach to interpreting the Charter's terms.[2] Certainly, the judiciary would be active in the constitutional transformation that Trudeau envisioned, and, as I outline below, arguments expressing concern about this judicial role would have been familiar to him. I turn, subsequently, to several factors that may have contributed to Trudeau's lack of concern about the judicial role under a bill of rights. I then discuss occasions when the Supreme Court of Canada became a focus of concern, largely for polemical reasons, and, finally, I situate Trudeau's understanding of the judicial role in constitutional-theoretic terms, drawing on the idea of constitutional culture through a Madisonian lens. The argument, to repeat, is not that Trudeau gave no thought to the judicial role – it turns out that he gave some, but not very much, thought to this subject – only that it did not at all concern him in the run-up to patriation. I turn now to a discussion of why he would have been aware of reasons to worry about that expanded judicial role.

Reasons to Worry

Despite the scarcity of references, Trudeau revealed some of his thinking about the judicial role in his academic writing. He acknowledged, for instance, the paramount importance of the Judicial Committee of the Privy Council (JCPC) in preserving Canada's unity. Had they not "leaned" in a provincial-rights direction, he maintained, Quebec separatism would already have been "an accomplished fact" (Trudeau 1965b, 30). This was less an observation about how the JCPC decided federalism cases than a sociological observation that the JCPC's "decentralizing impulse" was "harmonious" with the evolving nature of Canadian federalism (Cairns 1988, 63).

Both of Trudeau's leading intellectual influences at Harvard (Carl Friedrich) and the London School of Economics (Harold J. Laski) would have alerted him to the centrality of the judicial function in managing a bill of rights. From Friedrich (1941, 224–25), he would have learned that the judicial branch is the "guardian" of the constitution, maintaining an equilibrium between old and new norms. "Only through the neutralizing and rationalizing influence of such judicial interpretation," Friedrich wrote, "will the various interests, groups, and classes in the community be sufficiently balanced" (234). Friedrich warned his readers about the conservative disposition of judges, noting that, for some time in the United States, judges were allied with "big business interests opposed to the reforms desired by farmers and workers" (229). A passage in his *Constitutional Government and Democracy* (1941)[3] is devoted to the *Lochner* era, named after the US Supreme Court decision in *Lochner v. New York* (1905), famously invalidating a New York state law limiting the working hours and days of bakery workers. In this era, the "conservatism of the law held out against these forces of a new industrial revolution," observed Friedrich (1941, 225–26), becoming so "dogmatic" that it "threatened seriously to upset the equilibrium" between old forces and new interests. Trudeau acknowledged these difficulties in his 1967 CBA speech. "At times," he observed, "the courts have construed [due process of law] so broadly as to invalidate some social legislation which we would now accept as essential" (Trudeau 1968a, 56). Judicial philosophies, it turned out, were critical to the success of any new or ongoing constitutional enterprise.[4]

Trudeau had reason to be anxious about courts standing in the way of progressive social change. To the extent that he was beginning to lean leftward politically, all of this should have been worrisome, just as it was for his mentor at the London School of Economics, Professor Harold J. Laski. Laski articulated precisely such reservations in *A Grammar of Politics* (1948). Although he acknowledged that individual rights were key to democratic life (for this reason, Laski preferred to confine constitutionally entrenched rights to freedom of speech and to local self-government), he was cautious about entrenching an omnibus bill of rights, as they act "as a serious lever against what may well be desirable change" (Laski 1948, 135).[5] As a result, Laski recommended against entrusting "the judge with the power to override the will of the legislature [which] is broadly to make him the decisive factor in the state" (304). As a written constitution "always reflect[s] the spirit of the time at which it is made," the judge will more perfectly respect that spirit, as Friedrich observed, than those of a novel ideology. Therefore, on questions concerning pressing economic legislation, judicial views "are no more likely to be right than those of the legislature." There "seems, therefore, no common sense in allowing his views to prevail," Laski concluded (304). Trudeau certainly read *A Grammar of Politics* – "an encyclopaedic work that for some unknown reason no longer gets any attention" (Trudeau 1993, 46) – and later acknowledged Laski's contributions to his thinking (English 2006, 171, 195, 224).

One can detect the influences of both Friedrich and Laski at work in Trudeau's writings. In his epilogue to *The Asbestos Strike* (1974), Trudeau describes Quebec society as being in a state of "unstable equilibrium ... torn between opposing lines of force" (343), in language reminiscent of Friedrich's description of stabilizing functions performed by the judicial branch. One wonders whether Trudeau, writing in 1956, was thinking about judicially enforceable collective bargaining rights as a way out of this impasse.[6] In his foreword to *Federalism and the French Canadians* (1968a), Trudeau again invokes the concept of equilibrium, giving practical effect to the theory of checks and balances that he associates with Montesquieu and de Tocqueville (xxiii). He appears to channel Laski in "Economic Rights," published in the *McGill Law Journal* (Trudeau 1962a).[7] "Economic reform is impossible so long as legislators, lawyers and businessmen cling to economic concepts which were conceived for another age" (125). The "erroneous concept of property" actively promoted by them "has erected a wall of prejudice against reform" (125).

Stephen Clarkson (2000) reports that "Trudeau's views in old age had returned to those more radical positions he had adopted in his younger years," those responding to economic inequality and the promotion of social justice. Despite these influences, however, Trudeau exhibited little interest, in this early period, in the judicial capacity to stifle legislative innovation. What appears to have stuck with him throughout his years of intellectual and political activity were unelaborated views about judicial review. I turn next to currents running in the opposing direction that help to explain this lack of interest.

Why He Did Not Worry

Centrality of Quebec

Trudeau's constitutional ambition was Quebec-driven and focused. If the project was one that emerged out of a "Citélibreist" narrative about French Canada's role in Canada (McWhinney 1984),[8] there appears not to have been much thinking in those circles devoted to the question of judicial politics. Nor would his education have nurtured an interest in questions associated with judicial review, as he loathed his legal studies, describing "infrequent courses in constitutional law" as "completely worthless" (Trudeau 1974, 37).

Overall, the judicial experience in Quebec under Premier Maurice Duplessis would have identified courts as unreliable stewards of change, until reversed, that is, by the Supreme Court of Canada in a series of key constitutional cases (e.g., *Roncarelli v. Duplessis* in 1959), a number of them involving Frank Scott of McGill Law School (Trudeau 1968, 171; 2010, 81). On this basis, judicial review by a national apex court represented a positive contribution to political life.

F.R. Scott

John English (2006, 329) observes that, although Trudeau "admired Scott, his papers suggest that Scott's influence was perhaps more personal than intellectual." I disagree: Scott's influence was, indeed, "intellectual" and it reached potentially into questions about the propriety of a judicial role under a bill of rights. Scott had been advocating for an entrenched bill of rights since 1935 (Adams 2006, 439). He knew of the American experience in the *Lochner* era, yet disregarded that experience in the socialist project he first outlined, with his co-authors, in *Social Planning for Canada* (League for Social Reconstruction 1935). Adams explains Scott's willingness to define away any tension between advocating for increased state action and the disabling effects of judicial review under a bill of rights (Scott 1949, 1959) as the product of Scott's belief in "legalism": in the judiciary's ability to rise above the fray and to respect "both democratic socialist initiatives and civil liberties" (Adams 2006, 440). Scott certainly differed from Trudeau on the merits of provincial autonomy, at least until Trudeau entered electoral politics (Scott 1947, 22; Trudeau 1965a, 33; Macdonald 1997).[9] Nevertheless, Scott was a substantial intellectual influence. Sandra Djwa (1987, 319) claims that Trudeau invoked Scott in the report he prepared during his short stint at the Privy Council Office for a September 1950 First Ministers' meeting in Quebec City. Trudeau later acknowledged that Scott was a "great hero of mine ... [It was from contacts with him] that I absorbed much of my constitutional thinking" (Djwa 1987, 326; Trudeau 1987, 47–48). Scott and Trudeau would find common cause in a project for a bill of rights.

Admiration of the United States

Like Scott, Trudeau was confident that Canada would not replicate American controversies over rights interpretation. At the February 1968 constitutional conference in Ottawa, Trudeau admitted that "some of the initial opposition in this country to a Bill of Rights was based upon the evidence of American experience ... We are aware of some of its shortcomings; I simply say that the American precedent with respect to those shortcomings is not valid in Canada" (Trudeau 1972, 90).

Like Prime Minister Stephen Harper after him (Harper 2001), Trudeau admired the US constitutional system. In those same proceedings in Ottawa, he declared that "it would be most unfortunate if our criticism of some aspects of American society caused us to forget that there has been created in the United States one of the great legal systems of the world. In our natural desire to borrow some of what is good from that system, we should not be inhibited by those who warn us of what is bad" (Trudeau 1972, 90). In a 1968 *New York Times* interview, Trudeau (1972, 172) declared his "very great respect for the legal thought" in the United States, referring to the "institutions which grew around your political institutions, the Supreme Court, the federal system of government, and so on." André Burelle (2005, 79, 257) noted that Trudeau's advisers were enamoured of the United States, resulting in a 1980 draft preamble declaring "We the People of Canada." Trudeau was sufficiently proud of this preamble ("it was pretty hard to beat") that he referred to it in his submission to the Senate Committee on the Meech Lake Accord (Trudeau 1988, 77–78). Evidently, he was not overly concerned with the influence of the elephant to the south.

France

In promoting a bill of rights, Trudeau imported both American and French constitutional ideas into Canada. In his 1990 "Values of a Just Society" essay, he expressly referred to "the grand tradition of the 1789 *Declaration of the Rights of Man and the Citizen* and the 1791 *Bill of Rights of the United States of America,*" which "implicitly established the primacy of the individual over the state and all government institutions and, in so doing, recognized that all sovereignty resides in the people" (Trudeau 1990, 363). It is not clear why Trudeau would describe these rights as "implicit" – in both instances they are quite explicit. There was, however, no judicial review to speak of in France until 1971. It was only then that the *Conseil constitutionnel* announced an ability to declare unconstitutional legislation that had been proposed by President Charles de Gaulle (Decision no. 71–44 DC of 16 July 1971). In 1971, the *Conseil* also incorporated into the preamble of the 1946 French Constitution the whole of the 1789 declaration, enhancing greatly the scope of judicially enforceable rights in the Fifth Republic (Stone 1992, 66).

In Chapter 8, Guy Laforest and Rosalie Readman note the extent to which "personalist" philosophical influences – in particular, the Catholic thinkers Emmanuel Mounier and Jacques Maritain – had a significant influence on Trudeau's thinking (Trudeau 1972, 88; 1993, 40). It is not evident, however, that their work would have triggered greater reflection on the judicial role under a bill of rights.[10] Personalism, represented by a divergent set of interwar thinkers, contrasts the "human person" with the atomized "individual" (Berdyaev 1943, 35). The latter signifies isolation and fleshy materialism; the former emphasizes the spiritual dimension and that every human person is deserving of dignity "by virtue of the existence of its soul" (Maritain 1942 (2011), 3–4; Mounier 1938, 68–69). Personalism represented a sort of "communitarian third way" between capitalism and totalitarianism, appealing to a Christian Europe seeking moral, not just economic, reconstruction after the Second World War (Moyn 2011, 90). The system of thought associated with personalism not only differed among its leading thinkers but also evolved over time. Max and Monique Nemni maintain that the "communitarian personalism" associated with Mounier – anti-capitalist and anti-American (Mounier 1938, 171–72) – was rejected by Trudeau[11] in favour of Maritain's version, emphasizing the individual over the community and pluralist democracy over more collectivist forms of political organization (Nemni and Nemni 2011, 231). Although Maritain is credited with facilitating the rise of an international human rights discourse and helping to draft, as head of the French delegation, the *Universal Declaration on Human Rights* (Moyn 2011, 64), he had nothing to say about enforcement mechanisms.[12] He spent many years in exile in the United States and so must have been familiar with judicial review, but he did not theorize how human rights would be realized beyond its force as a "moral" code (Maritain 1951, 112). I return to the theme of a "bill of rights as moral code" below.

International Human Rights Movement

Relevant international declarations, conventions, and treaties are continually referenced in the documentation associated with a proposed bill of rights for Canada (e.g., Trudeau 1968b, 52). To the extent that these developments influenced Trudeau's constitutional thinking, he would have derived little understanding about the judicial role in rights enforcement from the international human rights movement. As David Kennedy (2004, 13) observes, the movement "propagates unduly abstract ideas" that can be used for all variety of purposes and by all variety of political actors. The rise of an international human rights discourse and its assimilation into international instruments provides little context for the meaning of those rights and the manner in which the judicial branch is to enforce them.

All of these influences would have pointed Trudeau away from a preoccupation with judges and judicial review. Each elides or is silent about the judicial role in the construction of constitutional human rights projects.

Legal Polemics and the Supreme Court

Rather than a sophisticated articulation of the judicial function in fulfilling his vision for an entrenched bill of rights, what we find, particularly in Trudeau's later days, are simplistic and opportunistic explanations of judicial interpretation. The record from 1980 to 1982 suggests that Trudeau, in the single-minded pursuit of his objective, would use virtually any tactic, including clumsy legal arguments, to undermine the recalcitrant "Gang of Eight" premiers. In the acrimonious 1980 First Ministers' conference, he disingenuously compared provincial human rights codes to an entrenched bill of rights. He proudly recounted his exchange with Sterling Lyon in his *Memoirs:* to Lyon's claim that Trudeau's constitutional project would tear the country apart, Trudeau replied: "Because we have asked for a Canadian charter of rights, when most of you already have provincial charters? Then the country deserves to be torn up!" (Trudeau 1993, 306). Yet only Saskatchewan, Alberta, and Quebec had statutory codes that included the hallmarks of bills of rights, such as rights to free speech, religion, and association (Lang 1978, 500). Moreover, none of these "provincial charters" was entrenched. They were, Trudeau (1968a, 5) acknowledged in 1968, merely "statutory in character" and so could be amended or repealed at any time.

A fine example of opportunistic legal argument can be found in the "Kirby Memo," intended to guide federal strategy in advance of the 1980 First Ministers' meetings. Although Trudeau did not author the memo, his actions at the time were consistent with its content.[13] Michael Kirby (1980, 116), principal secretary in the Prime Minister's Office, wrote in his memo that the People's Package of constitutional reform (representing the proposals Trudeau would promote after the failure of the 1980 negotiations) "[is] clearly very popular with the Canadian public." "The premiers who are opposed should be put on the defensive very quickly," he advised, "and should be made to appear that they prefer to trust politicians rather than impartial and non-partisan courts in the protection of basic rights ... It is evident that the Canadian people prefer their rights protected by judges rather than politicians" (Kirby 1980, 116). The label "People's Package" entirely elides the matter of judicial review under the bill of rights. This contributes to the fantasy that judges stand in the shoes of "the people" when they enforce the constitution's terms (Bickel 1986, 33). Few constitutional provisions are so clear and self-executing that they can represent the people's will without escaping judicial discretion.

These examples, it must be admitted, look more polemical than legal. They do not negate the possibility that Trudeau had a fully worked-out understanding of the judicial role under a bill of rights. His powerful interventions in the Meech Lake and Charlottetown Accord debates more closely resemble legal argumentation, although they also verge on the polemical. For instance, Trudeau homed in on the implications of judicial review of the "distinct society" clause in the Charlottetown Accord. He observed that "courts will be called upon to define these words" and would then have to "determine what new powers the constitution intends to give Quebec in order to better enable it to 'promote its distinct society'" (Trudeau 1988, 82; 1996, 268). Yet Trudeau did not acknowledge that the Charlottetown Accord (in both Charlottetown's "consensus report" and "draft legal text") declares that "nothing in this section [in which the clause appears] derogates from the powers, rights or privileges of the Parliament or the Government of Canada" (section 2[3]). Admittedly, the clause could play a role when courts classify new laws as valid exercises of federal or provincial authority, but this has always been an unstable interpretive exercise, driven as much by non-legal considerations as by legal resources such as text and precedent (Schneiderman 2012). The degree of uncertainty contributed by a distinct society clause in cases of division-of-powers cases seemed negligible, if non-existent. Charlottetown may indeed have been "a mess that deserved a big no" (Trudeau 1992), but my point here is that Trudeau's legal analysis, though skillful, was not entirely forthright.

It is not the case, then, that Trudeau did not care about the judicial function in a constitutional democracy. Rather, the claim is a narrower one: that he did not take an intellectual interest in judicial review during the constitutional reform efforts leading up to patriation. His concern about the Supreme Court as an institution is evinced by memoranda he prepared while employed at the Privy Council Office (1949–50) (Nemni and Nemni 2011, 197),[14] and by a string of sparkling judicial appointments in which he had a personal hand, including Bora Laskin (Girard 2005, 367), Bertha Wilson (Anderson 2001, 125), and Jean Beetz (an old acquaintance).[15] Trudeau read Justice Wilson's rulings on the Ontario Court of Appeal, which "[seem] to be very good in commercial law," he observed (Anderson 2001, 125). But "what about human rights and civil liberties, what would she be like there?" he inquired of his friend Alan Linden in advance of her appointment (Anderson 2001, 125). The subsequent elevation of Laskin to the position of Chief Justice, Trudeau's hope that federal power might be vindicated in the *Anti-Inflation Act Reference* (1976), and his subsequent disappointment in the *Patriation Reference* (1980) all point to Trudeau's appreciation of the judicial function in Canada's constitutional democracy. In his only detailed treatment of a judicial decision, Trudeau's convocation speech at the opening of the Bora Laskin Law Library at the University of Toronto in 1990, he delivered a brusque attack on the Supreme Court's decision in the *Patriation Reference* ten years earlier. This was an instance of bare "judicial lawmaking" (Trudeau 1991, 303) – "inventing" a constitutional convention requiring substantial provincial consensus, "blatantly manipulat[ing] the evidence before them so as to arrive at the desired result" (302). Yet there is precious little evidence that "judicial lawmaking" had concerned him previously. There is little evidence, in other words, that Trudeau thought about the judicial role in a sophisticated and sustained way during much of his academic or political career.

What Was the Worry?

How might we characterize Trudeau's thinking about judicial review in constitutional-theoretic terms? Many have focused on entrenchment of the Charter as a "nation-building" exercise in which the Charter appears intended to counteract the centrifugal forces of Quebec nationalism (Russell 1983; Knopff and Morton 1985; Laforest 1995). Human rights, it is believed, are uncontroversial values that citizens of every democratic society would want to make their common cause. Others have, relatedly, characterized the project in Habermasian terms, as being about generating a "constitutional patriotism" (Fossum 2007; Ipperciel 2008). We have seen that Trudeau's attraction to a bill of rights project significantly predated any secessionist threat and is traceable to his early embrace of "personalist" Catholic thought, but he also saw the uses of constitutionalism in a nation-building context, as evident in his early broadsides against separatism in *Cité libre* and, of course, thereafter (Trudeau 1968, 166). Whatever the case, nation-building hypotheses speak hardly, if at all, to the judicial function under a bill of rights.

I propose that we think about Trudeau's project in terms that would have been familiar to James Madison, one of the principal architects of the 1787 US Constitution; that is, that we displace the courts as the central referent in constitutional ordering. For Madison, the judiciary had no special power to determine the constitutional "outer limits" of any of the other coordinate branches (Madison 1789, 464). This was a common eighteenth-century understanding associated with what is called "popular constitutionalism," where the people, and not the judiciary, are the supreme authority (Kramer 2004, 105–7). Admittedly, this is an understanding at odds with the one assumed by Trudeau and his cohort in 1980–82 (Romanow 1982, 114–15). Trudeau, after all, understood Canada's federal arrangements as continuously evolving under judicial supervision. To be lasting, the constitution "must be a living thing," he maintained (Trudeau 1965b, 26), invoking language reminiscent of Lord Sankey's "living tree" in the "Persons Case" (*Edwards v. R.* 1930).

A Madisonian account, however, resonates well with Trudeau's understanding of rights where courts are of less central significance. Madison, like Trudeau, emphasized the cultural functions served by a bill of rights. If the judicial branch could not bind other departments on questions of constitutional consistency, a bill of rights could at least serve an educative role (Rakove 1996, 336). In Virginia, Madison observed, the bill of rights had been "violated in every instance where it has been opposed by popular current" (Madison 1788, 420). When, he asked in a letter to Thomas Jefferson, "can a bill of rights serve in popular Governments?" First, when these "political truths ... become incorporated within the national sentiment" and so can "counteract the impulses of interest and passion." Second, when dangers of oppression "spring" from "acts of Government" rather than "interested majorities of the people," in which case a bill of rights provides "good ground for an appeal to the sense of community" (Madison 1788, 421–22; Rakove 1996, 335).[16] Bills of rights served valuable functions, then, when assimilated into popular understandings or as grounds for checking factionalism. In either event, rights are principally rhetorical resources.

This cultural function of a bill of rights complements the "personalist" position promoted by Jacques Maritain. In *Man and the State,* Maritain (1951, 110) identified what a common "secular faith" in a "genuine democracy" would look like. It would "bear within itself a common human creed; the creed of freedom" (109), which gives expression to "practical points of convergence" around which a pluralist society would rally (111). The body politic would keep alive this democratic sense by promoting a "code of social and political morality" that would include "rights and liberties of the person" and political and social rights, in addition to a long list of other rights and duties, resulting in "a society that is truly free and ruled by laws whose change and evolution depend on the popular majority" (112). Again, there is no discussion of mechanisms of enforcement by apex courts, only reference to majoritarian rule. Instead, the emphasis is on the cultural force and binding nature of a moral charter that would increasingly deepen, to the extent that the body politic adheres to "Christian convictions" (113).

Trudeau did not think that the Charter was self-executing – the rhetoric of the People's Package suggested that it was not. The judiciary was expected to play an active role in the constitutional transformation Trudeau had in mind. Nor would it have been expected that judges would engage in sterile and technical interpretations of rights and freedoms. As suggested above, framers like Trudeau would have been schooled in Lord Sankey's "living tree" (*Edwards v. R.* 1930; Trudeau 1965b, 26) and so would have favoured "large and liberal" interpretations that gave courts reasonable room to adjust judicial interpretation in light of changing socio-political realities. He knew, then, that the judiciary would be obliged to resolve vexing rights questions that had no obvious legal answers and that would require the weighing of complex policy options in particular social, political, and economic contexts (Romanow 1982, 114). The risk of judicial politicking would have been considered tolerable given the promise of checking oppressive state action. Moreover, there was the prospect of changing hearts and minds so as to generate new "national sentiments," adjusting constitutional culture so as to "counteract the impulses of interest and passion" (Madison 1788, 421; cf. Trudeau 1965b, 27).

Conclusion

Trudeau understood that Canada was an evolving polity, a continuing experiment. As circumstances change, "the terms of the federative pact must be altered," he admitted, "and this is done as smoothly as possible by administrative practice, by judicial decision, and by constitutional amendment, giving a little more autonomy here, a bit more centralization there, but at all times taking great care to preserve the delicate balance upon which the national consensus rests" (Trudeau 1965b, 26). This balance was achieved in Canada by modest constitutional reform, the general direction of JCPC jurisprudence, and some administrative centralization (Trudeau 1965b, 30). Bruce Powe reports that Trudeau, in a conversation touching on the Charlottetown Accord, held on to this view: "The point is, don't stop change by putting us in a bind with these deals" (Powe 2007, 246).

Powe is attracted by the idea of openness, which he associates with his friend Trudeau's "Just Society." "Imagine an era," Powe (2007, 52) writes, "where everything is possible because everything is open." Powe elaborates a pluralist vision – a state without "one dominant and curbing view" (120) and so "lacking a single identity" (Powe 2006, 123) – that he associates with Trudeau's constitutional project. For Powe (2006, 122), this "rootlessness" can be "liberating." He concludes his *Towards a Canada of Light* (2006, 156) with this observation: "An overly formulated and detailed constitution is a recipe for fanaticism."

It is curious that both Powe and Trudeau exempt the 1982 patriation exercise from their considerations. To the extent that this was an "overly formulated" project, determining the shape and direction of constitutional politics ever since, we will not have succeeded in achieving this openness. They would have been better advised to reread Laski's *Grammar of Politics* (1948). In contrast to the draining effect of a bill of rights on political life, Laski reflects on the beneficial effects of the English constitutional system, which "makes for a flexibility that has enormous advantages in a period of great social change. It means that new ideas can make their way without being compelled to pass through the complicated sieve devised to protect ideas deemed fundamental by an earlier period" (Laski 1948, 303). For the Trudeau generation, this was not anything they needed to worry about.

Acknowledgments

I benefited greatly from exchanges on this subject with Stephen Clarkson, Barry Strayer, and John Whyte, and from comments by Lois Harder, Steve Patten, Brian Peckford, and Peter Russell. Many thanks to Patricia Paradis for initiating this endeavour.

Notes

1 The CBA speech was written by Carl Goldenberg but "revised extensively" by Trudeau (Clarkson and McCall 1990, 261).

2 On constitutional culture, see Schneiderman 2005, 2006.

3 I draw here on the 1941 edition of Friedrich's book, assuming that this was the edition Trudeau would have read. The first edition, published in 1937, did not include the *Lochner*-era discussion (Friedrich 1937).

4 Friedrich mentions in passing, for instance, the US Supreme Court's denuding of the Fourteenth Amendment as a source of federal authority in the Civil Rights cases (1883), a position it reversed only in the 1960s (Friedrich 1968, 212).

5 References are to the fifth edition of *A Grammar of Politics*, published the year after Trudeau arrived at the London School of Economics to study with Laski. It is likely that Trudeau would have had access to the fourth edition, issued in February 1938. For my purposes, there are no material differences between this edition and the fifth one.
6 Trudeau's draft Declaration of Principles adopted by the "Rassemblement provincial des citoyens" in September 1956 suggests that this was the case. The declaration recommends "freedom of association in labour unions without hindrance" (Nemni and Nemni 2011, 381).
7 See also Trudeau's "The Practice and Theory of Federalism" (1961).
8 On the origins of *Cité libre* and its contributors (the "Citélibreists"), see Nemni and Nemni (2011, c. 8).
9 "I believe in provincial autonomy," Trudeau wrote (1965a, 33).
10 The Nemnis date Trudeau's first encounter with Maritain's writing to 1942. Trudeau found him unimpressive although Maritain was, in reality, "defending before his [Trudeau's] very eyes the same propositions that he would be defending himself many years later" (Nemni and Nemni 2006, 242).
11 Burelle (2005, 23–24) accuses Trudeau of abandoning this communitarian personalism, the foundation for their friendship, for a "juridical liberalism, individualist and republican".
12 Among such instances, Maritain (1947, 88) elaborates on the "rights of the civic person," which would include "equality before the law, implying an independent judiciary power which assures to each one the right to call upon the law".
13 Michael Kirby, principal secretary in the Prime Minister's Office, was a self-acknowledged constitutional novice (McCall and Clarkson 1990, 281), one of the anglophone "nation-building militants" derided by fellow adviser Burelle (2005, 67).
14 Trudeau would later have occasion to promote the institutional innovation of the Supreme Court in his capacity as legal counsel to the Fédération des unions industrielles du Québec (1953, 41), as public intellectual (1961, 392), as minister of justice (Pearson 1968), and as prime minister of Canada (Trudeau 1968c; Victoria Charter 1971, Part IV).
15 See Nemni and Nemni 2011, 413.
16 Madison anticipated "no tendency in our governments to danger on that side" under the administration of the widely revered George Washington (Madison 1788, 422).

References

Adams, Eric M. 2006. "Canada's 'Newer Constitutional Law' and the Idea of Constitutional Rights." *McGill Law Journal/Revue de droit de McGill* 51: 435–74.

Anderson, Ellen. 2001. *Judging Bertha Wilson: Law as Large as Life.* Toronto: University of Toronto Press.

Berdyaev, Nicolas. 1943. *Slavery and Freedom.* London: Geoffrey Bles.

Bickel, Alexander M. 1986. *The Least Dangerous Branch: The Supreme Court at the Bar of Politics.* 2nd ed. New Haven, CT: Yale University Press.

Blakeney, Allan E. 2010. "The Notwithstanding Clause, the Charter and Canada's Patriated Constitution: What I Thought We Were Doing." *Constitutional Forum constitutionnel* 19 (1): 1–9.

Burelle, André. 2005. *Pierre Elliott Trudeau: L'intellectuel et le politique.* Montreal: Fides.

Cairns, Alan C. 1988. "The Judicial Committee and Its Critics." In *Constitution, Government, and Society in Canada: Selected Essays by Alan C. Cairns,* edited by Douglas E. Williams, 43–85. Toronto: McClelland and Stewart.

Clarkson, Stephen. 2000. "The Legacy of Pierre Elliott Trudeau: Charisma and Contradictions." Unpublished manuscript (25 September; revised 15 August 2005).

Cohen, Lenard, Patrick Smith, and Paul Warwick, eds. 1987. *The Vision and the Game: Making the Canadian Constitution.* Calgary: Detselig Enterprises.

Djwa, Sandra. 1987. *The Politics of the Imagination: A Life of F.R. Scott.* Toronto: McClelland and Stewart.

Edwards v. R., [1930] A.C. 124 (JCPC).

English, John. 2006. *Citizen of the World: The Life of Pierre Elliott Trudeau.* Vol. 1, *1919–1968.* Toronto: Alfred A. Knopf Canada.

Flanagan, Tom. 2002. "Canada's Three Constitutions: Protecting, Overturning, and Reversing the Status Quo." In *The Myth of the Sacred: The Charter, the Courts, and the Politics of the Constitution in Canada,* edited by Patrick James, Donald E. Abelson, and Michael Lusztig, 125–46. Montreal/Kingston: McGill-Queen's University Press.

Fossum, John Erik. 2007. "Constitutional Patriotism: Canada and the European Union." RECON Online Working Paper 2007/4. http://www.reconproject.eu/projectweb/portalproject/RECONWorkingPapers.html.

Friedrich, Carl Joachim. 1937. *Constitutional Government and Politics: Nature and Development.* New York: Harper and Brothers.

—. 1941. *Constitutional Government and Democracy: Theory and Practice in Europe and America.* Boston: Little, Brown.

—. 1968. *Constitutional Government and Democracy: Theory and Practice in Europe and America.* 4th ed. Waltham, MA: Blaidsell Publishing.

Girard, Philip. 2005. *Bora Laskin: Bringing Law to Life.* Toronto: University of Toronto Press.

Harper, Stephen. 2001. "One Crucial Flaw in Canadian Government Is the Ineptitude of Federal Cabinets." *Report Newsmagazine* 28 (May): 13.

Ipperciel, Donald. 2008. "Where Did Trudeau Go Wrong? On the Question of Nationalism and Charter Patriotism in Canada." *Constitutional Forum constitutionnel* 17 (2): 39–47.

Kennedy, David. 2004. *The Dark Sides of Virtue: Reassessing International Humanitarianism.* Cambridge, MA: Harvard University Press.

Kirby, Michael. 1980. "Excerpts from the Kirby Memorandum, August 30, 1980." In *The Vision and the Game: Making the Canadian Constitution*, edited by Lenard Cohen, Patrick Smith, and Paul Warwick, 113–27. Calgary: Detselig Enterprises, 1987.

Knopff, Rainer, and F.L. Morton. 1985. "Nation-Building and the Canadian Charter of Rights and Freedoms." In *Constitutionalism, Citizenship and Society in Canada*, edited by Alan Cairns and Cynthia Williams, 133–82. Toronto: University of Toronto Press.

Kramer, Larry D. 2004. *The People Themselves: Popular Constitutionalism and Judicial Review*. New York: Oxford University Press.

Laforest, Guy. 1995. *Trudeau and the End of a Canadian Dream*. Translated by Paul Leduc Browne and Michelle Weinroth. Montreal/Kingston: McGill-Queen's University Press.

Lang, Hon. Otto [Minister of Justice]. 1978. "Constitutional Reform: Canadian Charter of Rights and Freedoms" (August 1978). In *Canada's Constitution Act 1982 & Amendments: A Documentary History*, edited by Anne Bayefsky, 499–511. Toronto: McGraw-Hill Ryerson, 1989.

Laski, Harold J. 1948. *A Grammar of Politics*. 5th ed. London: George Allen and Unwin.

League for Social Reconstruction (LSR Research Committee). 1935. *Social Planning for Canada*. Toronto: Thomas Nelson and Sons.

Lochner v. New York, 198 US 45 (1905) (S. Ct.).

Macdonald, Roderick A. 1997. "F.R. Scott's Constitution." *McGill Law Journal/Revue de droit de McGill* 42 (1): 11–28.

Madison, James. 1788. "To Thomas Jefferson" (17 October). In *Writings, James Madison*, edited by Jack N. Rakove, 418–23. New York: Library of America, 1999.

—. 1789. "Speech in Congress" (17 June). In *Writings, James Madison*, edited by Jack N. Rakove, 457–65. New York: Library of America, 1999.

Maritain, Jacques. 1942 (2011). *Christianity and Democracy; and, The Rights of Man and Natural Law*. Translated by Doris C. Anson. San Francisco: Ignatius Press. Original published in New York: Éditions de la Maison Française.

—. 1947. *La personne et le bien commun. [The Person and the Common Good]*. Translated by John J. Fitzgerald. New York: Charles Scribner's Sons.

—. 1951. *Man and the State*. Chicago: University of Chicago Press.

McCall, Christina, and Stephen Clarkson. 1990. *The Magnificent Obsession*. Vol. 1, *Trudeau and Our Times*. Toronto: McClelland and Stewart.

McWhinney, Edward. 1962. *Comparative Federalism: States' Rights and National Power*. Toronto: University of Toronto Press.

—. 1984. "Constitutional Patriation as Prologue: Phase Two Constitution-Making and Reform of Federal Institutions." *Les Cahiers de droit* 25 (1): 165–71. doi:10.7202/042590ar.

Mounier, Emmanuel. 1938. *A Personalist Manifesto*. London: Longmans, Green.

Moyn, Samuel. 2011. "Personalism, Community, and the Origins of Human Rights." In *Human Rights in the Twentieth Century*, edited by Stefan-Ludwig Hoffman, 85–106. Cambridge, UK: Cambridge University Press.

Nemni, Max, and Monique Nemni. 2006. *Trudeau, Son of Quebec, Father of Canada.* Vol. 1, *Young Trudeau, 1919–1944.* Translated by William Johnson. Toronto: McClelland and Stewart.

—. 2011. *Trudeau, Son of Quebec, Father of Canada.* Vol. 2, *Trudeau Transformed: The Making of a Modern Statesman, 1944–1965.* Translated by George Tombs. Toronto: McClelland and Stewart.

Pearson, The Right Hon. L.B. 1968. "Federalism for the Future: A Statement of Policy by the Government of Canada." In *Canada's Constitution Act 1982 & Amendments: A Documentary History*, edited by Anne Bayefsky, 61–74. Toronto: McGraw-Hill Ryerson, 1989.

Posner, Richard A. 2008. *How Judges Think.* Cambridge, MA: Harvard University Press.

Powe, B.W. 2006. *Towards a Canada of Light.* Toronto: Thomas Allen Publishers.

—. 2007. *Mystic Trudeau: The Fire and the Rose.* Toronto: Thomas Allen Publishers.

Rakove, Jack N. 1996. *Original Meanings: Politics and Ideas in the Making of the Constitution.* New York: Vintage Books.

Re: Anti-Inflation Act, [1976] 2 S.C.R. 373 [*Anti-Inflation Act Reference*].

Re: Resolution to Amend the Constitution, [1981] 1 S.C.R. 753 [*Patriation Reference*].

Robertson, Gordon, Donald G. Lenihan, and Roger Tassé. 1994. *Canada: Reclaiming the Middle Ground.* Montreal: Institute for Research on Public Policy.

Romanow, Roy. 1982. "Making Canada's Constitution: Reflections of a Participant." In *The Canadian Charter of Rights: Law Practice Revolutionized*, edited by A. Wayne MacKay, 106–20. Halifax: Faculty of Law, Dalhousie University.

Roncarelli v. Duplessis, [1959] S.C.R. 121.

Russell, Peter H. 1983. "The Political Purposes of the Canadian Charter of Rights and Freedoms." *Canadian Bar Review* 61 (1): 30–54.

Schneiderman, David. 2005. "Banging Constitutional Bibles: Observing Constitutional Culture in Transition." *University of Toronto Law Journal* 55 (3): 833–52. doi:10.1353/tlj.2005.0026.

—. 2006. "Property Rights and Regulatory Innovation: Comparing Constitutional Cultures." *International Journal of Constitutional Law* 4 (2): 371–91. doi:10.1093/icon/mol009.

—. 2012. "Making Waves: The Supreme Court of Canada Confronts Stephen Harper's Brand of Federalism." In *What's Next for Canada? Securities Regulation after the Reference*, edited by Anita Anand, 75–94. Toronto: Irwin Law.

Scott, F.R. 1947. "The Special Nature of Canadian Federalism." *Canadian Journal of Economics and Political Science* 13 (1): 13–25. doi:10.2307/137599.

—. 1949. "Dominion Jurisdiction over Human Rights and Fundamental Freedoms." *Canadian Bar Review* 27 (5): 497–536.

—. 1959. *Civil Liberties and Canadian Federalism.* Toronto: University of Toronto Press.

Stone, Alec. 1992. *The Birth of Judicial Politics in France: The Constitutional Council in Comparative Perspective.* New York: Oxford University Press.

Trudeau, Pierre Elliott. 1953. "On Constitutional Problems ... in 1953." In *Against the Current: Selected Writings 1939–1996,* 36–41. Toronto: McClelland and Stewart, 1996.

—. 1961. "The Practice and Theory of Federalism." In *Social Purpose for Canada,* edited by Michael Oliver, 371–93. Toronto: University of Toronto Press.

—. 1962a. "Economic Rights." *McGill Law Journal/Revue de droit de McGill* 8 (2): 122–25.

—. 1962b. "The New Treason of the Intellectuals." In *Federalism and the French-Canadians,* 151–81. Toronto: Macmillan, 1968.

—. 1968. "The New Treason of the Intellectuals." In *Federalism and the French Canadians,* by Pierre Elliott Trudeau, 151–81. Toronto: Macmillan, 1968.

—. 1965a. "Quebec and the Constitutional Problem." In *Federalism and the French Canadians,* by Pierre Elliott Trudeau, 3–51. Toronto: Macmillan, 1968.

—. 1965b. "Federalism, Nationalism and Reason." In *The Future of Canadian Federalism: L'avenir du fédéralisme canadien,* edited by P.-A. Crepeau and C.B. Macpherson, 16–35. Toronto: University of Toronto Press.

—. 1968a. *Federalism and the French Canadians.* Toronto: Macmillan.

—. 1968b. "A Canadian Charter of Human Rights." In *Canada's Constitution Act 1982 & Amendments: A Documentary History,* edited by Anne Bayefsky, 51–61. Toronto: McGraw-Hill Ryerson, 1989.

—. 1968c. "The Constitution and the People of Canada: An Approach to the Objectives of Confederation, the Rights of People and the Institutions of Government." In *Canada's Constitution Act 1982 & Amendments: A Documentary History,* edited by Anne Bayefsky, 78–98. Toronto: McGraw-Hill Ryerson, 1989.

—. 1972. *Conversation with Canadians.* Toronto: University of Toronto Press.

—, ed. 1974. *The Asbestos Strike.* Translated by James Boake. Toronto: James, Lewis and Samuel. Original published in 1956.

—. 1987. "On the Occasion of Frank Scott's Seventieth Birthday." *Brick: A Literary Journal.* A special issue on F.R. Scott (Summer): 47–48.

—. 1988. "We, the People of Canada." In *With a Bang, Not a Whimper: Pierre Trudeau Speaks Out,* edited by Donald Johnston, 36–105. Toronto: Stoddart.

—. 1990. "The Values of a Just Society." In *Towards a Just Society: The Trudeau Years,* edited by Thomas S. Axworthy and Pierre Elliott Trudeau, 357–85. Markham, ON: Viking.

—. 1991. "Convocation Speech at the Opening of the Bora Laskin Law Library." *University of Toronto Law Journal* 41 (3): 295–330. doi:10.2307/825837.

—. 1992. *Trudeau: "A Mess That Deserves a Big No."* Translated by George Tombs. Toronto: Robert Davies Publishing.

—. 1993. *Memoirs.* Toronto: McClelland and Stewart.

—. 1996. *Against the Current: Selected Writings 1939–1996.* Toronto: McClelland and Stewart.

—. 2010. *Approaches to Politics.* Translated by Ivon Owen. Don Mills, ON: Oxford University Press.

Victoria Charter. 1971. In *Canada's Constitution Act 1982 & Amendments: A Documentary History,* edited by Anne Bayefsky, 214–22. Toronto: McGraw-Hill Ryerson, 1989.

Weinrib, Lorraine Eisenstat. 1998. "Trudeau and the Canadian Charter of Rights and Freedoms: A Question of Constitutional Maturation." In *Trudeau's Shadow: The Life and Legacy of Pierre Elliott Trudeau,* edited by Andrew Cohen and J.L. Granatstein, 257–82. Toronto: Random House Canada.

8

More Distress than Enchantment: The Constitutional Negotiations of November 1981 as Seen from Quebec

Guy Laforest and Rosalie Readman

The title of this chapter is borrowed from the autobiography of the great French Canadian writer Gabrielle Roy (1909–83). In *La détresse et l'enchantement* (1984), Roy delivers a powerfully moving narrative of her childhood in Saint Boniface and the Winnipeg area in the early decades of the twentieth century. Paraphrasing her incomparable prose, we argue that, from the perspective of the majority of Quebecers, the constitutional negotiations of November 1981 and their legal sequel – the *Constitution Act, 1982* – represent much more "distress than enchantment." In those negotiations, and in much historical lore since, the province of Quebec and the government of René Lévesque were left in isolation; Quebec's National Assembly withheld its consent and has remained steadfast in its refusal ever since. In Quebec and elsewhere in Canada, this story now informs a substantial portion of scholarship in many disciplines of the social sciences and humanities.

Without diminishing the value of such scholarship, we take up the question of what share of responsibility for Quebec's isolation and alienation can be attributed to the key players in the constitutional negotiations: Pierre Elliott Trudeau, René Lévesque, and the premiers of the nine other provinces. At the University of Alberta's Patriation Negotiations Conference in November 2011, a great deal of attention was accorded to the roles and responsibilities of the nine other premiers. As Howard Leeson, Peter Meekison, Peter Lougheed, and Brian Peckford coherently argued, at some point during the 1981 negotiations Trudeau and Lévesque lost the initiative, and the other premiers dictated the terms that transformed the conference. It is clear that, in the end, the *Constitution Act, 1982* was far from being solely Trudeau's deed; it was the other premiers', as well. We thus agree that some rebalancing must be done as we re-evaluate the scale of responsibilities. However, given the existence of important scholarship that has not been fully considered by English-language audiences, there is good reason to pay additional attention to a re-evaluation of the roles of Trudeau and Lévesque, including some consideration of its normative dimension. It is this re-evaluation that dominates the analysis in this chapter.

Much has been written in French and in English about Trudeau's role in the entire constitutional business of the 1970s and early 1980s, which was, in the words of Clarkson and McCall (1990), his "magnificent obsession." It is our conviction, however, that English-language historiography of Trudeau has almost completely disregarded the insights of André Burelle, a philosopher and federal civil servant who was also a Trudeau speechwriter and adviser from 1977 until the months following patriation, and whose books have not been translated into English. One important contribution we hope to make in this chapter is to fill a void in the English-language scholarship by using Burelle's analysis to make sense of Trudeau's behaviour and motivations up to and during the constitutional negotiations of November 1981. Most significantly, we draw on Burelle for insights into the long-term importance of the intellectual tradition of "communitarian personalism" to Trudeau's political philosophy, a political philosophy that has too often been depicted in overly simplistic liberal individualist and anti-nationalist terms.

A second contribution that we hope to make is to fill a different void, one that can be felt in the scholarship provided in French by Quebecers over the past thirty years. We will elaborate on the much-neglected roles and responsibilities of René Lévesque and his Parti Québécois government in the events of 1981. In our judgment, a nuanced explanation of Quebec's exclusion from the negotiations that produced the agreement must allocate more blame to Lévesque than the popular Night of the Long Knives image has permitted. We contend that the performance of Lévesque and his team was a disaster, and they must bear a greater share of responsibility than has typically been the case. We will present a series of facts and arguments to substantiate our claim.

In addition to the in-depth re-evaluation of the roles played by Trudeau and Lévesque, we hope to contribute to an understanding of the larger picture of the patriation debate by assessing, in the next section, the major factors leading to the patriation negotiations of 1981 and by reviewing, in the final section, the most important political consequences of those negotiations and the adoption of the *Constitution Act, 1982*. With this in mind, we now delve into the challenge of identifying the factors and forces that led to the patriation negotiations of November 1981.

Causes

The identities and political evolution of countries and societies owe a lot to structural economic forces and anonymous macro-social forces. At times, however, they can be massively changed through the actions and willpower of individuals whose qualities of political leadership reach the level of once-in-a-generation skills or abilities. We would argue, for example, that the first, crucial cause leading to the 1981 First Ministers' Conference on the Constitution was the re-election of Pierre Trudeau in February 1980. Fortune provided Trudeau with one more opportunity to bring his "magnificent obsession" to fruition. André Burelle argues that after his re-election, Trudeau pursued a nation-building dream built along two fundamental dimensions. The first dimension involved fostering a form of government-by-judges, through a national charter that would reign supreme over provincial charters, reduce the importance of the collective rights of various partners of the federation (first and foremost, Quebec), and standardize the law and political culture of the country through an idea of symmetrical equality linked to the supremacy of individual rights. The second dimension was designed to implement a form of government through the "people of Canada," enabling the federal government to circumvent the old constitution and intrude, however indirectly, in provincial powers in the name of a superior national interest (Burelle 1994, 64). It would be a mistake, however, to reduce the whole affair to a matter of Trudeau's individual agency.

A second cause was the political pressure resulting from the social and political evolution of Quebec in the preceding two decades. The Quiet Revolution and related social and political circumstances in Quebec were also important engines of change as they helped to foster a sense that constitutional reform was urgently needed (McRoberts 1997, 31). Burelle argues that from the 1971 Victoria Charter to the failed constitutional conference of September 1980, Trudeau worked to reconcile his views about contemporary Canada with the 1867 constitution and with the aspirations of modern Quebec. From 1976 onward, René Lévesque and his Parti Québécois government expressed these aspirations, even if their independentist drive and much of the social dynamism of Quebec were exhausted by their failure to secure a majority in the 1980 sovereignty association referendum.

The third cause, which had its roots in the 1970s, was the realization among the political and intellectual elites that the old Loyalist English Canadian brand of Canadian nationalism had reached a stalemate. Regarding the crucial matter of Canadians' collective ability to modify substantial elements of their constitution dealing with power sharing between the central and provincial governments, Canada remained a British colony fifty years after the *Statute of Westminster, 1931.* Canada had become officially bilingual in 1969, and the steady transformation of the country through immigration had been at least partially recognized through the adoption of a policy on multiculturalism in 1971. There was thus a social and political appetite for a new kind of Canadian civic nationalism that would modernize the image and the identity of the country (Burelle 2005, 74).

Of course, despite the force of Trudeau and the social and political changes discussed above, the immediate cause of the First Ministers' Conference on the Constitution was the September 1981 decision of the Supreme Court of Canada, which recognized the legality of the federal government's unilateral constitutional initiative but seriously questioned its legitimacy by positing the necessity of substantial provincial consent.

This forced all the players, including Trudeau and Lévesque, to come to the negotiating table one more time.

Responsibilities

Making Sense of Trudeau's Role

Trained as a philosopher, André Burelle joined Prime Minister Trudeau's team of advisers in 1977, and also worked as his primary speechwriter in French. After the nomination of their common friend Gérard Pelletier as Canadian ambassador in Paris in 1975, Burelle provided a voice of continuity in the evolution of Trudeau's thinking. The three men were united around a moral philosophy of Christian (Catholic) humanism. Owing a lot to European thinkers such as Emmanuel Mounier, Jacques Maritain, and Denis de Rougemont, this form of Christian humanism inspired a number of postwar European federalist thinkers and the development of the doctrine of *personnalisme communautaire* (communitarian personalism), which gives moral primacy to the human being as a person, without neglecting the communities that are essential to the full development of the human personality.

As a political philosophy for federalism, communitarian personalism espouses a combination of four principles: substantive rather than formal equality for persons and groups; subsidiarity as a principle for the division of powers; non-subordination as a principle for the division of sovereignty between levels of government; and finally, co-decision as a principle for the management of interdependence between the partners of the federation (Burelle 2005, 44). Burelle is very insightful in showing that until the constitutional conference of September 1980, this doctrine occupied a fair share of Trudeau's mind, competing with the more abstract, doctrinaire brand of liberal individualism and its anti-nationalist and anti-communitarian leanings, which Trudeau absorbed during his years of training in England and the United States. The trajectory of Pierre Trudeau is often depicted as showing the edifying triumph of liberal reason over nationalist passion. On this matter, Burelle invites us to think more carefully. According to him, there was indeed a struggle between reason and passion in Trudeau's mind, but it was different and more complicated than is commonly assumed. Having worked for Trudeau and studied the evolution of his thinking throughout the years, Burelle concludes that Trudeau's mind was passionately liberal-individualistic, but his rational side restrained this by introducing the nuances of communitarian personalism (Burelle 2005, 68). Through a careful analysis of Trudeau's thinking from the 1950s to the late 1970s, Burelle shows the spiritual struggle that resulted in an equilibrium in his thinking between these principles, at least until 1980. According to Burelle, this spiritual equilibrium left room for the distinctiveness of the constitutional requirements of Quebec.

For instance, as late as the constitutional conference of September 1980, Trudeau was willing to propose a preamble to the constitution that would define Canada as a federation protecting individual and collective rights (including those of Aboriginal peoples) and recognizing the distinct character of Quebec society with its French-speaking majority. Reflecting such major documents of renewed federalism as the 1978 Pépin-Robarts Report and the 1980 *Livre beige* of Claude Ryan's Liberals, Trudeau was also prepared to recognize Quebec's distinctiveness in federal institutions, including granting Quebec a right of veto on future amendments. He was equally ready to consider constitutionalizing a coherent and cooperative structure for intergovernmental negotiation, and forms of asymmetry on matters such as culture, language, immigration, and telecommunications (Burelle 2005, 63). It was only after the failure of the September 1980 constitutional conference that he abandoned these elements and that, according to Burelle, a break in equilibrium emerged in his mind between the various sources and principles fighting for primacy in his very soul. In a lengthy lament, Burelle inquires into the reasons for this change. Since his book remains unpublished in English, the translation is ours:

> Why such absence of any recognition of the distinct character of Quebec society in the *Constitution Act, 1982*? How to justify the enshrinement of a charter of rights limiting, without the consent of the National Assembly, the sovereign powers of Quebec on matters of language? How to explain the abandonment by Mr. Trudeau of the requirement to extend to Ontario and to New Brunswick the obligations imposed on Quebec by section 133 of the 1867 constitution, in contradiction to the federal proposal of September 1980? How to

> explain the decision to withdraw the offer made to Quebec to decentralize powers in the fields of language, culture and telecommunications, while maintaining similar decentralizing offers to the Western provinces in matters relating to natural resources? Why in the end did Mr. Trudeau accept a constitutional amending formula depriving Quebec of its historic veto after having struggled so hard and for so long for the Victoria formula of regional vetoes? (Burelle 2005, 66)

In his search for explanations, Burelle seeks to distinguish between, on the one hand, a superficial and immediate rationale and, on the other hand, a wide array of personal, intellectual, and political reasons. The failure of the September 1980 constitutional conference offered Trudeau a pretext to change his mind, to adopt a tougher position towards provinces and particularly towards Quebec, and ultimately to attempt a unilateral approach. As that conference unravelled, the Quebec delegation played a key role in the formulation of a vastly decentralizing interprovincial agreement known as the "Chateau consensus." It was only four months since Trudeau had promised that a "non" vote in the referendum on sovereignty association would result in immediate action to renew the constitution. However, in the memorandum documenting the Chateau consensus, Trudeau discerned a clear strategy on the part of the Quebec delegation, led by Lévesque and Claude Morin, to prevent substantial constitutional reform (Burelle 2005, 65). And it was in this context, according to Burelle, that Trudeau committed himself to a Jacobin, liberal-individualistic refounding of the Canadian nation. Following Burelle, we will now enumerate and examine the more complex personal, intellectual, and political causes of Trudeau's change of mind.

Although we are persuaded by Burelle's depiction of the intellectual equilibrium that existed for many years between Trudeau's liberal individualism and his communitarian personalism, others have suggested that his anti-nationalist – even anti-communitarian – individualism was more visceral and deep-rooted. This may partially explain why, after September 1980, his rational, intellectual commitment to communitarian personalism could no longer restrain the passion of his individualism. Burelle points to other, external causes, however. He explains how, by

1980, there had been a changing of the palace guard in Trudeau's personal and intellectual support network. Gérard Pelletier and Jean Marchand had always been moderating influences, coaxing Trudeau away from his anti–(Quebec) nationalism. They had disappeared from the scene by the early 1980s, however, and in their place were more liberal-minded influences, including Jim Coutts and Tom Axworthy in the Prime Minister's Office, Michael Pitfield at the Privy Council Office (in place of Gordon Robertson), and Michael Kirby serving as secretary to the Cabinet for Federal-Provincial Relations. Trudeau had also removed Burelle from close contact with the constitutional file because he no longer wanted to be paralyzed by Burelle's troubling memos appealing to the communitarian part of his mind that was a waning influence on his constitutional politics (Burelle 2005, 81–82).

Also important to Trudeau's change of mind was the fact that, by the early 1980s, English-speaking Canada was increasingly ready for a redefinition of itself as a multicultural and bilingual nation. Quebec was also changing, but Burelle (2005, 76) laments Trudeau's unwillingness to recognize the emergence in Quebec of an authentic civic nationalism open to the values of pluralistic modernity. Instead, with his eye on English-speaking Canada, Trudeau saw political opportunity for his new, more liberal individualist nation-building resoluteness.

Yet much of Burelle's explanation of Trudeau's intellectual shift and changing constitutional strategy focuses on Trudeau's personality and personal political situation. It must be recalled that in the summer of 1979, Trudeau looked like a spent force in Canadian politics. He had lost the federal election to Joe Clark and announced his retirement. Analysts were pointing out that, despite his achievements, Trudeau had failed on the two issues that mattered most to him: patriating a reformed constitution and fighting Quebec separatism. This affected him deeply, and so when he returned to politics and won another majority government, he was determined to fight even more implacably than before – he had a renewed sense of historic mission (Burelle 2005, 88). Moreover, he had an opportunity to define the constitutional battle in polarized terms, which was exactly the sort of political battle he relished. Trudeau had, at least figuratively speaking, vanquished René Lévesque in the Quebec referendum of 20 May 1980. For a while, it seemed he would have to negotiate constitutional reform with the referendum's winner, the federalist Quebec Liberal leader, Claude Ryan, but Lévesque's subsequent electoral victory allowed Trudeau to go head-to-head with his old nemesis. The political moment enabled him to elevate Ottawa as a champion of individual rights against power-hungry provinces, and to fight unyieldingly against Lévesque and all forms of Quebec nationalism. As such, the political moment and Trudeau's personality supported his change of mind and embrace of an implacably liberal constitutional strategy.

André Burelle's insights help us to understand the events leading to the 1981 patriation conference and to the new constitution. In particular, his contribution deepens our understanding of Trudeau's behaviour and motivations, and sheds light on his responsibilities. Politically resurrected in February 1980, and liberated spiritually from the need to integrate the complexities of communitarian personalism, Pierre Trudeau launched a fresh constitutional offensive aimed at founding the Canadian nation anew and settling his score with Lévesque and Quebec nationalism.

Understanding the Role of Lévesque and His Government

We turn now to navigate more uncharted waters, trying to explain the responsibilities of René Lévesque and his government. Some thirty years after these events, no single study (book-length monograph, chapter, or article), in either English or French, has focused on tackling this crucial task as a primary objective. Certainly, Claude Morin, Lévesque's minister of intergovernmental affairs and right-hand man at the time of the conference, has written books touching on the issue (Morin 1988, 1994). However, his main objective was to attack Trudeau and the federal government, and to engage in critical dialogue with his counterparts from elsewhere in Canada to underline and to bemoan the fact that they had abandoned Lévesque, his government, and Quebec. We believe it is high time for a lucid analysis of Quebec's performance in 1981–82.[1]

Lévesque and his government suffered a resounding defeat (59.5 percent to 40.5 percent) in the 20 May 1980 referendum on sovereignty association. Guy Laforest (2004, 332–33) has drawn an analogy between the referendum and Quebec provincial election of 1980–81, on the one hand, and the rebellions of 1837–38 on the other, calling the latter the failed rebellions of the imperial age and the former the failed rebellions of the democratic age. In both eras, leaders of a national minority who embarked upon a major initiative to reform or break out of the state system had to deal with the strategic fact that they would be weaker when they failed. Historical documents, memoirs, and autobiographies by Quebec's political leaders of the 1980s reveal a deep and looming pessimism pervading the period leading to the patriation conference and to the promulgation of the new constitution. Lévesque and his government never recovered from the political defeat of the referendum. Of course, they had some good days, making some tactical gains in the aftermath of the referendum, but at most key moments, their behaviour was characterized by unsuccessful improvisation. Clearly, the failed referendum diminished Lévesque, the stature of his government, and, in the end, the place of Quebec in Canada.

Lévesque's biographer, Pierre Godin, establishes that Lévesque and his government had not carefully considered any strategy in the event of a referendum defeat. It is clear from Godin's retelling of the first post-referendum meetings of Lévesque with his top advisers, cabinet, and caucus that they had no idea what their next steps should be. They were manifestly on the defensive, reacting to the initiatives of Trudeau and of his justice minister, Jean Chrétien. Indeed, constitutional strategy took a back seat as Lévesque and his colleagues decided that they would continue to govern Quebec until the end of their mandate, and that their key priority would be to defeat Claude Ryan and the Liberals in the next Quebec general election, which took place on 13 April 1981. Lévesque and Ryan had known each other since the early days of the Quiet Revolution. In the 1960s, as editor of *Le Devoir*, Ryan was respected in Quebec and throughout Canada as a careful thinker and éminence grise of renewed federalism. In 1979, Ryan's Quebec Liberal Party published its *Livre beige*, one of the era's key documents of renewed federalism. Given that Ryan and Trudeau did not see eye to eye on the issue of reforming the Canadian constitution, Lévesque could have made much greater use of Ryan's advice – and of his legitimacy as a federalist leader and thinker – in the negotiations leading to the patriation conference. Quite naturally, there was some acrimony between these men who had fought on the battlefields of the referendum and a tough electoral campaign in the spring of 1981. Following the election, and even during the patriation conference, Ryan made efforts to get in touch with Lévesque, but Lévesque did not return his calls (Godin 2005, 152). Ignoring Ryan throughout the process was Lévesque's first major mistake.

The second major mistake occurred barely three days after the 1981 election, when Quebec chose to endorse a major interprovincial ("Gang of Eight") proposal aimed at derailing the unilateral strategy that Trudeau had announced in the House of Commons on 2 October 1980. With this decision, the Lévesque government abandoned Quebec's historic constitutional veto (a veto that many observers from outside Quebec, including eminent constitutional scholar Donald Smiley, thought that it had at the time) and endorsed an amending formula that required the consent of two-thirds of provinces for most changes, enriched by an opting-out clause with fiscal compensation. The Lévesque government could have explained clearly that its agreement would remain valid only if, in the end, Quebec deemed a full constitutional reform package acceptable, and thus explicitly retained the province's historic veto in the event that an acceptable agreement did not materialize. Discussions towards this decision began during the election campaign, when the task of overseeing the constitutional file rested exclusively with the minister in charge, Claude Morin, and his deputy minister, Robert Normand. The cabinet, then overburdened by the campaign, and much of the supporting bureaucratic team were completely left out (Tremblay 2006, 262–63). The decision to abandon the veto was thus made by Morin, Normand, and Lévesque, and we believe they acted precipitately.

We turn now to Quebec's strategic behaviour on the judicial front. As Philip Girard details in Chapter 6, Quebec, Manitoba, and Newfoundland moved the issue to their courts of appeal soon after Trudeau announced his desire to act unilaterally. Decisions on these references were handed down in the spring of 1981, with the Quebec government losing in its own court (4–1), while Trudeau's unilateralism suffered a crucial defeat in Newfoundland (3–2). From there, the issue moved to the Supreme Court of Canada, with Quebec joining the opposing provinces. The Supreme Court justices rendered their judgment in the *Patriation Reference* on 28 September 1981. In late December and early January 1982, two months after the November First Ministers' conference on the Constitution, the Quebec government went once more to its own court of appeal on the issue of whether there existed a veto right for the province, and once again, it was defeated in a judgment that was rendered in early May 1982. The Supreme Court of Canada then confirmed the decision of the Quebec Court of Appeal in early December 1982.

There were at least two strategic missteps in Quebec's manoeuvres before the courts. First, likely out of solidarity with the Gang of Eight, Quebec did not submit a reference to its own court of appeal about the existence of a specific right of veto for the province immediately after the Supreme Court rendered its decision in September 1981. When Quebec finally chose to do so, it was more than two months after the First Ministers' conference, when preparations were already under way for promulgation of the *Constitution Act, 1982* by the Queen in Ottawa in early April. This indecisiveness was a strategic error.

The second misstep occurred earlier. In the fall of 1980, for reasons that remain unknown, Lévesque and Morin made changes to the leadership of Quebec's team of constitutional lawyers. Former Supreme Court justice Yves Pratte replaced Laval University constitutional expert Henri Brun. Although an experienced lawyer and judge, Pratte did not have much time to prepare Quebec's brief in the *Patriation Reference*. The resulting problem was not what Quebec pleaded (traditional arguments about duality and founding peoples, and historical precedents – 1964 and 1971 – supporting the idea that Quebec, indeed, had a veto) but rather what it did *not* plead. Donald Smiley outlined an important argument at the time of patriation that was available to Quebec lawyers in the early 1980s. The *Constitution Act, 1867*, then known as the *British North America Act*, contained a clause allowing federal authorities to homogenize or standardize the legal space of common law provinces on matters of property and civil rights, provided that these provinces would give their explicit legislative consent. There was no mention of Quebec in this article, section 94 of the constitution. But considering that Quebec had just codified its civil law, and taking into account the fact that George-Étienne Cartier viewed the securing of article 92(13), which granted the control of property and civil rights to provinces, as a triumph for Quebec's autonomy, it was clear to Smiley, as it should have been to Lévesque's government and its constitutional lawyers, that the overall meaning of section 94 was a recognition of Quebec's particularity (Smiley 1983, 77).

In 1981–82, Quebec should have argued that, at the very least, any constitutional reform touching provincial powers in the field of property and civil rights (something recognized by every court in the key judgments of the times) required its explicit legislative consent (see also LaSelva 1995, 62–63). Not to have done so was a strategic error.

Although our assessment is severe, we are far from suggesting that the Quebec government did everything wrong between the spring of 1980 and the First Ministers' conference of November 1981. First, Quebec played an undeniably positive and key role in the Gang of Eight, the interprovincial alliance opposed to Trudeau's unilateralism. For a while, particularly after the September 1980 constitutional conference, which proved to be a disaster for the Trudeau government, many provincial premiers appeared more comfortable with Lévesque than with the prime minister. Aside from the issue of the amending formula and the matter of a veto right, previously discussed, the Lévesque government managed to act both in its own interests and for the sake of the alliance until the 1981 First Ministers' conference on patriation. Moreover, as many analysts have recognized, the Quebec delegation in London, led by Gilles Loiselle, played a crucial role in the manoeuvres of the provincial alliance that was lobbying British authorities and whose arguments ultimately prevailed in the February 1981 Report of the Parliamentary Committee led by Anthony Kershaw (Clarkson and McCall 1990, 320).

We have argued that there was much improvisation on the part of the Quebec government at the beginning of the process that led to the 1981 patriation conference. The same observation applies to the behaviour of the Quebec delegation during the conference itself. In addition to Lévesque, the team featured Minister of Intergovernmental Relations Claude Morin and Deputy Minister Robert Normand – two experienced people who had been in charge of the file since the referendum. Surprisingly, however, the remaining two positions were filled by ministers with limited experience with the file: Marc-André Bédard, the minister of justice, and Claude Charron, at the time the government's parliamentary leader, who was included primarily because Lévesque liked his dynamism and appreciated his company at such meetings (Godin 2005, 152). Senior Quebec ministers such as Jacques Parizeau, Bernard Landry, and Pierre-Marc Johnson (all of whom would become premiers of Quebec in subsequent years) were left out. Amazingly, Parizeau invited himself to the conference, was brought in for a day, but returned home totally distressed by the chaotic atmosphere surrounding the Quebec delegation (Godin 2005, 159).[2] All observers, including those like Martine Tremblay who were quite sympathetic and loyal to Lévesque, noted that he often looked tired, confused, at times enraged, and even depressed during the conference.

The greatest and most fateful instance of improvisation took place late in the morning of 4 November. Trudeau proposed to Lévesque that the paradigm or model for the whole constitutional business could be changed, suggesting that the matter should be submitted to the people in a referendum. Amazingly, without consulting anybody, Lévesque seemed to indicate that this was a very good idea and that he was willing to explore it in greater detail. Notwithstanding all of the other proposals that were being discussed in the heated atmosphere of the conference, involving, among others, the federal delegation and Jean Chrétien, the Ontario and Saskatchewan delegations, and the British Columbia delegation, Lévesque's response to Trudeau's referendum gambit signalled that he was willing to go his own way, beyond the agreements among the members of the Gang of Eight.

When the conference reconvened that afternoon and Trudeau made public the details of his prospective referendum, it soon became clear to Lévesque and the Quebec delegation that this new project was unpalatable. Apparently, the day ended with an impasse, and the Quebec delegation retired to their hotel across the Ottawa River, where they spent the night with no communication whatsoever with their allies or adversaries at the conference, except for a brief phone call from BC premier Bill Bennett informing them that breakfast the next morning would take place half an hour later than scheduled. The rest is history. As Howard Leeson (2011, 81) explains in his lucid and useful book *The Patriation Minutes*, the nine English-speaking premiers took matters into their own hands and seized the initiative – which had long rested with Trudeau, Lévesque, or both – by agreeing on a constitutional package that suited their interests. A compromise was worked out with Trudeau that same night but was never reached with Lévesque and his government. For the Quebec delegation, the patriation conference was a catastrophe of the greatest proportions. As a political actor and possibly as a human being, René Lévesque would never recover.

Weakened by his referendum defeat and disheartened by the disaster at the conference, Lévesque learned shortly afterwards that his main adviser on constitutional affairs, Claude Morin, had accepted money and acted as an informant for the RCMP before and after the election of the PQ government in November 1976. Morin had met twenty-nine times with RCMP officials between 1975 and late 1977 (Godin 2001, 460, 612). Lévesque was now indeed a broken man, and this helps explain why he could never resolve to use the democratic referendum card to prevent the patriation of the Canadian constitution without Quebec's consent. Trudeau had his own reasons for not submitting the "People's Package" to the Canadian people. Insofar as Lévesque was concerned, however, he appears to have been simply too discouraged to even consider this option.

Without Trudeau's forceful actions and willpower, there certainly would have been no patriation conference or meaningful constitutional reform for Canada in 1982. Contrary to hegemonic interpretations in English-speaking Canada, however, his behaviour on constitutional affairs, particularly his approach towards Quebec, showed clear contradictions. André Burelle sheds much-needed light on some of Trudeau's complex motivations. The nine English-speaking premiers were key constitution makers even though they seized the initiative only very late in the process, on 4 November. In the end, Trudeau and these premiers were jointly responsible for imposing constitutional reform on Quebec. As shown by the missteps and miscalculations described above, however, it is also fair to say, at least in our judgment, that René Lévesque and his government must also be held responsible for the constitutional isolation of Quebec.

We now turn to an examination of the consequences of the First Ministers' 1981 patriation conference.

Consequences

The negotiations of November 1981 led to the adoption of the *Constitution Act, 1982.* We wish to explore, however briefly, six consequences of these fateful events. The first was the judicialization of Canadian politics. In the equilibrium among the executive, legislative, and judicial branches of government, the 1981 negotiations led to constitutional reform that substantially reinforced the role of the courts, particularly the Supreme Court of Canada. The Supreme Court has become much more than the umpire of federalism: it now sees itself as our primary constitutional guardian, steward of the actions of governments, and protector of the rights of citizens. In their analysis of the judicialization of Canadian politics, Kelly and Manfredi (2009, 6) identify four major factors at work: "constitutional provisions explicitly authorizing judicial participation in public policy; judicial approaches to governing with the Charter; changing approaches to governance by parliamentary actors; and finally, greater recourse to the courts by citizens seeking policy changes denied by parliamentary politics."

As Peter Russell argues in Chapter 11, the second consequence was, perhaps surprisingly, the securing of a strong constitutional anchor for the rights of Aboriginal peoples. While Quebec fuelled the constitutional reform of the late 1970s with its societal and political energy, it came out of the process with reduced powers and no constitutional provision explicitly addressing its requirements. Paradoxically, whereas Aboriginal peoples where left out of the processes of constitutional dialogue, they came away with a strong legal anchor through section 25 of the Charter and section 35 of the *Constitution Act, 1982.*

Third, the patriation process and the passage of the *Constitution Act, 1982* transformed Canadian national identity and reinforced the allegiance of citizens to the federal government and the Canadian state. André Burelle (2005, 440–41) believes that the reforms of 1981–82 amounted to the abandonment of the social contract flowing from the 1867 constitution and its understanding of Canada as a multinational polity, and other constitutional scholars support this perspective. Alan Cairns (2011, 370) argues that the "Charter was a nationalizing, Canadianizing constitutional instrument intended to shape the psyches and identities of Canadians." Its objective, he contends, was to constrain the diversities that federalism is meant to reflect and sustain. Sujit Choudhry's work (2009, 239, 241) echoes this interpretation:

> The Charter relies on both the regulative and constitutive conceptions of a bill of rights to serve as an instrument of nation building. In regulatory terms, the Charter imposes legal restraints on minority

> nation building by Quebec, through the rights to inter-provincial mobility and to minority language education for children ... However, the Charter was also intended to function constitutively as the germ of pan-Canadian constitutional patriotism.

An increase in Quebec's political alienation was almost certainly a fourth consequence of the 1981 constitutional agreement and patriation. A number of political columnists, including Chantal Hébert and Jeffrey Simpson, have commented on the gradual estrangement of Quebec and Quebecers from Canadian political life, but this troubling reality has not been the subject of careful empirical analysis. Still, we believe that the two global societies of French-speaking Quebec and English-speaking Canada are even more indifferent to one another than they were thirty years ago. This estrangement has resulted in some perplexing political developments. For example, when Quebecers abandoned the Bloc Québécois in the federal election of 2 May 2011, they voted en masse for a party with which they were largely unfamiliar, Jack Layton's New Democratic Party.

The fifth significant consequence is that constitutional reform is now more difficult to achieve. The complex amending formula adopted in 1981–82 has subsequently been rendered even more rigid by the idea of regional vetoes introduced by the Chrétien government, the requirement for provincial referenda prior to ratification in some provinces, and the need to secure the involvement of all concerned, including Aboriginal peoples, which stems from the 1998 Supreme Court decision in *Reference re Secession of Quebec*. Our constitution remains amendable (for instance, in 1997, Ottawa and Quebec agreed on a modification to section 93 of the *Constitution Act, 1867*), but both legally and politically, it is now extraordinarily difficult to secure and ratify changes.

Sixth, as Alain-G. Gagnon and Alex Schwartz suggest in Chapter 12, the 1981 patriation agreement had the effect of reducing the importance of federalism within the Canadian political regime. The idea of an equilibrium between self-rule for provincial communities and shared rule across Canada, granting substantial policy autonomy to provinces while preserving solidarity and interdependence, was weakened by the purposeful centralizing and standardizing reforms of 1981–82. This has implications for issues like language rights. And, as Burelle (2005, 446) explains, on these issues, justice and fairness result from an ethics of equivalence of treatment, not the ethics of symmetrical or standardized treatment that shaped so much of the patriation agreement. José Woehrling (2009) has also explored the consequences of this for Quebec. For example, insofar as rights protection through a constitutional instrument is an anti-majority mechanism, it limits the political autonomy of minorities that control territorial entities. A minority controlling such an entity sees its political power restricted for the benefit of its own minorities. The most problematic situation occurs when "the minority within the minority" is part of the majority at the national level, as is the case for minority English speakers in Quebec, who are part of the English-speaking majority in Canada. The majority at the national level can then give in to the temptation to use its power to impose on its minority compliance with excessive guarantees benefiting "the minority within the minority" (Woehrling 2009, 125).

Conclusion

Canada's English-speaking First Ministers, working through the institutions of executive federalism, negotiated the patriation agreement of November 1981. There was no ratifying referendum or election to give democratic legitimacy to the agreement, and only one province (Alberta) allowed for a legislative debate prior to ratification. Without Quebec's consent, or democratic legitimacy, the English-speaking Canadian majority essentially abused its powers to put in place an agreement that, as Peter Russell has argued over the years, challenged the understanding of Canada as a fundamentally federal community (Russell 2004). This is the normative point that we alluded to in the introduction to this chapter. The primary responsibility for the way the constitutional saga unfolded in the fall of 1981 belongs to Prime Minister Trudeau, but, in truth, all the premiers were complicit. They knew there were risks associated in proceeding without Quebec, but individually and collectively they were willing to accept those risks. Donald Smiley (1983, 77) disagreed; he considered the whole affair a "dangerous deed":

> In my view, the first-line protection of the rights of the francophone community of Quebec is and has been since Confederation among the powers of the Legislature and government of that province, and

> on this basis Canadian constitutional convention dictates that these powers should not be restricted without Quebec's assent.

Nevertheless, as we have shown in this chapter, there were mitigating circumstances. First, Trudeau came from Quebec; his voice carried significant legitimacy; and in the vote that took place in the House of Commons, seventy-three out of the seventy-five MPs from Quebec voted in favour of patriation. Technically speaking, they were in no way authorized to reduce the powers of Quebec's National Assembly without the consent of their counterparts in that assembly, but many members of the public would see this as an obscure normative point, particularly today, when the federal element in the political culture of the land carries less weight than before. Second, the performance of Quebec authorities throughout 1980 and 1981 was marked by significant strategic missteps. René Lévesque and his associates must accept a greater share of the responsibility than has been admitted up to now. Third, in the political and symbolic circumstances of the time, many people sensed that patriation offered Canada a glorious opportunity to found anew its idea of nationhood. Fourth, we should not forget that the patriation experiment was draped in the language of rights, the dominant idiom of moral and political philosophy in the world after 1945. In their seminal study, Clarkson and McCall (1990, 187) captured very clearly both this aspect and its major flaw as seen by many in Quebec:

> The notion of an entrenched charter of rights and freedoms would appeal to the legal establishment and civil libertarians among the country's liberal-minded intellectual elite ... With all these favourable aspects of the package diverting attention, the "constitutionalization" of the official languages law and the entrenchment of minority-language education rights would be camouflaged.
>
> While this canny move to outwit Lévesque and the separatists was well understood in Quebec, it was not perceived as deceptive in English Canada, where the idea of citizens' rights was so popular that it overrode other considerations.

We have attempted to demonstrate that in 1981–82, aided and abetted by the misjudgments of Lévesque and his government, Pierre Trudeau and the premiers of the majority English-speaking provinces joined forces to transform Canada's constitutional order and national identity without the consent of Quebec. As with all complicated social phenomena, there were many causes, responsible agents, and consequences. In the conclusion to his wonderful 2005 book, André Burelle indicates that there are ways to act politically beyond the legacy of the patriation agreement and its legal consequences. Even now, however, Canadians, and Quebecers in their midst, have failed to embark on such a journey. In the end, the enchantment of Burelle's prose affords precious little consolation for the political and constitutional distress of many Quebecers, including us authors, in contemporary Canada.

Notes

1 For a partial attempt at this endeavour, see Dion 1995, 42–43.

2 For a dissenting view on this assessment, see Tremblay 2006, 268–69.

References

Burelle, André. 1994. *Le mal canadien.* Montreal: Fides.

—. 2005. *Pierre-Elliott Trudeau: l'intellectuel et le politique.* Montreal: Fides.

Cairns, Alan. 2011. "Reflections on the Political Purposes of the Charter." In *Essential Readings in Canadian Constitutional Politics,* edited by Christian Leuprecht and Peter H. Russell, 370–73. Toronto: University of Toronto Press.

Choudhry, Sujit. 2009. "Bills of Rights as Instruments of Nation Building in Multinational States: The Canadian Charter and Quebec Nationalism." In *Contested Constitutionalism: Reflections on the Canadian Charter of Rights and Freedoms,* edited by James B. Kelly and Christopher P. Manfredi, 233–50. Vancouver: UBC Press.

Clarkson, Stephen, and Christina McCall. 1990. *The Magnificent Obsession.* Vol. 1, *Trudeau and Our Times.* Toronto: McClelland and Stewart.

Dion, Léon. 1995. *Le duel constitutionnel Québec-Canada.* Montreal: Boréal.

Godin, Pierre. 2001. *René Lévesque: l'espoir et le chagrin.* Montreal: Boréal.

—. 2005. *René Lévesque: l'homme brisé.* Montreal: Boréal.

Kelly, James, and Christopher P. Manfredi, eds. 2009. *Contested Constitutionalism: Reflections on the Canadian Charter of Rights and Freedoms.* Vancouver: UBC Press.

Laforest, Guy. 2004. *Pour la liberté d'une société distincte.* Quebec City: Presses de l'Université Laval.

LaSelva, Samuel V. 1995. *The Moral Foundations of Canadian Federalism: Paradoxes, Achievements and Tragedies of Nationhood.* Montreal/Kingston: McGill-Queen's University Press.

Leeson, Howard. 2011. *The Patriation Minutes.* Edmonton: Centre for Constitutional Studies.

McRoberts, Kenneth. 1997. *Misconceiving Canada: The Struggle for National Unity.* Toronto: Oxford University Press.

Morin, Claude. 1988. *Lendemains piégés.* Montreal: Boréal.

—. 1994. *Les choses comme elles étaient: Une autobiographie politique.* Montreal: Boréal.

Re: Resolution to Amend the Constitution, [1981] 1 S.C.R. 753 [*Patriation Reference*].

Roy, Gabrielle. 1984. *La détresse et l'enchantement.* Montreal: Boréal.

Russell, Peter H. 2004. *Constitutional Odyssey: Can Canadians Become a Sovereign People?* 3rd ed. Toronto: University of Toronto Press.

Smiley, Donald. 1983. "A Dangerous Deed: The Constitution Act, 1982." In *And No One Cheered: Federalism, Democracy and the Constitution Act, 1982*, edited by Keith Banting and Richard Simeon, 74–95. Toronto: Methuen.

Tremblay, Martine. 2006. *Derrière les portes closes: René Lévesque et l'exercice du pouvoir (1976–1985).* Montreal: Quebec Amérique.

Woehrling, José. 2009. "La Charte canadienne des droits et libertés et ses répercussions sur la vie politique." In *Le parlementarisme canadien*, 4th ed., edited by Réjean Pelletier and Manon Tremblay, 88–127. Quebec City: Presses de l'Université Laval.

9 Tracking Justice: The Constitution Express to Section 35 and Beyond

Louise Mandell and Leslie Hall Pinder

September 1980

In a spacious but unpretentious office, sitting at a large, old wooden table, is an Indigenous man. His hair, black as a raven's wing, is cut in bangs across his forehead – unchanged since he was a boy at his grandmother's knee. The dark, unblemished skin on his full-moon face shows the glowing effects of a summer spent meeting his people at fish camps, hunting places, and powwow grounds. His brow is permanently furrowed from deep thought, but the hollowed creases around his mouth promise an expansion into laughter. His age is difficult to determine.

He is leaning over – more like leaning into – a legal-sized document, which he has just removed from an unmarked brown envelope. He has thick black-rimmed glasses because his eyesight is poor.

This is Grand Chief Dr. George Manuel, the powerful Secwepemc leader and president of the Union of BC Indian Chiefs (UBCIC), former president of the National Indian Brotherhood (NIB), and founding president of the World Council of Indigenous Peoples.

George hands the document to me, Leslie Pinder. I am sitting beside Louise Mandell and Mary Lou Andrew, an elder from Seabird Island Reserve, who is our immediate boss. Cautious, skillful – with a mother's love for the Fraser River – Mary Lou teaches us how to use our legal skills to be effective advisers for UBCIC. I have learned to trust that whatever George does is guided by a wise and wily intuition that he employs every day to manage the difficult course of politics – a course made even more complicated by the avowed intention of Prime Minister Pierre Trudeau to patriate Canada's constitution without the involvement of First Nations. The work we are doing for the UBCIC is uncharted in every sense; George is our astonishing guide.

The document is a briefing to the federal cabinet, with no indication of its authorship; in bold letters, it is marked "STRICTLY CONFIDENTIAL." As I read aloud, it is obvious that this document should not be in our possession.

> *There is likely to be a major effort by Canada's Native Peoples to win national and international support (especially at Westminster) for their stand against patriation. If the Native peoples press forward with their plans and if they succeed in gaining support and sympathy abroad, Canada's image will suffer considerably. Because Canada's Native peoples live, as a rule, in conditions that are very different from those of most other Canadians – as sample statistics set out below attest – there would be serious questions asked about whether the Native peoples enjoy basic rights in Canada:*
>
> *a. Indians have a life expectancy 10 years less than the Canadian average.*
> *b. Indians experience violent deaths at more than three times the national average.*
> *c. Approximately 60 percent of Indians in Canada receive social assistance.*
> *d. Only 32 percent of working-age Indians are employed.*
> *e. Less than 50 percent of Indian homes are properly serviced.*
> *f. In Canada as a whole, the prison population is about 9 percent Native, yet Native peoples make up only 3 percent of Canada's population. In 1977, there were 280 Indians in jail per 100,000 population, compared with 40, the national average.*
>
> *Native leaders realize that entrenching their rights will be enormously difficult after patriation, especially since a majority of the provinces would have to agree to changes that might benefit Native peoples at the expense of provincial power. They, therefore, demand an entrenchment of Native rights before patriation (cited in Mandell 1984, 171–72; O'Connell, n.d.).*

Silence takes hold. The four of us do not yet understand how foreboding our speechlessness is. We are about to enter an era where the issues of voice and entitlement to speak, as well as to be heard, are the dominant metaphors of the political discourse. Subsequently, this was perhaps best epitomized during the first lengthy test case on Aboriginal title in British Columbia – in the case of Delgamuukw *(1986). Mary Johnson, a Gitksan-Wet'suwet'en elder, was giving evidence of her* adaawk *(oral history), part of which was expressed in a dirge song. Despite the significance of the song's showing of ancient territorial ownership, the trial judge didn't want to hear it. "I have a tin ear," Judge McEachern said. "It's not going to do any good to sing to me." Indeed, it didn't do any good. He ruled that Aboriginal title in BC had been extinguished.*

The silence between us is broken by George. With clarity and precision, he describes the powerful leaders who were the masterminds of this newly minted, draconian strategy to eliminate the Indigenous peoples' voice from the patriation conversation. He sees the roots of the strategy in Trudeau's White Paper of 1969, which was Canada's own Final Solution to the "Native problem" (Canada 1969). He recalls Trudeau's words when Jean Chrétien, then minister of justice, introduced this policy and outlined the constitutional change which was needed to implement it – full jurisdictional powers over "Indians and Indian lands" would be transferred to the provinces; Indigenous peoples would become "Canadians as all other Canadians" (cited in Cumming and Mickenberg 1972, 331). Trudeau said:

> *perhaps the treaties shouldn't go on forever ... We must be all equal under the laws and we must not sign treaties amongst ourselves ...*
>
> *But Aboriginal rights, this really means saying, "We were here before you. You came and you took the land from us and perhaps you cheated us by giving us some worthless things in return for vast expanses of land ... We want you to preserve our Aboriginal rights and to restore them to us." And ... our answer is "no." (Cited in Cumming and Mickenberg 1972, 331–32)*

I sense another collective presence in the room. Over two hundred Indigenous leaders, immaculately dressed, look on as witnesses to our meeting. In the photograph above the table, they are standing on the steps of the former residential school in Kamloops in 1969; they've just formed the UBCIC for the purpose of opposing the White Paper, which was threatening their very survival.

George Manuel sounds the alarm. Trudeau's proposal for constitutional change is "beyond consultation, beyond administrative battles with government, beyond petty politics. It is hitting at the roots – the very existence of the

Indian nations." If passed, the Canada Bill *would enable Canada to get rid of the special constitutional status of Indigenous peoples, just as Trudeau and Chrétien had tried to do in 1969.*

Over 100 chiefs at a UBCIC assembly in November 1980 stated their position on the proposed constitutional reform. While resolute, their position is inclusive, conciliatory, seeking harmony and cooperation between the nations. How different its tone is from the devious confidential briefing to cabinet.

> *Indian nations in Canada were never conquered. European traders, and in later years, settlers, were made welcome in the land and environment that was alien to them. Throughout years of European settlement and expansion, Indian nations sought a mutual accommodation, one that would permit a bountiful land to be shared to the benefit of all.*
>
> *Indian rights to land, resources, culture, language, a livelihood, and self-government are not something conferred by treaties, or offered to Indians, or concessions by a beneficent government. These are the rights that Indian nations enjoy from time immemorial. These rights are pre-existing and inviolable. A Canadian constitution can accommodate Indian rights – it cannot diminish, alter, or eliminate them.*
>
> *Indian nations understand the constitution to be a pact among founding peoples, among which we include ourselves. We understand our special constitutional relationship with the federal government to be in the nature of a partnership with the federative system, which was intended to permit us to survive and prosper as Indian nations, while contributing to Canada's total development.*
>
> *a new constitution can have two alternative results insofar as Indian nations are concerned. It can have the effect of entrenching poverty, dependency, and alienation; or it can re-open avenues to Indian development in terms consistent with the rights recognized and affirmed in all previous transactions with the Crown ...*
>
> *exclusion of Indian participation from a broad constitutional review [is] the first mistake which federal authorities have to correct. Until this is done, Indian nations reject the proposed federal resolution in total as a hostile and aggressive measure and are prepared to employ all means to resist its implementation. (Cited in Mandell 1984, 164–65)*

To place these two documents side by side (the government briefing and the UBCIC's resolution) is to view a conversation. For the UBCIC, it is one between the peoples of two founding nations. In effective conversation, both parties not only have to have a voice, they must hear one another. The UBCIC chiefs are speaking to Canada about a partnership anchored in the past and extending, with mutual benefit, into the future. Canada's audience, however, is not the Indigenous nations. It is the international community, which, if it learns about the treatment of Indigenous peoples by Canada, will question "whether the native peoples enjoy basic rights." Canada's image will be tarnished. The First Nations' voice must be silenced.

This conversation is broken.

The Living Tree of Confederation

In the fall of 1980, Mary Lou Andrew organized meetings across British Columbia where Leslie and I explained the proposed constitutional reform. The gymnasiums where they were held were so full that, with characteristic wry humour, one chief commented that we drew a bigger crowd than bingo night. We were all on an unfamiliar path. One early morning, I was on a float plane dock, scheduled to attend a meeting in a north coast community that had no electricity. The morning was still until I heard the sound of a motorboat. Ducks scattered. The young man operating the boat shouted, "Are you a lawyer?" I hollered, "Yes." "Do you know anything about this so-called *BNA Act*?" "Yes." He swung the boat around and said, "OK. Get in." I jumped in.

Although many at the meetings had never heard of the *British North America Act,* they had a deep understanding of what they called "the Queen's law," which was transmitted orally from generation to generation. In the Okanagan, the elders would say what sounded like "Ha'Queen," which meant, "the Queen said." "Ha'Queen – the government cannot bring down their law against the people for living from the land. Ha'Queen – the government cannot take charge of our people and our lands without a treaty." They also spoke eloquently about how Canada broke the Queen's law – denied Aboriginal title, disrespected Aboriginals' ancient laws, and dishonoured treaties. As we listened, our instructions became clear: the lawyers should ask Britain to deny the patriation of the constitution without Aboriginal involvement, because to do so ignored the original peoples and their special constitutional relationship with the British sovereign.

These instructions sounded a legal chord – Indigenous societies with legal orders pre-existed and survived the assertion of Crown sovereignty; this is the golden thread of recognition by the common law, woven through Canada's living constitution by the doctrine of continuity, creating a bedrock of legal pluralism. This was the law governing the assertion of Crown sovereignty, stated in the *Royal Proclamation of 1763,* which required Crown governments to recognize the pre-existing rights of Indigenous peoples to their lands and laws as legal rights and the incremental perfecting of Crown title and sovereignty through treaties. The 1764 *Treaty of Niagara* and other agreements had woven relationships of peace, friendship, and respect into the Canadian constitutional fabric (Borrows 1994, 23–24). This law and the treaties endowed Canada with an Indigenous foundation based on the rule of law (Henderson 2007).

These principles are also woven into the *Constitution Act, 1867* (as the *British North America Act* is now known) through sections 91(24) and 109. In 1888, the Privy Council, in *St. Catherine's Milling and Lumber Co. v. The Queen,* relying on section 109 of the *Constitution Act, 1867,* held that the "lands, mines, minerals and royalties" become available to provinces as a source of revenue only when Aboriginal title has been addressed. Yet in most of British Columbia, the province took control over the land and resources anyway, without treaty.

Under subsection 91(24), the federal government was assigned jurisdiction over "a trust which could [not] conveniently be confided to the local Legislatures,"[1] who would be in a conflict of interest over resources until the lands were dealt with by treaty. The *Royal Proclamation* is an implied term of subsection 91(24),[2] vesting in the federal government the primary constitutional responsibility ... "to safeguard one of the most central of Native interests – their interest in their lands (*Delgamuukw* at para. 176)." Nevertheless, Canada pursued assimilation goals under the *Indian Act.* Access to justice was foreclosed by making it illegal to raise money for Indigenous peoples to go to court about the land question. By outlawing the potlatch, Canada sought to undermine Indigenous laws and legal orders. Cultural suppression and dispossession continues. The chiefs hoped the British courts would recognize their plight and bring justice and peace through constitutional renewal.

Looking through the cracks, we can see what the chiefs were up against. Accompanying the colonizers to North America was a racist world view that assumed the superiority of European-derived nations and the inferiority of Indigenous nations – a social Darwinism ladder of human endeavour and of ascending stages of civilization. Through this lens, Indigenous peoples are illusions – savage Indians without laws – their territories a juridical vacuum, available for the superior law of the Europeans to rule. The myths were many – that law arrived in Indian territories with the first colonial legislature and governors; that Indians did not have effective control of their territories, since their law-making powers were extremely limited; that the new settler legal order lived by the rule of law, whereas Indians lived more by custom; that the settler governments brought their economy, whereas Indians had trade; that warfare, disease, scarcity, and inter-tribal conflict constantly altered the living arrangements of Indians. The arrival of the Europeans and association with Crown sovereignty, it was believed, gave Indians the evolutional advantages of the European experience.

Assumed Crown sovereignty and superiority coalesced into legal doctrines – the doctrine of discovery and of *terra nullius,* where ancient civilizations are portrayed as too primitive to possess legal rights to land cognizable under the common law, justifying the denial of Aboriginal title without treaty making; and the doctrine of parliamentary supremacy, where the solemn promises made in treaties could be modified through laws of general application, by legislative assemblies where Indigenous peoples were denied the right to vote.

I described this as an encounter with "The Ghost" in a paper prepared for the fortieth anniversary of the UBCIC (Mandell 2009). The Ghost is the thing from the past that troubles the present and continues to cause a disturbance, subverting the goals of Indigenous peoples as long as it is being nourished.

> Most Ghosts begin their sojourn in fine fettle. This Ghost was a stowaway in the enterprise of European colonial imperialism. It landed in the newly claimed British Columbia with the first settlers. The Ghost created the kind of thing that a Ghost is really good at building: illusions. The first illusion: by planting the flag, the Crown claimed complete ownership and jurisdiction over everything.

> The Ghost then began to spread lies about the Indigenous peoples who had stewarded the land beautifully and successfully for generations and centuries. As with all good lies, they came with many alternative fallbacks. The Ghost's mantra is denial and its favourite illusion is *terra nullius:* the land was unoccupied; or if occupied, it was by people who were not really civilized; or if civilized, they did not have concepts of land ownership, they did not have real laws; or if they did have laws or rights, they were all extinguished; or if not extinguished, the land they used was just small, spotty, postage stamp-sized parcels (just the size of reserves, actually). And the Ghost was a boaster. The Crown represented a superior race of people with a real government that made real laws and had real state power. The Ghost whispered: "First Nations are primitive – without laws. The Crown is superior – worthy of the greatest respect and absolute deference."
>
> There were, however, other voices that softened and ameliorated the hubris and manifest destiny extolled by the stowaway. The Queen would not take the land and then just turn her back on the Indigenous peoples. No, the Crown would bring great benefits to the Natives, the Ghost proclaimed. The Crown was committed to bringing civilization to these less evolved and less fortunate races. The benevolent goal of assimilation would take time. Meanwhile, the Crown would watch over her Indians and protect them. They were better off living on Indian reserves, but the children should be separated from the regressive influence of their Native communities, put in residential schools where they would be suitably educated. Until the Natives were fully civilized, they could continue their hunting, gathering, and fishing for food – as long as the Crown did not need the land and resources for development. The Crown would let them. The Crown was honourable (Mandell 2009, 55).

What the Indigenous nations sought from Britain in 1981–82 was justice – honouring of treaties and respect for the simple fact that Canada's constitutional makeup is built on the recognition of Indigenous societies who were here first, and whose title to the land and legal orders is woven into the fabric of Confederation, coexisting with, and imposing constraints on, Crown sovereignty. They saw their unique and historical constitutional status as the key to their survival as distinct peoples and to their achievement of self-determination within Confederation. George Manuel wrote that "remaining Indian means that Indian people gain control of the economic and social development of our own communities, within a framework of legal and constitutional guarantees for our land and our institutions" (Manuel and Posluns 1974, 221). Yet Canada's negotiations excluded Indigenous voices from the forums of debate. One elder put it this way: "Canada is inside playing hockey with us, but they won't let us in the door. All we hear from the outside is the call of them scoring."

The Train Leaves the Station

George Manuel often said that a successful strategy brings together action on three levels – political, legal, and in the press. He warned against fighting "bare bones political" or "bare bones legal." He would illustrate this by reference to the *Calder* case (Manuel 1973), where the Nishga went to court in response to the White Paper policy while UBCIC formed to advance Aboriginal title. The campaign to stop the *Canada Bill* was a stunning example of this three-pronged play.[3]

In November 1980, UBCIC and Treaty 9 Nations from northern Ontario made written submissions to the Fourth Russell Tribunal on the Rights of the Indians of the Americas on the plight of the Canadian Indians in the constitutional debate. The tribunal's report condemned Canada's treatment of Indigenous peoples and their exclusion from constitutional reform:

> A significant number of Indian Nations ... in the Americas have preserved their own identity and cultural initiative, in spite of the unremitting efforts of genocide and ethnocide directed against them. The program of cultural destruction and social oppression of the native people of the Americas did not cease when the several countries of the American continent declared their independence. On the contrary ... the machinery of internal colonialism has been continuously consolidated, ruthlessly seeking the disintegration of Indian communities. (Fourth Russell Tribunal 1980, 3)

Before Christmas 1980, hundreds of Indigenous peoples scraped together funds and boarded a train in Vancouver, which they called the Constitution Express. The Express rolled across the country, picking up supporters and support along the way, making headlines day after day. When the train pulled into the Ottawa station, Trudeau announced that the Special Joint Committee on the Constitution, which had previously excluded Indigenous participation, would extend its timetable to February 1981 to hear from Indigenous representatives (Mandell 1984, 173). Instead, the Constitution Express headed to Governor General Ed Schreyer's residence and presented a petition and bill of particulars to be delivered to the Queen, seeking internationally supervised negotiations. Leslie and I created this legal format to serve contemporary purposes, continuing the tradition of the many elegant petitions and powerful letters that had been addressed to heads of Crown governments and to the Queen over the centuries.[4] The petition and bill also went to the Government of Canada, and the Express then journeyed to New York to deliver the bill to the United Nations. The document was inclusive and solution-oriented.

> An opportunity exists to elevate the constitutional amendment to an exercise in statesmanship and nation building. This is a course which we would welcome because it offers the possibility of creating a place for us in Canada's federal system consistent with our rights as Indian Nations. We have given long and serious consideration in many assemblies of our people to the ways in which our special status can be integrated into Canada's federal system. We are convinced that this aim can be accomplished with the result of strengthening our Indian Nations and of strengthening the Government of Canada. This process, however, must take place before the Constitution is amended. (Cited in Mandell 1984, 173–75)

From the government, silence.

UBCIC and the Federation of Saskatchewan Indians (FSI) set up headquarters in London. I took my baby son, Max. Many from the Express headed to Europe, and in the months ahead they lobbied in major

European cities, advising that Canada was misrepresenting the position of the Indigenous nations abroad, and describing the lack of basic human rights and Indigenous peoples' exclusion from constitutional reform.

When Leslie and I arrived in London, a Special Foreign Affairs Select Committee, chaired by Conservative MP Sir Anthony Kershaw, was investigating the role of Westminster with regard to Canada's request to patriate the *BNA Act.* The British Foreign and Commonwealth Office (FCO), led by Secretary of State Lord Peter Carrington, rendered a decision, publicly declaring that any outstanding obligations to the Indigenous peoples of Canada were no longer Britain's responsibility. In spite of the fact that the select committee was an all-party parliamentary advisory body, it deferred to the legal advice of the FCO and advised Parliament that it would be inappropriate to even discuss "Indian issues" during debates on the *Canada Bill.* The committee relied on Mr. J.R. Freeland, a lawyer from the FCO. When asked whether the British courts had ever ruled on whether the Crown had existing legal responsibilities under treaties made with the Indians, Freeland replied: "Not to my knowledge."

UBCIC engaged Ian Brownlie, professor of international law at Oxford University, to provide an opinion about the legal advice of the FCO, and made written submissions, but was refused permission to make representations to the committee (Mandell 1984, 176–77; O'Connell n.d., 4). FSI retained Rosalyn Higgins, professor of international law at the University of London, who wrote a memorandum asking a series of questions: Which obligations devolved? Had notice ever been given to the Indigenous peoples? Could the treaties, as a matter of constitutional and international law, have become the responsibility of Canada? The memorandum was picked up by the London press but was omitted from the official list of submissions to the select committee (Mandell 1984, 177–78; O'Connell n.d., 4–6).

UBCIC prepared two memoranda of law, endorsed by the Indian Association of Alberta and the Four Nations Confederacy of Manitoba, addressed to the attorney general of the United Kingdom. As the attorney general can refrain from placing before Parliament a bill that is legally flawed, the memoranda set out arguments to support this course of action and to seek a judicial opinion about the bill's legality. One memorandum outlined objections to the request from the Indigenous perspective, the second from the perspective of the provinces that opposed patriation for different reasons.

The first memorandum was used for a parliamentary lobby – a huge undertaking, since there were 635 MPs and about 400 "working peers" of the House of Lords. Chiefs and elders from all parts of Canada participated in a spontaneous working coalition, attended prearranged, daily meetings at Westminster, took their case to the press, and met with church and support groups. One challenge was how little was known about Indigenous peoples and their legal and political circumstances. This was apparent at one meeting, jointly attended by chiefs from Saskatchewan and British Columbia. A member of the House of Lords turned to the gathered group and asked where they were from. One chief responded, "Saskatoon, Saskatchewan." The British politician looked at his researcher and said, alarmed: "They don't speak English."

The legal historian Frederic Maitland commented: "So long as law is unwritten, it must be dramatized and acted. Justice must assume a picturesque garb or she will not be seen" (cited in Berman 1983, 58). Those in London dramatized their relationship with the Crown in their own beautiful ways. I can still see the late John Tootoosis, the Cree-speaking elder from Saskatchewan who was eighty-two years old when I was introduced to him in the corridor of Parliament. He was wearing a treaty medal, which had been presented to his great-uncle Poundmaker, one of the chief negotiators of *Treaty No. 6* in 1876. Dancers, drummers, and singers from FSI performed in London, Liverpool, and Birmingham. A delegation attended the annual conferences of both political parties in Blackpool and Brighton, and then travelled to Edinburgh and Glasgow. At these events, they urged that letters be written to MPs to oppose the bill, and many were.

These events contributed to political pressure, which was also building in Canada, to include a provision in the constitution recognizing Aboriginal and treaty rights. But the initial draft bill reflected the Canadian government's legal position, based on the doctrine of discovery, qualifying Aboriginal title – positing that Crown sovereignty is presumed and complete, while Aboriginal title is denied or acknowledged only when proven in court. The draft read: "The aboriginal and treaty rights of the aboriginal peoples of Canada *as they have been or may be defined by the Courts are hereby recognized and affirmed* and can only be modified by amendment" (emphasis added). This passage was later removed from the proposed bill (see Waddell 2003, 18).

The Constitution Express arrived in London in November 1981 and held a potlatch in Westminster. The potlatch was a chaotically stunning ceremony, celebrating ties with the Queen. I hold an enduring memory of my son, Max, now a musician, with a bowl on his head and a wooden spoon in his chubby little hands, drumming on his head in time to the Constitution Express song, which carried the heartbeat of the movement to the world. Members of Parliament as well as church and community groups were invited to witness Indigenous law in action. Families opened up their homes, showing great hospitality and personal support. Through this performance, Britain was reminded about the Queen's word, and about reciprocating the loyalty shown by the Indigenous nations, who honoured their relationship with the Queen through the generations. The British press was fascinated.

Meanwhile, at home in British Columbia, Indigenous women occupied the offices of the Department of Indian Affairs in what was called "the black tower." They demanded an inquiry into the deplorable living conditions on the reserves. After ten days, all the demonstrators were arrested and charged, but all were later acquitted. News of the black tower occupation reached London.

In November 1981, Canada's first ministers reached an agreement acknowledging Aboriginal and treaty rights and the *Royal Proclamation of 1763*. Section 35 read: "Existing Aboriginal and Treaty Rights are hereby recognized and affirmed." Indigenous nations were still on track to stop patriation.

The Court Cases in London

In the English courts, three representative actions were brought or joined by Indigenous nations from Alberta, New Brunswick, Nova Scotia, Ontario, Manitoba, Saskatchewan, British Columbia, and the Northwest Territories. These cases were a testament to the opposition to the *Canada Bill* in Indian country clear across Canada. The cases were *The Queen v. The Secretary of State for Foreign and Commonwealth Affairs* (the Alberta case), *Manuel v. A.G. England* (the Chiefs' case), and *Noltcho v. A.G. England* (the Saskatchewan case).

The Alberta Case

The Alberta case was a judicial review of the FCO decision that all Crown treaty obligations had become obligations of Canada. The case proceeded on law alone. The court found that the treaty partner was now Canada, but the judges offered no coherent explanation of how the treaty relationship could devolve to Canada without the consent, let alone knowledge, of the Indigenous partners.

Lord Denning held that the treaty partner originally was the British Crown, who, at the time, was single and indivisible. But that changed in the first half of the century by constitutional usage and practice. The British sovereign transformed – she became divisible and then divided. The Crown in right of Canada became a sovereign entity, recognized by the Imperial Conference of 1926 and the *Statute of Westminster, 1931,* which gave legal force to that recognition. Lord Denning concluded that the treaty obligations were transferred to Canada without requiring the formal consent of the Indigenous nations. Lord Justice Kerr's theory was that the treaty partner was Canada all along, since by 1867 there was a government in Canada. Crown obligations, therefore, rested with that government, whether the First Nations were told this or not. The question of independence did not matter. Lord Justice May held that independence was the key to the question. When Canada became independent as a result of the *Statute of Westminster, 1931,* whoever the original treaty partner may have been, Canada assumed responsibility for treaties.

Try explaining this at a Band meeting! For the Indigenous treaty nations, their treaty partner was the British sovereign – affectionately referred to as "the Queen." Their relationship to the Queen created transgenerational obligations, sealed by ancient fidelity to one's word (Henderson 2007, 1–3). The Queen's representatives had said as much to them at the time of treaty:

> The Queen has to think of what will come long after to-day. Therefore, the promises we have to make to you are not for to-day only but for to-morrow, not only for you but for your children born and unborn, and the promises we make will be carried out as long as the sun shines above and the water flows in the ocean. (Morris 1880, 96)

They now learned that their Queen had been excused from the marriage, leaving them in perpetual political union with a royal personality who has only ever wanted to steal their land.

At one point in the proceedings, Lord Denning asked, "What do the Indians want?" He wanted to help. And he did. In his last judgment, he assured Indigenous peoples that they had nothing to fear, since fundamental principles of British justice expressed in the *Royal Proclamation* are an implied term of the constitution.

> To my mind, the Royal Proclamation of 1763 was equivalent to an entrenched provision in the Constitution of the colonies in North America. It was binding on the Crown "so long as the sun rises and the river flows." There is nothing, so far as I can see, to warrant any distrust by the Indians of the Government of Canada. But, in case there should be, the discussion in this case will strengthen their hand so as to enable them to withstand any onslaught. They will be able to say that their rights and freedoms have been guaranteed to them by the Crown – originally by the Crown in respect of the United Kingdom, now by the Crown in respect of Canada – but, in any case, by the Crown. No Parliament should do anything to lessen the worth of these guarantees. They should be honoured by the Crown in respect of Canada "so long as the sun rises and the river flows." That promise must never be broken (Alberta case, at paras. 91, 99).

The *Canada Act* was proclaimed on 17 April, and three days later the British government served motions to strike both the Saskatchewan and Chiefs' cases.

The Saskatchewan Case

Like the Alberta case, the Saskatchewan case raised the issue of whether the treaties were binding on the British Crown and whether they imposed obligations that constituted trusts remaining in force (Mandell 1984, 185–89). However, the Saskatchewan case was brought as an action, and would proceed based on evidence that the nations would never have concluded a treaty with Canada – the treaties were concluded with the British sovereign as a protection against Canada. Nonetheless, Vice

Chancellor Megarry relied on Lord Diplock's decision in the House of Lords in the Alberta case:

> In the result, my conclusion is that the Alberta case is decisive of the present case, despite the suggested distinctions, and the language of emphasis of the Appeal Committee in that case requires me to strike out the statement of claim in the Noltcho action, or at the very least justifies me in doing so, and this I do.

The Chiefs' Case

The Chiefs' case (involving UBCIC, the Four Nations Confederacy in Manitoba, and the Grand Council of Treaty 9 in Ontario), also an action, was based on an interpretation of the *Statute of Westminster, 1931.* Section 4 provided that the laws passed by the British Parliament for the overseas dominions would apply only at the request of and with the consent of a dominion. Section 7 stated that the *BNA Act* might be amended only at the request of the Dominion of Canada. The question raised was: Who is the Dominion of Canada? The Chiefs pleaded that the Dominion of Canada included the Indigenous nations, and they were not consulted and did not consent to this request.

The writ was served on 10 December 1981, one day after Jean Chrétien brought the request for patriation from Canada to London. On 25 February, the Chiefs successfully made an application for a speedy trial, and 8 June was set for the hearing (Mandell 1984, 188). On the first day of the second reading of the *Canada Bill,* MP David Ennals, a minister in the Labour government, urged Parliament to await the decision in the Chiefs' case before debating the bill:

> Last week Mr. Justice Vinelot ordered the British Government, who had been pleading for more time, to prepare their defence by March 16. The pressure is on the British Government in the same way as the British Government is putting pressure on us to pass the legislation. Mr. Justice Vinelot said that the Indian case raised issues of great constitutional importance that must be clarified at the earliest moment. He noted that if the Indians succeeded, the Canada Bill would be declared unconstitutional and of no effect. He recognized

> the supremacy of Parliament but noted that it was the proper function of the courts to interpret that supremacy. (United Kingdom 1982)

The British government chose instead to outrun the courts. Prime Minister Margaret Thatcher had made a controversial promise to Trudeau that her government would use its parliamentary majority to secure passage of the *Canada Bill* as quickly as possible, subject to the formalities of due process. On 29 March, the bill was passed by Parliament, and on 31 March, the British government served the motion to strike both the Saskatchewan and Chiefs' cases.

Ironically, the Chiefs' case was struck based on the doctrine of parliamentary supremacy – the very doctrine that Trudeau argued justified the need for a charter of rights and freedoms that would place basic human rights and freedoms beyond the power of any government to override. The *Canada Bill* recited that it was passed by the "Dominion of Canada"; the British Parliament passed it, and that was good enough for the courts.

The debate over the *Canada Act,* as the new legislation was now called, was unlike any other in Canada's history. When the *BNA Act* was passed in 1867, Indigenous peoples were absent from the discussion, as they were on fourteen other occasions until 1975, when amendments to the *BNA Act* were debated in Westminster. By contrast, twenty-seven of the thirty hours spent debating the bill in both Houses of Parliament dealt with the Indigenous peoples of Canada. David Ennals summed up the debate:

> The Indians are not asking for material assistance from us or for money. They are asking us to ensure, as we promised, that their constitutional status is protected in the renewed Canadian Federation. They have asked us for the constitutional tools to enable them to develop their own nationhood, their own forms of self-government and to preserve their traditions. (Cited in Mandell 2009, 31)

And so it came to pass that Indigenous nations were not included in constitutional renewal in 1982, but their objections to the *Canada Bill,* including section 35, were placed on the record through the London legal cases. Constitutional renewal between Crown and Indigenous governments remains Confederation's unfinished business.

Thirty Years Later: 2012

The courts have interpreted section 35 in unfolding layers of dynamic jurisprudence, which no one imagined. The premiers thought the word "existing" meant "extinguished," and argued that the provision was an empty box in *R. v. Sparrow* (1990). But the Supreme Court of Canada held the opposite: "existing" means "unextinguished." In *Haida Nation v. British Columbia* (2004) the court held that section 35 holds the promise of reconciliation of "pre-existing Aboriginal sovereignty with assumed Crown sovereignty" (*Haida Nation v. British Columbia [Minister of Forests]* at para. 20).

Then the courts turned to whether Aboriginal title had been extinguished in British Columbia. In *Delgamuukw* (1997), the governments had every opportunity to establish legitimacy for their century of denial, and the Ghost spoke eloquently in their defence: the doctrines of discovery and *terra nullius* were argued in all of their declining alternatives, and were rejected. The Supreme Court concluded that Aboriginal title has not been extinguished in British Columbia, and it is protected in its full form by section 35; it includes jurisdictional and economic components.

In this way, the jurisprudence accommodates the co-existence of different cultural narratives, titles, laws, and jurisdictions. This is legal pluralism: two legal orders operating on the same landscape. We do not need to choose one of two competing visions. Each way of understanding the world and living in it has important contributions to make to our common future, and this will be accomplished through reconciliation; a process that the Court described as lying at the heart of Aboriginal Crown relations. "We are all here to stay" (*Delgamuukw*, 186). Jurisdiction is not exhaustively divided between Crown governments. Laws that emanate from Indigenous societies form part of the Canadian legal landscape and are part of the rich soil in which the living tree of Canada's constitution is rooted.

Governments never liked what the Supreme Court of Canada had to say, never implemented *Delgamuukw*, and focused their efforts on overturning it. They maintained legal positions based on the repudiated doctrines of discovery and *terra nullius*, and continued the systemic abuses of assumed Crown sovereignty. Then the governments turned the tables through the decision in *William v. British Columbia* (2012). The BC Court of Appeal held that Aboriginal title exists where it can be proven (mirroring the rejected draft of section 35), and confined Aboriginal title to small spots, such as village sites, salt licks, and fishing rocks. The Supreme Court rejected the governments' legal position, which the BC Court of Appeal affirmed – a legal position that finds expression in legislation, policy, government negotiation mandates, and litigation positions. "There is no suggestion in the jurisprudence or scholarship that Aboriginal title is confined to specific village sites or farms" (*Tsilhqot'in*, 42). And the Supreme Court of Canada rejected governments' arguments that a territorial claim of Aboriginal title is legally untenable, declaring Aboriginal title over a sizable portion of Tsilhquot'in territory.

In spite of constitutional developments, the dream of justice is illusive. This is not just the struggle of Indigenous peoples. To borrow from Justice Marshall Rothstein's caution in *R. v. Ipeelee*, the goal of Aboriginal title jurisprudence should not be to "separate Canadians into two camps with two competing interests, but rather to unite them together with the shared goal of 'a just, peaceful and safe society.'" Recognizing the rights of Indigenous peoples does not diminish Canadian society but rather enriches it. Making room for a legal and constitutional future in which we truly are "all here to stay" requires not the finality of Aboriginal title restriction or mitigation (salt licks, fishing stations, and narrow defiles) but the vitality of constitutional recognition through a just federalism built on legal pluralism that acknowledges the legal traditions not only of newcomers, but also of Indigenous peoples.

In meeting rooms on and off reserve, there are current negotiations to settle claims. It is not uncommon for Indigenous communities to spend hours telling Canada's appointed representatives, in passionate and precise detail, of the importance of their territory, the significance of its loss, the troubled state of their communities, the young people killing themselves. At the end of this, the representative pulls out a sheet of paper and begins reading a prepared speech.

The government has made itself into the Ghost with a tin ear. He doesn't even have to say "no." He sits there impassive, waiting. He does not listen. He does not care.

It takes thousands of events and many generations to create a cultural figure, someone who represents the values of the times. The Ghost with the tin ear reading the heartless speech to the Indigenous peoples has become a cultural figure.

While the Ghost is sent out by Canada to meet the Indigenous communities, in reality it is a full-body mask for the more menacing face of government, revealed in Canada's policies to resolve the "Indian Question" since Confederation, expressed in the confidential briefing to cabinet in 1980, and given full voice by Canada's lawyers in court.

What is needed today, right now, without delay, is more than the reconciliation mandated by the courts and ignored by government. Reconciliation is about compromise, making one thing compatible with another. The time for such an achievement is long past. What is needed has a higher purpose with a deeper resonance, because the treatment of First Nations by Canada has been murderous. What is needed is the redemption of the relationship.

Redemption is not possible unless one feels seen. Redemption is not possible unless the other actually understands one's sorrow and views it with compassion.

To have a real conversation is to be changed, because two isolated world views open up and are transformed, like the emerging of an overtone when two melodies are sung. The overtone is not made by either of the singers; it is the magical creation of the two, together. We must get beyond the judge saying, "It's not going to do any good to sing to me." It is time to make a new song, with many voices, sung with inspiration and hope.

Dreaming

Ancient cultures have foretold the coming of an age when domination and control by humanity's fearful ego will pass, when there is no social Darwinian hierarchy of cultures but different narratives, legal orders, and world views coexisting. Here the adaptive genius of Indigenous societies can contribute to our collective survival and evolution.

We are already part of this global shift in consciousness. The United Nations *Declaration on the Rights of Indigenous Peoples* (2008)[5] has been birthed from this dream. It provides a human rights framework that views Indigenous rights as inherent, inalienable human rights, and rests on notions of justice, equality, good faith, self-determination, and rights to culture, language, habitat, and Indigenous institutions. The doctrine of discovery has been repudiated as "racist, scientifically false, legally invalid, morally condemnable and socially unjust."[6]

Canada is a young country with ancient roots. Indigenous laws and legal systems are the deepest roots of our living tree of Confederation.

A strength of Canada's constitution is the development of principles that allow for meaningful interaction and relationship between spheres of law – such as the adoption of the living-tree approach to Canadian federalism – and in Indigenous law, the adoption of the golden thread of the common law, which continues to be alive in a core sense of values. These doctrines are powerful legal metaphors for building bridges of respect, equality, and harmonious reciprocity.

Imagine that a constitutional conference is under way. This is the first time ever that Crown and Indigenous governments are discussing jurisdictional arrangements leading to the attainment of self-determination for Indigenous peoples within Canada. Section 35 holds jurisdictional space for Indigenous legal orders and laws, and subsection 91(24) is also engaged. The federal government, which has wanted out of the "Indian business" for decades, surrenders powers to Indigenous governments to pursue self-government and healing, rather than delegating them to the provinces, which pursued assimilation. New institutions are endorsed for dispute resolution and for shared decision making regarding the use and management of land and resources, providing stewardship solutions for the benefit of seven generations of all cultures, and revenue and benefit sharing and transfer payment agreements will finance Indigenous governments, to compensate for the past, and to vitalize economies.

We cannot erase the past, but we can change history by the stories we tell. We can tell a new story – where Indigenous legal orders, with their sacred connections and transmitted ancient consciousness, have constitutional space to grow and deepen, and our collective endeavour can shine like a light as an example to the world.

If not now, when?

Note: Louise Mandell and Leslie Pinder practised law together as partners at Mandell Pinder for a quarter of a century. Pinder's voice appears in italics, Mandell's in regular font.

Notes

1 *Jules v. Harper Ranch Ltd.* at para. 89, citing the 1837 Resolution of the Select Standing Committee.

2 See *Ontario Mining Co. v. Seybold* at para. 30; *Daniels v. Canada (Minister of Indian Affairs and Northern Development)* at para. 539.

3 The *Canada Bill* would become the *Canada Act* 1982 (U.K.). 1982 c. 11.
4 Examples of declarations and petitions from British Columbia Aboriginal peoples can be found in Maracle 1994, 109–16.
5 http://www.un.org/esa/socdev/unpfii/documents/DRIPS_en.pdf.
6 Similarly, see United Nations *International Convention on the Elimination of All Forms of Racial Discrimination.*

References

Berman, H.J. 1983. *Law and Revolution: The Formation of the Western Legal Tradition.* Cambridge, MA: Harvard University Press.

Borrows, John. 1994. "Constitutional Law from a First Nations Perspective: Self Government and the Royal Proclamation." *University of British Columbia Law Review* 28 (1): 1–47.

Calder v. Attorney General of British Columbia, [1973] S.C.R. 313.

Campbell et al. v. AGBC et al., [2000] BCSC 1123, 79 B.C.L.R. (3d) 122.

Canada. Minister of Indian Affairs and Northern Development. 1969. *Statement of the Government of Canada on Indian Policy.* 28th Parliament, 1st Session. Ottawa: Queen's Printer.

Cumming, Peter, and Neil Mickenberg, eds. 1972. *Native Rights in Canada.* Toronto: Indian-Eskimo Association of Canada.

Daniels v. Canada (Minister of Indian Affairs and Northern Development), [2013] F.C. 6.

Delgamuukw v. British Columbia, [1997] 3 S.C.R. 1010 [*Delgamuukw*].

Fourth Russell Tribunal. *Report of the Fourth Russell Tribunal on the Rights of Indians of the Americas*. 1980. Rotterdam: Workgroup Indian Project.

Haida Nation v. British Columbia (Minister of Forests), [2004] 3 S.C.R. 511.

Henderson, James (Sákéj) Youngblood. 2007. *Treaty Rights in the Constitution of Canada.* Toronto: Thomson Canada.

International Convention on the Elimination of All Forms of Racial Discrimination, New York, 7 March 1966, 660 U.N.T.S. 195 (entered into force 4 January 1969).

Jules v. Harper Ranch Ltd., [1989] 3 C.N.L.R. 674 (BCSC).

Mandell, Louise. 1984. "The Union of British Columbia Indian Chiefs Fights Patriation." *Socialist Studies: A Canadian Annual* 2: 164–95.

—. 2009. "The Ghost." In *Aboriginal Law since Delgamuukw,* edited by Maria Morellato, 55–85. Aurora, ON: Canada Law Book.

Manuel v. A.G. England, [1982] 3 W.L.R. 821; [1982] 3 C.N.L.R. 13 [Chiefs' case].

Manuel, George, and Michael Posluns. 1974. *The Fourth World: An Indian Reality.* Don Mills, ON: Collier-Macmillan.

Maracle, Lee, ed. 1994. *We Get Our Living Like Milk from the Land.* Penticton, BC: Theytus Books.

Morris, Alexander. (1880) 1991. *The Treaties of Canada with the Indians of Manitoba and the North-West Territories.* Reprint, Toronto/Saskatoon: Belfords, Clarke/Fifth House, 1991.

Noltcho v. A.G. England, [1982] 3 All E.R. 786 (Ch.D.) (U.K.) [Saskatchewan case]

O'Connell, Victor. n.d. "The Indian Condition on the Canadian Constitution." Chapter of unpublished manuscript, on file with authors.

Ontario Mining Co. v. Seybold, (1900) 31 O.R. 386.

R. v. Ipeelee, 2012 S.C.C. 13; [2012] 1 S.C.R. 433.

R. v. Sparrow, [1990] 1 S.C.R. 1075.

Tsilqot'in v. British Columbia [2014] S.C.C. 44.

St. Catherine's Milling and Lumber Co. v. The Queen (1888), 14 App. Cas. 46 (P.C.).

The Queen v. The Secretary of State for Foreign and Commonwealth Affairs, [1981] 4 C.N.L.R. 86 (Eng. C.A.).

United Kingdom. House of Commons. 1982. *Debates*. 23 February. http://hansard.millbanksystems.com/commons/1982/feb/23/canada-bill#S6CV0018P0_19820223_HOC_234.

Waddell, Ian. 2003. "Building a Box, Finding Storage Space." In *Box of Treasures or Empty Box? Twenty Years of Section 35*, edited by Ardith Walkem and Halie Bruce, 14–20. Penticton, BC: Theytus Books.

William v. British Columbia, 2012 B.C.C.A. 285.

"28 – Helluva Lot to Lose in 27 Days": The Ad Hoc Committee and Women's Constitutional Activism in the Era of Patriation

10

Marilou McPhedran, Judith Erola, and Loren Braul

> On the view of justice as participatory parity, overcoming injustice means dismantling institutionalized obstacles that prevent some people from participating on a par with others, as full partners in social interaction. (Fraser 2007, 16)

The executive federalism that characterized over fifty years of constitutional negotiations in Canada is not consistent with participatory parity – that is, with the idea that individuals and groups can participate "on a par with others in social interaction" (Fraser 1996, 25). While never claiming the roles of elected First Ministers, leaders of equality-seeking constituencies, including Aboriginal peoples and women, were driven by their commitment to bring participatory parity to the process of building a more inclusive, rights-based constitution for Canada in the early 1980s. This chapter is drawn from the disparate experiences of the co-authors regarding the twenty-seven days that followed the signing, by First Ministers, of the federal-provincial "Kitchen Accord" that became the foundation for the *Constitution Act, 1982.* Tabled in the House of Commons by Prime Minister Pierre Trudeau on Thursday, 5 November 1981, the accord was subsequently modified by the signatories in response to extensive but largely undocumented social mobilization. The final version was adopted in the House on Wednesday, 2 December 1981. From the diverse experiences of co-authors Marilou McPhedran, a legal counsel and strategist for the Ad Hoc Committee of Canadian Women on the Constitution (Ad Hoc Committee or Ad Hockers) throughout the 1980s and 1990s, and the Honourable Judith Erola, minister responsible for the status of women in the 1981 Trudeau cabinet, with research contributions from Loren Braul, we weave together the perspectives of a Trudeau cabinet "insider" (Erola) with an "outsider" citizen (McPhedran). This chapter is derived from speeches at the November 2011 Patriation Negotiations Conference at the University of Alberta, archival materials, redacted federal cabinet documents recently released by the Privy Council Office under the federal *Access to Information Act*, as well as media commentary, to recapture the context and significance of the negotiations on women's constitutional rights. We examine the significance of women's rights among the public and the media, and how tensions between sections 33 and 28 (override provisions, otherwise known as "notwithstanding" or "*non obstante*" clauses) shaped debate, and we conclude that section 28 has played an integral, although understated, role in advancing equality jurisprudence, with considerable potential for further positive influence.[1] With former cabinet minister Erola providing her insider recollections in such detail for the first time, and with recently released cabinet documents from those twenty-seven days (some extensively redacted), we offer additional evidence of the relevance of "drafters' intent" when assessing the impact and value of section 28. We are more optimistic than Ad Hocker Linda Ryan-Nye, who concluded, immediately after the twenty-seven days of struggle arising from the Kitchen Accord: "Twenty-eight was a helluva lot to lose ... but it wasn't a helluva lot to win" (Kome 1983, 95).

Context for the Patriation Negotiations of November 1981

As is carefully documented by Philip Girard in Chapter 6, Quebec's May 1980 referendum on sovereignty association generated political momentum for Trudeau to advance constitutional negotiations. The prime minister sought to exercise the federal government's right to act unilaterally with the passage of a constitutional resolution in the House of Commons and Senate in April 1981, but several provinces, and ultimately the Supreme Court of Canada, disagreed. In September, the Supreme Court advised that the "constitutional convention" of consensus would be preferable to the federal government's imposition of the unilateral "old machinery one more time (Patriation Reference, 789)." It held that constitutional amendments affecting the provinces required "a substantial measure of provincial consent" (Patriation Reference, 905). What became the patriation agreement began to take shape once all ten premiers arrived in Ottawa on 2 November 1981. Leery of Trudeau's proposed endgame of a national referendum on a "People's Package" of constitutional rights and preferring the exercise of executive federalism, nine of the ten premiers formulated an agreement on their own terms.

The Kitchen Accord: Is Equality Burning?

McPhedran: *As the November 1981 negotiations unfolded, women constitutional activists began to "smell" the Kitchen Accord before seeing it. Word leaked from under closed doors that Attorneys General Jean Chrétien (Canada), Roy McMurtry (Ontario), and Roy Romanow (Saskatchewan) had triumphed in securing a consensus of first ministers. Those of us who led the women's rights lobby in the period preceding the April 1981* Canada Act *bill knew we were not a priority during the November 1981 negotiations, but we never contemplated that the prime minister would back away from core Charter protections; he had driven its entrenchment by force of will. Soon we saw how the accord with its new override clause, signed by nine of ten premiers, was their antidote to the allergic reaction many of them had to an entrenched charter of rights – a version of what Harvard law professor and Canadian Paul Weiler (1980, 231) had suggested the year before:*

> *We should entrench our fundamental rights in the Canadian constitution in order to give them the legal and symbolic authority which would be conducive to their flourishing. But we should include in the constitutional Bill of Rights the kind of non obstante provision now contained in our statutory bill, a provision which would allow Parliament to enact (or to re-enact) a statute which would then be legally valid irrespective*

> *of a judicial holding that it is incompatible with the Bill of Rights if and when Parliament states explicitly that this is what it is doing. In typical Canadian fashion, I propose a compromise, between the British version of full-fledged parliamentary sovereignty and the American version of full-fledged judicial authority over constitutional matters.*

The long-term costs of the Kitchen Accord ingredients and who would bear those costs were not clear, but Aboriginal rights had disappeared and the wording in clause 3 of the accord was disturbingly vague on women's rights: "The entrenchment of the full Charter of Rights and Freedoms now before Parliament with the following changes ... (c) A 'notwithstanding' clause covering sections dealing with Fundamental Freedoms, Legal Rights and Equality Rights. Each 'notwithstanding' provision would require reenactment not less frequently than once every five years."

Sharing the Ad Hockers' concern that sex equality had been subjected to the new notwithstanding clause, NDP Member of Parliament Pauline Jewett addressed the prime minister in the House on Friday, 6 November, the day after he tabled the Kitchen Accord version of what became the patriation agreement:

> Clause 28 of the constitutional resolution is a paramountcy clause ... saying *Notwithstanding anything in this Charter, the rights and freedoms referred to in it are guaranteed equally to male and female persons.* What I would like to ask the Prime Minister is if he can tell the House whether clause 28 will continue to have paramountcy. That is, will it override any attempts made to deny equality to women? (Canada, House of Commons 1981a, 12594)

To which Trudeau responded: "Mr. Speaker, I can only answer my impression is that the clause would continue. I have not been involved in the drafting that went on between provincial and federal officials yesterday afternoon and, I believe, during the night as well" (Canada, House of Commons 1981a, 12594). Cabinet documents released in 2012 indicate that, just hours before Ms. Jewett questioned him in the House, Trudeau had presided over a meeting of his cabinet at which no women members were listed as present, and no mention was made of women's rights (Canada, Cabinet Documents 1981a).

Over the weekend, the drafting of the patriation agreement based on the accord continued, and on Monday, 9 November, the prime minister gave an alarming response to a query from the leader of the opposition. The Right Honourable Joe Clark asked him "to confirm ... the opt-out or override provisions do not apply to the guarantee of equality of male and female persons which ... was set down deliberately in a separate section, Section 28." Trudeau replied: "My understanding is that in the work done by federal and provincial officials the 'notwithstanding' clause would indeed apply to that particular section" (Canada, House of Commons 1981b, 12634). At 3:30 p.m. that day, the Cabinet Committee on Priorities and Planning met, again with no women ministers recorded as present. The redacted minutes state:

> On the question of general strategy and tactics, Ministers noted that: a) in any move to amend the Accord (and accordingly to seek the agreement of the other provinces to the particular change(s) proposed), the government must exercise extreme caution to ensure that the amendments did not precipitate a more broadly-based unraveling of the agreement (e.g. in relation to Indians and women). (Canada, Cabinet Documents 1981b, 5)

McPhedran: *Ad Hoc women rejected the accord's new override as an odious surtax on the price of their hard-won constitutional rights. For the First Ministers to shove section 28, which begins "Notwithstanding anything in this Charter" under the new clause, which also began with "notwithstanding" seemed absurd and treacherous. I joined other Ad Hockers bound for Ottawa, hoping our strategy could be to free both section 15 and section 28 from section 33, confident that we would fight, fast and hard – yet again with no funding – for women's constitutional rights.*[2]

Erola:[3] *My personal involvement began just a few months earlier when I was appointed the minister responsible for the status of women – the first woman to hold that post, which caused something of a stir. Imagine! A woman! At this point, the constitution was in its final stages, and due to the brilliant efforts of so many women drafters, it seemed it was now a fait accompli. Then came the final glitch – the fatal Kitchen Accord – the Night of the Long Knives. Gone was section 28, emasculated by a new override. But I was unaware of this change until I was summoned to attend the official ceremony, to sit, along with a number of fellow cabinet ministers, behind the prime minister to indicate solidarity. I was seated beside Mr. Eddie Goldenberg, Mr. Chrétien's adviser, who had a copy of the text. I asked to see it and much to my horror, discovered what had taken place. Shaken, and terribly angry, I rose to leave. I was quietly restrained by Mr. Goldenberg, and in retrospect, by staying I had time to think through future action. Should I resign immediately, or stay to fight another battle? I thought of Emily Murphy,[4] and, choosing to fight – in a cold, quiet rage – I attended a meeting that followed the ceremony.*

My cabinet colleagues were in a celebratory mood, full of compliments to the prime minister and the justice minister on this historic achievement. Without preamble, I expressed my shock and horror that 52 percent of the Canadian population had been left out of the Charter by the override. The prime minister was taken aback. It was obvious that he had not had time to consider all of the implications of the new draft, but he was quick to point out that the provinces had demanded the change, not the federal negotiators. We then proceeded to have a heated argument. No one else participated. They watched, as everyone did when anyone challenged the prime minister. He insisted that it was the fault of the provinces ... the provinces took it out ... there was nothing to be done ... the accord had been agreed to ... it was the provinces that were guilty. He then went on with the all too familiar argument: that rights of women were implicit in the Charter. I responded that that was not good enough (sometimes cold rage is a good ally), that women's rights must be explicit – free and clear as in section 28. No more, no less. The women would not accept less, I insisted.

Then I suggested that we would convince the nine provincial premiers to change their positions; they would withdraw the override on women's rights. Astonished by the suggestion, the prime minister replied, to this effect: "You, Judy, are going to change the premiers' positions? When all of the might of the federal negotiators could not?" "Not me, prime minister. The women of Canada," I brashly asserted. I recall he said, "And how are you going to do that?" I outlined the strength of the powerful lobby that existed as a result of the work leading up to the Charter. We would work together to take on this huge task. We had no tweets in those days, but we did have telephones. To say that the prime minister was dubious is an understatement. He pointed out to me that I, as a member of the federal cabinet, could not be seen actively opposing the patriation agreement, thereby breaking cabinet solidarity. My public statements would have to be careful, I could not participate in press conferences, and my work had to be underground. With that, we had a deal, but it was understood that should this blow up or fail, my resignation would be expected. I recall saying at the time, "Who would want to be the minister responsible for the status of women if women had no status?" The meeting came to an end, and I sensed that, with the exception of my friend and cabinet colleague Monique Bégin, others did not hold much hope for me.

And so began the campaign. Every resource in my political office, in the Status of Women, in the Canadian Advisory Council on the Status of Women and our provincial counterparts was activated. The Rolodexes were mined and the lines began to ring. Lucie Pépin (now a senator), then the new head of the Canadian Advisory Council on the Status of Women, swung into action: travelling, cajoling, connecting. What started as a small group of "elite feminists" became a mass movement of women from just about every socio-economic level.[5] *Volunteers from the Ad Hoc Committee arrived at my offices in the evenings to staff the telephones and arrange meetings. Many, including me, barely slept. Every known women's organization in the country was contacted, urging them to lobby their provincial representatives and premiers. Many activists organized marches to the provincial legislatures. From Quebec came powerful allies – the "Yvettes," that incredible women's movement that mobilized on behalf of Canada in the 1980 Quebec referendum. We had support from the Imperial Order Daughters of the Empire (IODE), nurses unions, the Federation of Women Teachers, the Catholic Women's League, the Business and Professional Women's Clubs, the University Women's Clubs, the Women's Institutes (WI) (oh, I did love them – as a rural child of a WI stalwart, I knew what potent pests they could be), and many others.*

Internally, the Liberal Women's Commission led by Lauris Talmey integrated their network with the lobby. As well, women in the House of

Commons, including Flora MacDonald (PC), Pauline Jewett, and Margaret Mitchell (NDP) whipped (and I mean whipped) their respective caucuses and coaxed their provincial counterparts into agreement. They also kept up the pressure in the House. This was non-partisan cooperation at its finest, and all with one common objective: the sex equality clause had to be free and clear.

It is interesting to note that at no time in this debate did the prime minister, or any of the other ministers, with the exception of Monique Bégin, acknowledge the efforts of women across Canada. Nonetheless, women marched on the provincial legislatures; they flooded the provincial MLAs' offices and their premiers' offices with phone calls. It was quite magnificent.

McPhedran: *The dominant narrative of the patriation negotiations, as a story of executive federalism, with ongoing "dialogue" between legislatures and courts (Hogg and Bushell 1997; Hogg, Bushell Thornton, and Wright 2007), misses a crucial third contributor to democratic constitution making: citizens. Those who tend to control the historical narrative – Canada's mainstream journalists and academics – have seldom acknowledged the role of women constitutional activists as crucial.*[6] *I introduced the "trialogue" metaphor to acknowledge the influence of social movements in constitution making, such as the strengthening of equality rights in section 15 and section 28 of the Charter – for a more inclusive, accurate understanding of how the Canadian constitution was built. Making our constitution work requires sustainable citizen participation in the "living" of the rights and freedoms articulated in the Charter (McPhedran 2007, 101).*

Section 28 – A Helluva Lot to Lose?

In the weeks following the Kitchen Accord, Trudeau continued to deflect criticism to the premiers. "Anything taken out [was] taken out because of the accord ... not because we wanted to take them out but ... as the price of an agreement"; he advised critics of the accord to "get hold of the nine premiers and get them to interpret the accord" (Canada, House of Commons 1981b, 12635).

Lysiane Gagnon immediately challenged the prime minister in her 10 November *La Presse* column titled "Trudeau et les femmes." After recounting the exchange between Jewett and the prime minister over section 28, Gagnon (1981, A8) derided Trudeau's inattention to sex equality rights; while he was clear that the accord limited the rights of Aboriginal peoples, he could not recall clearly the fate of women's rights.[7]

With Gagnon and other journalists advocating women's constitutional equality, section 28 took on separate significance during those twenty-seven days before the accord was tabled in the House of Commons. On 10 November, Trudeau set the goalpost for the women's rights lobby: "If I have the entire support of ... the province of Saskatchewan, and a couple of other provinces, we will revert" (Canada, House of Commons 1981c, 12692). Erola and the Ad Hockers were soon to discover, however, that the goalpost would be moved by the prime minister – from "a couple of other provinces" to unanimity among the accord signatories. When the cabinet met on 12 November, Erola was listed as present, and the un-redacted portions of the cabinet minutes state:

> In opening up the item for discussion, the Prime Minister proposed that the three specific issues for decision be dealt with *in reverse order of political importance and complexity*, i.e. 1) women's rights; 2) aboriginal rights and 3) Quebec.
>
> With reference to the women's rights issue, the Minister of Justice reported that considerable progress had been made on the central question in dispute – i.e., the addition of a *non obstante* clause to Section 28 of the Charter, with all but three of the provinces having indicated their willingness to have the clause withdrawn. Mr. Chrétien noted that the problem seemed initially to have arisen as a consequence of misdirected negotiations at the officials' level, and he was accordingly reasonably confident that the issue could be resolved without reopening the substance of the Accord. (Canada, Cabinet Documents 1981c, 5; emphasis added)

Those cabinet minutes also note:

> Although a number of other Ministers were considerably less sanguine about the possibility of avoiding the heat, the Minister Responsible

> for the Status of Women suggested that even in the absence of a successful resolution of the Section 28 issue, it might be possible for the government to deflect much of the pressure from women's groups to the provincial level, where in fact it was already beginning to focus. (Canada, Cabinet Documents 1981c, 6)

Erola: *Premiers began to accede to our campaign, with Alberta and Ontario leading the way. But we also faced some challenges. Premier Buchanan of Nova Scotia, for example, was nowhere to be found. When I called to ask Flora MacDonald to use her impeccable Conservative Party connections to locate him, she said, "I'll find him ... he used to take my sister out."*[8] *Find him she did – in New York City, where he was meeting with investment bankers. She delivered his agreement as well.*

Day by day, we tracked the progress. Though the official communication between the provinces and the federal government was conducted through the Ministry of Justice, we were generally aware of success before others were. At one point in the heat of battle, the senior bureaucrat at the Status of Women informed me that using the Status of Women resources for political purposes violated the rules. Did I worry? I would face whatever consequences would follow after the war was over.

By 16 November, in response to a question from NDP leader Ed Broadbent, I was able to respond, "I should like to advise honourable members that we are optimistic at this stage, and hope that clause 28 in the general section will remain intact. We may know by the end of the day." However, on 18 November, in response to a question put to him by Flora MacDonald, the prime minister answered that there was lack of unanimity, but refused to name Saskatchewan as the lone holdout. Premier Blakeney was stubbornly holding the equality clause hostage to Aboriginal rights. Behind the scenes, women New Democrats like Pauline Jewett and Marion Dewar went to work. They sought to convince the premier that the equality clause was as important to Aboriginal women as to other Canadian women, perhaps even more so. Outside the legislature in Regina, on a cold, cold night, a massive rally of women demanded that Premier Blakeney support section 28.

McPhedran: *After a flurry of calls to Saskatchewan, we thought we had won. But as Carol Goar reported, on 18 November,*

> *Erola walked, beaming, into ... Question Period ... confident that a full-strength women's rights provision would be in the re-drafted constitutional resolution ... Her aides had ordered champagne ... At 2:50 p.m. Erola sent a brief note to the women "No. It's no go" ... The champagne was cancelled, the press release destroyed. (Goar 1981, A10)*

Media samplings from this period of the patriation negotiations belie retrospective assertions that women's rights received little attention, that they were not considered important, or that the women's lobby was weak, with few credible male allies. All parties supported a motion by Liberal MP Ursula Appolloni calling on NDP MPs to petition Saskatchewan Premier Blakeney (Canada, House of Commons 1981d, 12916). The next day, Premier Blakeney released his telex replies to criticism from the newly elected NDP government in Manitoba (which included women in cabinet), and federal NDP leader Ed Broadbent also weighed in:

> *It is inconceivable to us that in 1981 we could be writing a constitution that ignores the legitimate claims of Canada's original people and denies equality to women. (Maser 1981, A4; Canadian Press 1981, A5)*

Blakeney and the other premiers supported the new section 33 override as a "legislative safety net ... [a] distinctively Canadian [means] of reconciling the British tradition of responsible democratic government with the American tradition of judicially enforced constitutional rights" (Russell and Weiler 1989, B3). Section 33 was also described as a "compromise within a compromise," and its supporters argued that it protected legislative supremacy by allowing the federal and provincial governments to pass legislation notwithstanding certain sections of the Charter, while protecting "language, education, and mobility rights ... the core of Trudeau's 'Just Society'" (Axworthy 2011, 109).

Opposition leader Joe Clark argued that although the accord created "a 'notwithstanding' clause covering sections dealing with Fundamental Freedoms, Legal Rights and Equality Rights ... section 28 is not referred to in the list of exceptions" (Canada, House of Commons 1981b, 12635). But Trudeau remained firm and required unanimity among the signatories to lift section 33 from section 28, and in the revised resolution to adopt the Charter, tabled on 20 November 1981, section 28 was explicitly diminished:

> 28. Notwithstanding anything in this Charter *except section 33*, the rights and freedoms referred to in it are guaranteed equally to male and female persons. (Canada, House of Commons 1981e, 12992; emphasis added)

At that point, the section 33 wording dominated; the social mobilization of thousands of Canadian women across the country during the two weeks following the accord appeared to have failed:

> 33. (1) Parliament or the legislature of a province may expressly declare in an Act of Parliament or of the legislature, as the case may be, that the Act or a provision thereof shall operate notwithstanding a provision included in section 2 or sections 7 to 15 of this Charter, *or s. 28 of this Charter in its application to discrimination based on sex referred to in section 15.* (Canada, House of Commons 1981e, 13042; emphasis added)

Clark immediately moved to "reinstate, without qualification, the guarantee in Section 28 of the equality of male and female persons" (Canada, House of Commons 1981e, 13047) by "[removing] the *non obstante* clause from Section 28" (13050).

Pressure continued to be exerted on Saskatchewan to accede. On 20 November, prominent NDP supporter Stephen Lewis, responding to the province's refusal to lift section 33 from section 28, was quoted as saying: "I'm so disappointed in Blakeney, I can't tell you. I've never heard such addle-pated sophistry on that women's issue stuff as has come from Saskatchewan ... I wouldn't have believed it if I hadn't heard it and watched it – it is junk" (Butler 1981, A5). The *Globe and Mail* published a letter on 21 November from another prominent male ally, retired Senator Eugene Forsey: "Clause 15 is now at the mercy of the 10 provincial legislatures, and Clause 28 has been placed in the same position. This last is a flagrant violation of the accord itself ... Clause 28 is now being disemboweled with the others ... The accord has poisoned the charter" (Forsey 1981, A3). That same day, a *Globe and Mail* article titled "Women Mount Campaign against Charter" noted active resistance by numerous groups and a telegram from the Canadian Civil Liberties Association, "demanding that parliamentary debate on the constitution be postponed because of the 'broken promises to women and natives'" (Mironowicz 1981, A6). Outside Ottawa, 500 women marching in Manitoba against the "barter of rights" in Saskatchewan made the front page of the *Winnipeg Free Press* (Cole 1981, A1). Other front page stories featured "women's groups who have been lobbying furiously" (Hunter and Robb 1981, A1), referencing "mounting pressures" on Premiers Blakeney and Buchanan, with unnamed federal officials described as "watching in astonishment" that intense pressure from lobby groups "appears to be accomplishing what we have been unable to do in the backrooms with quiet persuasion" (Sheppard 1981, A1).

On 23 November, *Toronto Star* columnist Michele Landsberg (1981, D1) drew lessons from how the prime minister had moved the goalpost for liberating section 28 from the section 33 override:

> It's been an extraordinary two weeks. Never before in Canada's history has the moral authority of women stood so high. Never before have so few women accomplished so much on behalf of so many. Never before have the political lessons we must learn been so starkly clear.

Her first lesson was women's self-reliance in safeguarding their rights:

> The Kitchen Constitution, concocted by amateur chefs Jean Chrétien (Liberal), Roy Romanow (NDP) and Roy McMurtry (Tory) showed that all three parties were capable of brushing off equality rights as casually as they might swat a fly. (Landsberg 1981, D1)

The second lesson was the necessity of women's political participation, exemplified by the coordinated efforts of Flora MacDonald (Progressive Conservative), Pauline Jewett (NDP), and Judith Erola (Liberal).

> It is particularly worth noting that there is not a single woman in the legislative caucus of the Saskatchewan New Democrats. I have no

> doubt whatever that this helps to account for Premier Allan Blakeney's obtuse inability to see that women's equality is not a chip in a poker game, to be traded or gambled away. (Landsberg 1981, D1)

For lesson three, Landsberg (1981, D1) declared:

> Every protest counts. The Ad Hoc Committee has clout now because of Doris Anderson's [former chair of the Canadian Advisory Council on the Status of Women] resignation-on-principle last fall, the triumphant Ad Hoc conference on the Constitution, and then the brilliant coup of getting women's equality clauses into the proposed charter. All year, women's rights have enjoyed a snowballing legitimacy.

But she cautioned women against complacency:

> This whole astounding reversal that had the premiers backpedalling so fast that they nearly fell off their tricycles was engineered by a handful of women who took unpaid time off their jobs to do it. No limos, no flunkies, no Telex machines for them ... Canadian women have to snap out of their apathy. Because the Ad Hoc (committee) had to work on a shoestring, there was neither time nor research depth to prepare for battle. Had there been more time, we might have concentrated our fire on the provincial over-ride of Section 15 (anti-discrimination clause) instead of solely on Section 28 (general equality). As it is, we may have irretrievably lost an important legal protection. In the next week or so, we will probably win back Section 28. But we've been burned three times by now and we should have learned **Lesson Number Five**: In the coming days of constitutional wrangle, we must have a women's watchdog in Ottawa to protect our equality rights. (Landsberg 1981, D1)

Back in the House of Commons, the debate persisted, with MPs such as Pauline Jewett poignantly asking on 23 November: "What does this tell us about the position of Canadian women in society? Are we simply a detail, a drafting error?" (Canada, House of Commons 1981f, 13130).

By then, thankfully, the tireless efforts of women across the country had demonstrated that women's rights could not be so easily traded away. That evening, Chrétien finally announced: "I am pleased to be able to inform the House that I have obtained from all provinces which are parties to the accord their agreement that Section 28 on the equality of men and women should apply without the override clause" (13140).

Before adjourning on the evening of 2 December, parliamentarians from all parties stood together in the House of Commons to sing "O Canada," thus marking their acceptance, on behalf of the peoples of Canada, of the resolution that would become the *Constitution Act, 1982*. As a result of extensive social mobilization and political engagement over just twenty-seven days, the resolution restored section 28, which guaranteed all rights in the Charter to male and female persons equally, unfettered by section 33, and reinstated section 35, which recognized the Aboriginal and treaty rights of the Indian, Inuit, and Métis peoples, to be further developed in future constitutional talks with Aboriginal leaders.

Was Section 28 a Helluva Lot to Win?

Three decades after the accord, section 33 has been used sparingly – sixteen times, mostly in Quebec (Kahana 2006, 555).[9] When Alberta proposed to use section 33 to resist Supreme Court–mandated protections against discrimination on the basis of sexual orientation in *Vriend v. Alberta* (1998), there was significant public backlash and the government stood down (Cosh 2004, A21). The threat of section 33 being used to override section 15 equality rights has also largely failed to materialize, which begs the question of whether protecting section 28 from section 33 was a "helluva lot to win." The protective role of the sex equality guarantee cannot be fully quantified, particularly since occasions when the clarity and simplicity of section 28 gave pause to legislators or judges are unlikely to be in any public record.

Among legal scholars, opinion about the usefulness of section 28 remains divided. While equivocal in her personal assessment, noting that section 28 "is seldom alluded to in current *Charter* literature and cases," Diana Majury (2002, 307–9) gave examples of authors with positive views: that section 28 is an enhancement of the section 7 protection of liberty and security of the person for women (citing Sheppard 1986); that section 28 ensures a high level of justification under section 1 for any sex-based distinction (citing Eberts 1985); and that section 28 ensures that gender equality is an immutable right (citing Abella 1986).

Katherine de Jong (1985, 528) argues that section 28 is not the "weak sister," dependent on section 15 for its meaning:

> Section 28 should not be dismissed as being a "mere application" of section 15. The two sections perform different functions and have different legislative histories. Unlike section 15, section 28 is limited to the rights referred to in the *Charter.* Unlike section 15, section 28 is not subject to section 1 or to the section 33 override. Unlike section 15, section 28 came into effect on April 17, 1982 ... The principle of sexual equality is now a legal standard of the highest priority.

In his 1982 annotation of the *Canada Act,* constitutional expert Peter Hogg (1982, 72) forecast that section 28 would have advantages over section 15, including the fact that section 33 cannot override section 28 – an opinion that he maintained in subsequent editions (Hogg 2007, 37, 667). In one of the early decisions referencing section 28, *Boudreau v. Family Benefits Appeal Board* (1984, para. 12), the Nova Scotia Supreme Court Appeal Division affirmed that "legislators have treated sexual discrimination as the most odious form of discrimination and taken away from legislative bodies the right to perpetrate it in the future." Newman (2010b) interpreted this observation to mean that "s.28 prevails over s.33 and a s.33 derogation cannot violate sex equality," although Gibson (1990, 208) argued that section 28 only protects rights guaranteed in the Charter, not equality rights generally. That the prophylactic role of section 28 for other Charter rights is acknowledged leaves scope for its integrative potential as "a substantive part of each right and freedom referred to in the *Charter*" (de Jong 1985, 520). In *R. v. Kapp* (2008), a majority of the Supreme Court of Canada found that although a section has a "confirmatory purpose" in relation to subsection 15(1), this "does not preclude an independent role" for it.

Newman's view (2010a) is that section 28 does not provide substantive rights but merely requires that existing rights under the Charter be applied equally to male and female persons (*McIvor v. Canada [Registrar, Indian and Northern Affairs]* at para. 64). Justices Claire L'Heureux-Dubé,

Charles Gonthier, and Beverley McLachlin attributed the strength of a guarantee to section 28: "The principles of equality, guaranteed by both ss.15 and 28, are a significant influence on interpreting the scope of protection offered by s.7" (*New Brunswick [Minister of Health and Community Services] v. G.[J.]* at para. 60). Baines (2005, 45), who was a key constitutional expert during the intense lobbying to secure section 28 both before and during the patriation negotiations, proposes "that we treat s.28 as neither independently rights bearing nor dependently interpretive, but rather as independently rights enhancing."

If section 33 has so far been just a "paper tiger" (Leeson 2000; Axworthy 2011), would it have mattered if section 28 had been fettered by section 33? Even without jurisprudence on the question, the presence of section 28 as the first "notwithstanding clause" within the Charter means something politically and legally; its strong wording cannot logically be ignored or consigned to merely interpretative status. As affirmed by Justice John Sopinka, for the majority of the Supreme Court of Canada, non-conformity with section 28 is "antithetical to the *Charter* (*R. v. Butler* at para 28)." Nevertheless, the question concerning the relative strength of section 28 in the context of a section 33 application remains to be judicially considered.

McPhedran: *If the Parti Québécois had passed its proposed charter of values, which, among other things, prohibits the wearing of religious symbols in the performance of public duties, we may have seen a contest between section 33 and section 28.*[10] *In the event that such a charter has become law in Quebec and section 33 was invoked, in keeping with past practice for protecting French-language primacy laws, section 33 cannot be used by Quebec to override section 28. In the event of a challenge on behalf of Muslim women for whom wearing a niqab is presented as their protected choice, consistent with their section 15 equality rights and their section 2 fundamental freedom of religious expression in the Canadian Charter, then they may ask the courts to adjudicate their claim against the Quebec law, potentially arguing for the Baines view of section 28 as independently rights enhancing, free of the section 33 override.*

Conclusion: Still a Helluva Lot to Lose

Because sections 15 and 28 were shaped by trialogue, with intense and sustained citizen engagement, much more is at stake in the freeing of section 28 from the clutches of the section 33 override than rarefied judicial or academic interpretation of the Charter. Dodek (2009, 91) warns:

> If those voices, their efforts, are ignored, we send the message that political mobilization is not worth it; that constitutionalism is elitism; that their work has no relevance to the important task of constitutional interpretation. This is a potentially dangerous message to send, especially in a society with decreasing levels of political engagement and increasing levels of public cynicism towards government and public affairs. We need to recognize and celebrate the efforts of our leaders, government officials and our citizens in giving us a constitutionally-entrenched bill of rights. We should be doing this in our classrooms, in the press and in the courts as well.

McPhedran: *Understanding that trialogue is essential to democratic constitution making reinforces the value of section 28, our "made-in-Canada Equal Rights Amendment" (ERA), even as American women gear up to try yet again to achieve an ERA.*[11] *As one of the feminist framers of section 28, I confirm that section 28 was intended to be rights bearing, not to muscle out other rights but to enhance them with gender equality so that the rights of women are equal, not secondary. And I predict that section 28 has an influential future yet to come, likely as an "integrator" protecting and embedding sex equality in complex discrimination scenarios. For example, Aboriginal women can use sections 15 and 28 of the Charter, as well as section 35(4) of the* Constitution Act, 1982: *"Notwithstanding any other provision of this Act, the aboriginal and treaty rights referred to in subsection (1) are guaranteed equally to male and female persons." A "purposive interpretation suggests that section 28 is consistent not only with substantive equality but also with intersectionality" (Baines 2005, 45). We could see Aboriginal women successfully claiming race equality under section 15(1) and sex equality under section 28, "revealing that neither section need be condemned as redundant" (Baines 2005, 67).*

Erola: *I'll end with a quote from Pauline Jewett ... who said in the House of Commons in reference to the Kitchen Accord: "If ever there was a time when a woman should have been in the kitchen!" (Canada, House of Commons 1981f, 13131).*

Notes

1 Section 33 enables the federal and provincial legislatures to pass legislation contrary to section 2 (fundamental freedoms) and sections 7–15 (legal and equality rights) of the *Canadian Charter of Rights and Freedoms* for a period of five years, after which the section must undergo a new process of legislative approval. Section 28 insists that whatever else the Charter may guarantee or limit, the equality of men and women is paramount.

2 The Ad Hoc strategy to focus on liberating section 28 is documented in my 1981 notebook, on loan to the Canadian Museum for Human Rights from York University Libraries, Clara Thomas Archives and Special Collections, Marilou McPhedran fonds. http://archivesfa.library.yorku.ca/fonds/ON00370-f0000514.htm.

3 At the November 2011 Patriation Negotiations conference, Judith Erola spoke publicly, for the first time, about her experiences within cabinet during the twenty-seven days of the Ad Hoc women's lobby against the section 33 override.

4 "Whenever I don't know whether to fight or not, I fight" is attributed to Judge Emily Murphy, who in 1916 presided over the new Women's Police Court as the first woman police magistrate in the British Empire. After her authority was challenged, referencing the *British North America Act* – solely because she was a woman and therefore not entitled to the privilege of her appointment – she became the leader of the "Famous Five" in the "Persons Case," launching *Edwards v. Canada (Attorney General)* through a petition to the Supreme Court of Canada on 27 August 1927 (Millar 1999, 9–15).

5 See Mironowicz 1981, A6, and Cole 1981, A1, discussed further below.

6 As a recent example, in *Canadian Women and the Struggle for Equality* (2012) by Lorna Marsden (a former Trudeau adviser and Liberal senator), the Ad Hoc Committee of Canadian Women on the Constitution is not even mentioned.

7 "J'ai accepté les conditions des sept premiers ministres. Ils proposaient certaines suppressions dont l'une visait les droits des autochtones. L'autre article [28] dont vous parlez en faisant peut-être partie. Je n'en suis pas certain. Je vais verifier ... Les droits des autochtones, M. Trudeau se souvenait de les avoir bradés. Mais les droits des femmes, c'était flou dans sa mémoire. Les femmes, on sait bien, c'est si peu important." (Gagnon 1981, A8)

8 At this point in Erola's speech at the November 2011 conference, Premier Buchanan called out from the audience: "First young lady I kissed in my life was her sister Sheila."

9 In the spring of 1982, as an act of protest against the entrenchment of the Charter without its consent, the Quebec government repealed all provincial legislation and then re-enacted it to include section 33 notwithstanding provisions. Legislation enacted during the rest of the Parti Québécois government's tenure (until December 1985) included section 33 declarations. See Centre for Constitutional Studies, "Notwithstanding Clause," *Constitutional Keywords,* http://ualawccsprod.srv.ualberta.ca/ccs/index.php/i-o/755-notwithstanding-clause.

10 National Assembly of Quebec, Bills – 40th Legislature, 1st Session (20 October 2012 – 5 March 2014). The Explanatory Note to Bill 60 states: "A further purpose of the bill is to specify, in the Charter of human rights and freedoms, that the fundamental rights and freedoms guaranteed by that Charter are to be exercised in a manner consistent with the values of equality between women and men and the primacy of the French language as well as the separation of religions and State and the religious neutrality and secular nature of the State, while making allowance for the emblematic and toponymic elements of Québec's cultural heritage that testify to its history." http://www.assnat.qc.ca/en/travaux-parlementaires/projets-loi/projets-loi-40-1.html.

11 On 22 June 2011, Representative Carolyn B. Maloney (D-NY-14) introduced H.J.Res. 69, Equal Rights Amendment [112th Congress] stating in Section 1: "Equality of rights under the law shall not be denied or abridged by the United States or by any State on account of sex." *Congressional Record,* 112th Congress (2011–12), Library of Congress, http://www.thomas.loc.gov. On 1 August 2013, Rep. Maloney reintroduced the resolution as H.J.Res. 56 in the First Session of the 113th Congress: http://maloney.house.gov/issue/equal-rights-amendment.

References

Abella, Rosalie. 1986. "Limitations on the Right to Equality Before the Law." In *The Limitation of Human Rights in Comparative Constitutional Law,* edited by Armand L.C. de Mestral, 223–32. Cowansville, QC: Yvon Blais.

Axworthy, Thomas S. 2011. "Sword of Damocles or Paper Tiger: Canada's Continuing Debate over the Notwithstanding Clause." In *Recreating Canada: Essays in Honour of Paul Weiler,* edited by Randall Morck, 108–18. Kingston: Queen's Policy Studies Series, School of Policy Studies, Queen's University.

Baines, Beverly. 2005. "Section 28 of the *Canadian Charter of Rights and Freedoms:* A Purposive Interpretation." *Canadian Journal of Women and the Law* 17 (1): 45–70. doi:10.1353/jwl.2006.0004.

Boudreau v. Family Benefits Appeal Board (N.S.), [1984] N.S.J. No. 489, 16 D.L.R. (4th) 610.

Butler, Don. 1981. "Lewis Tears Strip Off Blakeney." *Ottawa Citizen,* 20 November, A5.

Canada. Cabinet Documents. 1981a. 6 November. Serial No. 39–81CBM, Copy No. 162.

—. 9 November. Serial No. 28–81CMPP, Copy No. 161.

—. 12 November. Serial No. 40–81CBM, Copy No. 162.

Canada. House of Commons. 1981a. *Debates.* 32nd Parliament, 1st Session. 6 November.

—. House of Commons. 1981b. *Debates.* 32nd Parliament, 1st Session. 9 November.

—. House of Commons. 1981c. *Debates.* 32nd Parliament, 1st Session. 10 November.

—. House of Commons. 1981d. *Debates.* 32nd Parliament, 1st Session. 19 November.

—. House of Commons. 1981e. *Debates.* 32nd Parliament, 1st Session. 20 November.

—. House of Commons. 1981f. *Debates.* 32nd Parliament, 1st Session. 23 November.

Canadian Press. 1981. "NDP, PCs Want Accord to Cover Natives, Women." *Winnipeg Free Press,* 20 November, A5.

Cole, Brian. 1981. "Women's Rights March Expected to Attract 500." *Winnipeg Free Press,* 20 November, A1.

Cosh, Colby. 2004. "Klein's Eye for the Queer Guy." *National Post,* 16 December, A21.

de Jong, Katherine J. 1985. "Sexual Equality: Interpreting." In *Equality and the Canadian Charter of Rights and Freedoms,* edited by Anne F. Bayefsky and Mary Eberts, 493–528. Toronto: Carswell.

Dodek, Adam M. 2009. "Where Did (Section) 1 Come From? The Debates over the Limitations Clause at the Special Joint Committee of the Senate and the House of Commons on the Constitution, 1980-81." *National Journal of Constitutional Law* 27 (Suppl. Constitutional Update): 77–91.

Eberts, Mary. 1985. "Sex-Based Discrimination and the Charter." In *Equality and the Canadian Charter of Rights and Freedoms,* edited by Anne F. Bayefsky and Mary Eberts, 183–218. Toronto: Carswell.

Edwards v. Canada (Attorney General), [1929] U.K.P.C. 86; [1930] A.C. 124.

Forsey, Eugene. 1981. "Charter 'Shot Full of Holes' by Provinces." *Globe and Mail,* 21 November, A3.

Fraser, Nancy. 1996. "Social Justice in the Age of Identity Politics: Redistribution, Recognition, and Participation." The Tanner Lectures on Human Values, Stanford University. http://tannerlectures.utah.edu/_documents/a-to-z/f/Fraser98.pdf.

—. 2007. "Abnormal Justice." *Critical Inquiry* 34 (3): 393–422. doi:10.1086/589478.

Gagnon, Lysiane. 1981. "Trudeau et les femmes." *La Presse,* 10 November, A8.

Gibson, Dale. 1990. *The Law of the Charter: Equality Rights.* Toronto: Carswell.

Goar, Carol. 1981. "Erola Bloody but Unbowed." *Toronto Star,* 20 November, A10.

Hogg, Peter W. 1982. *Canada Act 1982 Annotated.* Toronto: Carswell.

—. 2007. *Constitutional Law of Canada.* 5th ed., supplemented. Scarborough, ON: Thomson Carswell.

—. and A.A. Bushell. 1997. "The Charter Dialogue between Courts and Legislatures (or Perhaps the Charter of Rights Isn't Such a Bad Thing After All)." *Osgoode Hall Law Journal* 35: 75–124.

Hogg, Peter, A.A. Bushell Thornton, and W.K. Wright. 2007. "Charter Dialogue Revisited – Or 'Much Ado about Metaphors.'" *Osgoode Hall Law Journal* 45: 1–67.

Hunter, Iain, and Jim Robb. 1981. "Fight Looms over Rights Issue." *Ottawa Citizen*, 20 November, A1.

Kahana, Tsvi. 2006. "Legalism, Anxiety and Legislative Constitutionalism." *Queen's Law Journal* 31: 536–77.

Kome, Penney. 1983. *The Taking of Twenty-Eight.* Toronto: Women's Educational Free Press.

Landsberg, Michele. 1981. "Help Wage War for Women's Equality." *Toronto Star*, 23 November, D1. Reprinted in *Writing the Revolution*, by Michele Landsberg, 285–87. Ottawa: Feminist History Society, 2011.

Leeson, Howard. 2000. "Section 33, the Notwithstanding Clause: A Paper Tiger?" *Choices* (New York) 6: 3–24.

Majury, Diana. 2002. "The *Charter*, Equality Rights, and Women: Equivocation and Celebration." *Osgoode Hall Law Journal* 40 (3–4): 298–334.

Marsden, Lorna R. 2012. *Canadian Women and the Struggle for Equality – The Road to Equality since 1867.* Don Mills, ON: Oxford University Press.

Maser, Peter. 1981. "Unanimous House Pressures Blakeney on Sexual Equality." *Ottawa Citizen*, 20 November, A4.

McIvor v. Canada (Registrar, Indian and Northern Affairs), [2009] B.C.J. No. 669 (BCCA).

McPhedran, Marilou. 2007. "A Truer Story: Constitutional Trialogue." *Supreme Court Law Review* 36 (2d): 101–23.

Millar, Nancy. 1999: *The Famous Five: Emily Murphy and the Case of the Missing Persons.* Cochrane, AB: Western Heritage Centre.

Mironowicz, Margaret. 1981. "Women Mount Campaign against Charter." *Globe and Mail*, 21 November, A6.

New Brunswick (Minister of Health and Community Services) v. G.(J.), [1999] 3 S.C.R. 46.

Newman, Dwight. 2010a. "HCHR-7 Charter Values." In *Halsbury's Laws of Canada – Constitutional Law: Charter of Rights*, 31. Markham, ON: LexisNexis Canada.

Newman, Dwight. 2010b. "HCHR – 24 Application of Override." In *Halsbury's Laws of Canada – Constitutional Law: Charter of Rights.* Markham, ON: LexisNexis Canada.

R. v. Butler, [1992] S.C.J. No. 15 [*Butler*].

R. v. Kapp, [2008] 2 S.C.R. 483 [*Kapp*].

Re: Resolution to Amend the Constitution, [1981] 1 S.C.R. 753 *[Patriation Reference]*.

Russell, Peter H., and Paul C. Weiler. 1989. "Don't Scrap the Override Clause – It's a Very Canadian Solution: SU2 Edition." *Toronto Star*, 4 June, B3.

Sheppard, N. Colleen. 1986. "Equality, Ideology and Oppression: Women and the *Canadian Charter of Rights and Freedoms*." *Dalhousie Law Journal* 10: 195–223.

Sheppard, Robert. 1981. "NDP, Tories Vow to Fight for Rights." *Globe and Mail*, 20 November, A1.

Vriend v. Alberta, [1998] 1 S.C.R. 493.

Weiler, Paul C. 1980. "Of Judges and Rights, or Should Canada have a Constitutional Bill of Rights?" *Dalhousie Review* (Summer): 205–34.

PART 4
The Political and Constitutional Consequences of Patriation

Patriation and the Law of Unintended Consequences

11

Peter Russell

It is the nature of big historical events that many of their most important consequences were not intended by those who planned and promoted them. This is the law of unintended consequences, and it applies – in spades – to the patriation of Canada's constitution in 1982. Certainly, the primary aim of those who pushed for patriation was accomplished. The passage of the *Canada Act* by the Parliament of the United Kingdom meant that Canada's formal constitution came home at last to its *patria*, its native land. It now could be amended entirely and solely in Canada. Small-minded legalists might quibble that in cold black-letter law, the Parliament at Westminster could rescind the *Canada Act* and recover its custody of Canada's constitution. But if we can be sure about anything in the future of Canadian politics, it is that we Canadians would simply not succumb to such a crazed rebirth of British imperialism.

The other primary *intended* product of patriation was the *Canadian Charter of Rights and Freedoms*. For Pierre Trudeau, adding a constitutional bill of rights was the priority item in the "People's Package" of constitutional reforms his government presented to the country on 2 October 1980. His insistence that the patriation amendments must include the Charter was the greatest obstacle to securing the substantial measure of provincial support for patriation that the Supreme Court ruled was a constitutional requirement. Although Trudeau either did not anticipate or did not care about the extent to which the Charter would significantly increase the power of the judiciary, as David Schneiderman argues in Chapter 7, that was not the consequence of entrenching a bill of fundamental rights and freedoms in the constitution that mattered to him. He was always most concerned about the broad symbolic power of the Charter to enhance citizens' attachment to the constitution and to the country. As he put it in his final parliamentary speech on the Charter: "Lest the forces of self-interest tear us apart, we must now define the common thread that holds us together" (Canada 1981, 8519). The evidence is clear that the Charter was and remains popular with Canadians, anglophone and francophone, in all parts of the country (Sniderman et al. 1996). How much that contributes to strengthening Canadian unity remains to be seen, and depends to a large extent on one of patriation's unintended consequences, the alienation of Quebec nationalists from Canada's constitutional process. The risk to Canadian unity arising from a repudiation of patriation by Quebec nationalist politicians is the first negative unintended consequence of patriation that I wish to examine in this chapter. The second is much more positive in nature, namely, the important gains made by Canada's Aboriginal peoples through the patriation amendments to the constitution.

Quebec and the Risk to National Unity

Bringing the constitution home was accomplished in a manner that posed great risk to Canada's federal union. In the words of the late Donald Smiley (1983), patriation was a "dangerous deed." For the fathers of patriation – Prime Minister Trudeau and the nine provincial premiers who supported the patriation package – going ahead without the support of the province of Quebec was a calculated risk. They knew there would be trouble from Quebec, but it is very doubtful that they anticipated just how much.

This was partly because of their – particularly Trudeau's – mistaken belief that the force of their rationality could overcome the patriotism of the Québécois and their sense of their place in Canada. After all, Quebec premier René Lévesque, as a member of the "Gang of Eight," had been willing to support an amending formula that, like the one in the patriation package, did not give Quebec a veto. Moreover, to assuage

Quebec's fears that the other provinces and Ottawa might gang up and use their amending power to strip Quebec of its historical powers, the formula contained provision for a dissenting province to opt out of an amendment reducing its powers, and receive fiscal compensation if such an amendment related to education or other cultural matters. And finally, to remove any angst about English-speaking immigrants flooding into Quebec's English-language schools, the Charter section prescribing the right to minority language education would come into force only when the legislature and government of Quebec agreed to it. With these protections, from a logical, rational point of view, surely there was nothing in the patriation package for Quebec's francophone majority to worry about.

And yet, on 25 November 1981, Quebec's National Assembly passed a "decree" by a vote of 78 to 38 rejecting the patriation package. In the final hours of the 1981 constitutional conference, the sponsors of patriation broke the bond of trust between English and French Canada on which Confederation in 1867 had been based, by presenting the Quebec premier with an agreement that the other provinces had negotiated with the federal government, and then going ahead without Quebec's support (Graham 2011). That bald, ugly fact trumps all the arguments about whether Premier Lévesque had been stabbed in the back; or whether Lévesque, by supporting Trudeau's idea of breaking the intergovernmental deadlock with a referendum, broke his bond with the other premiers; or whether Trudeau, by bringing forward constitutional proposals that reduced rather than increased Quebec's powers, broke the promise he had made to Quebec voters in the 1980 referendum campaign. The Supreme Court of Canada might pronounce in the *Quebec Veto Reference* (*Re: Objection by Quebec to a Resolution to Amend the Constitution*) that there was no constitutional convention requiring Quebec's consent to constitutional amendments affecting its powers, but Canada's constitutional politics would demonstrate otherwise – and it is through politics, not the courts, that conventions are made (Dicey 1961).

In 1971, when patriation on the basis of the Victoria Charter appeared imminent, Trudeau and the provincial premiers agreed that patriation would be consummated by the passing of identical resolutions in the Parliament of Canada and all of the provincial legislatures (Russell 2004,

123–24). Although there was no legal requirement for this, it was felt that approval by the elected legislatures of Canada would give the patriated constitution a stronger democratic root in Canada. Approval by the country's elected legislatures was regarded as a requirement of political legitimacy rather than legal legitimacy. That this kind of political legitimacy was not attempted for patriation in 1981 reflects the patriation patrons' fear of displaying a fundamental division in the Canadian body politic. The unwillingness to even try to win democratic approval for Canada's patriated constitution should not blind us to the fact – ugly as it may be – that in 1982, Canadians, in their deep diversity, did not and could not act as a sovereign people. Those, like Eric Adams in Chapter 3, who see patriation as an exercise in constitutional nationalism should bear that reality in mind.

Canada's complex multinational nature makes constitutional nationalism a problematic aspiration (Gagnon and Tully 2001). While the national allegiance and national identity of a majority of English-speaking Canadians attaches strongly and solely to Canada, that is not the case for a majority of Québécois and a majority of First Nations Canadians. These two groups of Canadians harbour a dual sense of national identity. Most members of these groups identify with Canada and have an allegiance to it, but they also identify with a historic nation, Québécois with Quebec and First Nations people with their particular nation (Mi'kmaq, Haida, Mohawk, etc). When causes presented under the banner of Canadian nationalism conflict with loyalty to their historic nations, it is the latter that for many is likely to prevail. This was the case for much of French Quebec in the patriation crisis. The great majority of francophone Quebecers liked the Charter and were in favour of patriating Canada's constitution from Great Britain. For many of them, however, these constitutional changes were drained of legitimacy when they appeared to have been carried out in a manner that denied Quebec's special place in Canada as the home of one of its founding peoples.

Soon after patriation, Canadians – or, more accurately, their political leaders – took up the challenge of patching the tears in Canada's constitutional fabric. The country entered a long season of mega-constitutional politics designed to win the support of Quebec, the

Aboriginal peoples, and everyone else for a constitution that all could endorse: four First Ministers' conferences with Aboriginal leaders, the three-year agony of Meech Lake, and the mammoth effort of the Charlottetown Accord prompted by Quebec's Estates General and ending in rejection by Canadian voters in the first nationwide referendum. These exhausting and ultimately futile efforts to achieve a popular constitutional accord were, in large measure, the unintended consequence of patriation, and in the end all they gave us was a serious case of constitutional constipation.

On the heels of these mega-constitutional failures came the 1995 Quebec referendum on another convoluted proposal for Quebec independence. This time, it came within 31,000 votes of winning the support of a majority. The closeness of that vote, which fed so much on the Québécois sense of betrayal and the futility of seeking their constitutional objectives within the federation, was perhaps the greatest unintended consequence of patriation and a measure of the risk its sponsors took in 1981.

At the 2011 Patriation Negotiations Conference at the University of Alberta, Edward Goldenberg, who served as special constitutional adviser to Justice Minister Jean Chrétien from 1980 to 1982, challenged the view that the failed efforts at constitutional reform that followed patriation and the closeness of the vote in the 1995 Quebec referendum had anything to do with the decision of Trudeau and nine premiers to proceed with their patriation package without the support of the Quebec government or legislature. He argued that it was Prime Minister Brian Mulroney's foolishness in responding positively to Premier Robert Bourassa's 1985 proposals to accommodate Quebec that plunged the country into the messy constitutional negotiations that followed, the failure of which prompted the 1995 referendum. I find this a difficult argument to accept. One would have to believe the counterfactual proposition that if Mulroney had turned Bourassa down and said that Quebec must learn to live with patriation and give up its nationalist agenda of securing stronger recognition of Quebec's special status in the Canadian federation, Quebec's constitutional discontent would have simmered down and we Canadians would have lived happily ever after. Admittedly, counterfactuals are impossible to prove either way, but I find it difficult to believe that rejecting Bourassa's proposals would have ushered in an era of constitutional peace in Canada.

A number of those who spoke at the 2011 Patriation Negotiations Conference, including former premiers and some of the officials who participated in the 1981 negotiations, argued that the risk of patriation without Quebec had to be taken; otherwise, patriation would have been indefinitely postponed. Those who took that position were convinced that Lévesque, in the end, would not agree to anything that would strengthen Canada. I question the certainty of that belief.

Before the November 1981 First Ministers' conference, Lévesque had agreed with seven other premiers on an amending formula that would not give Quebec a veto and that was similar to the amending formula that was actually enacted in the *Constitution Act, 1982*. However, when he met with the Gang of Eight on the morning of Thursday, 5 November, the package that had been put together overnight was missing the clause from the amending formula that would compensate provinces that opted out. This infuriated Lévesque. He was even more infuriated that Quebec was not involved in putting together the package that his Gang of Eight allies were now supporting. We will never know what would have happened if Trudeau and the premiers had taken more time that Thursday – perhaps adjourning their meeting for a while and giving Lévesque some time to calm down. In a less heated atmosphere, there might have been a real effort to see whether changes could be made that would win Lévesque's support. In the days that followed the First Ministers' conference, Trudeau did offer two changes aimed at meeting Quebec's concerns: compensation for provinces that opted out was restored to the amending formula, and the right of English-speaking immigrants to English-language education in Quebec would not take effect until Quebec's National Assembly gave its consent. Inserting these changes into the *Constitution Act, 1982* did not win Lévesque's support for patriation, however. By the time Trudeau made these concessions, Lévesque had taken a strong political stand and aroused such furor over Quebec's betrayal during the so-called Night of the Long Knives that there was no turning back. But can we be sure that if those concessions had been offered later in the day on 5 November Lévesque would still have opposed patriation?

In her presentation to the 2011 Patriation Negotiations Conference, Chantal Hébert reminded us that after patriation, when Lévesque was opposition leader in Quebec, he took *le beau risque* in supporting the Meech Lake proposals. I doubt that her point swayed those who believe Lévesque would never have made a deal short of Quebec independence. The discussion at the 2011 conference left no doubt that back in 1981 many of the key players, in their heart of hearts, believed Lévesque was not bargaining in good faith. They did not trust him and, in the end, he did not trust them. Thus, the loss of political trust between the leaders of English Canada and Quebec was another unintended consequence of the patriation moment. Whether or not that trust ever existed is another question. I doubt that it does today.

The Gains of Aboriginal Peoples

Unlike the risk to national unity that stemmed from patriation of the constitution without Quebec's consent, another unintended consequence of patriation was positive – namely, the constitutional resources secured by Canada's Aboriginal peoples through the patriation process. Indeed, I would argue that the Aboriginal peoples were the greatest beneficiaries of patriation. It is deeply ironic that a constitutional reform process that was initiated to meet Quebec's aspirations, and from which the Aboriginal peoples were largely excluded, culminated in a package of reforms that ignored Quebec's demands, on the one hand, but yielded substantial gains for Aboriginal peoples, on the other.

As constitutional politics heated up in the late 1960s and again after the election of a sovereigntist government in Quebec in 1976, Aboriginal leaders sensed that the opening up of Canada's constitutional reform agenda might give them an opportunity to secure their vital constitutional interests. Associations and networks of Aboriginal peoples prepared to place their aspirations on the agenda. During Joe Clark's brief tenure as prime minister, Aboriginal organizations came close to getting a seat at the constitutional table, but when intergovernmental constitutional negotiations resumed after Trudeau's return to power and the 1980 Quebec referendum, Aboriginal peoples and their issues were left off the table. In Chapter 9, Louise Mandell and Leslie Hall Pinder discuss how, at this point, status and non-status Indian, Métis, and Inuit organizations worked hard outside the First Ministers process to mobilize support for Indigenous concerns. These efforts included a "Constitution Express" to Ottawa and establishment of a lobbying base in London (Sanders 1983).

Aboriginal organizations scored effectively when they participated in the joint parliamentary committee's televised hearings on Trudeau's 1980 "People's Package." The Trudeau government sensed that it could increase public support for its constitutional proposals by responding positively to this pressure. In January 1981, it agreed to add amendments that were in line with proposals of the National Indian Brotherhood, the Native Council of Canada, and the Inuit Committee on National Issues. Both opposition parties supported this agreement.

The three amendments were (1) a section of the constitution recognizing Aboriginal and treaty rights, (2) a section of the Charter of Rights and Freedoms protecting the rights and freedoms of Aboriginal peoples recognized in the *Royal Proclamation of 1763* and subsequent treaties from being abrogated or derogated by other rights and freedoms enumerated in the Charter, and (3) another section of the constitution requiring a First Ministers' conference involving Aboriginal representatives within a year, to discuss constitutional matters affecting Aboriginal peoples. Although the commitment to add these three amendments to the patriation package was strongly challenged over the next year, eventually, with a little bit of tweaking, they became part of the *Constitution Act, 1982.*

The most notorious tweak was the insistence of Alberta's Premier Peter Lougheed that the word "existing" be inserted before the "aboriginal and treaty rights" recognized and affirmed in section 35 of the *Constitution Act, 1982.* At the time, no one knew what this meant, but it seemed to save Lougheed and perhaps other premiers from having nightmares about Aboriginal peoples having too many rights. At the 2011 Patriation Negotiations Conference, I asked Lougheed about his intentions in having the word "existing" inserted in the clause. He told me and the other conference attendees that he wanted the rights that were recognized to be those that applied in the contemporary context, without dragging in a lot of history. Given that Aboriginal rights stem from the situation of Aboriginal peoples before the assertion of sovereignty by European powers and from historical treaties, it is not easy to understand Premier Lougheed's thinking.

The three amendments relating to Aboriginal peoples by no means met all the constitutional concerns of Aboriginal peoples. Some groups, notably the Union of British Columbia Indian Chiefs, argued that it was a mistake for Indians to participate in a Canadian constitutional process. Since their nations' relationships were with the British Crown, they would pressure the government of the United Kingdom to prevent provisions in the Canadian constitution relating to Indians, notably sections 91(24) and 109, from coming under Canadian control without their consent (Sanders 1983). Their arguments got a much fuller hearing in London than in Canada. Indeed, nearly 80 percent of the time the British Parliament spent dealing with the *Canada Act* was devoted to Aboriginal matters. In the end, the Indian lobby in London failed to persuade either Lord Denning in the High Court or British parliamentarians that their concerns were grounds for delaying patriation.

Even for Aboriginal leaders who accepted participation in Canada's constitutional process, the amended package failed to meet two critical constitutional needs: recognition of Aboriginal peoples' inherent sovereignty and, corollary to this, the need for their consent to any modification of their constitutional rights. In the end, only one Aboriginal organization, the Métis Association of Alberta, supported the wording of the section recognizing Aboriginal and treaty rights. All three national Aboriginal organizations opposed the entire constitutional package. Despite this widespread opposition, I contend that the 1982 constitutional package has been of considerable value to Aboriginal peoples.

Consider first the recognition clause, section 35 of the *Constitution Act, 1982,* and the modification of its wording to state that it affirmed and recognized "existing aboriginal and treaty rights." For quite some time after 1982, many Aboriginal people held the not unreasonable belief that "existing" was truly a weasel word that would be used by governments and courts to deny that section 35 changed anything so far as giving effect to their peoples' rights was concerned. At the three constitutional conferences held in the mid-1980s with First Ministers, Aboriginal leaders struggled to explain that they had never given up, and indeed could not give up, the obligation inherent in their creation to be responsible for their societies (Hawkes 1989). Their failure to secure support for constitutional recognition of this "inherent right" underscored their fears that what they had in section 35 was not even a glass half full. In 1990, however, when the Supreme Court of Canada, in *R. v. Sparrow*, made its first pronouncement on the status and nature of the rights recognized in section 35, it became clear that the glass was not empty and might be more than half-full.

The Supreme Court's rhetoric in *Sparrow* – and it was a unanimous court – was splendid. The justices acknowledged that it was strong presentations made by Aboriginal organizations in the patriation process that put section 35 in the constitution, and reasoned that for the courts to drain it of meaning would be an act of betrayal. "A generous, liberal interpretation" of the words in section 35 was required (*R. v. Sparrow* 1990, 1106). The court went further and delivered some substance: "existing" did not mean that Aboriginal peoples' only constitutional rights were those that survived years of regulation by federal and provincial governments. Aboriginal rights could be extinguished only when legislation expressed a clear intention to do so and met a high justificatory standard that demonstrated to Aboriginal peoples "that their rights are taken seriously." Similarly, in *R. v. Sioui* (1990), the Supreme Court held that courts must "adopt a generous and liberal approach" in interpreting treaties (1036).

After *Sparrow* and *Sioui*, the judicial treatment of section 35 went through what I have described elsewhere as a roller-coaster ride (Russell 1998). There were certainly some real gains, as in *Delgamuukw v. British Columbia* (1991), where the Supreme Court, overriding previous jurisprudence, held that Aboriginal title, where it applies and has not been extinguished, constitutes a real proprietary right of an Aboriginal people that includes subsurface mineral rights. But mixed in with this sweet for Aboriginal peoples there was a lot of bitter. Non-Aboriginal judges would be the ones to identify the practices and activities that are essential to Aboriginal societies and that warrant constitutional protection. Non-Aboriginal justices would be the arbiters of the Crown's and the Indians' treaty obligations. And all this would be done, in Chief Justice Antonio Lamer's words, with the aim of reconciling Aboriginal peoples with the sovereignty of the Crown. However, despite the justices' condescension and doctrinaire commitment to a continuation of imperial British/Canadian state sovereignty over Aboriginal peoples – what Grace Woo (2011) refers to as "Ghost Dancing with Colonialism" – many of these decisions on section 35 enhanced Aboriginal peoples' power to protect their interests.

Section 37.1 of the *Constitution Act, 1982* required a First Ministers' conference within a year to deal with matters of concern to Aboriginal peoples. This resulted in the one and only time that the general procedure for amending the constitution has been used since patriation. This in itself was surely not what the patriation leaders expected or intended, but it was useful for securing Aboriginal interests. The 1983 conference produced an amendment, spelled out in the *Constitutional Amendment Proclamation, 1983,* that added subsection 3 to section 35, removing any doubt that constitutionally protected treaty rights include rights incorporated in modern land claims agreements. This amendment constitutionalized the land claims process, ensuring that agreements with Aboriginal peoples on land issues and on self-government provisions contained in such agreements are entrenched and cannot be unilaterally altered by the federal government or Parliament. This provision goes some way towards meeting the Aboriginal principle that the consent of an Aboriginal people is required for constitutional changes relating to them. The 1983 amendment added a further subsection to section 35 ensuring that Aboriginal and treaty rights "are guaranteed equally to male and female persons."

The real sleeper in the troika of constitutional changes relating to Aboriginal peoples was section 25 of the *Canadian Charter of Rights and Freedoms.* This section reads as follows:

> The guarantee in this Charter of certain rights and freedoms shall not be construed so as to abrogate or derogate from any aboriginal, treaty or other rights or freedoms that pertain to the aboriginal peoples of Canada including
>
> a) any rights or freedoms that have been recognized by the Royal Proclamation of 7 October 1763; and
> b) any rights or freedoms that now exist by way of land claims agreements or may be so acquired.

In effect, this section protects the rights and freedoms of Aboriginal peoples that Britain recognized in the *Royal Proclamation of 1763* from being eroded or lessened by the application of the constitutional rights and freedoms newly recognized in the Charter.

Section 25 must be the part of the Charter least known to the non-Aboriginal population. Most non-Aboriginal Canadians are unaware of the *Royal Proclamation* or the circumstances under which it was presented to, and negotiated with, nations native to North America. Many Canadians who have an Aboriginal background and identify with one of the historic nations regard the proclamation as their Magna Carta, however. Further, they regard the 1764 Treaty of Niagara, through which representatives of native North Americans accepted the proclamation's terms as conditions for maintaining peaceful relations with Great Britain and her colonists, as their fundamental constitutional agreement with Britain and its successor state, Canada (Borrows 1997).

Three points in the *Royal Proclamation* are of crucial importance. First, the proclamation recognized that these nations indigenous to North America possessed – that is, owned – the lands and waters on which they lived and which sustained them. Second, the British monarch committed to not permitting settlement on Indian lands that had not been ceded to the Crown through a proper meeting or assembly of the nation concerned. In effect, that is a commitment to a treaty process for obtaining access to First Nations' historical territory for settlement or economic development. Third, King George III addressed the Native peoples to whom this part of his 1763 proclamation was directed, not as his subjects but as "the several Nations or Tribes of Indians, with whom We are connected and who live under our Protection." In effect, this language recognized that the Indian nations were being invited to enter into a relationship with Britain that did not require the surrender of their political independence. The reference to the Indians living under the King's protection was a tad presumptuous, given that the strategic purpose of the Indian sections of the proclamation was to persuade the nations participating in the Pontiac uprising to cease burning British forts and attacking British settlements. Nonetheless, this recognition of the Indian nations' independence was crucial to the twenty-four nations whose representatives met with the British emissary, Sir William Johnson, at Fort Niagara in July 1764. Later that year, Johnson wrote to General Thomas Gage, upbraiding him for referring to Indians as British subjects:

> You may be assured that none of the Six Nations or Western Indians ever declared themselves *subjects,* or will ever consider themselves in that light, while they have any men or an open country to retire to ... The very idea of subjection would fill them with horror. (Stone 1865)

In my view, the treaty made at Fort Niagara in 1764 should be regarded as our first Confederation. I say this even though the terms of that agreement were not respected by Britain or Canada for a very long period. The part of the *Royal Proclamation of 1763* pertaining to relations with Aboriginal peoples, and the principles underlying it, discussed and achieved in Covenant Chain at Fort Niagara in 1764, remain good law – good Canadian constitutional law – and a sound foundation for a just and mutually beneficial relationship between Aboriginal peoples and Canada.

Conclusion

Patriation of Canada's constitution in 1982 shows how wonderfully interesting and unpredictable history can be. Only through the workings of the law of unintended consequences could a constitutional process – originally initiated to accommodate a post–Quiet Revolution Quebec with the Canadian federation, and excluding Aboriginal peoples – have resulted in alienating Quebec's francophone majority and risking the unity of the country, while taking a giant step towards recovering the basis on which Aboriginal peoples originally consented to sharing their country with newcomers.

In constitution making, we truly know not what we do. This has been true of Canada since its beginning in the 1760s. The foundations of Canada as a political community are Great Britain's incomplete conquests of New France and nations native to North America. After Wolfe defeated Montcalm on the Plains of Abraham, the British did not completely conquer *les canadiens* in the way that just a few years earlier they had totally conquered and expelled the Acadians. They made their peace with the French Canadians, who vastly outnumbered them, by allowing them to maintain their language, their civil law, and their religion, which at that time defined their distinct society. Similarly, the British did not try to conquer the Indian nations who resisted their invasion of the Indian territory after the fall of New France. Instead, the British made peace with Indian nations at Niagara in 1764 on terms set out in the *Royal Proclamation of 1763.* In both cases, the British chose accommodation rather than conquest mainly for practical reasons. It was the easiest and least expensive way of consolidating their position in the northern and western reaches of North America. Little did British policy-makers foresee that this policy of accommodation would over time yield a constitutional ethic of national pluralism that would become a fundamental principle of the Canadian constitution. There were times when the British and Canadian governments were prepared to abandon this national pluralism and, so to speak, complete the conquests. The attempt, following Lord Durham's report, to assimilate French Canadians into a political community dominated by English-speaking people, and the efforts of Canada through the *Indian Act* to destroy the historical Indian nations and totally assimilate their people into the Canadian mainstream are the leading examples. The nations within Canada survived, however. At Confederation, French Canadians got a province in which they would be a majority with the power to protect and nurture their distinct society. After the Second World War, a Canada that was supporting decolonization internationally and repudiating racism was more open to recognizing the rights of colonized Aboriginal peoples within Canada.

Although the Québécois were unable to secure more powers for their province in the patriation process, by repudiating patriation they made it clear that they would not accept a situation that appeared to leave what they had won at the time of Confederation in the hands of Canada's English-speaking majority. On the other hand, the Aboriginal peoples, who were entirely left out of Confederation, managed to secure through patriation formal recognition of their rights and their role in Canada's constitutional process. Although the consequences of patriation that I have discussed may have been unintended, they surely have deep roots in Canadian history. The lesson of patriation is that any efforts in the future to reform Canada's constitution cannot afford to ignore the principles embedded in the incomplete conquests on which Canada was founded.

References

Borrows, John. 1997. "Wampum at Niagara: The Royal Proclamation, Canadian Legal History and Self-Government." In *Aboriginal and Treaty Rights in Canada*, edited by Michael Asch, 155–72. Vancouver: UBC Press.

Canada. House of Commons. 1981. *Debates*. 32nd Parliament, 1st Session. 2 March.

Delgamuukw v. British Columbia, [1997] 3 S.C.R. 1010.

Dicey, A.V. 1961. *Introduction to the Study of the Law of the Constitution*. 10th ed. London: Macmillan.

Gagnon, Alain-G., and James Tully, eds. 2001. *Multinational Democracies*. Cambridge, UK: Cambridge University Press.

Graham, Ron. 2011. *The Last Act: Pierre Trudeau, the Gang of Eight and the Fight for Canada*. Toronto: Allen Lane.

Hawkes, David. 1989. *Aboriginal Peoples and Constitutional Reform: What Have We Learned*. Kingston: Institute of Intergovernmental Relations, Queen's University.

R. v. Sioui, [1990] 1 S.C.R. 1025.

R. v. Sparrow, [1990] 1 S.C.R 1075.

Re: Objection by Quebec to a Resolution to Amend the Constitution, [1982] 2 S.C.R. 793 [*Quebec Veto Reference*].

Russell, Peter H. 1998. "High Courts and the Rights of Aboriginal Peoples." *Saskatchewan Law Review* 61: 247–76.

—. 2004. *Constitutional Odyssey: Can Canadians Become a Sovereign People?* 3rd ed. Toronto: University of Toronto Press.

Sanders, Douglas. 1983. "The Indian Lobby." In *And No One Cheered: Federalism, Democracy and the Constitution Act*, edited by Keith Banting and Richard Simeon, 301–32. Toronto: Methuen.

Sniderman, Paul M., Joseph F. Fletcher, Peter H. Russell, and Philip E. Tetlock. 1996. *The Clash of Rights: Liberty, Equality, and Legitimacy in Pluralist Democracy*. New Haven, CT: Yale University Press.

Smiley, Donald. 1983. "A Dangerous Deed: The Constitution Act, 1982." In *And No One Cheered: Federalism, Democracy and the Constitution Act*, edited by Keith Banting and Richard Simeon, 74–95. Toronto: Methuen.

Stone, William L. 1865. *The Life and Times of Sir William Johnson, BART*. Vol. 2. 228. Albany, NY: J. Munsell.

Woo, Grace Li Xiu. 2011. *Ghost Dancing with Colonialism: Decolonization and Indigenous Rights at the Supreme Court of Canada*. Vancouver: UBC Press.

12

Canadian Federalism since Patriation: Advancing a Federalism of Empowerment

Alain-G. Gagnon and Alex Schwartz

The patriation agreement of November 1981 was intended to provide Canadians with a founding constitutional moment, one that would inaugurate new constitutional practices. Pierre Trudeau's commitment to "renew the constitution" following a "No" victory in the 1980 Quebec referendum on sovereignty association was a central motivator for constitutional reform. However, a large proportion of Quebecers of all political stripes felt that the country was no longer in tune with their aspirations as a founding people. Indeed, as Peter Russell argues in Chapter 11, the patriation agreement actually exacerbated tensions between Quebec and its partners in the Canadian federation. If anything, patriation reopened old wounds and undermined federal practices. This chapter advances a normative approach for diagnosing and addressing the main inadequacies of Canadian federalism in the post-patriation era.

The argument proceeds in three stages. First, we outline how federalism can serve various goals or functions and so should not be reduced to any single telos. Second, we sketch a set of criteria for a federalism that is pluralistic in the sense that it can be endorsed from various philosophical and normative positions and, at its best, serve diverse values and purposes. Third, we explain how Canadian federalism has failed to satisfy these criteria with respect to the place of Quebec in Canada. We argue that Canada's constitutional order has been stubbornly unresponsive to the expression of Quebec identity, and prone to a centralizing and monistic focus on functional efficiency at the expense of other federal values. Finally, we consider how one of the main theoretical discourses to have emerged in response to the constitutional settlement – what might be called dialogic recognition – may, paradoxically, be perpetuating the impoverished state of Canadian federalism. This approach tends to prioritize indefinite constitutional conversation above substantive outcomes. In brief, we contend that the procedural emphasis of dialogic recognition encourages unhealthy federal dynamics that could be overcome by a substantive approach inspired by the idea of a "federalism of empowerment."

Competing Conceptions of Federalism

At the most abstract and general level, federations are polities that combine elements of shared rule and self-rule through at least two territorial orders of government constituting distinct but overlapping political communities endowed with distinct (if sometimes overlapping) powers and obligations (Elazar 1987; Gagnon 1993). However, there is no academic consensus regarding the general purpose or telos of federalism. Indeed, rather than appealing to a single purpose or value as an ultimate or universal justification for federalism, political theorists have sought to advance federalism in terms of various and sometimes contradictory goals. Generally speaking, these reflect three overarching normative conceptions of federalism: (1) utilitarian, (2) liberal, and (3) democratic-communitarian.

Utilitarian Conceptions of Federalism

Utilitarian conceptions of federalism are those that justify federalism as a means of maximizing general utility (where utility is understood primarily as a function of economic efficiency). In this view, federalism promotes efficiency through interjurisdictional competition within the context of a common economic market. Presuming that people are reasonably mobile, federalism allows individuals to move and settle in those jurisdictions that offer them the best "deal" on their preferred "bundle" of public goods (Breton 1965). Thus, federalism promotes an optimal pairing of people to laws and public policies while simultaneously encouraging the constituent units of the federation to compete with one another to provide the most attractive package of desired public goods (Inman 2007). Even in the absence of a reasonably mobile citizenry, "politically independent provinces may engage in efficiency-enhancing 'yardstick competition' as citizens observe what their neighbours are doing and demand comparable service or tax performances from their own elected leaders" (Inman 2007, 525). In turn, competition among diverse jurisdictions promotes innovation, the constituent units serving as a kind of "laboratory" for "novel social and economic experiments" (see *New State Ice Co. v. Liebmann* 285 U.S. 262 (1932), 311, *per* Brandeis J. in dissent). In the Canadian context, policy experimentation at the level of the constituent unit of the federation has often become the model for federation-wide social programs (Gagnon 1993; Hogg 2009, 343).

Liberal Conceptions of Federalism

Liberal conceptions of federalism justify federalism as a check against the abuse of centralized state power. These conceptions are united by the idea that federalism prevents the concentration of power in one place. One version of this argument, expounded by James Buchanan, builds on the possibility that intrafederal mobility assures citizens of an exit option should their "local" or "state" government become their oppressor (Buchanan 1995). Thus, federalism "serves as a disciplinary device to limit government inefficiency and corruption" (Inman 2007, 525). Of course, mobility within the federation is not helpful if it is the federal government itself that has become the oppressor – this is why Buchanan advocated a right of secession for the constituent units of the federation (Buchanan 1996). Within the liberal conception, a more influential strain of argument values federalism's capacity to counterbalance governments against one another. This view features prominently in the *Federalist Papers*, which insisted that the natural loyalty of citizens to their states would counteract whatever power was placed in the hands of the federal government; the federal government could be trusted "in part because, and perhaps just to the degree that, the people are inclined to be loyal and attached to their states rather than to the center" (Levy 2007, 465). Jacob Levy has recently breathed new life into this *Federalist*

Papers line of argument by augmenting it with a plurinational dimension. Liberty, Levy (2007, 466) suggests, is best protected where loyalties are divided between competing nationalisms: "The unity of nation and state encourages an unhealthy veneration of the state; it joins together loyalties that are more safely separated."

Democratic-Communitarian Conceptions of Federalism

Democratic-communitarian conceptions understand federalism primarily in terms of collective self-government. Some of these variants have a decidedly civic republican flavour, where federalism is seen as a means of enhancing the "voice" of citizens and communities. According to this view, federalism's units of government allow citizens more opportunity for active and effective participation in politics (Weinstock 2001, 77). Multiple sites of government create "more opportunities for the people to express themselves democratically through the ballot box, increase the weight of each vote, and foster enlightened and informed democratic participation by situating certain political decisions at a level that is cognitively more accessible to the average citizen" (Weinstock 2001, 77). A more communitarian variant of this position emphasizes the capacity of decentralized government to be more expressive of a local community's interests or values than a remote centralized government could ever be. Thus, many see federalism as a vital mechanism for minority self-government in plural societies (Gagnon 2001, 2014). This type of argument can be prudential in its emphasis (Horowitz 2008), or it may be more explicitly normative (Kymlicka 1998; Norman 2006; De Schutter 2010). From this perspective, the ideal is a fully fledged multinational federation where one or more constituent units is empowered as a locus of national allegiance and as an instrument of collective action in its own right (even though it continues to participate in the larger encompassing state) (Gagnon 2010).

Advancing a Meta-Normative Theory of Federalism

Rather than endorsing any one of these theories on its own, we argue for a kind of meta-normative theory of federalism – a model that does not reduce federalism to utilitarian, liberal, or democratic-communitarian objectives but looks instead to how the various values and functions of federalism can be pursued concurrently within the same polity. To this end, we identify three key principles for the realization of a truly pluralistic federalism. The first principle is *flexibility*, or "the capacity to change in relation to changing conditions, to accommodate change" while respecting the environment (Thompson 2007, 195). Flexibility means that the balance between shared rule and self-rule can adapt to an evolving set of conditions. Flexibility is essential to the long-term health of a pluralistic federation because the perceived costs of any balance between the various values of federalism will change with time. The introduction of new technologies, for example, may increase the need for centralized coordination. However, changing socio-political conditions can also raise the costs that centralized coordination exacts upon the realization of collective self-government for communities.

The second principle, *robustness*, requires that the federal principle of combining shared rule and self-rule endures over time.[1] Robustness "is a capacity for self-maintenance, self-adjustment, and self-organization in the face of change" (Thompson 2007, 195). Without robustness, a flexible federal system may become so decentralized that the benefits of coordination are lost or, conversely, the state becomes so centralized that it ceases to be a federation in all but name. In short, the principle of robustness demands that the federal nature of the state – the coexistence of two distinct orders of government, with neither subordinated to the other – persists regardless of how the federal balance evolves.

The third principle is *versatility*. This principle underpins the first two. If federalism is going to be flexible and robust in the face of changing and complex circumstances, then no single value of federalism should be allowed to preclude the realization of the others. One value may impose a cost on another – the realization of individual liberty, for example, may impose a legitimate cost in terms of efficiency – but no value can have a monopoly on the meaning of federalism. This is especially important in the Canadian context, where the sense of membership in the Canadian federation is mediated by a "plurality of ways of belonging" (Taylor 1993, 183; see also Karmis 2009). In short, the principle of versatility means that federalism ought to be "prismatic," that is, capable of reflecting the full spectrum of "ways of belonging" that are meaningful to people (Elazar 1987).

Taken together, the principles of flexibility, robustness, and versatility provide criteria against which actual federal systems might be appraised. Applying these principles in our evaluations of the health of federal systems enables us to identify the specific ways in which they may or may not be deficient.

As we see it, the best way to realize these three principles together is through a "federalism of empowerment." Federalism as empowerment is an approach that has been championed by Erwin Chemerinsky in the United States, where it is intended to counter the overly legalistic interpretation of federalism advanced by the Rehnquist-led United States Supreme Court (Chemerinsky 1996, 1997, 2004). Instead of seeing federalism as a set of rules limiting power, federalism as empowerment seeks to maintain an open space in which multiple orders of government may or may not move in response to changing needs. As Chemerinsky explains:

> "A key advantage of having multiple levels of government is the availability of alternative actors to solve important problems. If the federal government fails to act, state and local government actions are still possible. In other words, the greatest beauty of federalism is its redundancy: multiple levels of government over the same territory and population, each with the ability to act" (Chemerinsky 1996, 538).

For our purposes here, the central point of empowerment is this: the distinctive contribution of federalism with respect to the values of general utility, individual liberty, and collective self-government depends, in each case, upon the effective empowerment of more than one order of government. General utility is enhanced by interjurisdictional competition, but genuine competition is possible only if the constituent units of the federation actually have the autonomy to innovate and to speak for themselves. If policy is dictated from the centre, then the constituent units are at risk of being reduced to mere branches of the central government, and this sort of "field station" federalism precludes effective interjurisdictional competition. Similarly, as Levy's argument suggests, federalism can act as a bulwark against tyranny only if each community is sufficiently empowered as an independent locus of legitimate authority. From the national perspective of Quebec, the potential benefits of federalism as empowerment are substantial, and correspond to the redistribution of power to the Quebec state in accordance with the needs and obligations of Quebec as a modern pluralistic nation.

In what follows, we evaluate Canadian federalism in terms of its adherence to the three principles of flexibility, robustness, and versatility. Our analysis concentrates on the place of Quebec within Canada. We focus on Quebec for good reason. The growth of Quebec nationalism is the single greatest challenge to the theory and practice of Canadian federalism to arise in the last fifty years. The "Quebec question" is an existential question, not only for Quebecers but also for the rest of Canada; while it remains the impetus for Quebec sovereigntists, it was also an underlying motivation behind Trudeau's patriation process and the central theme in subsequent debates about constitutional reform in Canada. Arguably, some of the problems we diagnose extend beyond the relationship between Quebec and Canada, but it is with respect to Quebec that the differences between competing visions of Canada are most acute.[2] No other province has challenged the meaning of Canada the way Quebec has.

Our evaluation of Canadian federalism also pays special attention to the role of the Supreme Court of Canada as a mechanism for enforcement of the three principles of pluralistic federalism. Canada lacks an effective second legislative chamber to perform this role. As our analysis shows, however, the Supreme Court also falls short of serving as a reliable guardian of federalism. The root of the problem is a function of faulty institutional design: the fact that the Supreme Court is appointed by the federal government with no input from Quebec or the other provinces (Ferejohn, Rakove, and Riley 2001). This was recognized as early as 1956 by the Royal Commission of Inquiry on Constitutional Problems (the Tremblay Commission), which argued that the Supreme Court was too beholden to the federal government and so could not be reliably regarded as impartial in disputes about federalism (Quebec 1956). Not surprisingly, then, the following analysis illustrates that Canadian federalism has – at least for the last thirty years – failed to adequately approximate the three principles of flexibility, robustness, and versatility.

Impoverishing Federalism
When Rigidity Trumps Flexibility

The original federal pact of Confederation may have been adequate for the circumstances of English/French cultural and linguistic pluralism that existed in 1867. The bare fact of a province with a francophone majority, coupled with provincial jurisdiction over "property and civil rights," allowed for a substantial degree of minority self-government, the maintenance of the French civil law tradition, and the continuing development of a predominantly francophone and Catholic society. These conditions were, from the outset, enough to mark Quebec as a "distinct society" within the wider Canadian context, and they may have sufficed had Quebecers continued to understand themselves in essentially ethnocultural terms.

Before the early 1960s, the *Constitution Act, 1867* was generally seen in Quebec as a bulwark against the centralizing ambitions of the federal government (Bernier and Lajoie 1986, 71). However, the rapid ascent of a self-confident, secular, and territorially based Quebec nationalism in the 1960s changed matters considerably. This "neo-nationalism" was spearheaded by an educated secular middle class that came to see the Quebec state as a key vehicle for progressive change, for "modernizing Quebec's human and physical resources and in affirming its existence as a nation" (Bernier and Lajoie 1986, 23). Overt calls for an independent Quebec grew alongside efforts to rethink the terms of Confederation. Quebecers increasingly came to see the original constitution of 1867 not as a guarantee of autonomy but as "an obstacle, a brake on Quebec's dynamism, and a major weakness in the legal system" (Bernier and Lajoie 1986, 34). The vast majority of Quebecers now look to the Quebec state as a primary institutional nexus of solidarity and as the appropriate medium for the pursuit of a distinct nation-building project with wide-ranging socio-economic and cultural ambitions (Gagnon and Iacovino 2007). A significant portion of Quebecers reject the possibility of pursuing this project within the existing arrangements of the Canadian federation, and many sectors of society remain attracted to the idea of an independent and sovereign Quebec.

The patriation of the Canadian constitution in 1982 was an opportunity to amend federal arrangements in response to the rise, maturation, and institutionalization of Quebec nationalism – arguably the single most important change in the political environment of Canadian federalism during the last 100 years – but that opportunity was squandered. Rather than recognizing the reality of Quebec, the agreement that emerged from the November 1981 First Ministers' conference represented a stubborn reaction against it (Smiley 1983; Russell 1983). Most importantly, the fact that the settlement was imposed without the consent of Quebec's political representatives was an implicit denial of the claim that there is something constitutionally significant about Quebec's distinctiveness. In addition, the substantive content of the settlement subsumes the national reality of Quebec within a vision of coast-to-coast bilingualism, a multicultural mosaic, and "pan-Canadian constitutional patriotism" centred on the *Canadian Charter of Rights and Freedoms* (Laforest 1995; Choudhry and Gaudreault-Desbiens 2007, 168). As James Tully (1995, 8) explains, the Charter is not neutral vis-à-vis the respective national projects of Quebec and Canada:

> When the [Quebec] National Assembly seeks to preserve and enhance Quebec's character as a modern, predominantly French-speaking society, it finds that its traditional sovereignty in this area is capped by a Charter in terms of which all its legislation must be phrased and justified, but from which any recognition of Quebec's distinct character has been completely excluded. The effect of the Charter is thus to assimilate Quebec to a pan-Canadian national culture, exactly what the 1867 constitution, according to Lord Watson, was designed to prevent.

It is this inflexibility, as well as the associated unravelling of federal practices in Canada, that causes Quebecers to question their relations with the Canadian polity. Formal constitutional amendment recognizing and accommodating the national reality of Quebec has been blocked and, in this respect at least, the Canadian federation has failed to satisfy the principle of constitutional flexibility.

To be sure, formal constitutional change is not the only way of satisfying flexibility; absent formal amendment, the constitution might be adapted to the reality of Quebec nationalism by means of judicial decision (Leclair 2005). In other words, the Supreme Court could take the lead and reinterpret the Constitution in multinational or plurinational terms, achieving the otherwise elusive recognition and accommodation of Quebec. To do so would be in keeping with the dominant school of constitutional interpretation, which understands the constitution as "a living tree which, by way of progressive interpretation, accommodates and addresses the realities of modern life" and thus embodies the principle of flexible federalism (*Same-Sex Marriage Reference,* para. 22).

To allow the federation to evolve in light of changing conditions, the "living tree" approach instructs us to interpret legislative competencies as "essentially dynamic," in the words of Justice Jean Beetz in (*Martin Service Station Ltd. v. M.N.R.* [1976], 1006). In this way, the federal balance of power has, in fact, been "adjusted" by judicial interpretation in response to the imperatives of a modern and industrial social democracy on several occasions: to accommodate new technologies (see, for example, *Toronto Corporation v. Bell Telephone Co. of Canada* [1905]); to regulate business activity (see *General Motors of Canada Ltd. v. City National Leasing*); to expand the power over employment insurance in light of the increased participation of women in the labour market (*Reference re Employment Insurance Act [Can.], ss. 22 and 23*); and to reflect contemporary norms about the institution of marriage (*Same-Sex Marriage Reference*).

In the *Same-Sex Marriage Reference,* the Supreme Court expounded the rationale behind the "living tree" approach to constitutional interpretation:

> A large and liberal, or progressive, interpretation ensures the continued relevance and, indeed, legitimacy of Canada's constituting document. By way of progressive interpretation our Constitution succeeds in its ambitious enterprise, that of structuring the exercise of power by the organs of the state in times vastly different from those in which it was crafted. (2004, para. 23.)

This passage draws a link between progressive interpretation and political legitimacy. The idea here is that if the constitution falls too far out of step with the world it purports to preside over, then it will cease to be a source of political legitimacy.

Unfortunately, while progressive interpretation has been used to expand the powers of the federal government (Swinton 1992, 128), the greatest challenge to the constitution's legitimacy – the reality of Quebec nationalism – has been largely ignored by the Supreme Court of Canada. This is not for lack of opportunities to recognize the national reality of Quebec. In the 1982 *Quebec Veto Reference,* the government of Quebec essentially asked the court whether, given the dualist theory of Canadian federation, there was a constitutional convention requiring the consent of Quebec for any amendment to the constitution, a question of crucial political importance:

> In the context of this reference, the word "duality" covers all the circumstances that have contributed to making Quebec a distinct society, since the foundation of Canada and long before, and the range of guarantees that were made to Quebec in 1867, as a province which the Task Force on Canadian Unity has described as "the stronghold of the French-Canadian people" and the "living heart of the French presence in North America." These circumstances and these guarantees extend far beyond matters of language and culture alone: the protection of the British North America Act was extended to all aspects of Quebec society – language, certainly, but also the society's values, its law, religion, education, territory, natural resources, government and the sovereignty of its legislative assembly over everything which was at the time of a "local" nature (para. 813).

According to the dualist theory, Quebec, being a nation in its own right, ought not to have its constitutional status determined by the unilateral will of a pan-Canadian national majority.

The Supreme Court chose to sidestep the issue of Quebec's national distinctiveness and resolved the dispute against Quebec on the grounds that it could not be demonstrated that a Quebec veto power had ever been explicitly accepted by the other actors in the Canadian federation (*Quebec Veto Reference,* para. 184). But there is a tension (even a contradiction) between the court's insistence on explicit acknowledgment of a Quebec veto in this case and the lack of explicit statements acknowledging the convention requiring a "substantial degree" of provincial consent in the earlier *Patriation Reference*. Moreover, in the *Quebec Veto Reference*, the court was unmoved by the fact that the two earlier attempts to patriate the constitution (in 1964 and 1971) were abandoned precisely because of the failure to obtain the consent of Quebec (Russell 1983; Smiley 1983). Based on the criteria applied in the *Patriation Reference*, those precedents alone should have been sufficient to establish the convention in question (Choudhry and Gaudreault-Desbiens 2007, 176–77).

There is more one could say against the Supreme Court's decision in the *Quebec Veto Reference*. For one thing, the decision certainly undermined the legitimacy of the Supreme Court in the eyes of many Quebecers. For our purposes, however, the main issue is that the court's decision contravened the principle of flexibility. A constitutional practice related to a Quebec veto *had* emerged in response to the national reality of Quebec. That practice was to ensure that constitutional reform proceeded on an essentially plurinational basis (i.e., with the consent of Quebec). By denying this practice the status of a convention, the court effectively annulled what had been occurring at the sub-constitutional level before the 1981 patriation agreement (Tarr et al. 2004).

In 1998, the *Quebec Secession Reference* provided the Supreme Court with yet another opportunity to reconsider the national reality of Quebec. The court was asked whether or not the government of Quebec could proceed with a unilateral secession from Canada. The court ruled that unilateral secession was unconstitutional, although it did find that the federal government would be obligated to negotiate terms of secession in good faith in the event of a majority vote in favour of secession. Once again, however, the Supreme Court sidestepped the question of Quebec's national distinctiveness and the political repercussions of Quebec nationalism. On the question of whether there was, in international law, a "Quebec people" with the right of self-determination, the court stated (somewhat opaquely) that "the Quebec population certainly shares many of the characteristics (such as a common language and culture) that would be considered in determining whether a specific group is a 'people,' as do other groups within Quebec and/or Canada" (para. 125). To be sure, there was some acknowledgment that Quebec is a unique province. On the principle of federalism and Quebec's original place in the federation, the Supreme Court went on at length:

> The principle of federalism facilitates the pursuit of collective goals by cultural and linguistic minorities which form the majority within a particular province. This is the case in Quebec, where the majority of the population is French-speaking, and which possesses a distinct culture. This is not merely the result of chance. The social and demographic reality of Quebec explains the existence of the province of Quebec as a political unit and, indeed, was one of the essential reasons for establishing a federal structure for the Canadian union in 1867 (para. 59).

The Supreme Court (para. 47) also noted that despite the refusal of the Quebec government to endorse the patriation process, the province is bound "to the terms of a Constitution that [are] different from that which prevailed previously, particularly as regards provisions governing its amendment, and the Canadian Charter of Rights and Freedoms". However, the ruling contains no discussion of the history of constitutional conflict – the rise of Quebec nationalism, the *Quebec Veto Reference*, and the failure of the Meech Lake and Charlottetown Accords – that ultimately paved the way for the referendum on secession in 1995 (Choudhry and Gaudreault-Desbiens 2007, 93). Thus, once again, the Supreme Court's reasoning remains aloof from the reality of Quebec, displaying a stubborn detachment that violates the principle of constitutional flexibility we have outlined here.

When Centralization Trumps Robustness

As explained earlier, the principle of robustness requires that federal systems maintain their federal character over time. To some extent, the Canadian federation is stronger than the United States in this respect (Gagnon and Simeon 2010). Canadian provinces enjoy more exclusive competencies than their American counterparts. Moreover, under the Canadian constitution, where federal and provincial jurisdictions overlap, federal law trumps provincial jurisdiction only in the event of an actual conflict, either because dual compliance with federal and provincial law would be impossible (see Justice Dickson in *Multiple Access Ltd. v. McCutcheon* [1982], 191) or because provincial law frustrates the objectives of federal law (see Justice La Forest in *Bank of Montreal v. Hall* [1990], 155). Despite formal bulwarks against the expansion of federal jurisdiction, the Canadian government has used its spending power and other strategies to influence and control provincial governments in ways that undermine the federal character of Canada generally and obstruct the national life of Quebec more specifically.

The best example of this is surely the Social Union Framework Agreement (SUFA). SUFA is part of a nation-building project that seeks to build a pan-Canadian political community. The issue here is not centralization versus decentralization, but distinct and competing visions of federalism (Gagnon and Iacovino 2007, 49), statecraft, and the expression of legitimate sovereignty (Burgess and Gagnon 2011). SUFA's insertion of mobility as a defining characteristic of the Canadian federation trumps all other political claims. Article 2 states: "All governments believe that the freedom of movement of Canadians to pursue opportunities anywhere in Canada is an essential element of Canadian citizenship" (Gagnon 2000, 244). By entrenching this position, Ottawa manages to intrude into a field of exclusive provincial jurisdiction and, concomitantly, reinforce its presence in the field of citizenship that, as a result, applies identically across the country. This undermines the robustness of federal practices to the extent that it reduces the scope for variation within the federation.

When Monism Trumps Versatility

Until 1949, the Judicial Committee of the Privy Council in the United Kingdom served as the ultimate tribunal in disputes about the distribution of federal and provincial powers in Canada (Lajoie 2009). The Privy Council generally adopted an interpretation of the division of powers that favoured the provinces against the federal government (Brouillet 2005; Hogg 2009, 339). The federal powers to make laws relating to "trade and commerce" (*Reference re Board of Commerce Act Canada 1919 and Combines and Fair Prices Act* [1922]) and for "the peace, order, and good government of Canada" were interpreted narrowly, the latter authorizing legislation only where there was an identifiable gap in the division of powers or where federal law was needed in response to some emergency situation (*Reference re legislative jurisdiction of Parliament of Canada to enact the Employment and Social Insurance Act* (1935, c. 48), [1936]

S.C.R. 427; *Re: Anti-Inflation Act*, [1976] 2 S.C.R. 373; *R. v. Crown Zellerback Canada Ltd.* [1988] 1 S.C.R. 401). Meanwhile, the provincial power over "property and civil rights" was given a comparatively generous interpretation. The Privy Council's decidedly decentralist jurisprudence was based in part on a formalistic reading of federalism, which assumed that legislative powers should be assigned exclusively to one order of government pursuant to the "heads" of power listed in the *Constitution Act, 1867.* This left little room for additional powers to be "read into" the federal scheme.

The formalistic approach continued for some time after judicial authority over the constitution was transferred to the Supreme Court of Canada. In 1951, the Supreme Court still spoke the language of formalism:

> Parliament can legislate only on the subject matters referred to it by section 91 and ... each Province can legislate exclusively on the subject matters referred to it by section 92. The country is entitled to insist that legislation adopted under section 91 should be passed exclusively by the Parliament of Canada in the same way as the people of each Province are entitled to insist that legislation concerning the matters enumerated in section 92 should come exclusively from their respective Legislatures. In each case the Members elected to Parliament or to the Legislatures are the only ones entrusted with the power and the duty to legislate concerning the subjects exclusively distributed by the constitutional Act to each of them. (*Attorney General of Nova Scotia v. Attorney General of Canada* [1951], 34)

By the early 1960s, however, commentators, political scientists, and jurists were already forecasting the imminent end of "classical federalism of 'water-tight compartments' with provincial legislatures and federal parliament carefully keeping clear of one another" (see the discussion in *Multiple Access Ltd. v. McCutcheon* [1982]).

Now one might imagine that a shift from formalism to a more evaluative approach would be conducive to flexibility, making it easier to adjust the federal balance in light of changing conditions, including the circumstances of national pluralism. From the perspective of the principle of versatility, however, there is a real danger here because open-ended evaluation may allow the system to be captured for certain purposes or values to the exclusion of others. As Jean Leclair (2003, 431) reminds us, "the Privy Council's presumably more formal approach to federalism had the virtue of forcing courts to define what lay within the exclusive power of the provincial polities." However, the Supreme Court's subsequent jurisprudence has generally reflected a single-minded utilitarian concern with functional efficiency at the expense of democratic-communitarian concerns. This has allowed federal power to encroach on what would otherwise be provincial jurisdiction. Two decisions of the Supreme Court warrant particular attention here.

In *General Motors of Canada Ltd. v. City National Leasing* (1989), the Supreme Court held that the federal power to make law for "the general regulation of trade" could support federal competition legislation even though the regulated business activity in question was intraprovincial in its scope. The government of Quebec argued before the court that, while the trade and commerce power may well allow for pan-Canadian competition legislation, the legislation should be "read down" so as to apply only to international and interprovincial commercial activity; competition within Quebec ought to be governed by Quebec's power over property and civil rights. The court rejected Quebec's argument and, in doing so, departed from "more than 100 years of constitutional interpretation in which the federal government's power to regulate trade and commerce in section 91(2) of the Constitution was limited to the interprovincial and international flow of commerce" (Swinton 1992, 127).

The Supreme Court justified its decision on utilitarian-functionalist grounds. The object of the impugned legislation was pan-Canadian in scope: "the economy as a single integrated national unit rather than as a collection of separate local enterprises." This object, the court reasoned, required a uniform effort because "the failure to include one or more provinces or localities would jeopardize successful operation of the legislation in other parts of the country" (*City National Leasing* [1989], para. 680). The court, being skeptical about the ability of the provinces to act collectively for the sake of the "national interest" (understood in a pan-Canadian sense), held that the incursion into provincial jurisdiction was justified. Significantly, the decision was a function of the perceived inability of the provinces to adopt a truly "national perspective that could transcend their own regional interests" (Swinton 1992, 133).

The second important decision was *R. v. Crown Zellerbach Canada Ltd.* (1988). In this case, the Supreme Court held that the federal government's power to make laws for "peace, order, and good government" included a plenary power over marine pollution, even within provincial boundaries, on the basis that the matter in question was of "national concern." Again, a kind of utilitarian functionalism underpins the decision. The regulation of marine pollution was characterized as functionally indivisible, and therefore a matter that could be effectively regulated only from the centre by the federal government. The consequences in *Crown Zellerbach* are even more drastic than those in *City National Leasing*, however, because the jurisdiction it supports is exclusively federal. The unwieldy centralizing potential of this doctrine was the focus of Justice La Forest's admonitory dissent:

> By conceptualizing broad social, economic and political issues in that way, one can effectively invent new heads of power under the national dimensions doctrine, thereby incidentally removing them from provincial jurisdiction or at least abridging the provinces' freedom of operation ... Here, it must be remembered that in its supposed application within the province the provision virtually prevents a province from dealing with certain of its own public property without federal consent. (*Crown Zellerbach* [1988], 452)

These concerns were later vindicated in *Ontario Hydro v. Ontario (Labour Relations Board* [1993]*)*, where the standard was further relaxed to allow for federal jurisdiction over labour relations at Ontario's nuclear power plants. Significantly, whether or not the object of legislation was part of a single and indivisible subject matter was not treated as the threshold question of national concern but as a limiting condition "to determine which provincial powers the existence of a national concern allowed Parliament to plunder" (Baier 2006).

The Supreme Court's reliance on a utilitarian-functionalist criterion of "provincial inability" has been criticized as vague and "highly subjective" (Leclair 2003, 428–29). Functionalism can easily come to dominate the meaning of federalism, to the detriment of other federal values. As Katherine Swinton (1992, 132) has argued:

> Applying either the national dimensions doctrine or the new general regulation of trade doctrine shifts powers to the federal government which the provinces would otherwise have exercised exclusively. When the Court invokes these doctrines, it acts as a constitutional reformer or designer. In the case of the national concerns doctrine, the Court reforms or designs with no textual guidance as to what is national, in contrast to the interpretation of the distribution of enumerated powers, where there is some indication of criteria of national and provincial salience.

The consequences of a centralizing constitutional drift for the national interests of Quebec are especially serious. The idea of provincial incapacity is not objective or value-neutral as between different conceptions of the Canadian federation; in *City National Leasing*, for example, provincial inability was understood in part as the inability to adopt a "national" pan-Canadian perspective (Swinton 1992, 133). This doctrine leaves little or no room for the "national" perspective of Quebec. For this reason, not only is the triumph of utilitarian functionalism over other normative conceptions of federalism in the jurisprudence of the Supreme Court a deficiency in terms of versatility, but it also undermines the ability of the Canadian federation to respond to the circumstances of national pluralism and further contributes to the alienation of Quebecers.

Conclusion: Recognition versus Empowerment

We have argued here that the Canadian federation has some major deficiencies insofar as it has failed to respect the principles of flexibility, robustness, and versatility. We have also illustrated that, to a large extent, these deficiencies stem from, or follow, the 1981 patriation agreement. Flexibility was compromised in a missed opportunity to adapt the federation to the national reality of Quebec. The robustness of Canadian federalism has been further eroded by the centralizing efforts of the federal government. The Supreme Court has undermined the versatility of the Canadian federation by overexpounding a utilitarian jurisprudence emphasizing functional efficiency at the expense of other federal values. Such deficiencies have political consequences.

Because the patriation agreement was premised on a failure (or refusal) to acknowledge the distinctive national reality of Quebec, scholarly criticism has often focused on the question of recognition (Seymour 2010). We agree that recognition (or its lack) is a crucial element in this story, but the discourse of recognition may actually have negative consequences in theory and in practice. There is a danger of "fetishizing" recognition, of elevating symbolism and idealizing perpetual dialogue, while sidelining what are arguably more important concrete questions of power and power relations.

The precise significance of recognition in constitutional politics has been ambiguous. Is recognition a means to an end, or is the struggle for recognition valuable regardless of the outcome? James Tully (2008) seems to suggest the latter, describing "the intersubjective activity" of struggling over recognition as "an intrinsic public good" (189) and "the continuous contests of mutual disclosure and acknowledgment" as "ends in themselves" (208). What is the actual benefit for minority nationalists? Tully argues that "participation in the intersubjective negotiation of identity" is an essential prerequisite to development of "the sense of self-worth of individuals and groups which empowers them to become free, equal and autonomous agents in both private and public life" (169).

We see two dangers in Tully's understanding of the issue. First, despite his emphasis on egalitarian dialogue, the relationship between the participants in such "agonic games" remains vertical – there are those who are in a position to benevolently bestow recognition, and there are those who seek it. In other words, it is a contest where one team has a numerical advantage and writes the rules of the game as it is being played, to serve its own interests (Noël 2011). Second, in thinking of the dialogue of recognition as an end in itself, we (as theorists, social scientists, jurists, or citizens) may abandon the tough work of actually thinking through the problem of national pluralism in substantive terms (Gagnon 2010, 2011; Seymour and Gagnon 2012). The alternative we endorse prioritizes empowerment instead of recognition. This approach aims to articulate a substantive vision of what the endgame ought to look like: a multinational federal vision in which different national communities are equipped with the powers they need to flourish, to develop legitimate contexts of choice, and to realize comparable possibilities. Federalism, as we have argued here, can be endorsed from utilitarian, liberal, and democratic-communitarian perspectives and simultaneously enlisted to serve each of these goals or values. The idea of a federalism of empowerment embraces this pluralism. The practical challenge in a modern federation such as Canada is to find a balance between the pursuit of various goals and values while remaining flexible, robust, and versatile (Requejo 2010). Naturally, this is easier said than done.

Notes

1 Our use of the idea of "robustness" is similar in spirit but narrower than Jenna Bednar's (2009). For Bednar, robust federalism is a function of "compliance, to dissuade transgressions; resilience, an immunity to design flaws and external shocks; and adaptation, an ability to adjust the rules to meet changing needs" (13).

2 We acknowledge that the governments of Alberta and Newfoundland and Labrador have periodically challenged the dominant model of Canadian federalism over the past thirty years.

References

Attorney General of Nova Scotia v. Attorney General of Canada, [1951] S.C.R. 31.

Baier, Gerald. 2006. *Courts and Federalism: Judicial Doctrine in the United States, Australia, and Canada.* Vancouver: UBC Press.

Bank of Montreal v. Hall, [1990] 1 S.C.R. 121.

Bednar, Jenna. 2009. *The Robust Federation: Principles of Design.* Cambridge, UK: Cambridge University Press.

Bernier, Ivan, and Andrée Lajoie. 1986. *Family Law and Social Welfare Legislation in Canada.* Toronto: University of Toronto Press (in cooperation with the Royal Commission on the Economic Union and Development Prospects).

Breton, Albert. 1965. "A Theory of Government Grants." *Canadian Journal of Economics and Political Science* 31 (2): 175–87. doi:10.2307/140062.

Brouillet, Eugénie. 2005. *La négation de la nation: l'identité culturelle québécoise et le fédéralisme canadien.* Sillery, QC: Septentrion.

Buchanan, James M. 1995. "Federalism as an Ideal Political Order and an Objective for Constitutional Reform." *Publius: The Journal of Federalism* 25 (2): 19–28.

—. 1996. "Federalism and Individual Sovereignty." *Cato Journal* 15 (2–3): 259–68.

Burgess, Michael, and Alain-G. Gagnon, eds. 2011. *Comparative Federalism and Federation.* Toronto: University of Toronto Press.

Chemerinsky, Erwin. 1996. "Dunwoody Distinguished Lecture in Law: The Values of Federalism." *University of Florida Law Review* 47: 499.

—. 1997. "Federalism As Empowerment, Not Limits." *University of Kansas Law Review* 45: 1219.

—. 2004. "Empowering States When It Matters: A Different Approach to Preemption." *Brooklyn Law Review* 69: 1313.

Choudhry, Sujit, and Jean-François Gaudreault-Desbiens. 2007. "Frank Iacobucci as Constitution Maker: From the Quebec Veto Reference to the Meech Lake Accord and the Quebec Secession Reference." *University of Toronto Law Journal* 57 (2): 165–93. doi:10.1353/tlj.2007.0010.

De Schutter, Helder. 2010. "Federalism as Fairness." *Journal of Political Philosophy* 19 (2): 167–89. doi:10.1111/j.1467-9760.2010.00368.x.

Elazar, Daniel. 1987. *Exploring Federalism.* Tuscaloosa, AL: University of Alabama Press.

Ferejohn, John, Jack N. Rakove, and Jonathan Riley. 2001. *Constitutional Culture and Democratic Rule.* New York: Cambridge University Press. doi:10.1017/CBO9780511609329.

Gagnon, Alain-G. 1993. "The Political Uses of Federalism." In *Comparative Federalism and Federation,* edited by Michael Burgess and Alain-G. Gagnon, 15–44. Toronto: University of Toronto Press.

—. 2000. "Working in Partnership for Canadians." In *The Canadian Social Union without Quebec: 8 Critical Analyses,* edited by Alain-G. Gagnon and Hugh Segal, 129–54. Montreal: Institute for Research on Public Policy.

—. 2001. "Quebec: The Emergence of a Region-State." *Scottish Affairs* (Special Issue): 14–28.

—. 2010. *The Case for Multinational Federalism.* London: Routledge.

—. 2014. *Minority Nations in the Age of Uncertainty: New Paths to National Emancipation and Empowerment.* Toronto: University of Toronto Press.

Gagnon, Alain-G., and Raffaele Iacovino. 2007. *Federalism, Citizenship and Québec: Debating Multinationalism.* Toronto: University of Toronto Press.

Gagnon, Alain-G., and Richard Simeon. 2010. "Canada." In *Diversity and Unity in Federal Countries,* edited by Luis Moreno and César Colino, 110–38. Montreal/Kingston: McGill-Queen's University Press.

General Motors of Canada Ltd. v. City National Leasing, [1989] 1 S.C.R. 641 [*City National Leasing*].

Hogg, Peter. 2009. *Constitutional Law of Canada.* Toronto: Carswell.

Horowitz, Donald. 2008. "The Many Uses of Federalism." *Drake Law Review* 55: 953–66.

Inman, Robert P. 2007. "Federalism's Values and the Value of Federalism." *CESifo Economic Studies* 53 (4): 522–60. doi:10.1093/cesifo/ifm018.

Karmis, Dimitrios. 2009. "The Multiple Voices of the Federal Tradition and the Turmoil of Canadian Federalism." In *Contemporary Canadian Federalism: Founda-*

tions, Traditions, Institutions, edited by Alain-G. Gagnon, 53–73. Toronto: University of Toronto Press.

Kymlicka, Will. 1998. "Multinational Federalism in Canada: Rethinking the Partnership." In *Beyond the Impasse: Toward Reconciliation,* edited by Roger Gibbins and Guy Laforest, 15–50. Montreal: Institute for Research on Public Policy.

Laforest, Guy. 1995. *Trudeau and the End of a Canadian Dream*. Montreal/Kingston: McGill-Queen's University Press.

Lajoie, Andrée. 2009. "Federalism in Canada: Provinces and Minorities – Same Fight." In *Contemporary Canadian Federalism: Foundations, Traditions, Institutions,* edited by Alain-G. Gagnon, 163–85. Toronto: University of Toronto Press.

Leclair, Jean. 2003. "The Supreme Court of Canada's Understanding of Federalism: Efficiency at the Expense of Diversity." *Queen's Law Journal* 28: 411–53.

—. 2005. "Reforming the Division of Powers in Canada: An (Un)achievable Endeavour?" In *Reforming Federalism: Foreign Experiences for a Reform in Germany,* edited by Gerhard Robbers, 93–134. Frankfurt am Main: Peter Lang.

Levy, Jacob. 2007. "Federalism, Liberalism, and the Separation of Loyalties." *American Political Science Review* 101 (3): 459–77. doi:10.1017/S0003055407070268.

Martin Service Station Ltd. v. M.N.R., [1977] 2 S.C.R. 996.

Multiple Access Ltd. v. McCutcheon, [1982] 2 S.C.R. 161.

Noël, Alain. 2011. "The Left, the Right, and Federalism." Paper presented at Richard Simeon's festschrift, "The Global Promise of Federalism: A Workshop to Honour Richard Simeon." University of Toronto, 3 September.

Norman, Wayne. 2006. *Negotiating Nationalism: Nation-building, Federalism and Secession in the Multinational State.* Oxford: Oxford University Press. doi:10.1093/0198293356.001.0001.

Ontario Hydro v. Ontario (Labour Relations Board), [1993] 3 S.C.R. 327.

Quebec. 1956. *Report of the Royal Commission of Inquiry on Constitutional Problems.* Quebec City: Government of Quebec.

R. v. Crown Zellerbach Canada Ltd., [1988] 1 S.C.R. 401 [*Crown Zellerbach*].

Re: Anti-Inflation Act, [1976] 2 S.C.R. 373.

Re: Objection by Quebec to a Resolution to Amend the Constitution, [1982] 2 S.C.R. 793 [*Quebec Veto Reference*].

Re: Resolution to Amend the Constitution, [1981] 1 S.C.R. 753 [*Patriation Reference*].

Reference re Board of Commerce Act Canada 1919 and Combines and Fair Prices Act, [1922] 1 A.C. 191.

Reference re Employment Insurance Act (Can.), ss. 22 and 23, [2005] 2 S.C.R. 669.

Reference re Legislative Jurisdiction of Parliament of Canada to Enact the Employment and Social Insurance Act (1935, c. 48), [1936] S.C.R. 427.

Reference re Same-Sex Marriage, [2004] 3 S.C.R. 698 [*Same-Sex Marriage Reference*].

Reference re Secession of Quebec, [1998] 2 S.C.R. 217 [*Quebec Secession Reference*].

Requejo, Ferran. 2010. *Fédéralisme multinational et pluralisme de valeurs.* Brussels: Collection Diversitas, Presses interuniversitaires européennes/Peter Lang.

Russell, Peter. 1983. "Bold Statecraft, Questionable Jurisprudence." In *And No One Cheered: Federalism, Democracy and the Constitution Act, 1982,* edited by Keith Banting and Richard Simeon, 210–38. Toronto: Methuen.

Seymour, Michel, ed. 2010. *The Plural States of Recognition.* New York: Palgrave Macmillan. doi:10.1057/9780230285569.

Seymour, Michel, and Alain-G. Gagnon, eds. 2012. *Multinational Federalism: Problems and Prospects.* Basingstoke, UK: Palgrave Macmillan. doi:10.1057/9781137016744.

Smiley, Donald. 1983. "A Dangerous Deed: The Constitution Act, 1982." In *And No One Cheered: Federalism, Democracy and the Constitution Act, 1982,* edited by Keith Banting and Richard Simeon, 74–95. Toronto: Methuen.

Swinton, Katherine. 1992. "Federalism under Fire: The Role of the Supreme Court of Canada." *Law and Contemporary Problems* 55 (1): 121–45. doi:10.2307/1191760.

Tarr, Alan, Robert Williams, and Josef Marko. 2004. *Federalism, Subnational Constitutions and Minority Rights.* Westport, CT: Praeger.

Taylor, Charles. 1993. *Reconciling the Solitudes: Essays on Canadian Federalism and Nationalism,* edited by Guy Laforest. Montreal/Kingston: McGill-Queen's University Press.

Thompson, Evan. 2007. *Mind in Life: Biology, Phenomenology and the Sciences of Mind.* Cambridge, MA: Harvard University Press.

Toronto Corporation v. Bell Telephone Co. of Canada, [1905] A.C. 52 (P.C.).

Tully, James. 1995. "Let's Talk: The Quebec Referendum and the Future of Canada." The Austin and Hempel Lectures. Dalhousie University and the University of Prince Edward Island, 23 and 27 March.

—. 2008. *Democracy and Civic Freedom.* Vol. 1, *Public Philosophy in a New Key.* Cambridge, UK: Cambridge University Press.

Weinstock, Daniel. 2001. "Towards a Normative Theory of Federalism." *International Social Science Journal* 53: 75–83.

13 An Indigenous Constitutional Paradox: Both Monumental Achievement and Monumental Defeat

Kiera Ladner

The patriation negotiations of November 1981 were like a game of constitutional poker. Eleven white men in suits played their cards in an attempt to distribute power and imbue their nation with a particular sense of itself. Particularly fascinating was the extent to which the aggressive gamesmanship sometimes unexpectedly forced the hands of some, while also revealing that key cardholders misread their ability to play the game. Perhaps even more fascinating was the fact that Indigenous people, who had neither cards to play nor an invitation to the game, proved themselves to be the most agile and ingenious players – and this despite the fact that the game was premised on perpetuating the colonial order through a reification of Canada as a nation bound together by the constitution (Churchill 1998). Although carried out on Indigenous lands, the men who engaged in this game of constitutional poker had no difficulty excluding those peoples on whose lands they sat. But Indigenous leaders held fast to that constitutional moment and found creative ways to force the players to acknowledge their existence, address their issues, and offer them a seat at future constitutional tables. They found a way to insert themselves into the governing processes of the settler-state without the leaders of the state fully realizing what had been done.

While deeply challenged by the task of dealing with the issues raised by Quebec's nationalist aspirations and vision of the country (Russell 2004), the political leaders negotiating patriation appeared completely unable to comprehend the idea of Indigenous nationalisms, nor could they grasp the moral and legal imperatives behind the demands of Indigenous leaders that Aboriginal and treaty rights be included in the constitution. After all, it should not be forgotten that only twelve years earlier, Pierre Trudeau had set forth a bold assimilation strategy for dealing with the "Indian problem." The 1969 White Paper on Indian Policy outlined his plan to abolish treaties, reserves, the "special" status of "Indians," and the *Indian Act* (Canada 1969). At the very moment when political leaders were struggling to understand the political and constitutional consequences of Québécois nationalism and multiculturalism, the white paper revealed a complete unwillingness to consider Indigenous aspirations. Ultimately, the mass mobilization of Indigenous peoples forced the government to abandon the white paper, but its assimilationist understanding of Canada continued to shape Aboriginal policy (Ladner and Orsini 2005, 194–99). A decade later, as Louise Mandell and Leslie Hall Pinder outline in Chapter 9, this assimilationist approach was profoundly challenged when Indigenous peoples and their constitutional concerns and aspirations dominated the patriation process in the United Kingdom. As Mandell and Pinder demonstrate, the attainment of constitutional change by Indigenous peoples was a monumental achievement given the assimilationist (even racist) context or paradigm within which such change was achieved. That said, what makes this even more fascinating is that the First Ministers who eventually yielded to pressure to respond to Indigenous constitutional claims did so without fully comprehending what it was that they had included in the 1982 constitutional package (Ladner and McCrossan 2009). It is this lack of understanding and lack of agreement that results in patriation being characterized by Indigenous peoples as both a monumental achievement and a monumental defeat.

The collective failure of political leaders to grasp Indigenous aspirations (let alone the constitutional provisions included in the *Constitution Act, 1982*) speaks not only to a reification of a unified constitutional nationalism that excludes Indigenous nationalisms and narratives from its purview but to these leaders' sheer lack of knowledge about Indigenous peoples, their histories, their quest for decolonization, and their resurgence outside of constitutional politics. Never was this lack of knowledge clearer than in the series of constitutional conferences held in the years following patriation when Pierre Trudeau professed: "I just don't know what you want" (Ladner and McCrossan 2009, 269). Few Canadian leaders showed any real desire or capacity to understand. The problem was not merely widespread ignorance of Indigenous history and politics but the active denial of that history and politics. The state encourages a historical amnesia that blocks questions about the country's colonial past and present. It is difficult to address this amnesia if one side is not willing to grapple with colonialism and admit that there is anything other than its own, singular narrative about nationalism in Canada. It should be noted that this historical amnesia and the incommensurability of Indigenous understandings of the past and visions of the future should be understood as a form of paradigm paralysis. It is the same paradigm paralysis that Ladner and Orsini (2005) argue defines the past, present, and foreseeable future of Canada's Aboriginal policy. It also defines and confines constitutional politics and thus is not simply a matter of incommensurable world views or an inability of Indigenous peoples to come to terms with the realities of constitutional negotiations.

Focusing on the mega-constitutional rounds and issues of judicial interpretation, this chapter argues that despite the tremendous potential for a paradigm shift opened by Indigenous constitutional interventions prior to 1982, patriation and the succeeding constitutional rounds achieved little for Indigenous peoples. The constitutional reforms associated with patriation recognized existing rights (*sui generis* rights that were not created by those eleven white men in suits), but the realization of those rights has been curtailed by the settler-state through its adherence to well-established policies and policy-making practices, legislative action, and judicial interpretation – indeed, there seems to have been a determined effort to limit the recognition and applicability of these rights within a Canadian context. In other words, this chapter seeks to demonstrate, through a discussion of judicial and constitutional politics, that despite the fact that patriation could have been a truly transformative moment for Indigenous peoples, the struggle to realize the decolonizing potential of the constitution has been an arduous journey with few real victories. As a result, Indigenous peoples continue to struggle to achieve recognition and implementation of their rights, to realize their constitutional demands, and to enact their vision of a decolonized and/or post-colonial Canada domestically through movements such as Idle No More and internationally using the United Nations *Declaration on the Rights of Indigenous Peoples* (UNDRIP).

Monumental Achievement, Monumental Defeat: Assessing Patriation

For Indigenous people, the *Constitution Act, 1982* represents a contradiction or a constitutional paradox. It is both an instrument of colonization and an instrument of decolonization. Despite all of the efforts to place their issues on the constitutional table and protect Indigenous rights (ultimately through the inclusion of sections 25 and 35 of the *Constitution Act, 1982*), most Aboriginal organizations viewed the amended constitution as a major defeat. All of the national and all but one provincial Indigenous organization (the Métis Association of Alberta) walked away from the constitutional table or rejected the amended constitution because it failed to offer sufficient protection to Indigenous peoples, or to enunciate an appropriate and detailed understanding of what sections 25 and 35 recognized, affirmed, and protected. Critics have argued that, as an instrument of colonization, the patriation agreement represented the domestication of Indigenous rights and responsibilities, that Indigenous nationalisms and sovereignties were remade in the image of Aboriginal rights cognizable to Canadian law (Borrows 2010).

Although easily construed as a monumental defeat, patriation also represented a monumental victory for Indigenous peoples. As Peter Russell argues in Chapter 11, the *Constitution Act, 1982* does afford some protection and recognition to Aboriginal and treaty rights (Ladner and McCrossan 2009, 267). It is true that the dreams of Indigenous constitutional activists were not fully realized, and Aboriginal organizations were unsuccessful in their efforts to insert a shield to protect Indigenous rights from the state and settler society within the patriation process. Still, given the political, conceptual, and attitudinal obstacles, those who waged this battle for constitutional recognition achieved something many believed impossible. With the entrenchment of section 35, Aboriginal and treaty rights were recognized and affirmed, arguably as *sui generis* rights originating within Indigenous nations or the agreements between Indigenous nations and the settler society. Moreover, section 25 affords these rights further protection from the *Canadian Charter of Rights and Freedoms.*

Although rejected by Indigenous leaders out of fear that the level of protection needed for Aboriginal and treaty rights was not attained, sections 25 and 35 achieved the impossible. Encrypted as Aboriginal and treaty rights, these sections represented the recognition and affirmation of Indigenous constitutional orders within the Canadian constitution and their subsequent protection from the Charter. As James (Sákéj) Youngblood Henderson, Marjorie Benson, and Isobel Findlay argue, "the spirit and the intent of section 35(1), then, should be interpreted as 'recognizing and affirming' Aboriginal legal orders, laws and jurisdictions unfolded through Aboriginal and treaty rights." In essence, Aboriginal and treaty rights are the manifestation of Indigenous constitutional orders and the means by which these orders are recognized and affirmed in the Canadian constitution (Ladner and McCrossan 2009, 268–69).

This was a monumental victory. The encrypting of rights opened a window of opportunity to reimagine the Canadian constitutional order and create the opportunities necessary for decolonization and the realization of a post-colonial Canada (Henderson 1994; Ladner and McCrossan 2009). Providing *sui generis* Indigenous rights (as vested in Indigenous constitutional orders and treaties) elevated their status within the new framework of constitutional supremacy and was a real achievement (Henderson 2004; Ladner and McCrossan 2009; Borrows 2010). Triumphalism is inappropriately overstated, however. The newly entrenched Indigenous rights are also limiting, insofar as they remake Indigenous peoples' nationalisms into something other than what they are. Section 35 provides recognition without articulating what, precisely, is recognized. This is a dangerous outcome, since these constitutionally enshrined rights rely on Canadian courts for their interpretation (Turpel 1989–90; Ladner 2003; Borrows 2010).

An alternative perspective on sections 25 and 35 views Aboriginal and treaty rights within the context of a meta-narrative of constitutional nationalism, one that construes the Charter as bringing citizens into the constitutional fold and thus shaping a new discourse of nationalism (Green 2005). Although this interpretation of the events and aftermath of 1982 ignores Indigenous peoples' mobilization and efforts to seek protection from the Canadian constitution and Trudeau's vision of constitutional nationalism, it nonetheless shows the magnitude of this victory. Simply by acknowledging that they have constitutional rights, sections 25 and 35 provide Indigenous peoples with a legal agency they had previously been denied, and establish a foundation upon which they can assert their pre-existing, *sui generis* rights within the Canadian state (whether in court or in negotiations).

Still, regardless of how one approaches the meaning of sections 25 and 35, their entrenchment was but a partial victory – a victory mitigated, confined, defined, and often defeated by the bureaucrats, politicians, lawyers, and judges who have tried to "give meaning" to these sections without an understanding of the Indigenous contexts that gave rise to these rights. In "Aboriginal Peoples and the Canadian Charter," Mary-Ellen Turpel-Lafond argued that Canadian and Indigenous rights traditions are "so fundamentally at odds that they could never be interpreted to co-exist under the Charter. As a result of this fundamental disjuncture, Turpel-Lafond argued that Aboriginal rights should never be subject to the conceptual frameworks, philosophical paradigms, and legal traditions of the other's discourse of rights" (Ladner and McCrossan 2009, 270).

Not a New Book: Judicial Responses to Aboriginal Rights

In *Mitchell v. M.N.R.* (2001), Justice Ian Binnie of the Supreme Court of Canada wrote in 2001: "The *Constitution Act, 1982* ushered in a new chapter but it did not start a new book. Within the framework of s. 35(1) regard is to be had to the common law ('what the law has historically accepted') to enable a court to determine what constitutes an aboriginal right" (para. 115). In many ways, Justice Binnie was right in suggesting that the Aboriginal and treaty rights provisions of the *Constitution Act, 1982* did not reset constitutional law in the country by throwing out the British constitutional tradition and starting afresh. By the same token, however, recognizing Aboriginal and treaty rights as "existing," *sui generis* rights suggests these rights have their origin outside of the settler-state or the

British constitutional tradition, and thus, arguably, find their roots in a not-so-new "book" that predates British constitutionalism in the Americas. The Indigenous constitutional orders within which Aboriginal and treaty rights are vested predate the extension of British common law into the Indigenous territories now occupied by Canada. They are, moreover, constitutional orders that several scholars and a number of early Canadian court cases recognized within the British common law tradition of *lex loci,* or the law of a place (Royal Commission on Aboriginal Peoples 1993; Barsh 2004). Thus, while not constituting a new book, *sui generis* Aboriginal and treaty rights populate the pages of unread chapters. Our failure to acknowledge those chapters obscures our understanding of political and constitutional history. In short, we cannot fully understand the well-worn constitutional book until we become familiar with these earlier chapters.

Viewed in this manner, 1982 and its aftermath represents a constitutional paradox, justifiably understood as both victory and defeat. Arguably, Indigenous people did not truly gain anything new in the *Constitution Act, 1982;* they simply had their existing rights recognized, affirmed, and protected within the constitution of the settler-state. However, rather than enabling the potential for a post-colonial order of which Henderson (1994) speaks, the state has spent much of the past thirty years attempting to retract, re-create, and refashion these rights in a manner more suited to maintaining colonialism. Brian Slattery (2005, 434) suggests that the Supreme Court's understanding of section 35 assumes that "the Crown's acquisition of sovereignty over indigenous peoples and their territories gave rise to Aboriginal rights in the Common law of Canada," but "Aboriginal peoples have to prove the existence of these rights on a case-by-case basis in order to gain judicial protection." This perspective – now dominant – not only rejects an Indigenous understanding of Indigenous constitutional orders, constitutional history, and the transformative potential of section 35 but also enables a recasting of Indigenous rights within the confines of a western-Eurocentric understanding of Indigenous peoples and their histories, thus making them subject to British/Canadian sovereignty (Borrows 2010).

It seems that Justice Binnie's proclamation that the Aboriginal provisions of the *Constitution Act, 1982* do not constitute a new book was intended to limit Aboriginal rights: no new rights were created, and those that were recognized could not be interpreted as being generative or transformative, for they were defined by "existing" expressions of such rights. This was likely what Premier Peter Lougheed had intended when he insisted on inclusion of the term "existing" within section 35 – namely, that "existing" meant those rights already recognized by the culturally biased common law up to 1982. Indeed, as an interpretive device, "existing" has generally tended not to invoke an understanding of Aboriginal and treaty rights as already existing outside the Canadian constitutional order. This has undermined the very real potential for section 35 to transform both Indigenous and settler nations and the relationships between them. The courts have, at times, departed from this restrictive view, asserting that section 35 rights developed out of a relationship between, and the reconciliation of, Indigenous peoples and Crown sovereignty (Slattery 2005, 435). However, cases offering a less restrictive interpretation of Aboriginal and treaty rights, such as *Haida Nation v. British Columbia (Ministry of Forests)* (2004) and *Taku River Tlingit First Nation v. British Columbia (Project Assessment Director)* (2004) are the exception. The restrictive view continues to dominate in political, legal, and even scholarly circles. Thus, while section 35 has decolonizing potential, restrictive readings of the Canadian constitution have undermined that potential, and even set the stage for the loss of "existing" rights associated with Indigenous constitutional orders. A review of the scholarship on some key cases is quite informative on this point.

In his frequently cited 1997 article on *R. v. Pamajewon* (1996), the case that gave rise to the notion of "permafrost rights," Bradford Morse (1997, 1014–16) argues that the Supreme Court has not taken positive advantage of its new-found capacity to define Aboriginal and treaty rights: "We have yet to see any increase in clarity or practical guidance beyond issues concerned with Aboriginal and hunting rights" because "our highest court [has] failed to enunciate these principles" in ways that promote balance within the Aboriginal-Crown relationship. The court, Morse (1997) adds, "has yet to articulate a clear statement of the legal status of the right of self-government, let alone on the scope of the right and its relationship to federal and provincial laws." According to Patricia

Monture-Angus (1999), not only have the courts failed to give meaning to Aboriginal and treaty rights, such as the right to self-determination, or to provide guidance for the type of renewed relationship that the Royal Commission on Aboriginal Peoples deemed essential, they have also chosen to use cases such as *R. v. Van der Peet* (1996), *Pamajewon*, *Mitchell*, and *R. v. Marshall* (1999) to reframe Aboriginal and treaty rights in a manner more amenable to Canadians, their governments, and the continuation of a colonial order.

Echoing Monture-Angus, Ladner and Dick (2008) suggest that "with the *Van der Peet* decision, the Supreme Court took Indigenous rights jurisprudence down a new and regrettable path, choosing to embrace a cultural justification for Aboriginal rights." In reframing the court's conceptualization of Aboriginal rights as mere cultural rights, Chief Justice Antonio Lamer stated in *Van der Peet* (1996, paras. 30–31):

> In my view, the doctrine of Aboriginal rights exists, and is recognized and affirmed by s.35(1), because of one simple fact: when Europeans arrived in North America, Aboriginal peoples *were already here*, living in communities on the land, and participating in distinctive cultures, as they had done for centuries ...
>
> ... [Therefore] the test for identifying the Aboriginal rights recognized and affirmed by s.35(1) must be directed at ... identifying the practices, traditions and customs central to the Aboriginal societies that existed in North America prior to contact with the Europeans.

Such reasoning freezes Aboriginal rights in some pre-colonial time of artificial authenticity. It further entrenches colonialism and the reification of a unified Canadian sovereignty by suggesting that the purpose of section 35 was to "reconcile the pre-existence of Aboriginal people with the sovereignty of the Crown" (Ladner and McCrossan 2009, 267–69) and link that with an extremely limited understanding of Aboriginal rights as the right to existing cultural practices that are (and have always been) "integral to the distinctive culture" (*R. v. Van der Peet* [1996], para. 6). This represents a rejection of Indigenous understandings of the patriation project as being one of constitutional pluralism, Indigenous nationalisms, and multiple sovereignties.

In promoting this "permafrost vision of rights," the Supreme Court has developed legal standards steeped in western-Eurocentric cultural perceptions of Indigenous peoples. Despite Lamer's insistence that his analysis of section 35 invokes principles that do not freeze Aboriginal rights, his writing of the majority decision in *Van der Peet* ignores such interpretive principles (as well as Aboriginal perspectives) and results in nothing less than the creation of permafrost conditions. It is interesting to note that even the High Court of Australia, a court that has never been known for its progressive interpretation of Indigenous rights or its treatment of Indigenous evidence, has been more intent and explicit in insisting that Aboriginal histories and perspectives need to be considered as creating an interpretive foundation (Russell 2005). In *Mabo and Others v. Queensland* (1992), for example, the High Court made it clear that Aboriginal laws (and thus Indigenous histories, legal and constitutional orders, and perspectives) provide the content of Aboriginal rights and title. This stands in striking contrast to the Supreme Court of Canada, which did not consider the substantive histories, jurisdictional or constitutional considerations, or Anishinaabe laws pertaining to the issues at hand in deciding *Pamajewon* – the court was content to limit its judicial purview to a written record comprising mainly historical and anthropological works of western-Eurocentric thinkers (Morse 1997, 1030–31).

The Canadian courts are freezing Aboriginal rights in accordance with western-Eurocentric notions of "Aboriginal culture" as it existed at some ill-defined (and possibly unknown) reference point in history. In so doing, they have not only denied the existence of Indigenous constitutional orders as the source (encryption) of the *sui generis* Aboriginal and treaty rights vested in the Canadian constitution post-patriation but have also completely failed to embrace and enable the realization of the post-colonial potential of the patriation deal. Instead, they have acted as if the constitutional book to which Justice Binnie referred remained unchanged after patriation.

Post-Patriation Constitutional Struggles

For the most part, both courts and politicians failed to recognize the potential of the *Constitution Act, 1982* with respect to issues of colonialism, the relations between settler and Indigenous nations, and Indigenous rights. Patriation need not have been a constitutional paradox; rather, it could have been a truly transformative moment, the apex of transitional justice (the point marking Canada's transition to a decolonized state). Instead, the struggle to realize the decolonizing potential of the constitution has been an arduous affair, with few real victories. This is because most of the legal and political victories that have "given meaning" to section 35 rights have come at great cost, and, in most cases, have limited the purview of the very Aboriginal and treaty rights that were being accorded constitutional recognition (*R. v. Marshall;* Borrows 2010; Monture-Angus 1999, 91). To resist postpatriation threats of retrenchment and restriction of rights through judicial action, policy change, and government inaction, Indigenous leaders and scholars have taken every opportunity to engage the state on constitutional matters and to bring clarity to the meaning of Indigenous rights in Canada. Such engagement has taken place on a variety of fronts and using a variety of venues, both domestic and international. The goal has been to educate settler societies and states about the realities of Indigenous peoples, nations, and rights, while forcing the transformation of colonialism and the relations between nations. The remainder of this chapter focuses primarily on the use of mega-constitutional politics to educate settler societies, engage decolonization, and transform the relationship, but other means have been and continue to be used, including grassroots struggles and protests such as Oka and Idle No More, and international mechanisms such as the United Nations *Declaration on the Rights of Indigenous Peoples.*

Having achieved some semblance of recognition of their rights, Indigenous peoples could have been forgiven for basking in a shared sense of achievement in the aftermath of the patriation agreement. They knew, however, that they had failed to educate Canadian leaders on the nature and meaning of Indigenous rights. They also recognized the magnitude of the challenge associated with enlisting Canadian political leaders, the institutions of the state, and Canadians in the resurgence of Indigenous nations and the realization of decolonization and the post-colonial potential of 1982. Educating Canadians and giving meaning to Indigenous rights through constitutional processes began in earnest in 1983, with the first constitutionally guaranteed First Ministers' conferences on the rights of Aboriginal peoples.

The Aboriginal constitutional conferences of 1983, 1984, 1985, and 1987 proved to be fraught with difficulty from the outset. The National Film Board documentary *Dancing around the Table* depicts the racism and intolerance shown to Indigenous peoples by Canadian politicians during these meetings. Canadian political leaders demonstrated a lack of understanding of Indigenous rights and unwillingness to engage Indigenous perspectives that contest the understanding of colonialism as a positive moment in Canadian history. Looking back, one cannot help but be struck by the interpretive disconnections surrounding sections 25 and 35. Indigenous demands and aspirations – including those that had recently been entrenched in the constitution – were apparently lost on Canadian politicians. This was never clearer than when, as mentioned above, Prime Minister Trudeau admitted, "I just don't understand what you want" (Ladner and McCrossan 2009, 269).

Despite these four full-fledged First Ministers' conferences and countless meetings with bureaucrats, the constitutional negotiating process that had been promised following patriation failed to advance the Indigenous agenda. Just as they had during the patriation process, the two sides continued to talk past each other, unable to overcome the paradigm paralysis that had long defined Indigenous/state relations. Although many would argue that such a paralysis resulted from the inability of Indigenous peoples and their "alternative world views" to come to grips with the actual constitutional negotiations, I would argue instead that it resulted from the inability of Canada to come to terms with its colonial self and of both sides to meaningfully engage in decolonization. Whichever way one chooses to characterize the paralysis, it defined this round of constitutional talks and perpetuated the constitutional paradox. Indigenous representatives spoke of an inherent right to self-determination that had existed since time immemorial and that would not (and could not) be defined and confined by the Canadian constitution, whereas non-Indigenous leaders denied that self-government was an Aboriginal or treaty right in the first place, suggesting instead that section 35 was an empty box that needed to be filled through intergovernmental agreements and, quite possibly, by the courts. Further, the organized voices of Indigenous women, embodied in organizations such as the Native Women's Association of Canada (NWAC), were not heard properly throughout these processes, even though the courts had ruled that such voices should be present (Russell 2004). Canada's federal and provincial leaders continued to define section 35 in the context of limited western-Eurocentric (individual) rights and had a hard time grasping notions of collective rights and non-western expressions of rights, history, and relations. As a result, Indigenous leaders faced a continuation of the ethos that had caused them to contest the patriation agreement – a lack of respect for the treaties and for their constitutional and political histories, and a lack of recognition of Indigenous rights that was exacerbated by a failure to grasp the decolonizing potential of section 35 and an unwillingness to protect Indigenous rights in the face of the Charter, the dominant society (the so-called common good), and colonial power.

There were successes, including agreement to amend section 35 to recognize its application to both men and women, but progress was limited. Over five long years, Indigenous leaders lobbied, negotiated, and persevered through four frustratingly unproductive First Ministers' conferences. To other Canadians, their expressions of displeasure appeared to represent the crumbling of the united Indigenous front in constitutional negotiations. In truth, however, Indigenous leaders never constituted a united front and never would. Divisions had always existed among and within the nations of the Americas, and colonization had not changed this. In their efforts to discover a simple (singular) expression of what Indigenous people wanted, Canada's political leadership found these divisions particularly vexing.

While the final First Ministers' conference on Aboriginal rights (1987) was intensely exasperating to and further fractured the Indigenous leadership, their cause was dealt an even harsher blow by the Meech Lake Accord – an accord that accommodated one of the "founding nations" of Canada while further alienating the original nations. Faced with the possibility that the terms of the accord would further amplify settler sovereignty and rights, Indigenous leaders did not want to risk jeopardizing the minor gains they had made by accepting an accord that could further entrench the colonial paradigm. They, therefore, set to work against Meech, and finally, found a window of opportunity when a parliamentary procedural technicality enabled Cree MLA Elijah Harper to block the accord's passage in the Manitoba legislature, effectively killing it (*Elijah* 2008).

In resisting the Meech Lake Accord's French/English (two-nation) conception of constitutional nationalism – and thus the deepening exclusion of Indigenous nations from Canada's constitutional foundations – Elijah Harper spurred a political awakening. One profound expression of this awakening comprised the events of the "Indian summer" of 1990 (Wagamese 1996; Peach 2011, 21). Images of Harper in the Manitoba legislature holding an eagle feather, and of the Mohawk men, women, and children standing behind barricades in defence of their lands and their sovereignty at Kanehsatà:ke (Oka) and Kahnawa:ke, were burned into the minds of all. Canadians were confronted by "Indians in unexpected places" (Deloria 2004), who had demands (constitutional and otherwise) that required an overhaul of the colonial project. Indigenous peoples responded to these rallying cries, transforming Indigenous political consciousness and solidifying Indigenous political demands in a manner inextricably embedded in the context of nationhood, sovereignty, and Indigenous laws, histories, and political traditions (Simpson and Ladner 2010). However, the unpredictable, even volatile, nature of this awakening also had the effect of further fracturing the so-called Indigenous community. These divisions were delineated by nations (e.g., Mohawk, Cree, and Dene), as well as political-institutional affinities with band councils, traditional governments, Christians, traditionalists, assimilationists, and nationalists.

As the events of 1990 unfolded, it was clear that any reopening of the constitutional negotiation process would have to include Indigenous peoples and their issues, and that Indigenous peoples' lack of support for the patriation deal could no longer be ignored (Peach 2011, 14–15). Thus, from the outset of the post-Meech "Canada Round" (sometimes called the Charlottetown round) of mega-constitutionalism, Indigenous peoples were included as active participants. This inclusion did not signify a meaningful end to the colonial approach to constitutionalism, however, nor did it alter the manner in which Canadian (and Quebec) constitutional nationalism obscured and denied Indigenous constitutional histories and decolonizing or post-colonial aspirations. Moreover, organized Indigenous women were excluded from the Charlottetown round until they took legal action pursuant to section 15 of the Charter (Russell 2004). This exclusion was particularly significant given that Indigenous women had been at the centre of Indigenous political systems and constitutional orders until colonialism, and the *Indian Act* excluded them and imposed western notions of gendered politics on Indigenous communities (Monture-Angus 1995; Smith 2005).

Once at the table, Indigenous leaders continued to face tremendous challenges in asserting their vision of Indigenous constitutional orders. These challenges were less intense than those faced by the previous generation of leaders who navigated the First Ministers' conferences of the 1980s, but Assembly of First Nations (AFN) constitutional adviser Mary-Ellen Turpel-Lafond and Grand Chief Ovide Mercredi documented the latent effects of colonialism on constitutional politics in their book *In the Rapids* (1993), and their experience shows just how difficult it is for Indigenous constitutional orders, sovereignty, nationalism, and understandings of treaties and Aboriginal rights to be adequately included in a constitution when they are poorly understood and neither taken seriously nor accorded respect because of the racism and colonialism that infuse Canadian society (Little Bear, Leroy, and Long 1984; Turpel 1989–90; Cairns and Williams 1991; Russell 2004).

Not surprisingly, then, the Charlottetown Accord was primarily a continuation of the dialogue of the deaf (or at least of the hard of hearing), concerning the (limited) meaning of Aboriginal and treaty rights that began with patriation. It was a multidirectional and multilevel discussion with the parties trying to scale the hurdle of incomprehension that had defined past conversations, yet they still managed to talk past each other. It was as though Indigenous leaders had finally been invited to participate in the constitutional poker game but continued to be excluded from actually playing the game, as both they and settler governments were playing two very different games while continuing to speak past each other, despite the use of the same language. In other words, although there appeared to be a commitment to inclusion of Aboriginals and to engagement with issues of incommensurability (of supposed "world views"), the paradigm paralysis persisted as the Canadian leadership showed no real commitment to dismantling colonialism. Arguably, the two sides' positions, their understandings of the past, and their visions of the future remained completely incommensurable. One party simply wanted to define and restrict the meaning of Aboriginal and treaty rights as part of a Canadian constitution- and nation-building project. The other wanted to protect and secure the rights of nations as separate yet intricately tied to this project through colonialism, and to redefine that relationship through self-determination and the unfolding of their own constitutional orders within section 35 (Mercredi and Turpel 1993; Henderson, Benson, and Findlay 2000; Ladner and McCrossan 2009). Despite these differences and the continuing challenges resulting from defining Aboriginal and treaty rights within the rubric and scope of western-Eurocentrism, the negotiations successfully brought issues to the table and ensured that they were addressed in the Charlottetown Accord. In fact, Aboriginal people were touted by most as the big winners of this round of mega-constitutional politics and, unlike in 1982, the Charlottetown Accord was acceptable to most Indigenous leaders (Cairns and Williams 1991; Russell 2004; Peach 2011, 19).

Once Canadian leaders got beyond questioning whether Aboriginal and treaty rights, such as the right to self-government, even – or, for that matter, ever – existed, Indigenous leaders were able to secure constitutional recognition of their peoples' inherent right to self-government; the right to participate in First Ministers' conferences; the development of a Métis Accord (a parallel accord pursuant to subsection 91[24] as well as sections 25 and 35); land rights; and the commitment of governments to hold biennial First Ministers' conferences on Aboriginal issues in order to move towards the implementation of treaties. This amounted, by most accounts, to a monumental achievement and a real victory for Indigenous peoples, particularly the Métis. Others, however, saw it as a monumental defeat. Indigenous leaders were chastised for selling out the remnants of Indigenous sovereignty and constitutional orders, for accepting the domination of western-Eurocentrism, and for agreeing to the continuation of colonialism as perpetuated through constitutional nationalism and the reification of Canadian sovereignty. Still others saw some Indigenous peoples as winning (Métis and, to a lesser extent, non–Treaty nations) and others as losing (Treaty nations and women). Most of the grassroots activists felt that the achievements were too limited, and the majority of Indigenous peoples seized the opportunity to vote "No" in the 1992 Charlottetown Accord referendum.

Reflecting on Thirty Years since Patriation

Ian Peach (2011, 19) has argued that the Charlottetown Accord's "provisions on Indigenous self-government and Métis issues, in particular, remain the 'high-water marks' in the willingness of governments to address Indigenous issues in Canada." Since then, momentum has diminished considerably among the general public, politicians, and the courts. No one seems willing to tackle Indigenous issues en masse and to work towards the transformation of the relationship between the settler-state and Indigenous nations, or to dismantle colonialism and its construction of nationhood and sovereignty, whether through mega-constitutional reform or other means (such as the Royal Commission on Aboriginal Peoples, the short-lived Kelowna Accord, or Prime Minister Stephen Harper's regressive legislative agenda). Indigenous peoples have been calling upon the federal and provincial governments to engage in constitutional discussions since they rejected the patriation deal in 1982. For the most part, however, settler governments have been reluctant to deal with Indigenous issues such as housing and education, even on a piecemeal basis. Even when success was attained through the 2005 Kelowna Accord, which sought to create a new relationship and close the socio-economic gap in housing, health care, and education, this success was short-lived as Paul Martin's government fell and Stephen Harper immediately retreated to the politics of old (characterized by reluctance and disregard). This disregard is all the more egregious when considered in the context of years of constrained budgets while population growth is making it increasingly difficult to tackle deteriorating socio-economic conditions on reserves.

Most scholars contend that renewed momentum towards real change requires a transformative event like the Oka Crisis of 1990 (Ladner 2010; Russell 2010; Peach 2011, 26). While the marches, social media blasts, round dances, and hunger strikes associated with Idle No More seemed capable of becoming a flashpoint with transformative potential even greater than Oka, momentum was surely lost through the cold days of winter following the 11 January 2013 meeting between Prime Minister Harper and the Assembly of First Nations. Still the flames of Idle No More may continue to inspire change, shift public opinion, and force governments into action, even if many remain doubtful that the resulting action would be consistent with the type of transformative shift that is required. The problem is that Canadians (and their governments and courts) are still acting as though 1982 changed nothing for Indigenous peoples, as though colonialism may have been modified slightly by constitutional nationalism but, in the end, the old book remains. Notions of the singular sovereign and western-Eurocentrism continue to define and restrict Indigenous nations and their ability to rebuild their nations and economies and to govern themselves in accordance with their own constitutional orders (be they existing, rebuilt, or newly created), protected by Aboriginal and treaty rights.

Despite the initial rejection of the patriation agreement by the Indigenous leadership – and their continued misgivings about the result – countless Indigenous and non-Indigenous scholars, including Peter Russell in Chapter 11, have argued that the *Constitution Act, 1982* has monumental transformative power and post-colonial potential (*Mabo and Others v. Queensland* [1992]; Slattery 1984; Ladner 2003; Henderson 2004; Russell 2004, 2005; Borrows 2010). However, the leaders who rejected the patriation package knew that they had not achieved enough to effectively alter the colonial paradigm. This is why leaders have continuously demanded Crown–First Nations gatherings (such as those held in January 2012 and 2013) or constitutional talks to address the meaning and implementation of Aboriginal and treaty rights, and why the grassroots activists have taken up issues of Aboriginal and treaty rights, nationhood, sovereignty, and Indigenous lands in Idle No More. Thus, even after over thirty years, patriation remains both a monumental victory and a monumental defeat. It remains a constitutional paradox despite its potential.

The substance of patriation should have resulted in the affirmation of Indigenous constitutional orders, but ultimately this was not realized, because of an absence of political will, inclination, and understanding on the part of Canadian politicians. Canada's political leaders have failed to recognize Aboriginal and treaty rights for what they are: encrypted or *sui generis* rights that flow from Indigenous constitutional (legal, political, and spiritual) histories defined by Indigenous languages, notions of territoriality, economies, spirituality, and histories. Instead, Canadian governments and courts have been intent on establishing their own doctrine of existing rights and reasserting a singular Eurocentric narrative of constitutionalism built on Canadian nationalism, a reification of sovereignty, colonialism, and patriarchy.

The patriation process, subsequent negotiations, and judicial interpretation over the last thirty years demonstrate a larger truth. Indigenous constitutional orders are currently incomprehensible to and incompatible with the Canadian constitutional order, with its roots in common law, civil law, and the "legal magic" of colonialism (Russell 2005). As scholars such as Mary-Ellen Turpel-Lafond have argued, a deep attachment to western-Eurocentrism has prevented Canadian politicians and judges from adequately understanding Indigenous peoples' laws, histories, and political traditions (Turpel 1989–90). Constitutional orders, like law and intellectual and political traditions, are culturally relative. The legal and interpretive tenets of one legal order cannot be used to understand another legal order without distorting and caricaturing that other. This is one reason why most Indigenous scholars and leaders have viewed the application of the Charter as problematic (although there is a very gendered debate over the Charter and its application). It is also one of the primary reasons why Indigenous leaders walked away from or rejected the patriation agreement: they doubted the capacity of section 25 to serve as a shield that would protect *sui generis* rights encrypted as Aboriginal and treaty rights (Turpel 1989–90; Ladner and McCrossan 2009).

Indigenous peoples are still struggling with or rejecting the *Constitution Act, 1982* for its perpetuation of colonialism and western-Eurocentrism, its promotion of an exclusionary constitutional nationalism, and its reification of a unified singular sovereign nation. They are struggling because, despite the act's tremendous potential for laying a foundation for decolonization or establishing a post-colonial constitutionalism, it is becoming increasingly doubtful that this potential can be realized in the face of Canada's apparent unwillingness to disengage from its colonial mentality of presumed authority and its paralyzying attachment to western-Eurocentrism. Indeed, it is increasingly argued that the *Constitution Act* as amended at patriation is a threat to Indigenous nations. The constitution itself becomes a threat to Indigenous societies when, for example, section 35 requires Indigenous peoples to prove their cultural integrity according to the standards of another dominant and historically antagonistic culture. Scholars such as Alfred (1999) contend that a threat like this should have been rejected in its totality right at the outset.

By rendering decisions in countless Aboriginal and treaty rights cases – such as *Van der Peet* (1996), *Marshall* (1999), and *R. v. Sappier; R. v. Gray* (2006) – the Supreme Court of Canada has, in essence, determined the "authentic Indian" past, present, and future based on the primacy of its own cultural bias. Viewed in this light, the implications of the court's interpretation of section 35 as constituting a new chapter but not a new book become crystal-clear. This book does not even attempt to cloak its cultural bias; it remains preoccupied with what Ward Churchill (1998) described as a "fantasy of the master race." It remains intent on sustaining domination, invoking reconciliation as a means of reifying a unified sovereign while denying Indigenous peoples agency or contemporary expressions of nationhood by locating their rights in some everlasting pre-colonial state. Unfortunately, the Supreme Court has not yet discovered the true spirit and intent of section 35 or the chapters in the history of constitutional law and politics in "Canada," which preceded the occupation of the Americas and the staging of colonial constitutional traditions. Instead of embracing the post-colonial potential offered by section 35 and the Indigenous constitutional orders that are encrypted within it, the courts have largely continued down the same well-worn track, pausing from time to time to retrench the old colonial paradigm. Admittedly, the courts have occasionally created windows of opportunity for the advancement of the post-colonial potential of the patriation project, and limited progress has been made through cases such as *Haida Nation* (2004) and *Delgamuukw* (1991), which challenge the colonial status quo. By and large, however, Indigenous peoples have gained very little from patriation and continue to suffer tremendous losses as a result of the courts' failure to explore the unread chapters on Indigenous constitutional, legal, and political histories.

Those who hoped section 35 might advance the sovereignty of Indigenous peoples within the Canadian constitution have had their optimism dashed by the Supreme Court's many misinterpretations – misinterpretations that repeatedly demonstrate the inevitable truth of incommensurability (Turpel 1989–90). Perhaps the inevitability of this truth can be altered, and we can find ways to realize the post-colonial potential inherent in the patriation project. Perhaps it can be altered if Canada and its constitutional foundations are rethought in such a way as to create a mutually beneficial and mutually agreeable future for Indigenous and settler nations alike. The fact of the matter, however, is that creating such a future will take much more than judicial victories based on section 35. It will require transformative constitutional change rooted in new understandings of constitutional histories, sovereignties, Indigenous nationalisms, and Indigenous constitutional orders. This will require that Canadians first recognize and then reject the realities of colonialism and the legal magic that has enabled the occupation, oppression, and dispossession of Indigenous lands and Indigenous peoples. In short, overcoming the incommensurability and paradigm paralysis that have defined Aboriginal constitutional politics (and Canada's Aboriginal policy more generally) requires truly transformative change. Truly transformative change will require that Canadians (their governments and their courts) be "Idle No More," or that, at the very least, they learn to play constitutional poker in a more honourable way!

References

Alfred, Taiaiake. 1999. *Peace, Power, Righteousness.* Don Mills, ON: Oxford University Press.

Barsh, Russell Lawrence. 2004. "Indigenous Rights and the *Lex Loci* in British Imperial Law." In *Advancing Aboriginal Claims,* edited by Kerry Wilkins, 91–126. Saskatoon: Purich Publishing.

Borrows, John. 2010. *Canada's Indigenous Constitution.* Toronto: University of Toronto Press.

Bulbulian, Maurice. 1983. *Dancing around the Table.* Part 1. http://www.nfb.ca/film/dancing_around_the_table_1.

Cairns, Alan, and D.E. Williams. 1991. *Disruptions.* Toronto: McClelland and Stewart.

Churchill, Ward. 1998. *Fantasies of the Master Race.* San Francisco: City Lights Books.

Delgamuukw v. British Columbia, [1997] 3 S.C.R. 1010 [*Delgamuukw*].

Deloria, Phillip. 2004. *Indians in Unexpected Places.* Kansas City: University Press of Kansas.

Elijah. 2008. Film. Paul Unwin, director. Produced for the CTV Television Network.

Government of Canada. 1969. "Statement of the Government of Canada on Indian Policy, 1969." Presented to the First Session of the Twenty-Eighth Parliament of Canada by the Honourable Jean Chrétien, Minister of Indian Affairs and Northern Development, Ottawa, 25 June.

Green, Joyce. 2005. "Toward Conceptual Precision." In *Insiders and Outsiders,* edited by G. Kernerman and P. Resnick, 227–41. Vancouver: UBC Press.

Haida Nation v. British Columbia (Ministry of Forests), [2004] 3 S.C.R. 511 [*Haida Nation*].

Henderson, James (Sákéj) Youngblood. 1994. "Empowering Treaty Federalism." *Saskatchewan Law Review* 58: 241–329.

—. 2004. "Aboriginal Jurisprudence and Rights." In *Advancing Aboriginal Claims*, edited by Kerry Wilkins, 67–89. Saskatoon: Purich Publishing.

Henderson, James (Sákéj) Youngblood, Marjorie Benson, and Isobel Findlay. 2000. *Aboriginal Tenure in the Constitution of Canada.* Scarborough, ON: Carswell.

Ladner, Kiera. 2003. "Rethinking Aboriginal Governance." In *Reinventing Canada*, edited by Janine Brodie and Linda Trimble, 43–60. Toronto: Prentice Hall.

—. 2010. "From Little Things ..." In *This Is an Honour Song: Twenty Years since the Blockades*, edited by Leanne Simpson and Kiera Ladner, 299–314. Winnipeg: Arbeiter Ring Publishing.

Ladner, Kiera, and Caroline Dick. 2008. "Out of the Fires of Hell." *Canadian Journal of Law and Society* 23: 63–91.

Ladner, Kiera, and Michael McCrossan. 2009. "The Road Not Taken." In *Contested Constitutionalism*, edited by James Kelly and Christopher Manfredi, 263–86. Vancouver: UBC Press.

Ladner, Kiera, and Michael Orsini. 2005. "The Persistence of Paradigm Paralysis." In *Canada: State of the Federation*, edited by Michael Murphy, 185–203. Kingston: Institute of Intergovernmental Relations, Queen's University.

Little Bear, Menno Boldt Leroy, and J. Anthony Long. 1984. *Pathways to Self-Determination.* Toronto: University of Toronto Press.

Mabo and Others v. Queensland (No. 2), [1992] HCA 23; (1992) 175 C.L.R. 1 [*Mabo*].

Mercredi, Ovide, and Mary-Ellen Turpel. 1993. *In the Rapids.* Toronto: Penguin Books Canada.

Mitchell v. M.N.R, [2001] 1 S.C.R. 911.

Monture-Angus, Patricia. 1995. *Thunder in My Soul.* Halifax: Fernwood Publishing.

—. 1999. *Journeying Forward.* Halifax: Fernwood Publishing.

Morse, Bradford. 1997. "Permafrost Rights: Aboriginal Self-Government and the Supreme Court in *R. v. Pamajewon.*" *McGill Law Journal/Revue de droit de McGill* 42: 1011.

Peach, Ian. 2011. "The Power of a Single Feather." *Review of Constitutional Studies* 16: 1–30.

R. v. Marshall, [1999] 3 S.C.R. 533 [*Marshall*].

R. v. Pamajewon, [1996] 2 S.C.R. 821 [*Pamajewon*].

R. v. Sappier; R. v. Gray, [2006] 2 S.C.R. 686.

R. v. Van der Peet, [1996] 2 S.C.R. 507 [*Van der Peet*].

Royal Commission on Aboriginal Peoples (RCAP). 1993. *Partners in Confederation.* Ottawa: Canada Communications Group.

Russell, Peter. 2004. *Canada's Constitutional Odyssey.* Toronto: University of Toronto Press.

—. 2005. *Recognizing Aboriginal Title.* Toronto: University of Toronto Press.
—. 2010. "Oka to Ipperwash: The Necessity of Flashpoint Events." In *This Is an Honour Song,* edited by Leanne Simpson and Kiera Ladner, 29–46. Winnipeg: Arbeiter Ring Publishing.
Simpson, Leanne, and Kiera Ladner, eds. 2010. *This Is an Honour Song.* Winnipeg: Arbeiter Ring Publishing.
Slattery, Brian. 1984. "The Hidden Constitution: Aboriginal Rights in Canada." *American Journal of Comparative Law* 32 (2): 361–91. doi:10.2307/840473.
—. 2005. "Aboriginal Rights and the Honour of the Crown." *Supreme Court Law Review* 20: 433–45.
Smith, Andrea. 2005. *Conquest: Sexual Violence and American Indian Genocide.* Cambridge, MA: South End Press.
Taku River Tlingit First Nation v. British Columbia (Project Assessment Director), [2004] 3 S.C.R. 550 [*Taku River*].
Turpel, Mary-Ellen. 1989–90. "Aboriginal Peoples and the Canadian Charter." *Canadian Human Rights Yearbook* 3: 4–45.
Wagamese, Richard. 1996. *The Terrible Summer.* Toronto: Warwick Publishing.

14

The Sad but True Story of a Shrinking Equality Opportunity Structure

Alexandra Dobrowolsky

In the early 1980s, women and other groups seized the patriation moment to launch equality struggles that shaped and significantly defined constitutionalism in Canada (Dobrowolsky 1998, 2000). Feminists latched onto the constitutional process and pried open its constrained notions of equality through a combination of rhetorical/strategic, descriptive/empirical, and normative claims (Hunter 2008a, 81).

Today, equality claims are on much shakier ground. On the one hand, equality seekers themselves express disappointment at the limited effects of constitutionalizing Canada's sex equality provisions (Jhappan 2002; McIntyre and Rodgers 2006). On the other hand, equality claims appear to have disappeared, as the detractors of gender equality have succeeded in popularizing the idea that equality between Canadian women and men is a given (Brodie 2008; Brodie and Bakker 2008; Jenson 2009).

What explains such glaring inconsistencies between dominant political discourses and empirical realities surrounding women's equality? There are two broad factors:

1 The opportunity created by the patriation of the constitution and women's efforts to entrench and expand notions of equality – the *constitutional opportunity structure* – has passed (Irving 2009, 79).

2 The *equality opportunity structure* – the discourses, institutional and noninstitutional political arrangements, and identity configurations that once bolstered gender equality struggles – has been so altered that equality claims have lost their rhetorical, empirical, and normative traction. The *erosion* of this structure, and the processes facilitating its *erasure,* are unprecedented.

This chapter interrogates the current *invisibilization* of gender equality by the governing Conservative Party and the problematic *instrumentalizing* (i.e., the politically calculated deployment) of gender equality by the opposition parties (Dobrowolsky 2008a). It highlights shifts in Canada's equality opportunity structure by tracing developments over the last three decades concerning discourse, identity, and voice. The first section explores the equality opportunity structure at patriation, while the next reviews the subsequent changes. The major campaign platforms from the 2011 federal general election are then analyzed to provide further evidence of the closure of the equality opportunity structure.

Relative Openness

As Chapter 10 attests, women were central players in the "macroconstitutional" activity leading to patriation and its consequences (see also Hosek 1983; Kome 1983; Dobrowolsky 1998, 2000). Through the 1980s and 1990s, women's "microconstitutional" engagement refined the meanings and mechanisms of equality (Manfredi 2004). This was a time in which the "idea of gender equality, as advanced by second wave feminism, was ... [emerging] out of the discourses of post-war social liberalism and the institutions of the welfare state" (Brodie 2008, 150).

Contemporary Canadian constitutional debates also evolved in this social liberal milieu. Indeed, in the years preceding the 1971 Victoria Charter, F.R. Scott (1977, 34) contended that Canada's constitutional maturity would be expressed not only through its disentanglement from Britain but also through a strong, activist, egalitarian state mindful of minority rights and multicultural composition. From the late '60s to the First Ministers' conference in 1981, federal constitutional proposals "were consistently informed, not by a desire to respond in an accommodative fashion to provincialism, but to weaken it, and to build a resurgent

Canadianism and a stronger Ottawa to fight it" (Cairns 1983, 32). Pierre Trudeau's Liberal government epitomized this commitment to "strong federal executive power as a counter to rapidly burgeoning French-Canadian nationalism," which in turn "seemed to confirm and reinforce Keynesian thinking which had preached the concentration of economic planning and decision-making powers in the central government" (McWhinney 1979, 94). Moreover, Trudeau's philosophical orientation towards a "Just Society" meant supporting social justice, expressed through both rhetoric and funding for multiculturalism, Aboriginal organizations, and women's groups. These community bases could, in turn, endorse Trudeau's vision of the constitution and Charter.

In this discursive setting, and indeed in the context of a broader post-war rights agenda (Clément 2008), social movements claimed legitimacy by both exposing the empirical realities of inequality and mobilizing equality as a rhetorical and normative tactic. In hearings around the *Canadian Bill of Rights, 1960,* for example, "the ordinarily disrespected became valued experts from whom elites had to learn. In their view, who better to explain the need for a charter than the groups most unhappily familiar with repression and tyranny" (James 2006, 62)? Miriam Smith (1999, 71) recounts how the "equality-seeking frame was drawn from the civil rights and counter-cultural movements of the sixties and from the opportunities provided by human rights commissions, before the advent of the Charter of Rights." And so, despite the limitations of the *Canadian Bill of Rights, 1960* and the doomed Victoria Charter, the equality opportunity structure had real substance.

The establishment of the Royal Commission on the Status of Women (RCSW) in 1968 reflected the tenor of the era. Women's lobbying and threats of mass protests led to the commission's formation, and its impact went far beyond endorsement of formal equality. It sparked a transformation within the state, with the development of status of women mechanisms such as the Canadian Advisory Council on the Status of Women (CACSW), and outside it, with the formation of the umbrella National Action Committee on the Status of Women (NAC), along with countless women's groups across the country (Newman and White 2012, 72–74).

This was a period of socio-economic and political transition. As post-war economic development slowed in the 1970s, Keynesian policy logic and the merits of an interventionist state were increasingly called into question, but the patriation process provided political space for the continued advance of social liberal discourses. Indeed, these discourses, and social movement activism around rights, ensured the prominence of foundational equality principles in the framing of the patriated constitution and the *Canadian Charter of Rights and Freedoms.* To the extent that the objectives of collective identities and communities aligned with Trudeau's constitutional project, they were regarded as useful in counterbalancing competing discourses, interests, and identities, particularly from the provinces, especially Quebec.

Not all rights-focused communities were equally prepared to intervene (Smith 1999, 71; Saunders 1983, 303), and so, beyond the Aboriginal mobilization recounted by others in this volume, it was mostly "English speaking feminist organizations and ethnocultural minority organizations" as well as disability activists that were "particularly successful in exploiting the political opportunity afforded by Trudeau's vision" (James 2006, 7).

Reservations concerning the Charter remained (Hosek 1983, 280). For example, NAC's submission to the 1980–81 Special Joint Committee on the Constitution (the Hays-Joyal Committee) asserted that "women could be worse off if the proposed charter of rights and freedoms is entrenched in Canada's constitution" (Dobrowolsky 2000, 47; Manfredi 2004, 44). Yet because patriation was viewed as a historic opportunity, feminists launched rhetorical, normative, and empirical equality claims. The process started with "legally knowledgeable women," moved to more "established women's groups working with the Ad Hoc Committee," and finally reached "far beyond activists to individual women" (Baines 2005, 50). Despite setbacks, feminists used both elite lobbying and mass protest tactics to mount a "successful campaign" to tighten existing equality provisions and entrench a new and "separate, overriding constitutional statement of women's equality" (James 2006, 85; Chapter 10).

The equality opportunity structure was workable in terms of both discourse and voice. Most notably, the CACSW and Status of Women Canada (SWC, established in 1971) provided a degree of internal leverage (Chappell 2002), and the Secretary of State's Women's Program resources enabled external lobbying efforts. Indeed, funding for the Women's Program rose from $700,000 in 1980 to $1.2 million in 1981 (Pal 1993, 143). As a result, women's groups enjoyed "unprecedented access to Canadian politicians and bureaucrats" (Brodie 2010).

Moreover, during the patriation process, fissures in party solidarity and the lack of consensus on evolving constitutional positions made it easier for feminists to breach party ranks (Dobrowolsky 2000). Women MPs were few in number, but they had a relatively high profile and many had movement connections. Thus, their actions in support of the gender equality struggle were noted inside and outside the parties. Seizing such political openings – intra- and intergovernmentally, as well as between and within the parties – women equality seekers created spaces to advance their agenda from within and from without.

Women's constitutional activism disrupted and challenged territorially based identities that had historically dominated discussions of federalism and constitutionalism. To be sure, the women's movement encompassed multiple, often conflicting identities, interests, and strategic priorities (Dobrowolsky 2008b). At this point, however, the leaders of women's groups were inclined to paper over differences to achieve the broader goal of constitutional entrenchment of gender equality. There were challenges from within the women's movement that were rooted in identity politics, just as there continued to be charter skeptics. However, national and local women's groups pragmatically united with a view akin to this one articulated over a decade later: "Criticisms of the *Charter*'s efficacy as a tool for egalitarian social change must be balanced against the realization that the *Charter* [would become] a fact of our legal and social universe" (LEAF 1996, xxv).

Taken together, the foregoing analysis points to favourable conditions in terms of discourse, voice, and identity that allowed women to use, and then enhance, the equality opportunity structure. The constitutional entrenchment of equality in sections 15 and 28 of the Charter acted as a springboard for feminists, who then deepened and widened equality in legal arenas, "microconstitutionally," in their campaign for substantive equality (Manfredi 2004, 49).

When section 15 came into force in 1985, the lower courts were overwhelmed with equality cases. Yet in "591 cases decided during the first three years, less than 10 percent were based on sex, thirty-five of which were brought by or on behalf of men, and only nine by or on behalf of women," and most of the litigation reflected formal equality (Baines 2005, 52–53). Nonetheless, "the Supreme Court decided equality should not be restricted to formal equality ... [and much] of the credit for persuading the Court to adopt substantive equality analysis belongs to the Women's Legal Education and Action Fund, better known as LEAF" (52–53). This national, nonprofit organization was founded in 1985 with the dual mandate of litigating to promote equality for women, and educating jurists and the wider public about this litigation and its relationship to women's equality (LEAF 1996, xi). As Baines (2005, 49) characterizes it, the Charter cast Canadian feminists as "lobbyists," but also as litigators working "to import the doctrine of substantive equality into *Charter* cases."

The Court Challenges Program (CCP) provided state support for litigation-based equality seeking. The CCP was first established under Trudeau in 1977 to support legal challenges by minority language groups, and its mandate broadened as the Charter's equality provisions came into force. Brian Mulroney's Conservative government initially expanded the program, but then cancelled it in 1992 to cut costs. The public outcry was fierce, and the Liberals committed themselves to reinstating the program as part of their 1993 election platform, which they did in 1994. The CCP's shifting fortunes foreshadowed strikes against the equality opportunity structure that would, in turn, destabilize feminist post-patriation macro- and microconstitutional efforts and lead to increasingly reactive equality struggles.

The Shrinking Equality Opportunity Structure

Today, the social liberal discourses of a strong welfare state, a positive disposition towards multiculturalism, equality seekers, and arguably even equality have weakened dramatically. Through the 1980s and '90s, critiques of "big government," together with growing individualism, and fiscal conservatism began undermining the equality opportunity structure, making gender equality more susceptible to challenge and, ultimately, even to practices of invisibilization. Conservative prime ministers Brian Mulroney and Kim Campbell embraced neoliberal rhetoric (Bashevkin 1998), which was then operationalized in public policy under the Liberal governments of Jean Chrétien (Bakker 1996; Brodie 1996; Bashevkin 2002). The turn to neoliberalism meant a move away from an activist state with an engaged interest in gender equity. Broadly speaking, equality-seeking voices were drowned out by the now-dominant neoliberal mantra of individualization, cost cutting, and streamlining of the state.

Changes were afoot within the women's movement at the same time. Diversity in women's movement priorities and leadership was taken more seriously, which made reaching consensus positions more challenging. It became harder to make blanket statements regarding gender equality, as such claims were vigorously disputed (Crow and Gotell 2000, 65–69). These identity and equality struggles were manifested in both the Meech Lake and Charlottetown Accord campaigns of the late 1980s and early 1990s. The former pitted Quebec's feminist organizations against those outside the province, while the latter resulted in even more deeply contentious identity politics disputes, with the focus of negotiations shifting from two nations to three (Quebec, the "rest of Canada," and First Nations).

Women's groups outside Quebec played a determinative role in the sinking of both accords (Dobrowolsky 2000) but with significant costs, not only in terms of state support but also at the expense of discourse, identity, and voice regarding gender equality. These unsuccessful reform processes sealed Canada's constitutional opportunity structure and shook the foundations of Canada's equality opportunity structure.

Because collective identity struggles became very complicated and fractious, especially with the sweeping scope of the "Canada Round" of constitutional negotiations, many women's groups hesitated to take a public stand on the Charlottetown Accord. NAC was a strong critic, however, and acted in solidarity with the Native Women's Association of Canada (NWAC), which argued that this agreement put Aboriginal women's equality rights at risk. As a result, NAC's representational legitimacy was fundamentally questioned. Buttons appeared declaring that "NAC does not speak for me" (Rebick 2002, 74), and when it took the "No" side in the Charlottetown referendum, the Mulroney government labelled NAC an "enemy of Canada" (Crow and Gotell 2000, 67). Rather than viewing the diversity in identities, ideas, and tactics among women's groups as an asset, detractors, including politicians, the mainstream media

(Rebick and Roach 1996, 118), and groups like Realistic, Equal and Active for Life (REAL) Women, used it in divide-and-conquer manoeuvres.

In response, coalition building became an important feminist organizational strategy. LEAF, for instance, adopted a diversification policy in 1990. Its objectives were to actively pursue "a broad representation of women" and to "broaden its knowledge and understanding of different women's lives" by increasingly working "as one member of a coalition" (LEAF 1996, xxii). Yet coalition work was both labour-intensive and time-consuming, and often produced complex compromises that were difficult to convey to the public. Moreover, the challenge of negotiating, resolving, and publicizing issues intensified as financial and personal resources waned. These factors help to explain LEAF's low profile during Charlottetown.

Increasingly defensive responses also arose in a context of political and policy change that de-emphasized "direct state intervention and prefer[red] to see social services provided either privately or as cash transfers to households" (Cohen and Pulkingham 2009, 22). This remaking of social policy lent credence to "an ideological attack on groups such as women, racial minorities, and the poor," now characterized as having costly, vexatious issues and demands that diverged from those of "ordinary Canadians" (Abu-Laban 2009, 151). Populist discourses disputed the merits of funding equality seekers. In stark contrast to the patriation period, then, feminist organizations were both publicly "dissed" and perfunctorily dismissed as "special interests" (Dobrowolsky 1998; Brodie 2002).

Governments removed routes to representational access to save money and, arguably, to stifle dissenting voices. Equality-seeking groups and agencies became prime targets for budget streamlining in response to their unwelcome evidence of the detrimental impact that neoliberal federal government initiatives (from free trade to the Charlottetown Accord's "economic union") would have on diverse women (Jenson and Phillips 1996; Dobrowolsky and Jenson 2004).

SWC continued to describe its mandate as advancing "'the equality of women by addressing women's economic, social, political, and legal situation" (as quoted in Brodie 2008, 153); outside its offices, however, these discourses were only weakly articulated. For example, although the federal government released its gender equality plan in 1995 (Bakker 2009, 229), by the late 1990s, the Liberal government's new buzzword was social exclusion, and how to combat it with social inclusion and social cohesion (Dobrowolsky 2009b). Women's rallying cry of equality had stopped resonating (Dobrowolsky 2008b, 2009a; Jenson 2009).

Such developments help explain the lack of public outrage when SWC actually removed equality from its mandate. Soon after the Conservatives took office in 2006, Beverley Oda, the new minister entrusted with the Status of Women portfolio, bluntly proclaimed that the problem of inequality of women had been resolved (Brodie 2008,145). The Conservatives also "downgraded" the position of the minister responsible for the status of women to that of a "minister of state," thus denying women's interests a designated voice in the federal cabinet (Brodie 2008, 156). They then proceeded to cut $5 million from SWC's $13 million annual operating budget (a decrease of almost 40 percent), closed most of its regional offices, and rescinded support for research and advocacy. As SWC's "pursuit of equality" was abandoned, the words "equality" and "advocacy" were erased from statements of SWC priorities and from its website. The Conservatives' assumption that equality already existed also appeared to motivate their decision in 2006 to shut down the CCP and the Law Commission of Canada. These cuts reduced the capacity of government agencies and advocacy groups to generate data on the nature and scope of existing inequalities, closed off strategic representational avenues for women (e.g., between women's groups and the state, and before the courts), and ultimately devalued equality's normative currency. While the word "equality" reappeared in the SWC mandate in 2008, the damage had been done. Women's groups inside and outside the state were in too perilous a condition to mobilize effective opposition to these developments (Bakker 2009, 226).

In the microconstitutional realm, the dual blows of the Harper government's cuts to SWC and its closure of the CCP took a significant toll on equality-seeking groups. By the late 1990s, LEAF was receiving over 25 percent of its revenue from a combination of the CCP and SWC (Manfredi 2004, 33). Although it managed to restructure and renew itself with the support of its membership base, other foundational equality-seeking organizations, including NAC, found survival more difficult. For women's groups outside of the state, any remaining public support was earmarked for service provision. As with SWC, research and advocacy by women's groups received little or no state support and was often actively discouraged (Philipps 2002). Scrambling for limited resources, feminist organizations lacked their former capacity, access, and influence; they had a lower public profile and were rarely called upon for policy advice.

Concomitantly, the real-life "returns" of these microconstitutional struggles were increasingly called into question (McIntyre and Rodgers 2006). Much of LEAF's "original proactive vision of initiating litigation" (Baines 2005, 53) became more reactive, as feminists' substantive equality strategy was getting "a far more vigorous workout as a shield than a sword" (MacIvor 2006, 207). Inequalities were all too apparent, however. Since the first equality decisions under section 15, "the number of single mothers living in poverty ... increased by more than 50 percent ... Food banks, a rare phenomenon in the early 1980s ... are now a critical means of survival ... Women and children have been most dramatically affected by the epidemic of homelessness" (Porter 2006, 42). Thus, from both practical (Sampson 2006) and theoretical (Hunter 2008b, 3) perspectives, many came to the conclusion that feminists' multiple approaches to the principle of equality had not resolved the multiple inequalities facing women.

These developments, in terms of discourse, identity, and voice, dramatically illustrate the erosion of Canada's equality opportunity structure. The process was set in motion soon after patriation and gained significant momentum in the decades that followed. This helps us to understand the ease with which the Harper government has been able to erase gender equality even when, in reality, inequalities are growing markedly. Now, however, as my examination of the 2011 election platform illustrates, along with this empirically incongruous invisibilization, Canada's other political parties have turned to instrumentalizing gender equality.

Equality and Party Platforms, 2011

Consider first a few points of comparison with 1984, the first post-patriation general election. The winds of change, blowing away from social liberalism and equality, could certainly be felt. And yet, while this was clearly a time of flux for the three main political contenders, social liberalism and women and equality were still very much on the agenda. To be sure, the newly installed Liberal leader and prime minister, John Turner, first worked to "distance himself from the Trudeau era" (Jeffrey 2010, 24), including "traditional Liberal policies of progress on issues of special importance to women, universality of social programs and improved retraining schemes" (Simpson 1985, 19). As one commentator described it, the Liberals were "a party in trouble. The creed of Liberalism, largely unexamined since the 1962 Kingston Conference ... [was] under serious attack from conservative ideologues in the United States and Britain" (Snider 1985, 71). The relatively new Progressive Conservative (PC) leader, Brian Mulroney, followed their lead and campaigned on a change from long-standing, "stale" Liberal policy legacies (Sears 1985, 31, 35). Even the New Democratic Party leader, Ed Broadbent, called for a dramatic shift in his party's orthodoxy, away from deficit financing towards cost cutting (Hills 1985, 40). In a confidential 1984 election "Strategic Overview," one of the nine NDP "disadvantages" identified as having to be addressed to gain electoral advantage was: "When we fight to preserve medicare and pensions, or when we emphasize women's issues, we are dismissed for recycling past policies" (Hills 1985, 38).

Nevertheless, all three parties expressed a lingering commitment to social liberalism. As the Liberal campaign began to flounder, it "moved from Turner's business Liberal platform to one that reiterated the left-wing Liberal concerns with social policy, if not the Trudeau vision of federalism" (Jeffrey 2010, 27), for the "Just Society" was still "in many respects, at the heart of Liberal political ideology" and it continued to be the "ideological stance that attracted the crux of the Liberal coalition" (Goldfarb and Axworthy 1988, 76).

At the same time, Mulroney found himself not only invoking the "sacred trust" of universal health care but also enriching certain social provisions:

> First, we extend the spousal allowance to eligible widows and widowers between the ages of 60 and 65, regardless of the age of their spouses at death. Second, we will restore at the earliest moment full

> indexing of the old age pension to the actual cost of living on a quarterly basis. Third, we will increase the guaranteed income supplement as soon as resources permit. (Sears 1985, 31)

Even Liberal stalwarts conceded that "while the Conservative party of Brian Mulroney disliked government and certainly no longer favored the extension of the social safety net and welfare state ... at the same time it held little real enthusiasm for a massive assault on social measures" (Goldfarb and Axworthy 1988, 72).

Although the NDP portrayed the Conservative and Liberal leaders as "the Chin and the Twin, the Bobbsey Twins of Bay Street," the two tried to outdo each other in expressing their commitment to social programs, especially in the "women's debate." Here "Turner accused Conservatives of being opposed to social programs that mainly involved women and Mulroney replied that he was 'earnestly and genuinely committed' to correcting past injustices to women in employment and social benefits" (Sears 1985, 33–34).

Still, in Broadbent's view, the voices of Bay Street had been "dancing around the concerns of Canadians on jobs, equality for women, fair taxes, social programs and nuclear disarmament ... They have created the Bay Street shuffle" (Hills 1985, 53). Worse, the NDP leader also found himself responding to Turner's two "bum-patting" incidents ("slapping Iona Campagnolo's bottom" as well as "the hind quarters" of a female campaign organizer), noting that it was "'a generational thing' and women find it offensive." Looking decidedly uncomfortable, Broadbent then pressed Turner to make "substantive commitments" on certain women's issues (Snider 1985, 123).

Bad behaviour aside, the immediate post-patriation context of the 1980s required a substantive policy discussion regarding women and equality. For example, Turner had made it clear that the Liberals' first priority was jobs, and their second priority was to "follow policies in the interests of the 'new majority women'" including equal pay for work of equal value. Turner had been primed. As one observer recalled (Lynch 1984, 67):

> His coaches on the gender issue were cabinet minister Judy Erola and Monique Bégin, and they let it be known that Turner was a quick

> learner, with a lot to learn. Rumour had it that it took him more than a day to get his tongue around the "equal pay for work of equal value" pledge, but he learned not only to say it with conviction but to believe it himself.

Leaping to Canada's 2011 general election, one immediately observes the erosion and even erasure of these earlier commitments to equality. The Conservatives' *Here for Canada* campaign platform provides the most blatant illustration of this development (Conservative Party of Canada 2011). Its style was austere, with few photographs and limited graphics. The snapshot of a bespectacled, suited, and solitary Stephen Harper striding purposefully was repeated, conveying the message of the singular man in control. In terms of its overall messages, "we're here for Canada" played up classic, small "c" conservative themes of patriotism, property, families, safety, and security. At the same time, neoliberal messages abounded around economic prosperity/growth, tax cuts, and more volunteerism/less state.

There was no mention of equality, however. The few scattered references to rights or allusions to courts reflected the Conservatives' law and order theme, religion, and property rights (57). These included a pledge to put victims' rights ahead of the rights of criminals (45), support for religious freedom (40), and protection against hate crimes.

Equality rights were out, but tax cuts and tackling the deficit, economic growth, and jobs were emphatically in. Social spending has been "taxified" (Bashevkin 2002), such that Conservatives could claim to support "hardworking Canadian families" (2) through tax breaks. Beyond the 120 tax cuts instituted by the Conservatives since 2006, the platform committed to a new round of tax "relief" measures that ranged from a new "Adult Fitness Tax Credit" to a "Children's Arts Tax Credit" (25–27). Other social policy initiatives evinced a peculiar populist mix of generality and specificity, vaguely pledging to provide more doctors and nurses for rural communities, along with very precise promises such as providing defibrillators for every hockey arena in Canada! Fleeting mention of enhancing Employment Insurance benefits was limited to parents of murdered or missing children. Instead of social security, we find "tough on crime" safety and security in various guises, from pledges to "crack down" on smuggling, to "combating" terrorism (34, 36).

While hailing families and addressing children, caregivers, and older Canadians, the platform did not discuss women, despite their disproportionate role in the realm of care. The direct references to women were meagre, appearing in Stephen Harper's opening acknowledgment of "our men and women in uniform" and the Conservatives' commitment to address maternal and child health issues in the "world's poorest countries" (43) – *not* Canada, however.

Collective identities were rarely invoked, with some revealing exceptions. First Nations received mention, but only in relation to promoting entrepreneurship and "First Nations Financial Transparency" (63), very much in line with contemporary neoliberal constructions of Aboriginal autonomy and accountability (MacDonald 2011). When the word "community" did appear, it related to "rural communities" or industry (52–60) in the sense of "creating jobs in our communities" (2). Civil society's role in advocacy went unremarked, but the platform strongly promoted volunteerism, including a Volunteer Firefighters Tax Credit (55).

In contrast to the staid style of the Conservative platform, the Liberal Red Book was stylized with glossy photographs, graphics, and tables. Unlike Harper's solitary image, Liberal leader Michael Ignatieff was portrayed with groups of diverse Canadians, and often with women and children. One photograph featured Ignatieff surrounded by a large, cheering group of Liberal women MPs. Substantively, the Liberal manifesto reflected a mixture of continuities and contrasts, with neoliberal themes mirroring some Conservative approaches, along with a strong reaction to or against the Conservative agenda. It was in the latter response that the Liberals' instrumentalization of equality became apparent.

The Red Books of previous Liberal leaders Jean Chrétien and Paul Martin were replete with "social investment" rhetoric, the figure of the child, and policies designed to enhance future outcomes for children and youth (Dobrowolsky and Jenson 2004; Jenson 2009). In 2011, the Liberals' main target shifted to the family as a whole. We see this in the platform's title: *Your Family. Your Future. Your Canada* (Liberal Party of Canada 2011), in pronouncements that "middle-class families are the bedrock of our economy," and in promises that Liberal policy would work to counteract a situation where families are "falling further behind, even though they're working harder" (7–8). Akin to the Conservatives, the Liberals also emphasized that "getting public finances under control goes hand in hand with smart investments in middle class families. Both will help to build a stronger economy" (19).

The Liberals' platform strategically deployed the rhetoric of equality and emphasized previous Liberal governments' efforts to provide the "foundations of equality – establishing universal medicare, a good public pension system, and a *Charter of Rights and Freedoms* guaranteeing equality of rights and responsibilities for all Canadians" (3). The fact that the Liberals had also undermined equality and equality seekers lent a certain irony to these claims. In any event, Ignatieff's main message became "It's time to put equal opportunity back at the centre of our idea of Canada" and that "Advancing equal opportunity is the work of a healthy democracy" (3).

Unlike the Conservatives, the Liberals acknowledged growing inequality between the richest Canadians and middle-class families. Their solution, however, was a quintessentially liberal response, that of pursuing fairness and equality of opportunity: a "fair and equal Canada, with a thriving middle class, will be a more competitive and productive Canada" (8). Thus, the Liberals' actual commitment was a limited one, that of equality of opportunity, not substantive equality.

Building on Trudeau-era themes, the platform featured the caption "A Creative, Bilingual, Diverse and More Equal Canada" (53). Some specific collective identities and the inequalities that befall marginalized groups were singled out – with a section devoted to the tragedy of missing and murdered Aboriginal women. Notably, in this context, civil society advocacy was positively portrayed in the sense that the NWAC's critical research on this issue was commended.

The Liberals referred to civil society in other sections as well, and, like the Conservatives, championed the voluntary sector. But they also blamed the Conservatives for the impoverished condition of state/civil society relations (59):

> The Harper government has been actively hostile to volunteer, non-governmental and community activist groups, particularly those who disagree with its right-wing ideology. However a healthy democracy

> requires a diversity of voices. The government does not have to agree with them, but should respect the role that they play.

Again, this critique is quite precious given past Liberal governments' complicity in cutting support for advocacy groups. However, it does highlight the Harper government's disparagement of civil society, especially equality rights seekers.

Equal opportunity for particular collective identities arises with respect to persons with disabilities and women. In terms of the latter, the platform stated that a Liberal government would "reverse the Harper government's decision to reduce pay equity to an ordinary labour relations and collective bargaining issue" and to recognize pay equity as a human right (63). Still, in the context of an eroded equality opportunity structure, this instrumentalization of equality does little more than reinstate the bare minimum, basic standards associated with equality-promoting institutions and policies.

The Bloc Québécois (BQ) platform echoed this instrumental use of equality. The BQ campaign had contrasted the Harper Conservatives' failure to win over many women and most Quebecers with its own successes among these groups, using witty advertisements to play up these differences. Its platform hit hard, polemically describing the Harper government's "demagogic, alarmist, and dogmatic positions," and suggesting that "when it comes to justice Stephen Harper's Canada is downright disquieting and even dangerous" (Bloc Québécois 2011, 19).

The BQ was distinctive both in its pursuit of sovereignty and in the paradoxical combination of neoliberal economic priorities with social justice scripts, and greater appreciation of the demands of various collective actors. Explicit references to women's rights and equality included: "defending women from attacks on their rights, such as their right to control their own bodies, by instituting pay equity and re-establishing the Equal Opportunities for Women Program and the Court Challenges Program. Let's talk equality" (21). But this commitment was strategic, providing a means of attacking the Conservative government. For instance, the BQ deployed its commitment to women's bodily autonomy as a means of alleging a Conservative "hidden agenda" on abortion.

Given the subsequent election of a Conservative majority and the banishment of the Liberals and the BQ to the political wilderness, one could posit that even such minimalist references to equality did not resonate with Canadians. However, the unprecedented rise in fortunes of the NDP suggests the need for a more nuanced analysis. Of the four major party platforms, the NDP's included the most expansive expressions of equality and human rights. For instance, it included domestic and international support for "gay, lesbian, bisexual, trans-gender and transsexual equality" (New Democratic Party 2011, 18) and "Increasing the Promotion of Health, Development and Human Rights" (20). It also devoted an entire section to "Moving Forward on Women's Equality" (17–18). Here, the NDP pledged to reverse "Stephen Harper's attacks on pay equity" (17) and decried violence against Aboriginal women. Overall, the NDP platform contained detailed discussion of equality-enhancing practices, from working with the provinces and territories to expand access to women's shelters and transition houses, to restoring pathways between women's groups and the state by, for instance, reinstating SWC as a full ministry responsible for advancing women's rights and supporting advocacy (18).

On social policy, the NDP platform contained a combination of "women-focused" and "family friendly policies" such as improving both maternity and family leave benefits. However, "the family" was the dominant theme: ensuring safe food for families; protecting the family farm; and "Helping to lift Children and Families out of Poverty" (6). Even the title of the platform, *Giving Your Family a Break: Practical First Steps*, reinforced this familial refrain.

The word "community" appeared often, but the discourse became contested in the context of Aboriginal peoples, where the platform resorted to talk of "partnership" and highlighted economic opportunities, including "increasing access to capital for aboriginal business developments" (15). Notions of entrepreneurialism evoke the Conservative response to First Nations, while the terminology of "partnerships" and "investment" here and elsewhere in the platform harks back to the Liberals' social investment perspective of the late 1990s and early 2000s (Dobrowolsky 2009b, 9–12).

Overall, the style of the NDP platform was extremely leader-focused, with a plethora of images depicting Jack Layton with women and children and as a man of the people. Photos of him with diverse groups, or with his shirt sleeves rolled up, invited the reader to understand that Layton was ready to work. In terms of policy substance, however, the NDP's platform contained the most robust response to the erosion and erasure of women's equality. Nevertheless, Conservative and Liberal platform themes reappear, especially around the family, and in relation to social investment and partnership, all of which have not augured well for women or equality (Jenson 2009).

Based on the behaviour of the major political parties during and around the 2011 election, it is clear that they once again calculated the electoral benefits of wooing women voters. And yet, there was a tendency across all the party platforms to treat women as an undifferentiated whole. When women did appear, they were seen in limited roles, such as mothers (or soldiers) or victims of circumscribed identities (e.g., Aboriginal women in crisis). All parties sang the praises of families, but there was little specificity in terms of the diverse nature of families, save for the tactical focus on "middle class" families. There was, for example, no recognition of the plight of single-parent families, usually headed by women and typically not middle-class. Further, the emphasis on tax benefits and tax credits showed little appreciation for the negative impact that indirect provision of social programs can have on women's equality.

Given these patterns, the parties' mention of women and/or equality appeared to be strategic. And, while the Conservatives reached out to women, particularly the so-called soccer moms (i.e., *mom*ipulation, Carroll 2006, 366), the connection was essentially made to those who either assume that equality exists or are its naysayers (such as REAL Women). Through such conjuring, the governing party could seek support from women while invisibilizing gender equality.

Conclusions

Beyond entrenchment and judicial recognition of equality, a favourable political, economic, and social environment, expressed in discourse, identity, and voice, is required in order to establish and expand an equality opportunity structure that is amenable to gender equality claims. This chapter has traced the very erosion and erasure of such fundamentals.

Yet the foregoing saga of a shrinking equality opportunity structure is not meant as a story of an inevitable, inexorable process. To be sure, the Conservatives' majority government and the almost total annihilation of the Liberals and BQ support the equality opportunity closure thesis. However, the NDP succeeded in becoming the Official Opposition for the first time in Canadian history. Its platform was often as instrumental as those of the Liberals and the BQ, but because it provided the most substantive articulation of equality, it may provide more of a toehold for rhetorical, descriptive, and normative equality claims. Whether the NDP can do more than refurbish a tattered equality opportunity structure remains to be seen, and much depends on the directions taken by its current leader. The space and capacity of partisan actors to advance an equality agenda will also depend on collective actors and social movements, as the patriation moment attests. Here, the Occupy and Idle No More protests that brought attention to outrageous levels of income and social inequality may provide a potential opening. For now, however, the only credible conclusion is that Canada's current equality opportunity structure is failing, and its future remains uncertain.

References

Abu-Laban, Yasmeen. 2009. "The Welfare State under Siege? Neo-Liberalism, Immigration, and Multiculturalism." In *Women and Public Policy in Canada: Neo-Liberalism and After?* edited by Alexandra Dobrowolsky, 146–65. Toronto: Oxford University Press.

Baines, Beverley. 2005. "Using the Canadian Charter of Rights to Constitute Women." In *The Gender of Constitutional Jurisprudence*, edited by Beverley Baines and Ruth Rubio-Marin, 48–74. Cambridge, UK: Cambridge University Press.

Bakker, Isabella, ed. 1996. *Rethinking Restructuring: Gender and Change in Canada.* Toronto: University of Toronto Press.

—. 2009. "'Show Us the Money': Tracking Gender-Equality 'Constraints' of Canadian Budgeting." In *Women and Public Policy in Canada: Neo-Liberalism and After?* edited by Alexandra Dobrowolsky, 226–43. Toronto: Oxford University Press.

Bashevkin, Sylvia. 1998. *Women on the Defensive: Living through Conservative Times.* Toronto: University of Toronto Press.

—. 2002. *Welfare Hot Buttons: Women, Work and Social Policy Reform.* Toronto: University of Toronto Press.

Bloc Québécois. 2011. *Parlons Qc.* Election Platform. Ottawa: Bloc Québécois.

Brodie, Janine. 1996. *Women and Canadian Public Policy.* Toronto: Harcourt Brace.

—. 2002. "Citizenship and Solidarity: Reflections on the Canadian Way." *Citizenship Studies* 6 (4): 377–94. doi:10.1080/1362102022000041231.
—. 2008. "We Are All Equal Now: Contemporary Gender Politics in Canada." *Feminist Theory* 9 (2): 145–64. doi:10.1177/1464700108090408.
—. 2010. "The 3Ds of the Canadian Women's Movement: Delegitimization, Dismantling and Disappearance." *FEDCAN blog*, 29 January. Posted under "Equity Matters." http://www.ideas-idees.ca/blog-category/equity-matters.
Brodie, Janine, and Isabella Bakker. 2008. *Where Are the Women? Gender Equity, Budgets and Canadian Public Policy.* Ottawa: Canadian Centre for Policy Alternatives.
Cairns, Alan C. 1983. "The Politics of Constitutional Conservatism." In *And No One Cheered: Federalism, Democracy and the Constitution Act*, edited by Keith Banting and Richard Simeon, 28–58. Toronto: Methuen.
Carroll, Susan J. 2006. "Moms Who Swing, or Why the Promise of the Gender Gap Remains Unfulfilled." *Politics and Gender* 2 (3): 362–74.
Chappell, Louise A. 2002. *Gendering Government: Feminist Engagement with the State in Australia and Canada.* Vancouver: UBC Press.
Clément, Dominique. 2008. *Canada's Rights Revolution: Social Movements and Social Change, 1937–82.* Vancouver: UBC Press.
Cohen, Marjorie Griffin, and Jane Pulkingham. 2009. "Introduction: Going Too Far? Feminist Public Policy in Canada." In *Public Policy for Women: The State, Income Security, and Labour Market Issues*, edited by Marjorie Griffin Cohen and Jane Pulkingham, 3–48. Toronto: University of Toronto Press.
Conservative Party of Canada. 2011. *Here for Canada.* Election Platform. Ottawa: Conservative Party of Canada.
Crow, Barbara, and Lise Gotell. 2000. "Canadian Women's Movements." In *Open Boundaries: A Canadian Women's Studies Reader*, edited by Barbara Crow and Lise Gotell, 65–69. Toronto: Prentice Hall.
Dobrowolsky, Alexandra. 1998. "Of 'Special Interest': Interest, Identity and Feminist Constitutional Activism." *Canadian Journal of Political Science* 31 (04): 707–42. doi:10.1017/S0008423900009616.
—. 2000. *The Politics of Pragmatism: Women, Representation and Constitutionalism in Canada.* Toronto: Oxford University Press.
—. 2008a. "Interrogating 'Invisibilization' and 'Instrumentalization': Women and Current Citizenship Trends in Canada." *Citizenship Studies* 12 (5): 465–79. doi:10.1080/13621020802337832.
—. 2008b. "The Women's Movement in Flux: Feminism and Framing, Passion and Politics." In *Social Movements in Canada*, edited by Miriam Smith, 159–80. Peterborough, ON: Broadview Press.
—. 2009a. "Charter Champions? Equality Backsliding, the Charter and the Courts." In *Women and Public Policy in Canada: Neo-Liberalism and After?* edited by Alexandra Dobrowolsky, 204–25. Toronto: Oxford University Press.
Dobrowolsky, Alexandra, ed. 2009b. *Women and Public Policy in Canada: Neo-Liberalism and After?* Toronto: Oxford University Press.

Dobrowolsky, Alexandra, and Jane Jenson. 2004. "Shifting Representations of Citizenship: Canadian Politics of 'Women' and 'Children.'" *Social Politics* 11 (2): 154–80. doi:10.1093/sp/jxh031.

Goldfarb, Martin, and Thomas Axworthy. 1988. *Marching to a Different Drummer: An Essay on the Liberals and Conservatives in Convention.* Toronto: Stoddart.

Hills, Nick. 1985. "The NDP Survivors." In *The Canadian General Election of 1984: Politicians, Parties, Press and Polls,* edited by Alan Frizzell and Anthony Westell, 38–53. Ottawa: Carleton University Press.

Hosek, Chaviva. 1983. "Women and the Constitutional Process." In *And No One Cheered: Federalism, Democracy and the Constitution Act,* edited by Keith Banting and Richard Simeon, 280–300. Toronto: Methuen.

Hunter, Rosemary. 2008a. "Alternatives to Equality." In *Rethinking Equality Projects in Law,* edited by Rosemary Hunter, 81–101. Oxford: Hart Publishing.

—. 2008b. "Introduction: Feminism and Equality." In *Rethinking Equality Projects in Law,* edited by Rosemary Hunter, 1–10. Oxford: Hart Publishing.

Irving, Helen. 2009. "More than Rights." In *Constituting Equality: Gender Equality and Comparative Constitutional Law,* edited by Susan H. Williams, 75–92. Cambridge, UK: Cambridge University Press. doi:10.1017/CBO9780511596780.005.

James, Matt. 2006. *Misrecognized Materialists: Social Movements in Canadian Constitutional Politics.* Vancouver: UBC Press.

Jeffrey, Brooke. 2010. *Divided Loyalties: The Liberal Party of Canada, 1984–2008.* Toronto: University of Toronto Press.

Jenson, Jane. 2009. "Writing Gender Out: The Continuing Effects of the Social Investment Perspective." In *Women and Public Policy in Canada: Neo-Liberalism and After?* edited by Alexandra Dobrowolsky, 25–47. Toronto: Oxford University Press.

Jenson, Jane, and Susan D. Phillips. 1996. "Regime Shift: New Citizenship Practices in Canada." *International Journal of Canadian Studies* 14: 111–45.

Jhappan, Radha, ed. 2002. *Women's Legal Strategies in Canada.* Toronto: University of Toronto Press.

Kome, Penny. 1983. *The Taking of Twenty-Eight: Women Challenge the Constitution.* Toronto: Women's Educational Press.

LEAF. 1996. *Equality and the Charter: Ten Years of Feminist Advocacy before the Supreme Court of Canada. Women's Legal Education and Action Fund.* Toronto: Emond Montgomery.

Liberal Party of Canada. 2011. *Your Family. Your Future. Your Canada.* Election Platform. Ottawa: Liberal Party of Canada.

Lynch, Charles. 1984. *Race for the Rose: Election 1984.* Toronto: Methuen.

MacDonald, Fiona. 2011. "Indigenous Peoples and Neoliberal 'Privatization' in Canada: Opportunities, Cautions and Constraints." *Canadian Journal of Political Science* 44 (02): 257–73. doi:10.1017/S000842391100014X.

MacIvor, Heather. 2006. *Canadian Politics and Government in the Charter Era.* Toronto: Thompson/Nelson.

Manfredi, Christopher. 2004. *Feminist Activism in the Supreme Court: Legal Mobilization and the Women's Legal Education and Action Fund.* Vancouver: UBC Press.

McIntyre, Sheila, and Sanda Rodgers, eds. 2006. *Diminishing Returns: Inequality and the Canadian Charter of Rights and Freedoms.* Toronto: Butterworths.

McWhinney, Edward. 1979. *Quebec and the Constitution 1960–1978.* Toronto: University of Toronto Press.

New Democratic Party. 2011. *Giving Your Family a Break: Practical First Steps.* Ottawa: New Democratic Party.

Newman, Jacquetta, and Linda A. White. 2012. *Women, Politics, and Public Policy: The Political Struggles of Canadian Women.* Toronto: Oxford University Press.

Pal, Leslie A. 1993. *Interests of State: The Politics of Language, Multiculturalism and Feminism in Canada.* Montreal/Kingston: McGill-Queen's University Press.

Philipps, Lisa. 2002. "Tax Law and Social Reproduction: The Gender of Fiscal Policy in an Age of Privatization." In *Privatization, Law and the Challenge to Feminism,* edited by Brenda Cossman and Judy Fudge, 41–85. Toronto: University of Toronto Press.

Porter, Bruce. 2006. "Expectations of Equality." In *Diminishing Returns: Inequality and the Canadian Charter of Rights and Freedoms,* edited by Sheila McIntyre and Sandra Rodgers, 23–44. Toronto: Butterworths.

Rebick, Judy. 2002. "Disappearing Act: The Women's Movement in Canada Has All but Vanished from the Public Conscience. Its Survival Is a Question of Commitment and Vision." *Elm Street,* Summer, 74.

Rebick, Judy, and Kiké Roach. 1996. *Politically Speaking.* Vancouver: Douglas and McIntyre.

Sampson, Fiona. 2006. "The Law Test for Discrimination and Gendered Disability Inequality." In *Making Equality Rights Real: Securing Substantive Equality under the Charter,* edited by Fay Faraday, Margaret Denike, and M. Kate Stephenson, 245–74. Toronto: Irwin.

Saunders, Douglas E. 1983. "The Indian Lobby." In *And No One Cheered: Federalism, Democracy and the Constitution Act,* edited by Keith Banting and Richard Simeon, 301–32. Toronto: Methuen.

Scott, Frank R. 1977. *Essays on the Constitution: Aspects of Canadian Law and Politics.* Toronto: University of Toronto Press.

Sears, Val. 1985. "The Buttery-Smooth Conservatives." In *The Canadian General Election of 1984: Politicians, Parties, Press and Polls,* edited by Alan Frizzell and Anthony Westell, 28–37. Ottawa: Carleton University Press.

Simpson, Jeffrey. 1985. "The Campaign: The Vincible Liberals." In *The Canadian General Election of 1984: Politicians, Parties, Press and Polls,* edited by Alan Frizzell and Anthony Westell, 15–28. Ottawa: Carleton University Press.

Smith, Miriam. 1999. *Lesbian and Gay Rights in Canada: Social Movements and Equality Seeking 1971–1995.* Toronto: University of Toronto Press.

Snider, Norman. 1985. *The Changing of the Guard: How the Liberals Fell from Grace and the Tories Rose to Power.* Toronto: Lester and Orpen Dennys.

Contributors

Eric M. Adams is an associate professor at the Faculty of Law at the University of Alberta. He teaches and writes in the areas of constitutional law and theory, legal history, and labour and employment law. He has published a number of articles on topics in Canadian constitutional history, including "Errors of Fact and Law: Race, Space, and Hockey in *Christie v. York*," *University of Toronto Law Journal* 63 (4) (2012); "Building a Law of Human Rights: *Roncarelli v. Duplessis* in Canadian Constitutional Culture," *McGill Law Journal* 55 (3) (2010); "The Constitutionality of Prorogation," *Constitutional Forum* 18 (1) (2009); and "Canada's 'Newer Constitutional Law' and the Idea of Constitutional Rights," *McGill Law Journal* 51 (3) (2006). Dr. Adams is currently completing a book on the intellectual history of the Canadian constitution over the course of the twentieth century.

Loren Braul serves as Crown counsel in the Constitutional Law Branch of Manitoba Justice. As a law student, he worked as a research assistant to Marilou McPhedran and attended the Patriation Negotiations Conference hosted by the University of Alberta Centre for Constitutional Studies on 3–5 November 2011. He is currently researching issues in constitutional legal history.

Janine Brodie is a Distinguished University Professor and Canada Research Chair in Political Economy and Social Governance in the Department of Political Science at the University of Alberta. She was awarded a Trudeau Fellowship in 2010 and acted as the director of the English Social Science Division of the Royal Society of Canada between 2007 and 2014. Dr. Brodie has written extensively on many of the core challenges in Canadian politics and public policy, including citizenship equality, gender politics, social policy, continental integration, and neoliberal governance. Her most recent publications include "Elusive Equalities and the Austerity Hypothesis," *International Journal of Law in Context* (2014); "New Constitutionalism, Neoliberalism and Social Policy," in *The New Constitutionalism and Global Order,* edited by S. Gill and C. Cutler (Cambridge University Press, 2014); and "Social Literacy and Social Justice in Times of Crisis," Pierre Elliott Trudeau Foundation Papers (2012). She is co-author of the popular introductory text *Critical Concepts,* now in its fifth edition. Dr. Brodie is currently researching austerity and the politics of crisis.

P.E. (Penny) Bryden is a professor of history at the University of Victoria, where she teaches twentieth-century Canadian history and writes about contemporary issues in Canadian politics. Her most recent book is *"A Justifiable Obsession": Conservative Ontario's Relations with Ottawa, 1943–1985* (University of Toronto Press, 2013). Dr. Bryden is currently at work on a book on the centralization of power in the Prime Minister's Office and Privy Council Office since the 1950s.

Alexandra Dobrowolsky is a professor of political science at Saint Mary's University. She teaches in the areas of Canadian politics, comparative politics, and women, gender, and politics. With research interests that revolve around themes of citizenship, Dr. Dobrowolsky has published widely on an array of topics including constitutionalism and rights; political parties; social movements; social policy; and security and immigration. Her first book was titled *The Politics of Pragmatism: Women, Representation and Constitutionalism in Canada* (Oxford University Press, 1999). It was followed by work on women's constitutional mobilization from a comparative perspective, including the co-edited collection (with Vivien Hart) *Women Making Constitutions: New Politics and Comparative Perspectives* (Palgrave Macmillan, 2004). Dr. Dobrowolsky's most recent edited volume is titled *Women and Public Policy in Canada: Neo-Liberalism and After?* (Oxford University Press, 2009). Her current research and writing deal with immigration, multiculturalism, and equality concerns at national and subnational levels.

Judith Erola was elected as member of Parliament for Nickel Belt in 1980 and served as minister responsible for the status of women from 22 September 1981 to 16 September 1984. She then took on a number of leadership positions and board directorships, including serving as the CEO of the Pharmaceutical Manufacturers Association and as the president of the Child Health Institute of Canada. She holds honorary doctorates from Mount St. Vincent University, Laurentian University, and the University of Ottawa.

Alain-G. Gagnon holds the Canada Research Chair in Quebec and Canadian Studies in the Department of Political Science at the Université du Québec à Montréal. He is director of the Interdisciplinary Centre of Research on Diversity and Democracy (CRIDAQ) and of the Research Group on Plurinational Societies (GRSP). He is the author of *L'Âge des incertitudes: essais sur le fédéralisme et la diversité nationale* (Les Presses de l'Université Laval, 2011) and *The Case for Multinational Federalism: Beyond the All-Encompassing Nation* (Routledge, 2010). Dr. Gagnon's many edited volumes include *D'un référendum à l'autre: le Québec face à son destin* (Les Presses de l'Université Laval, 2008); *Canadian Politics* (with James Bickerton, 6th ed., University of Toronto Press, 2014); *Federal Democracies* (with Michael Burgess, Routledge, 2010); *Political Autonomy and Divided Polities* (with Michael Keating, Palgrave Macmillan, 2012); and *Multinational Federalism* (with Michel Seymour, Palgrave Macmillan, 2012). Dr. Gagnon received a Trudeau Fellowship in 2010 and the Marcel-Vincent Award in 2008, and was elected a member of the Royal Society of Canada in 2008.

Philip Girard is a professor of law at Osgoode Hall Law School, York University. He has written on many aspects of Canadian legal history and is currently writing a history of law in Canada. In the year before the *Patriation Reference*, Dr. Girard clerked for Justice W.Z. Estey at the Supreme Court of Canada. He is the author of *Bora Laskin: Bringing Law to Life* (University of Toronto Press, 2005), which was recently reissued in paperback.

Lois Harder is a professor of political science at the University of Alberta. Her current research focuses on the law and politics of Canadian citizenship, both as a formal status and in the context of social policy. Her first book, *State of Struggle: Feminism and Politics in Alberta* (University of Alberta Press, 2003), examined the political economy of feminist organizing in Alberta, and subsequent research has considered the delivery of social policy through the tax system and, more recently, the political rationales for the regulation of intimate life. She is the co-author (with Jane Bayes and others) of *Women, Democracy and Globalization in North America* (Palgrave, 2006) and co-editor (with Steve Patten) of *The Chrétien Legacy: Politics and Public Policy in Canada* (McGill-Queen's University Press, 2006). In 2008, she held a Fulbright Visiting Professorship at the University of Hawaii, and in September 2014, she was the Eccles Centre Visiting Canadian Fellow in North American Studies at the British Library. She is currently writing a book on the birthright citizenship claims of the "Lost Canadians."

Kiera Ladner is an associate professor in the Department of Political Science at the University of Manitoba, a Canada Research Chair in Indigenous Politics and Governance, and a research affiliate with the University of Manitoba's Centre for Human Rights Research. Dr. Ladner's research focuses on constitutional reconciliation and decolonization. She is co-editor, with Leanne Simpson, of *This Is an Honour Song: Twenty Years since the Blockades* (Arbeiter Ring Publishing, 2010). She also authored, with Michael McCrossan, "The Road Not Taken" in *Contested Constitutionalism*, edited by James Kelly and Christopher Manfredi (UBC Press, 2009) and, with Michael Orsini, "The Persistence of Paradigm Paralysis" in *Canada: State of the Federation*, edited by Mike Murphy (Queen's University Institute of Intergovernmental Relations, 2005). Dr. Ladner's publications in scholarly journals include "Up the

Creek: Fishing for a New Constitutional Order," *Canadian Journal of Political Science* 38 (4) (2005); with Caroline Dick, "Out of the Fires of Hell: Globalization as a Solution to Globalization – An Indigenist Perspective," *Canadian Journal of Law and Society* 23 (1–2) (2008); "Understanding the Impact of Self-Determination on Communities in Crisis," *International Journal of Indigenous Health* 5 (2) (2009); and "Gendering Decolonisation, Decolonising Gender," *Australian Indigenous Law Review* 13 (2009).

Guy Laforest is a professor in the Department of Political Science at Université Laval, in Quebec City, where he has taught since 1988. His main areas of teaching and research are political theory, intellectual history in Canada and Quebec, constitutional politics in Canada, theories of federalism, and theories of nationalism. Dr. Laforest is vice-president of the International Association of Québec Studies. He co-edited, with Michel Seymour, *Le fédéralisme multinational: un modèle viable?* (Peter Lang, Brussels, 2011).

Louise Mandell, QC, LLD (hon.), is a founding partner of Mandell Pinder, a law firm specializing in Aboriginal and treaty rights law. She moved out of the day-to-day practice of law in 2011 but remains connected in the esteemed capacity of "counsel" to the firm. She was appointed Queen's Counsel in 1997, was awarded the Georges Goyer QC Memorial Award for exceptional contribution to the development of Aboriginal and treaty rights jurisprudence across the country in 2001, and received an honorary Doctor of Laws degree from Simon Fraser University in 2012. Louise Mandell was brought into the area of Aboriginal law when it was in its infancy by the late Grand Chief George Manuel, president of the Union of BC Indian Chiefs and the World Council of Indigenous Peoples, and her professional life has been devoted to the advancement of Aboriginal title and rights and treaty rights. She was legal counsel in UBCIC's fight against the patriation of the constitution and subsequently devoted herself to implementing constitutional change, advancing many of the leading cases, including *Van der Peet, Delgamuukw,* and *Haida Nation.* She is author of "The Ghost," in *Aboriginal Law since Delgamuukw,* edited by M. Morellato (Canada Law Book, 2009).

Marilou McPhedran is a professor and the director of the Institute for International Women's Rights at the University of Winnipeg Global College. Formerly the Ariel F. Sallows Chair in Human Rights at the University of Saskatchewan College of Law and chief commissioner of the Saskatchewan Human Rights Commission, she served as the principal of the University of Winnipeg Global College from 2008 to July 2012. She was named a member of the Order of Canada in 1985 in recognition of her co-leadership in the successful campaign for stronger gender equality protections in the Canadian constitution. McPhedran has long focused on human rights and systemic reform in Canada and internationally, and has published both scholarly and applied research in this area. Her publications include "Impact of S.15 Equality Rights on Canadian Society: Beacon or Laser?" *National Journal of Constitutional Law* (2005); "A Truer Story: Constitutional Trialogue," *Supreme Court Law Review* (2007); "Women's Constitutional Activism in South Africa and Canada," *International Review of Constitutionalism* (2009); and the equality rights chapter in *Pursuing Justice* (Fernwood, 2011).

Steve Patten is an associate professor in the Department of Political Science at the University of Alberta. He teaches and researches contemporary Canadian politics. His recent publications include "The Triumph of Neoliberalism within Partisan Conservatism in Canada" in *Conservatism in Canada,* edited by James Farney and David Rayside (University of Toronto Press, 2013), and "The Politics of Alberta's One-Party State" in *Transforming Provincial Politics: The Political Economy of Canada's Provinces and Territories in a Neoliberal Era,* edited by Bryan Evans and Charles Smith (University of Toronto Press, 2015). With Lois Harder, he edited *The Chrétien Legacy: Politics and Public Policy in Canada* (McGill-Queen's University Press, 2006). He is currently working on a book that examines the changing character of politics and governance in the Harper era. Dr. Patten serves on the editorial board of the *Review of Constitutional Studies.*

Leslie Hall Pinder practised law in the area of Aboriginal rights for twenty-seven years. She is currently engaged full-time as a novelist. In addition to essays on the law, she has published three novels, *Under the*

House (Random House, 1988), *On Double Tracks* (Bloomsbury, 1990), and *Bring Me One of Everything* (Grey Swan, 2012). *On Double Tracks* was nominated for a Governor General's Award. *Bring Me One of Everything* was described by David Roberts in *The Advocate* as being "up there with Gabrielle Roy and Margaret Laurence. It is worth reading just for the sheer joy of the author's literary talent." John Hulcoop in the *Vancouver Sun* said, "Like all great magicians in literature, Pinder conjures up a colourful multi-dimensional world of her own inhabited by characters who live their lives quite independently of their factual forebears." Leslie Pinder teaches writing and ethics in the Writer's Studio at Simon Fraser University.

Rosalie Readman holds a master's degree in political science from Laval University. Her primary research interests include Canadian federalism, the representation of women in politics, and the electoral system of Quebec. She is the co-author, with Guy Laforest, of "Plus de détresse que d'enchantement: les négociations constitutionnnelles de novembre 1981 vues du Québec" in *Le nouvel ordre constitutionnel canadien*, edited by François Rocher and Benoît Pelletier (Les Presses de l'Université du Québec, 2013). She has also worked as a research consultant for the chief electoral officer of Quebec.

Peter Russell is a professor emeritus at the University of Toronto, where he taught political science from 1958 to his retirement in 1996. He has held visiting professor positions at Australian National University, Harvard University, and the European Institute. He is a past president of the Canadian Political Science Association, the Canadian Law and Society Association, and the Churchill Society for the Advancement of Parliamentary Democracy. He has published widely on constitutional, judicial, and Aboriginal politics. He is an officer of the Order of Canada and a fellow of the Royal Society of Canada, and he holds honorary degrees from a number of universities and from the Law Society of Upper Canada. Dr. Russell's publications include *Constitutional Odyssey: Can Canadians Become a Sovereign People?* (University of Toronto Press, 3rd ed., 2004); *Recognizing Aboriginal Title: The Mabo Case and Indigenous Resistance to English-Settler Colonialism* (University of Toronto

Press, 2005); and *Two Cheers for Minority Government: The Evolution of Canadian Parliamentary Democracy* (Emond Montgomery Publications, 2008). He also edited, with Kate Malleson, *Appointing Judges in an Age of Judicial Power* (University of Toronto Press, 2006), and, with Lorne Sossin, *Parliamentary Democracy in Crisis* (University of Toronto Press, 2009).

David Schneiderman is professor of law and political science at the University of Toronto. He teaches Canadian and US constitutional law and international investment law. He has authored articles in such journals as *Citizenship Studies, Constellations, Law and Social Inquiry,* and *University of Toronto Law Journal.* His edited volumes on Canadian constitutional law include *Social Justice and the Constitution* (with Joel Bakan, Carleton University Press, 1992); *Charting the Consequences: The Impact of the Charter of Rights on Canadian Law and Politics* (with Kate Sutherland, University of Toronto Press, 1997); and *The Quebec Decision* (Lorimer Press, 1999). He also co-authored *The Last Word: Media Coverage of the Supreme Court of Canada* (UBC Press, 2006) and authored *Constitutionalizing Economic Globalization: Investment Rules and Democracy's Promise* (Cambridge University Press, 2008) and *Resisting Economic Globalization: Critical Theory and International Investment Law* (Palgrave Macmillan, 2013). He is presently at work on a book on the Americanization of Canadian constitutional culture. Professor Schneiderman has been Visiting Professor of Law at Georgetown University Law Center and at the Faculty of Law, Hebrew University, in Jerusalem, and Fulbright Visiting Scholar at the New School for Social Research and the School of Law, Columbia University.

Alex Schwartz is a lecturer in law at Queen's University of Belfast. He was previously Banting Fellow and adjunct assistant professor with the Department of Political Studies at Queen's University (Canada). He has also been a visitor at the Centre for the Study of Social Justice, University of Oxford, and a postdoctoral fellow with the Canada Research Chair in Quebec and Canadian Studies at L'Université du Québec à Montréal. He is co-editor (with Professor Colin Harvey) of *Rights in Divided Societies* (Hart Publishing, 2012).

Barry L. Strayer was professor of law at the University of Saskatchewan from 1962 to 1968 and taught constitutional law in the Faculty of Law, University of Ottawa from 1973 to 1978. He is the author of *Judicial Review of Legislation* (University of Toronto Press, 1968), which was revised as *The Canadian Constitution and the Courts* (Butterworths, 3rd ed., 1988), *Canada's Constitutional Revolution* (University of Alberta Press, 2013), and numerous articles on public law. Dr. Strayer served as an adviser to the government of Saskatchewan (1960–61) and to the government of Canada on constitutional reform and patriation of the constitution (1967–83). He was one of the federal counsels in the Newfoundland Court of Appeal and the Supreme Court in the *Patriation References*, and negotiated patriation arrangements with the United Kingdom. After leaving the federal government, Dr. Strayer was a judge of the Federal Court, both Trial Division and Court of Appeal (1983–2004); Chief Justice, Court Martial Appeal Court (1994–2004); and constitutional adviser to the Republic of Seychelles (1979) and the government of Hong Kong (1989). He also served on an advisory committee of the Canadian Bar Association that assisted the Nepal Bar Association in writing a new constitution for Nepal.

Index